## Praise for previous editions of *Global Health Watch*

'*Global Health Watch 3*, like the previous editions of the Watch, provides us with compelling evidence about all that is wrong with the governance of health care systems across the world. At the same time it also provides us with hope, in the many stories about what can be done and what is being done. The challenge before us is to act decisively on the evidence provided.' **Dr Halfdan Mahler, former director general of the World Health Organization**

'*Global Health Watch 3* provides the thorough and provoking overview of global health issues that we have come to expect from the series. The case studies of change in action provide powerful evidence that poverty and inequity are neither inevitable nor insurmountable, and my students are going to relish debating the feasibility of redesigning health and health care using the alternative blueprint suggested in the latter half of the book.' **Dr Jolene Skordis-Worrall, UCL Institute for Global Health**

'Since 2005, when the first edition of *Global Health Watch* was launched in Cuenca, Ecuador, each new edition has provided an entirely new and stirring account of creativity and courage from peoples and communities in all corners of the world, as they relentlessly struggle against the wide-ranging, criminal path of capitalism, rapaciously determined to cause ever more suffering and death. *GHW3*, surpassing its forerunners, masterfully addresses the relationship among health, health inequalities and their social determinants with exceptional scientific rigour, providing us with an indispensable reference for academics, activists, policy-makers, leaders, government officials, and students. Each section in the book objectively describes and supports the facts, while also unmasking the underlying processes, laying out new paths, and evaluating proposals. Reading *GHW3* is a necessary step in understanding how challenging and urgent change is, but that it is increasingly necessary for the survival of our planet Earth.' **Dr Eduardo Espinoza, vice-minister for health of El Salvador**

'Excellent … I highly recommend this treasure trove, which is full of food for thought, to scholars and health workers alike.' **Dr Maria Isabel Rodriguez, rector of the University of El Salvador, 1999–2007**

'*Global Health Watch* confirms the failure of the UN, capitalism and liberal democracy. It also convinces us that we shall need a radically new manner of thinking if mankind is to survive.' **Dr Suwit Wibulpolprasert, senior adviser on disease control, Ministry of Public Health, Thailand**

'An important contribution to understand the overwhelming health problems and their relation to the globalised oppressive world economy.' **Asa Cristina Laurell, former secretary of health of Mexico City and secretary of health of the Legitimate Government of Mexico**

'An incisive socio-political critique of contemporary global health issues which focuses on determinants rather than diseases, enables the reader to unravel the complexity of global economic governance of health, and helps us understand why appalling health inequities persist across and within nations – a must-read for anyone involved or interested in public health.' **K. Srinath Reddy, president, Public Health Foundation of India**

'A very good reference for people working in areas affecting the health of populations. It deals with some of the most important issues in today's world. I highly recommend it.' **Vicente Navarro, editor-in-chief, *International Journal of Health Services***

'Combines academic analysis with a call to mobilize the health professional community to press for improvements in global health and justice. I hope it will be read by many health professionals in rich and poor countries alike.' **Professor Andy Haines, dean, London School of Hygiene and Tropical Medicine**

'It is very good to see issues of trade and globalization reflected prominently in a report aimed at health professionals. *Global Health Watch* provides them with a resource to engage in debates about these non-clinical, structural determinants of poor health.' **Martin Khor, director, Third World Network**

'Governments and intergovernmental organizations have structured our social world so that half of humankind still lives in severe poverty. These global poor suffer vast health deficits. This greatest moral outrage of our time will continue until citizens reflect on its causes and firmly place the human rights of the global poor on the political agenda. Global Health Watch is a courageous and promising effort in this direction.' **Thomas Pogge, professorial research fellow, Centre for Applied Philosophy, Australian National University**

**The Global Health Watch** is a broad collaboration of public health experts, non-governmental organizations, civil society activists, community groups, health workers and academics. It was initiated by the People's Health Movement, Global Equity Gauge Alliance and Medact as a platform of resistance to the neoliberal dominance in health.

# GLOBAL HEALTH WATCH 4

## AN ALTERNATIVE WORLD HEALTH REPORT

People's Health Movement | CAPE TOWN

Medact | LONDON

Medico International | FRANKFURT

Third World Network | PENANG

Health Action International | AMSTERDAM

Asociación Latinoamericana de Medicina Social | MEXICO CITY

Zed Books | LONDON

*Global Health Watch 4: An Alternative World Health Report* was first published in 2014 by Zed Books Ltd, 7 Cynthia Street, London N1 9JF, UK

www.zedbooks.co.uk

Set in Monotype Plantin and FontFont Kievit by Ewan Smith, London
Index: ed.emery@thefreeuniversity.net
Cover designed by www.roguefour.co.uk

A catalogue record for this book is available from the British Library
Library of Congress Cataloging in Publication Data available

ISBN 978-1-78360-254-4 hb
ISBN 978-1-78360-253-7 pb

Printed and bound by CPI Group (UK) Ltd, Croydon, CR0 4YY

MIX
Paper from responsible sources
FSC  www.fsc.org  FSC® C013604

# CONTENTS

# BOXES, TABLES AND FIGURES

## Boxes

**Tables**

**Figures**

# IMAGES

# ACKNOWLEDGEMENTS

*Global Health Watch 4,* like the previous volumes, has been written collectively by a number of academics, scholars and activists. All those who have contributed to the contents are acknowledged at the end of the volume. We would like to particularly acknowledge all contributors and express our special gratitude to all of them for having worked without any honorarium, a spirit of volunteerism that we value immensely. Individual contributors have been involved in writing specific sections of the *Watch* and cannot therefore be held accountable for the views expressed in the whole volume.

We wish to thank our funding partners – Medico International and International Development Research Centre (IDRC) – for support provided. The views in the *Watch* are not necessarily those of our funding partners.

The production of the *Watch* is supported by a coordinating group of five civil society organizations – People's Health Movement, Asociación Latinoamericana de Medicina Social (ALAMES), Third World Network, Health Action International, Medico International and Medact. We would like to thank those involved, from all these organizations, in producing the *Watch*. Specifically, we would like to acknowledge the contributions of Rafael Gonzalez Guzman (ALAMES), K. M. Gopakumar (Third World Network), Tim Reed (Health Action International), Andreas Wulf (Medico International), Ruth Stern (Medact) and Anneleen de Keukelaere, Bridget Lloyd and Hani Serag (People's Health Movement). We also wish to acknowledge Susan Greenblatt for her translation of the Spanish contributions.

It has been a pleasure to work with the team at Zed Books associated with the production of the *Watch*. Specifically, we would like to thank Kim Walker, Ewan Smith and Ruben Mootoosamy for their patience, understanding and support.

Finally, we would like to express our deep appreciation to Susana Barria for the valuable research support and for her efficient coordination of the production of the *Watch*.

Amit Sengupta (on behalf of the *Global Health Watch 4* editorial group: Anne-Emanuelle Birn, Chiara Bodini, David Legge, David McCoy, David Sanders, N. B. Sarojini and Amit Sengupta)

# INTRODUCTION

The *Global Health Watch*, now in its fourth edition, is perceived widely as the definitive voice for an alternative discourse on health. It integrates rigorous analysis, alternative proposals and stories of struggles and change to present a compelling case for the imperative to work for a radical transformation of the way we approach actions and policies on health. It was conceived in 2003 as a collaborative effort by activists and academics from across the world, and is designed to question present policies on health and to propose alternatives. *Global Health Watch 4* has been coordinated by six civil society organizations – the People's Health Movement, ALAMES, Health Action International, Medico International, Third World Network and Medact.

*Global Health Watch 4*, like the preceding volumes published in 2005, 2008 and 2011, provides analysis of contemporary issues that impact on health. It provides policy analysis, debates technical issues, and provides perspectives on current global processes. The GHW does not limit itself to the 'health sector' but extends its scrutiny to all those areas that determine whether people are able to live healthy and fulfilling lives. We hope the contents will be of use to a wide range of readers – activists, academics, developmental agencies and policy-makers. *Global Health Watch 4* provides information and analysis, but it also takes sides. The analysis and alternatives that we present are embodied in a vision of a society that is more just, more equal and more humane. Many of the stories that we include inspire hope that change can happen, and is actually happening in many parts of the world.

As in the case of the previous editions, the contents of *Global Health Watch 4* are divided into five interlinked sections. The section on the 'The Global political and economic architecture' locates the decisions and choices that impact on health in the present structure of global power relations and economic governance. The section 'Health systems: current issues and debates' looks at contemporary debates on health systems in different parts of the world, to draw appropriate lessons and propose concrete actions. The third section, 'Beyond healthcare', engages with multiple social and structural determinants of health. The section on 'Watching' scrutinizes global processes and institutions which have significant impact on global health. The final section foregrounds stories of action and resistance, from different parts of the world.

## The global political and economic architecture

The section begins with a scrutiny of how and why neoliberal globalization has produced a global health crisis. It traces its forty-year history, describes three phases of neoliberalism (structural adjustment, financialization and austerity) and examines how these phases have affected health. It then looks at oppositional or countervailing forces to neoliberalism's orthodoxy, and discusses a number of policy options and political strategies that public health activists might support or pursue.

It also provides evidence from post-crisis Europe as a clear reminder of the need to defend public services. It is precisely at this juncture – when the economic crisis in Europe is eroding the livelihoods of millions of people – that public investment in education, healthcare and infrastructure is under attack.

The section further contends that the installation of several 'progressive' governments marks a new phase of transformation in the Latin American region, which could have far-reaching global repercussions. In each country, different power groups have emerged, giving rise to new contradictions and tensions. Concurrently, new forms of the 'welfare state' have started emerging, based on social rights and citizenship. New ways of defining social inequalities and what is 'socially good' are also emerging. Noteworthy, in this context, has been the rise of the idea of 'living well' (*vivir bien*) as a new paradigm, geared towards new forms of communal socialism.

The chapter 'After the Arab Spring' examines the aftermath of the spectacular fall of major Arab leaders in 2011. The uprising in the region was part of a revolutionary process against economic deprivation and political suffocation. The struggle for transformation in the region is now being forced to contend with renewed attacks by global capital, on welfare and social services.

### Health systems: current issues and debates

The chapter on 'Universal Health Coverage (UHC)' examines how existing public systems could be made truly universal. It argues that public systems need to be reclaimed by citizens, reformed in the interest of the people and made accountable. People's movements and organizations have much to lose from the present drift legitimized by a particular discourse in the name of UHC. Historically, healthcare systems worldwide have been shaped by labour's fight for better conditions of living – either through transformation of the capitalist system itself or through the extraction of better terms from the ruling classes. The fight for a just and equitable health system has to be part of the broader struggle for comprehensive rights and entitlements. To take this struggle forward, the dominant interpretation of UHC today – weakening public systems and the pursuit of private profit – needs to be understood and questioned.

The chapter on reforms in the UK's National Health Service (NHS) describes how the shift from NHS to 'National Healthcare Market' was made possible through various failures of democracy and professional leadership and reflects on the implications of the downfall of the NHS. The scale of the threat to the NHS – coupled with the UK government's lack of a democratic mandate to end the NHS and its propensity to misinform the public – suggests that we are in a situation where professional dissent is not just appropriate, but urgently required.

Countries in Latin America have been host to several 'experiments' designed to promote UHC, beginning with the health and social security reforms in Chile in the mid-1970s, carried out under the dictatorship of Pinochet. This trend continued with a wave of neoliberal reforms in most countries in the continent during the 1990s. The most celebrated was the Colombian reform of 1993, which was recommended to other countries as a successful model. With the virtual collapse of the Colombian health system, its place has been taken by the Mexican health reform and its 'Popular Health Insurance programme' (*Seguro Popular*). The chapter on Mexico discusses the supposed 'success story' of *Seguro Popular* and challenges the mainstream discourse about its 'success'.

Brazil's successes, in rapidly rolling out primary-care services to cover the entire country and in pioneering a model of social participation through its health councils, are discussed in the context of existing challenges. The chapter reflects about the need to overcome structural barriers that prevent the full implementation of reforms that would make the country's unified universal health system (SUS) the dominant form of healthcare provision in Brazil.

The chapter on South Africa discusses the country's commitment to the introduction of a tax-funded system with universal entitlements to comprehensive health services. The experience of South Africa could provide valuable lessons for other low- and middle-income countries (LMICs) that have large private health sectors.

The discussion on Tunisia looks at the current situation in the country, foreshadowed by the values of social justice and equity that were the underpinnings of the Tunisian revolution.

Community health workers (CHWs) were an important component of the original vision of a universal health system based on the principles of primary healthcare (PHC). However, over the past three decades CHW programmes have become bureaucratized and have lost the earlier intended focus on social mobilization. The chapter on CHWs looks at recent experiences from four countries – Brazil, India, Iran and South Africa – and argues that they demonstrate a number of commonalities. The most important of these is the relatively weak focus on and arrangements for inter-sectoral action on social and environmental determinants of health. The chapter discusses how CHW programmes can contribute to shaping healthcare to the expectations and reality of the community the health team serves.

In spite of some recent progress, the levels of maternal mortality and morbidity remain unacceptably high, and there are major inequities between and within countries. With a focus on Africa, the chapter on 'maternal mortality' discusses how universal access to reproductive and sexual health needs to be the cornerstone of programmes aimed at improving both maternal and women's health.

The chapter on the 'health workforce crisis' details how the availability of a strong health workforce, supported by public funds, is a prerequisite for strong, universal and quality health systems. The current focus on UHC carries the potential threat of reducing the role of health workers to undertaking selective diagnosis and treatment, rather than addressing the health of people and communities in a comprehensive and integrated way, combining public health and individual clinical approaches. It critically analyses recent trends in the role of health workers geared towards concerns of economic efficiency.

The final chapter in the section focuses on 'medical devices', a hitherto neglected area in public health discourse. While the medical-device industry makes claims about how new devices (and technologies) can 'revolutionize' healthcare, there are too few independent studies that examine such claims. The chapter argues for regulatory regimens based on better evidence as regards the cost-effectiveness of medical technologies.

### Beyond healthcare

The chapter on 'social protection' contests the mainstream discourse on development. It advocates for a transformative agenda where development implies an end to 'dual societies' engendered by neoliberal policies, and for a shift away from 'productivism' and an exclusively growth-oriented economy.

The rise in the incidence and prevalence of non-communicable diseases (NCDs) poses a complex challenge. The discussion on NCDs calls for vigilance to ensure that the agenda is not hijacked by very powerful interests who seek to profit from disease and suffering.

Two case studies (located in India and the Pacific Islands) individually and together illustrate the complex and dynamic global food and nutrition crisis. They are presented as stark reminders of the urgency of eliminating the 'double burden of nutrition' (under-nutrition and obesity), and of the clear and distressing explications of its national and global social, economic and political contexts. They underline the fact that this human crisis cannot be addressed without confronting and changing its social determinants.

The section also advocates that policy, law and guidelines on gender-based violence must incorporate a comprehensive health system response. Elimination of gender-based violence requires action at various levels, including steps to address societal issues related to power and dominance, access to resources and entitlements, among others.

The sanitation crisis is rapidly escalating, with a growing and urbanizing poor population in LMICs and a scarcity of fresh water and infrastructure. We discuss the embracing of a new strategy, termed 'Community Led Total Sanitation' (CLTS), by powerful international agencies and NGOs. The chapter argues that the strategy may be demeaning and represent a 'victim-blaming' approach to a basic health issue and human right.

The evidence demonstrating the causal relationship between exposure to mining hazards and adverse health outcomes is denied and suppressed by industry advocates. The same is true of the huge contribution of the mining industry to a high burden of disease. The chapter on 'extractive industries' contends, through an examination of several case studies, that current global governance structures are grossly inadequate in the face of the tremendous power imbalances that exist between communities and mining companies.

## Watching

The discussion on the World Health Organization (WHO) is located in the roots of the global health crisis in the contemporary regime of economic globalization. It argues for a theory of global (health) governance that goes beyond simply listing those international institutions that deal with health issues. An expanded theory of global governance, it is contended, should also recognize imperialism and big-power bullying; acknowledge the historic competition between the nation-state and the transnational corporation as the principal agent of governance; and contextualize governance within the emerging class relations between the transnational capitalist class, the diverse national middle classes and the more dispersed, excluded and marginalized classes of both the periphery and the metropolis. The chapter describes how the WHO is under continuing pressure to retreat to a purely technical role and to withdraw from any effective engagement with the political and economic dynamics that characterize the global health crisis.

Non-governmental organizations (NGOs) have been remarkably flexible in adapting to changing global power relations. A critical analysis of the role that NGOs play today, entitled 'A new "business model" for NGOs?', identifies some of the 'red lines' that are beginning to be defined quite sharply in relation to the activities of NGOs.

The chapter contends that 'pragmatism' guides many NGOs today as the current hegemonic discourse abhors utopian thinking by demanding realism. Consequently, as NGOs become increasingly beholden to donor funding, they are being overtaken by the agenda set by donors.

Public policy-making is being influenced on a global level by private actors, accountable only to their board members. We discuss the mounting evidence that clearly points to a clear nexus between different private actors – private foundations, consulting and accounting firms, private industry and global public–private partnerships. The precise role of this complex nexus in subverting public policy, it is argued, needs to be examined systematically.

The Trade Related Intellectual Property Rights (TRIPS) agreement harmonized laws that protect intellectual property (IP) in all countries and thus forced LMICs to allow patents on medicines, irrespective of the domestic situation. However, at the insistence of many LMICs, the TRIPS agreement incorporated a number of 'health safeguards' designed to mitigate the adverse impact of a strong patent regime in LMICs. The discussion on 'The TRIPS agreement: two decades of failed promises' takes stock of the experience of using the 'health safeguards' in the TRIPS agreement, and examines a number of emerging trends in the global trade environment that act as barriers to medicines access.

The analysis of the Haitian cholera epidemic contends that the popular consciousness of the epidemic, in donor countries, has been based on a fabricated narrative which has centred on the plight of the refugees affected by the January 2010 earthquake. This narrative is not only misleading, it misses out on the political context in which the epidemic took place. Haiti's story and its present plight need, instead, to be principally viewed in the context of how the country's political system and economy have been systematically undermined by its imperial neighbour.

Evidence is also presented to show that the World Bank's International Finance Corporation (IFC), through its Health in Africa initiative, works at odds with the commitment from the Bank's leadership to universal and equitable health coverage. While the initiative has failed to mobilize its target level of investment, of particular concern is the lack of focus on the poor. The Bank's response to the mid-term evaluation of the initiative does nothing to reassure critics that the IFC is genuinely committed to a pro-poor, evidence-based approach.

Finally, we analyse the growing trend of clinical trials being 'offshored' to LMICs. Case studies, presented in the chapter, reflect common trends in the preferred destinations of offshored clinical trials: weak regulatory systems and vulnerable populations that constitute a pliant pool of clinical trial subjects. The gross rights and ethical violations that are taking place reflect a nexus between multinational pharmaceutical companies, domestic regulatory agencies, pliant doctors leading clinical trials and regulatory agencies in the North.

### Resistance, actions and change

Three chapters in this section narrate the changing dynamics in Latin American countries that have witnessed significant social and political changes in the past decade. In Bolivia the concept of 'living well' (*vivir bien*) is contributing to the dismantling of colonial and neoliberal legacies of the past. El Salvador is embarking on a challenging process to ensure the irreversibility of the achievements made after the installation of a 'left' government in 2009. Venezuela faces the onslaught from the imperial US government and its allies in the country (the oligarchy, private media, the Catholic Church hierarchy, political parties now led by neo-fascist groups, etc.). The three countries represent different kinds of experiments, each in their own way attempting to chart a course that challenges and rejects the neoliberal framework. This contestation is being played out in the health sector as well, with entrenched neoliberal ideas being questioned and replaced by 'communitarian' approaches.

The analysis on two other countries in the region – Colombia and Peru

– represents a contrast. In both these countries, neoliberal hegemony is being challenged by popular movements. The two chapters narrate how such contestation is apparent in the struggles against reforms to the health system.

The global economic crisis has had a deep impact on people's lives in large parts of Europe. We carry vignettes, in this section, of the waves of protests and resistance movements that have started sweeping large parts of the continent. These target the austerity packages being imposed by the 'Troika' – the European Commission, the International Monetary Fund (IMF) and the European Central Bank – and also the EU–US negotiations for a new free trade agreement (the Transatlantic Trade and Investment Partnership, or TTIP). A linked case study narrates the story of Halkidiki – of a community in Greece that has collectively risen up in protest against a mining project.

We also focus, in this section, on the Right to Food (RTF) campaign in India. Over these years the RTF campaign has expanded into a wide network with members across the country representing different groups, including agricultural workers' unions, women's rights groups, Dalit rights groups, single women's networks, child rights organizations, those working with construction workers, migrant workers, homeless populations, etc. These groups have come together in the belief that 'everyone has a fundamental right to be free from hunger and that the primary responsibility for guaranteeing basic entitlements rests with the state'.

Finally the section foregrounds the story of the 'Aboriginal community-controlled health services in Australia'. This movement has been one of the key vehicles through which the Aboriginal community has been able to engage in the struggle for health. This struggle combines collective actions to access healthcare with those that address the social determinants of health.

**Towards a shared narrative for change**

We acknowledge that a single volume cannot encompass the wide range of issues that have a bearing on health in different parts of the world. Each community, country, region and continent has its own specificities, all of which need to be addressed. However, we do hope that the contents of *Global Health Watch 4* will stimulate readers to reflect more concretely about what needs to change, how things can be done differently, and how people can be at the centre of bringing about desired change. Above all, this volume is 'work in progress' towards the development of a shared narrative, located in a vision of equity and justice, and imbued with the urgency that the present global health crisis demands. Many of the ideas that are explored in this book are further detailed on the website of the Global Health Watch (www.ghwatch.org). Readers are invited to visit the website and contribute their own perspectives, so as to enrich this narrative that we seek to develop.

SECTION A

# THE GLOBAL POLITICAL AND ECONOMIC ARCHITECTURE

# A1 | THE HEALTH CRISES OF NEOLIBERAL GLOBALIZATION

## Introduction

The global economy has had a turbulent time over the past six years, creating greater inequities in health and in its social determinants. The Great Financial Crisis (GFC) began in 2007 and had deepened by 2008, sparking unprecedented public bailouts and stimulus spending by many of the world's richest and most powerful governments. This impressively rapid mobilization of public money forestalled a Great Depression but not a Great Recession (Box A1.1) from which much of the world has yet to recover. This period of powerful state intervention into the market economy, however, was very brief, and was quickly followed by the 'austerity agenda' adopted in most of the world's countries. Austerity was argued as being essential for reducing government debt, much of which was caused by the unregulated greed of global financial institutions that necessitated costly public rescues. Many are now questioning not only the health costs of austerity, but also its economic necessity. As the director-general of UNCTAD complained in that agency's 2011 report: 'Those who support fiscal tightening argue that it is indispensable for restoring the confidence of financial markets, which is perceived as key to economic recovery. This is despite the almost universal recognition that the crisis was the result of financial market failure in the first place' (UNCTAD 2011).

This recent tumultuous period is foreshadowed by a forty-year-old uncontrolled experiment in neoliberal globalization. The past forty years have seen a particular ideology, neoliberalism, dominate the norms or rules by which globalization has expanded. There are differing definitions of neoliberalism, but they distil to the same thing: a belief that free markets, sovereign individuals, free trade, strong property rights and minimal government interference are

---

### Box A1.1 Depression or recession?

There is no standard agreement on the difference between a depression and a recession, apart from the fact that a depression has a longer and more severe contraction in economic activity (usually measured by a decline in GDP approaching 10 per cent), usually accompanied by a sharp rise in unemployment rates.

the best recipe for enhancing human well-being. This belief, an extension of classical economic and political liberalism, was first promulgated by the Austrian economist Friedrich von Hayek in the 1940s. Hayek argued that the economy is too complex for governments to regulate, so markets should be allowed to regulate themselves through the 'rational' choices of hundreds of millions of individual producers and consumers. Two other economists of the same era, collaborators of John Maynard Keynes, expressed this somewhat differently as a belief that 'the nastiest of men for the nastiest of motives will somehow work for the benefit of all' (Robinson and Guillebaud 1941). The late Scottish-Australian health economist Gavin Mooney wrote in his last book: 'The best outcome in terms of bringing about real change would be to see an end to neo-liberalism. So many of the problems that beset societies today and their populations' health can be placed at its door ...' (Mooney 2012).

This chapter takes up Mooney's argument, and examines how and why neoliberal globalization has produced a global health crisis. It traces its forty-year history, describes three phases of neoliberalism (structural adjustment, financialization, and austerity), and examines how these phases have affected health. It then looks at oppositional or countervailing forces to neoliberalism's orthodoxy, and discusses a number of policy options and political strategies that public health activists might support or pursue to make globalization work for, or at least not against, greater equity in 'health for all'.

### From Neoliberalism 1.0 to Neoliberalism 3.0: an abbreviated history

*Neoliberalism 1.0: structural adjustment* Although neoliberalism's key tenets were defined by Hayek before the Second World War, Keynesian economics, with its emphasis on state intervention and regulation of private markets, held sway during the post-war reconstruction period and throughout much of the following three decades. The Cold War and the bipolar world provided decolonizing countries with options to experiment with mixed economies and with assigning a strong role for the state in economic planning and management. Neoliberalism's dominance in political and economic decision-making began to emerge only in the early 1970s. This was a decade marked by an increasing pace of economic recessions, oil embargoes and oil-price shocks that quadrupled the cost of capitalism's crude energy source. To help write off its Vietnam War debts and to stimulate its domestic economy, the USA in 1971 permanently unpegged the US dollar from the gold standard. This set financial exchanges adrift, allowing money to be made through currency speculation and entrenching the US dollar as the world's 'reserve currency' held by the central banks of governments and other financial institutions 'in reserve' as a means of paying off international debt obligations and of stabilizing the value of their own currency when needed. Two years later, the 1973 military coup in Chile gave the neoliberal economic disciples of Hayek and Milton Friedman their first experimental laboratory. In quick succession, Britain's

**Image A1.1** Children at a garbage dump in Rio: global poverty and inequality have risen (Camila Giugliani)

Margaret Thatcher, the USA's Ronald Reagan and Germany's Helmut Kohl joined Chile's Augusto Pinochet in ushering in neoliberalism 1.0. Although not yet a globally dominant discourse, the key tenet of Neoliberalism 1.0 was a belief that any form of state enterprise or service provision was 'second best' to private markets.

THE RISE OF NEOLIBERALISM 1.0 Neoliberalism 1.0 began its rapid ascent during the 1980s. This decade brought us the developing-world debt crisis, a result of oil-price shocks that had led many developing countries to borrow heavily to continue their post-colonial path to industrialization. First World banks flush with new 'petrodollars' lent indiscriminately, often to governments that were known or suspected to engage in corruption or misappropriation. Developing-world debt worsened dramatically when US-led monetary policy to control inflation led to huge increases in interest rates, rising from 11 per cent in 1979 to over 20 per cent in 1981. As the international debts of developing countries became due for refinancing, the super-high interest rates caused debt-servicing costs to skyrocket and debt loads to accelerate. Fearing sovereign defaults by heavily indebted countries (threatened first by Mexico) and an ensuing international financial crisis, the World Bank and the International Monetary Fund (IMF) stepped in with emergency loans and grants to keep the worst-affected nations afloat. Countries accepting these loans had to agree to several 'structural adjustment' conditionalities that embodied neoliberal economic principles, later codified as the 'Washington Consensus', named after the location of the head offices of the World Bank and the IMF. These conditionalities included:

- Privatization of state assets, in part to help governments pay off international loans;
- Deregulation, to enable rapid private-sector-led economic growth;
- Tax reform to attract foreign investment through lower corporate and marginal rates, or tax holidays, for foreign investments;
- Public deficit (the shortfall between revenues and expenditures in any single fiscal year) and debt (the total accumulated amount owed to creditors), in part to help governments pay off international loans; and
- Rapid liberalization of trade and financial markets on the theory that liberalization leads to economic growth (which it does sometimes but not always).

The health and social policy consequences of Neoliberalism 1.0 have been well documented, notably in Africa and Latin America, the two regions most affected by international debt obligations and most constrained by World Bank and IMF emergency loan conditionalities (Breman and Shelton 2001; SAPRIN 2004). These regions not only failed to grow economically (Figure A1.1), they also experienced severe retrenchments in public spending, upheavals in their domestic labour markets, and increased wealth inequalities within their borders. Central to structural adjustment was a reduction in social protection spending by governments, which subsequent analyses found to be the main cause of increases in poverty and inequality in the affected countries (UN Habitat 2003). Since poverty and inequality are the two greatest risk conditions for preventable disease, it is not surprising that structural adjustment led to

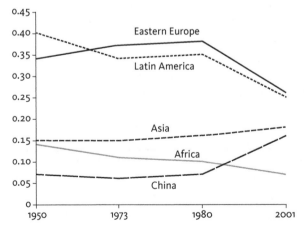

**A1.1** GDP per capita in developing regions relative to that in the developed world, 1950–2001 (*source*: UN DESA 2006)

**Image A1.2** Protests against the WTO at a G20 meeting in Paris in 2011 (Magali Delporte/ActionAid)

a slowdown or reversal of health gains, particularly affecting the poor, rural populations, women and children (SAPRIN 2004).

NEOLIBERALISM 1.0 AND THE 'FREE TRADE' AGENDA While structural adjustment was bringing many of the world's developing countries into alignment with neoliberal orthodoxy, negotiations on trade liberalization with high-income countries were doing much the same. The General Agreement on Tariffs and Trade (GATT) was originally a post-war mechanism for voluntary tariff reductions among wealthy countries, partly intended to decrease the risk of future world wars. Earlier periods of economic recession, followed by nationalist protectionism, including extremely high tariff barriers to imports, are considered part of the political and economic contexts that had led to the First and Second World Wars. Deeply entwining the economic fortunes of countries through trade (and later investment), liberalization is thought to act as a disincentive to war, since war would go against the interests of most economic elites. GATT negotiations, however, slowly deepened and expanded their purview, bringing more of the world's nations into the negotiating orbit and extending legally binding liberalization commitments beyond simply tariff barriers to encompass trade. The birth of the World Trade Organization (WTO) in 1995 introduced a much larger set of trade treaties, many of which went well beyond eliminating tariff barriers to incorporate extensive 'trade-related' domestic regulations, thereby reducing national space for policy-making (Lee

2006; Bond 2008; Koivusalo et al. 2008). Neoliberalism 1.0 began to transform the post-war mixed-economy welfare ('well/fair') state into the globalizing competitive state, with nations vying with each other to attract increasingly footloose capital (investment) and to enter or conquer new economic markets.

*Neoliberalism 2.0: financialization*

THE 'TRIUMPH' OF GLOBAL CAPITALISM Throughout this period, there were efforts by the global South to create a fairer 'new international economic order' to compensate for the wrongs of colonialism and foreign economic domination. A declaration on the new international economic order was actually endorsed by the United Nations in 1974, but then soon forgotten as neoliberal economics began its push to dominance. There were also exceptions to the general trend, with some regions of the world (notably such South-East Asian countries as Thailand, Malaysia, Singapore, Hong Kong, Taiwan and South Korea) not following the neoliberal path and performing economically much better over this period (Shin and Chang 2005). The erosion of national capitalisms with the deepening of internationalized trade and financial markets and the collapse of the Soviet Union, however, gradually entrenched Neoliberalism 1.0 while introducing us to Neoliberalism 2.0: the financialization of the economy.

Capitalism's inherent tendency towards a cyclical crisis of overproduction and under-consumption, leading to a declining rate of profits, accelerated in the 1970s. This led to a process of what Patrick Bond (2008) called 'shifting and displacing'. To boost their profit rates, corporations lowered their production costs by increasing the use of labour-saving technology and by outsourcing production to low-cost countries, and opened up new markets (by expanding the breadth and scope of trade treaties that lowered tariff and non-tariff barriers to goods and investment). Meanwhile, investors increased rapidly the financialization of the economy, made possible through new digital technologies, ideologically driven bank deregulation in the USA and the UK, and removal of capital controls that allowed rapid inflow and outflow of 'hot money' across borders. The global economy continued to grow during this period, but at a slower rate than in the 1960s (World Bank 2005). It was also far from stable, lurching from one regional recession or financial crisis to another (Cornia et al. 2008). The harmful effects on health of these episodic meltdowns caused by speculative capital flows were experienced first and most severely by those who were most vulnerable and least responsible for the genesis of these effects: women, children, the rural poor (Floro and Dymski 2000; Parrado and Zenteno 2001). The GFC of 2008 is the still-evolving outcome of Neoliberalism 2.0, a crisis whose inevitability was predicted by many heterodox (non-neoliberal) economists at least a decade before it occurred (Devarakonda 2012).

CAUSES OF THE GFC The immediate causes of the GFC are now fairly well known (see also GHW3, ch. A.1, www.ghwatch.org/sites/www.ghwatch.org/

files/A1.pdf). Corporate outsourcing led to large investment flows to low-wage countries. Despite China's efforts to retool its economy to increase domestic consumption (a response to the GFC's shrinking of its main export markets), its still-dominant 'factories for the world' continue to be fuelled by foreign investment, which accounts for over half of its exports and imports (World Bank 2010). Export-oriented developing countries (and especially China) accumulated huge amounts of foreign capital and banked this in low-interest-paying US treasury bills (the 'reserve currency'), while also having to borrow for short-term purposes on international markets at much higher interest rates. As a result of the interest-rate spread, developing countries by 2008 had transferred almost US$900 billion more annually to the USA and to other wealthy countries than they received in foreign investments or in foreign aid (UN DESA 2010). Investment banks and institutions in the rich world leveraged much of this new capital to bet on currencies, stocks and real estate, discovering that it was easier and faster to make money from money than lending it to the 'real economy' of production and consumption upon which most people rely for their livelihoods (Wade 2009). The USA and the UK were the two heavyweights when it came to staking their economic future on such financialization. 'Sub-prime' lending by banks led to the US housing bubble which helped the debt-financed consumption of cheap Chinese goods by that country's declining (outsourced) industrial working and middle classes. Imprudent loans that led to the real estate bubble in the south of Europe did much the same for the Eurozone.

The scale of this financialization is almost hard to imagine – the value of outstanding derivatives in 2011 exceeding US$700 trillion, or more than ten times the total value of the world's GDP (Figure A1.2) (see Box A1.2).

This represents an increase of over US$100 trillion in the six-month post-financial crisis period between 31 December 2010 and 30 June 2011, illustrating

---

### Box A1.2 What is a derivative?

A derivative, as its name implies, is a financial contract whose value derives from the performance of another 'underlying' entity, such as an asset (e.g. gold or other commodity), an index (related to stocks or bonds), interest rates and currency exchange rates. Derivatives can be futures (betting on a future price going up or down), options (to buy or sell a derivative at an agreed price during an agreed period of time), and swaps (exchanging different derivatives). Derivatives can be exchange-traded (on public financial exchanges) or 'over-the-counter' (private agreements between financial speculators). Over-the-counter trades, because they are less transparent, are sometimes referred to as the 'shadow banking system'.

## Box A1.3 Gambling in the casino of capitalism

Investor gambling with stocks and bonds or with other forms of derivatives is not new. Indeed, the 1600s witnessed a 'tulip mania' in the Netherlands, where widespread speculation led to the shooting up in the value of some tulip bulbs to more than ten times the average annual wage before the entire market collapsed, as all bubbles eventually do. Stock market gambling in the 1920s drove up the price of shares well beyond their relationship to their underlying value in the 'production and consumption' economy, precipitating the 1929 Wall Street Crash and the Great Depression. It also led to US legislation separating commercial banking (where people and firms make deposits and draw loans) from investment banking (where bankers leverage the value of their deposits and loans to 'play the markets'). The repeal of this 1933 legislation called the Glass-Steagall Act in 1999 is considered one of the precipitants of the GFC of 2008. What also distinguishes our more recent era of speculation is digital technology and financial market liberalization. The former allows instantaneous trades (most of the trades on many of the world's exchanges are now made by computers programmed to maximize short-term speculative capital gains) and new derivative instruments (increasing the gambling options almost exponentially). The latter allows for the free flow of capital and portfolio (speculative) investments in and out of countries, chasing short-term returns. For most economists, this is considered a recipe for chronic financial market instability, while for many countries experiencing the in- and outflows of 'hot money', it is a risk to their domestic economic security.

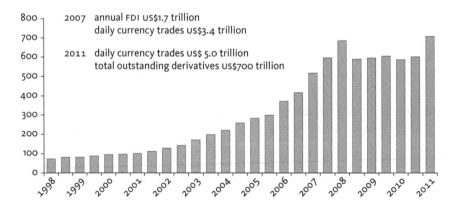

**A1.2** Total over-the-counter outstanding derivatives (in US$ trillions) (*source*: Zero Hedge 2011)

that what Susan George calls 'casino capitalism' (George 2008) and what David Korten (Korten 2001) describes as the 'funny money' game is far from being played out (Box A1.3).

To set the scale of this economic financialization in recent context: in 1980, the total value of *all* financial assets in the world was roughly equal to that of the world's GDP. In 2007, the total *annual* amount of foreign direct investment (FDI) that went into this real economy was US$1.7 trillion, a substantial amount but paltry when compared to the *daily* amount of currency exchanges in 2007 of US$3.4 trillion. In late 2011, and despite the GFC, this daily arbitrage clocked in at almost US$5 trillion (Bech 2012).

TRANSFERRING PUBLIC WEALTH TO CORPORATIONS The real toxicity of the financialized economy came in the form of 'asset backed commercial papers' (ABCPs), which bundled mortgage loans (debts) – many of them sub-prime and doomed to default – and aggressively sold them as sound investments. ABCPs allowed banks engaged in reckless lending practices to high-risk borrowers in an inflated housing market to offload their financial risks to others. Individuals, pension funds and other banks around the world bought into this scheme, partly on the strong endorsements of ABCPs by bond-rating agencies and by banks and their brokers selling them. This 'banking on bubbles'

**Image A1.3** Demonstration in Bali in December 2013: demands to curb corporate power have grown (Benny Kuruvilla)

began to unravel in 2007 with the collapse of the US housing market, leading to credit crunches (where banks refuse to lend to people, firms, countries or each other). The GFC was quickly followed by economic recession, counter-cyclical public spending (so called because the spending goes against, or is counter to, the business cycle) and publicly financed bailouts to cover the risks taken by private financiers. One estimate of the total amount of public financing that went into the bank rescues places it at US$11.7 trillion (Ortiz and Cummins 2013), several hundred billion of which were direct subsidies (Haldane et al. 2010). Less evident but more systemic are the interest-rate spreads on what governments provide to banks (whose credit rating assumes government bailouts when they fail), and what they then borrow back to cover this lending (with their own credit rating downgraded because of their rescues of banks, leading to higher borrowing costs). This interest-rate spread comprises a massive transfer of public wealth to the very corporations and individuals that were responsible for the GFC (Altvater and Mahnkopf 2012; Ortiz and Cummins 2013).

QUANTITATIVE EASING The rest of the recapitalization of banks came in the form of quantitative easing (QE). Governments in the most affected countries (the USA, the UK, Japan and several others) created new money *ex nihilo* (out of nothing) that was used to buy from distressed banks low-interest-bearing long-term government bonds or distressed ABCPs (sub-prime mortgages), and in the latter instance again effectively socializing the bad debts of private financiers. The amount of QE in the USA rose to US$3.8 trillion by year-end 2013 (Chapman 2013), almost half of it in the purchase of distressed ABCPs.

QE dramatically increases money supply, the intent being to encourage banks to lend to businesses (to produce) and to people (to consume), thereby reinvigorating the real economy. But this did not happen, because consumers, burdened with personal debt, and faced with the collapse of their housing equity and a surge in unemployment, were not borrowing and buying. Banks, instead, continued their practice of speculative portfolio and derivate investing (Hudson 2010), helping to drive up food prices globally (by betting on food futures) or to stall some of the growth in initially less affected middle-income economies by pouring in 'hot' money, driving up the value of the currencies of these countries ('Dutch disease') and depressing their export earnings (Box A1.5). Conversely, QE also suppressed the value of currencies in those countries that engaged in this practice (notably the USA and the UK), thereby making their exports more competitive globally.

Direct stimulus spending in the early year of the crisis (2008–09) is estimated at around US$2.4 trillion across fifty countries, most of them G20 or OECD members (Ortiz and Cummins 2013). The recessionary effects of the GFC on lost global income are enormously greater, and have been estimated at US$4 trillion annually (2008–12), with projections of medium-term losses ranging

---

**Box A1.4  Holding finance to account?**

The US banking company JP Chase Morgan in December 2013 agreed to a record US$13 billion civil fine, acknowledging 'it made serious misrepresentations to the public' about its residential mortgage-backed securities. Ironically, about half the fine (US$7 billion) will be a tax-deductible expense, so the public will partly subsidize the penalty (Chappell 2013). One of the more egregious examples of this pernicious practice was a 2007 bet placed by the Paulson Advantage hedge fund that the Goldman-Sachs' version of an ABCP would fail disastrously. It was actually designed to fail; yet one of Goldman-Sachs' trusted traders was busy selling this ABCP around the world as a solid, stellar investment. When it did fail, Paulson Advantage made US$3.5 billion on its hedge, eventually increasing to US$15 billion, about US$4 billion of which went directly to its CEO, John Paulson, who is reported as having assisted in creating the designed-to-fail ABCP in the first place. The Goldman-Sachs trader was eventually found liable on six counts of fraud, but faces no prison sentence. John Paulson was never charged for his role in the debacle, which launched him into Forbes' list of multi-billionaires (Stewart 2010). Burgle a house in dozens of American states three times (regardless of how minimal the value of the goods you have stolen) and you receive a life sentence in prison (the so-called three strikes rule). Burgle the global economy, thereby plunging millions into poverty, unemployment and poorer health, and you receive a slap on your wrist and/or enter the ranks of the world's wealthiest elites.

---

**Box A1.5  Dutch disease**

This term refers to the rise in the value of a country's currency. It was originally coined when the Netherlands experienced a (pre-euro) sudden increase in the value of its currency after the discovery of a large natural gas field in 1959. This led to a decline in its manufacturing exports, which made it more expensive for other countries to import because of the rise in the Dutch currency. The term now describes any development that leads to a large surge in foreign investment in a country, inflating the value of that country's currency.

---

between US$60 and US$200 trillion (Haldane et al. 2010; UNICEF 2012). The depth of global production chains meant that the GFC's credit crunch and the subsequent Great Recession (GR) rippled rapidly across supply chains in low- and middle-income countries. Estimates of the short-term social and health costs of the GR include:

- a rise in poverty (below $2/day) in developing countries of between 53 and 90 million (World Bank 2009a; ODI 2009a);
- an increase in childhood deaths due to increased food prices, declining incomes, decreased public health expenditures and lower rates of healthcare utilization, disproportionately affecting poorer populations;
- an increase in child labour and domestic violence (ODI 2009a);
- a decline in remittances (World Bank 2009a);
- a decline in net development assistance flows (CIDP 2013);
- a decrease in overall financial flows to developing countries (ODI 2009a); and
- a sharp rise in global unemployment of at least 69 million by the end of 2013, concentrated among young adults, creating a surplus (unemployed) labour pool of over 200 million, which is expected to rise even further to 210 million over the next five years (ILO 2011, 2013).

The story does not end with the GFC and the GR. Rather, the response to the 2008 crisis marks the advent of Neoliberalism 3.0 (Hendrikse and Sidaway 2010): the 'austerity agenda'.

*Neoliberalism 3.0: austerity*
RISING ECONOMIC INEQUALITY One of the effects of neoliberalism's earlier versions was the reversal of the post-war social contract in high-income countries (in Europe, for example, through the construction of the 'welfare state'), which had helped to flatten gross inequities in income distribution in most of these countries. Thus, a small group of people captured most of the gains of the past several decades of economic growth. While the 2008 GFC wiped out trillions of dollars in paper wealth, affecting the pensions and savings of many of the world's middle and working classes, the 24 million people whom investment banks refer to as 'high- and ultra-high net worth individuals' saw their balance sheets decline for a year or two, but then increase by over 20 per cent (Baxter 2011), a remarkable feat never accomplished by the pre-1929 oligarchs. Billionaire wealth rose by 20 per cent alone in 2012 over 2011, in what Forbes describes as 'a very good year for billionaires' (Forbes 2013). In 2012, the world's 1,426 billionaires between them had as much wealth (US$5.4 trillion) (ibid.) as the entire continent of Africa (US$2.3 trillion) and India (US$3.2 trillion) (Keating et al. 2012). Given Africa's and India's combined population of 2.2 billion in 2011, this represents an inequality ratio of roughly 1.5 million to 1, a ratio that does not even adjust for the wealth of the thirteen billionaires in Africa and of the fifty-five billionaires in India (see Figure A1.3).

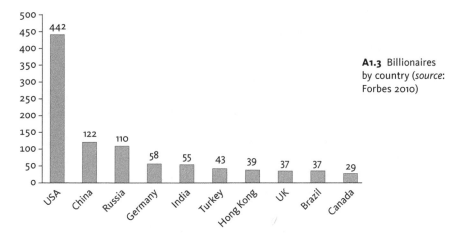

**A1.3** Billionaires by country (*source*: Forbes 2010)

In 2013, the world's eighty-five wealthiest people owned as much wealth as the bottom half (over 3.5 billion) of the world's entire population. By early 2014 only sixty-seven people had the same amount of wealth (equal to half the world's population) and even as the journalist with *Forbes* was finishing the article, this number had dropped to sixty-six! Each billionaire had as much wealth as the poorest 52 million of the world's population (Forbes 2014). By 2014, the number of the world's billionaires had surged to 2,170; and the amount of wealth they owned more than doubled between 2009 (the year after the GFC) and 2013 (Osborne 2014). Although some of the US-based billionaires have pledged to give roughly half of their fortunes to charity, this allows individuals to determine the where, what, why and how of future development for much of humanity, removed from the messy discourse of democracy and civil society engagement.

ATTACK ON THE PUBLIC SECTOR The stunning failure of the 2008 crisis to delegitimize neoliberalism reveals the extent to which public policy had been influenced by the private sector (and primarily financial institutions). Neoliberalism was never about eliminating the state; instead, it was about occupying it, 'a reconfiguring of both (state and market) so that they become thoroughly enmeshed' (Hendrikse and Sidaway 2010: 2039). The 'austerity agenda' is merely one of the means of completing this phase of neoliberalism. Its key tenets differ little from those of Neoliberalism 1.0 (structural adjustment):

- reduction in social protection spending and public sector employment;
- increased VAT (consumption) taxation;
- reduction or elimination of public deficits;
- reduction of public debt;
- increased user pay in public programmes (co-payments);
- privatization of state assets; and

• increased public–private partnerships (PPPs) characterized by the public absorbing most of the risk and enjoying little of the gain of private sector financing for public goods and services (Ortiz and Cummins 2013).

One key difference is that these policies are now a global phenomenon affecting high-income countries as well. Contrary to widely held assumptions, however, this fiscal contraction is still most severe in the developing world:

> Overall, 68 developing countries are projected to cut public spending by 3.7% of GDP, on average, in the third phase of the crisis (2013–15) compared to 26 high-income countries, which are expected to contract by 2.2% of GDP, on average … In terms of population, austerity will be affecting 5.8 billion people or 80% of the global population in 2013; this is expected to increase to 6.3 billion or 90% of persons worldwide by 2015. (Ibid.: i)

The biggest austerity cuts in public spending are anticipated in North Africa, the Middle East and sub-Saharan Africa. What is particularly disconcerting is that a comparison of the 2010–12 and 2005–07 periods reveals that nearly one quarter of developing countries appear to be undergoing excessive contraction, defined as cutting expenditures (as a percentage of GDP) to below pre-GFC levels (Ortiz et al. 2011). They are also being imposed by the 'troika' (the European Union, the European Central Bank and the IMF) in Europe, and the majority of IMF post-crisis loans continue to push for elimination of food and fuel subsidies; wage bill cuts; rationalizing (reducing) safety net expenditures; and pension reform to delay eligibility. Several countries have been advised to reform their public health systems and to increase labour market flexibilization, while many governments are attempting to generate revenue by broadening their consumption taxes to include items disproportionately consumed by poor households.

### Modelling health costs

The GFC and the ensuing Great Recession (GR) are expected to raise poverty rates for those in less secure employment settings (Bezruchka 2009; Quintana and Lopez-Valcarcel 2009); increase homelessness; and deepen reliance on low-cost, highly processed obesogenic foods. Stress levels related to unemployment, poverty and insecurity are also predicted to rise; and suicide rates since the crisis have indeed increased by 12 to 15 per cent in the worst-affected European countries (Stuckler et al. 2011). Figure A1.4 presents the different ways in which the GFC and GR are affecting health.

The most direct link between the GFC and health equity is the steep decline in overall economic activity. Financial crises reduce the tax base of governments, and hence limit their ability to spend on health, education, social protection and other important health-promoting programmes and sectors. Governments could respond to this revenue loss by increasing progressive

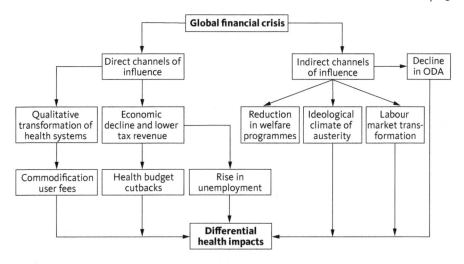

**A1.4** The global financial crisis and health (*source*: Ruckert and Labonté 2012)

taxation, thereby also reducing the extremes in wealth inequalities that have characterized neoliberal policies to date. Most governments have not done so, however, responding instead with austerity. Several countries have imposed healthcare budget cuts exceeding 20 per cent, with the most dramatic being in Greece, where the hospital budget has been cut by more than 40 per cent while demand (due to the health hardships induced by austerity measures) has increased by approximately 25 per cent (Kentikelenis et al. 2011). Diseases such as HIV and malaria are again on the rise in Greece; HIV rates among intravenous drug users have increased rapidly after healthcare budget cuts eliminated needle-exchange programmes (ibid.; see also Chapter A.2).

Similar health and social protection cutbacks and imposition of user fees, with similar harmful fallouts, are occurring throughout much of the developing world. The one notable exception to this declining trend is Latin America, where social spending has increased post-GFC (Bárcena 2012), primarily in the form of conditional (or unconditional) cash transfers. Latin American economies have largely been able to avoid having to rely on IMF and World Bank lending in the aftermath of the crisis, which partly explains their expansionary crisis response compared to financially dependent European and African countries.

Another important impact of the GFC, which has direct health effects, is the impact on employment. Not only has unemployment globally and throughout most of the world's regions increased, but social protection for the jobless has also decreased. Moreover, the quality of the employment that is still available has deteriorated, becoming increasingly insecure and precarious in the name of labour market 'flexibility' and global competitiveness. The growth of precarious working conditions is related to the wave of neoliberal policies implemented since the early 1980s, with their emphasis on 'reducing the constraints on the movement of workers into and out of jobs previously constrained by labour laws, union agreements, training systems, or labour markets that protect workers' income and job security' (Benach and Muntaner 2007: 276). This trend has given rise to a new term, the 'precariat', consisting of people 'working in short-term jobs, without recourse to stable occupational identities or careers, without reliable social protection support and without protective regulations' (Standing 2011).

Two-tiered systems of remuneration are increasingly emerging in the remaining sectors of industrial production in high-income countries, characterized by lower pay and fewer benefits for younger workers. The growth in insecure or part-time minimum wage 'McJobs' in the USA is projected to see four out of five Americans experience working poverty at some point in their lives (Helmore 2013). Many of these workers are skilled and highly educated, the 'education premium' in labour markets being increasingly confined to those working in the financial or digital sectors. Similarly, a quarter of Germany's employed workforce is trapped in insecure 'mini-jobs' (low-paid, part-time), the second-highest percentage of low-earning workers (defined as those earning wages that are less than two-thirds the average) in the Eurozone (Connolly and Osborne 2013). The UK is gaining notoriety for its surge in 'zero hours' contract employment (Goodley and Inman 2013), a post-GFC rise in new jobs that are only part-time or temporary, and a fall in the median wage, disproportionately affecting women workers (Helm 2013).

The erosion in labour markets is not just a rich-world phenomenon. Across Latin America, and despite a decrease in extreme poverty, the majority of those employed in cities work in the 'informal' (underpaid, lower-paid, insecure) sector (IADB 2011). Africa, despite posting some of the world's highest post-GFC economic growth figures and witnessing the rise of a small middle class, remains mired in income inequalities, with its economic growth failing to create new or sustainable jobs. China has experienced growing labour unrest as many employers (both foreign and domestic firms) have been unable or unwilling to meet their payroll obligations, or have threatened to move to lower-wage regions in the aftermath of the GFC's global economic slowdown or simply to avoid workers' demands for a fairer share of the wealth created by the country's manufacturing sector (Chan 2012). In late April 2013, the world was stunned by images of the collapse of the Rana Plaza textile factory in Bangladesh, which killed over 1,100 workers, mostly women. This was the worst, but not the first, such tragedy in the country, where textile workers earn less than half of what is considered a minimum living wage producing inexpensive clothing that makes life more affordable for the poor in wealthier countries (War on Want 2011).

### Towards a progressive public health agenda

What, then, are public health activists to do?

A first step is to recognize that we are not alone. Many multilateral agencies, including the World Health Organization (WHO), UNCTAD, the United Nations Children's Fund (UNICEF) and the International Labour Organization (ILO) are starting to express concern about the harmful effects of the financial crisis and the austerity agenda. There is a short (but challenging) list of actions that public health activists need to promote:[1]

- re-regulate global finance;
- reject austerity;
- increase progressive taxation;
- close tax havens;
- support global tax systems;
- confront the limits to growth;
- reclaim public discourse.


*Re-regulate global finance*  A key component of re-regulation is the re-establishment of legislative rules that clearly separate commercial from investment banking. A new US 'Volcker' rule, still to be finalized and scheduled to take effect in July 2014, would put some barriers between the two practices, but US banks and investors with deep pockets are protesting loudly and lobbying fiercely. An estimated US$5 billion was spent as lobbying costs between 1998 and 2008 to remove these barriers in the first place (Wall Street Watch 2009) and in increasing their loan leverage (see Box A1.6).

The UK is also contemplating banking re-regulation, but this would ring-fence only one third of commercial banking from its investment branches, and then not until 2015. Efforts to reduce bank leverage through Basel III rules (see Box A1.6) have been weak at best, with banks being required to retain just

---

### Box A1.6  Basel III and bank leverage

Bank leverage is the extent to which banks can lend money based on the assets they hold. In the run-up to the GFC the ratio of bank leverage in the USA was reduced from 1:17 to 1:40. This meant that while earlier with assets worth 100 dollars they could lend 1,700 dollars, now they were allowed to lend 4,000 dollars. This change in the US law was a major reason why the real estate bubble burst and why the banks considered 'too big to fail' started failing.

Basel III is a global, voluntary regulatory standard for global banks, developed in response to the deficiencies in financial regulation revealed by the GFC. Basel III is supposed to strengthen requirements for bank liquidity and decrease bank leverage. The standards were initially scheduled to be introduced from 2013 until 2015; but have now been postponed.

**Image A1.4** Austerity to rescue the big banks from failing (Indranil Mukhopadhyay)

3 per cent in assets relative to loans (a ratio of about 33:1). Moreover, assets include not just cash on hand, but also investments, such as BBB-rated bonds (otherwise known as 'junk bonds') (Kiladze 2014; Micossi 2013; Brunsden et al. 2013). Also, none of these rules takes full effect until 2019. The architect of even these modest reforms has publicly complained that the Conservative UK government has already watered them down in response to the US$150 million the financial sector spends lobbying politicians and treasury officials there each year (Treanor 2012). Clearly, banking re-regulation remains elusive; with no apparent political will to break banks (too big to fail) into smaller sizes.

*Reject austerity* When the GFC hit in 2008, governments around the world did not respond with austerity; instead, they became profligate spenders trying to save a collapsing world economy. But in less than two years, with some Eurozone countries rapidly accumulating high levels of debt, the neoliberal playbook has returned to rule. Explanations for this volte-face include ideology (politicians committed to neoliberalism and the 'minimal state'), desperation (politicians unable or unwilling to consider other ideas), mercantilism (the troika's austerity regime in the Eurozone, by driving down the value of the euro, makes Germany's exports globally more competitive) and econometric analyses (in particular, a study that found that government spending in affected Eurozone countries would have a negative impact on economic growth) (Reinhart and Rogoff 2010). All these explanations are fallacious. Austerity in most countries has failed to accelerate economic growth, even as it drives up unemployment and poverty rates and creates new direct and indirect health risks.

The initial assumption in the IMF's call for austerity in the Eurozone was that the 'fiscal multiplier' of new government spending would be between 0.4 and 1.2, which it averaged to 0.5. This meant that, according to the IMF's calculations, for every dollar spent by an indebted government, economic output would *shrink* by 50 cents. This was like music to the ears of neoliberal ideologues, keen to reduce the role of the state, and the IMF's projections formed the basis for prescriptions asking for savage cuts in public spending. The tragedy is (especially for the millions in the Eurozone who continue to suffer as a result of the austerity measures) the calculations were patently wrong! In 2012, the IMF recalculated its fiscal multiplier data and found that the range was actually between 0.9 and 1.7; and for Eurozone countries sinking deeper into recession owing to austerity, it was likely at the higher end of the estimate (Talley 2013; Blanchard and Leigh 2013). In other words the revised data show that increased public spending would actually lead to an *expansion* of the economy!

There is, in fact, robust evidence that every dollar in public spending can generate more than a dollar in economic growth in the 'real economy' of production and consumption, by purchasing goods and services that employ people, by employing people who purchase other goods and services, and by signalling stability to the private sector, which is then motivated to undertake its own increased activity (Stanford 2013b). In the post-GFC environment, government spending is thought to have an average fiscal multiplier effect of 1.6. Recent estimates of European public spending by sector show much greater multiplier impacts for investments in health, education and environmental protection than, for example, in defence. Other data from Eurozone countries show that governments with higher rates of spending are recovering faster from the 2008 GFC (Reeves et al. 2013). There is similar evidence available from the USA as well. Emergency unemployment benefits, extended by the US government in the wake of the GFC, are credited with reducing the economic impacts of the recession. These emergency benefits ended in December 2013 for 1.3 million Americans, which one economist estimated is costing the US economy US$1 billion a week, owing to decreased spending by the jobless (Lewis 2014).

Simply put, government spending in the health and social protection sectors is not only good for health equity and social stability, it is also good for the economy. Even the World Bank and the IMF have begun to accept the empirical evidence of the shortcomings of austerity, calling for government caution in implementing public sector cutbacks in recognition of the 'fiscal multiplier' effect of government spending.

The health-harmful effects of austerity are being better documented and becoming more widely known. This evidence in itself provides health activists with strong arguments to reject austerity. Even by the standards of very mainstream economics, austerity simply does not make any sense. Say it loudly. Say it often.

*Increase progressive taxation* Governments in the past have defaulted on their debts, with the IMF warning that this may occur again for many high-income nations carrying historically high debt loads. It is important to consider how and why these debts arose (Figure A1.5) and whether they are, in fact, unsustainable.

In the high-income countries, public debt rose rapidly after both the world wars owing to government-financed reconstruction. Public debt then fell dramatically over the next three decades, the result of high levels of economic growth, strong trade unions (which increased the share of economic wealth that went to labour) and progressive taxation. These were also decades of rapid expansion in government spending in education, health, housing and other public goods and services that played an important role in reducing income inequalities and health inequities within these countries. Public debt began to rise again only with the dawn of neoliberal globalization, and when governments spent to save global capitalism.

Beneath the broad contours shown in Figure A1.5 lies a trend that is extremely important: the decline in progressive taxation and government tax revenues (as a percentage of GDP) experienced by many high-income countries, which began almost three decades ago.

The argument for lowering taxes is that it stimulates economic growth (people spend more, companies invest more). But this argument ignores the fiscal multiplier effect of government spending, and evidence that corporations rarely invest all of their tax savings in new economic activity. A recent analysis in Canada found that, at best, corporations reinvest only 10 per cent of the savings generated by tax cuts (Stanford 2013a). Accounting for an average fiscal multiplier effect of 1.6, retained public revenue and spending outperforms

**A1.5** Public debt in advanced economies (as a percentage of GDP) (*source:* IMF 2012: 101)

corporate tax-cut reinvestment by almost 10:1. The net effects of such tax cuts, then, are a substantial redistribution of capital from public to private, and a further 'starving' of the redistributive welfare state. Canada's finance minister recently warned that 'Those that suggest that austerity should be abandoned … that's the road to ruin' (Engler 2013). Yet had the last six years of tax cuts in Canada not been implemented, there would have been no deficit and no need for austerity.

The same rebuttal applies to arguments for reducing tax rates for high-income earners. Most of their tax savings go into investing, and much of that goes into the 'funny money' financialized economy of derivatives and speculation. As a 2013 US review of econometric studies concluded, raising marginal tax rates in that country from their present historic low of 35 per cent to their previous high of 68 per cent would have no statistically significant impact on factors driving growth in the 'real economy' of production and consumption. It would, however, reduce poverty, shrink inequality, and stimulate growth through higher levels of public spending (Fieldhouse 2013). An IMF study was a little more cautious but reached the same conclusion, estimating that a marginal rate of 60 per cent would do no harm and more likely good to US economic growth (Elliott 2013).

Stated simply, there would be no financial crisis and no need for austerity in most of the world's high-income countries if progressive taxation rates had been retained. For many developing countries, the same would be true had they not followed decades of advice (or loan conditionalities) from the World Bank and the IMF to keep their tax rates low to attract foreign investment. Figure A1.6 provides a snapshot of what this means at a global level, and only for the most recent decade. Using global taxation data from the World Bank

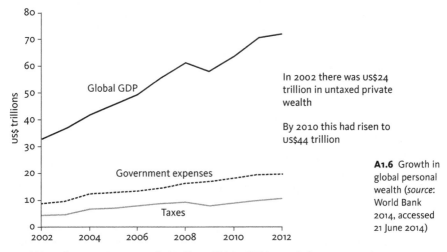

In 2002 there was US$24 trillion in untaxed private wealth

By 2010 this had risen to US$44 trillion

**A1.6** Growth in global personal wealth (*source*: World Bank 2014, accessed 21 June 2014)

*Notes*: 1. Government expenses calculated by multiplying GDP by reported expense percentage
2. 2002 and 2003 global GDP calculated by adding up country GDP as reported in table attached to: http://data.worldbank.org/indicator/NY.GDP.MKTP.CD/countries/ 1W?display=graph

data set (for years 2002 to 2010), and monetizing this taxation using constant dollar estimates of global economic product (GDP) for each of these years, three things are immediately apparent. First, although average global taxation revenues did increase between 2002 and 2007, revenues have been flat since. Secondly, government expenditures continued to rise over this period, but the gap between revenues and expenditures widened substantially after the GFC, creating the fiscal deficits now driving the austerity agenda. Thirdly, the value of global economic product (GDP) skyrocketed in comparison to both, dipping slightly after the GFC but quickly assuming its upward trajectory. Monetizing the difference between taxed and untaxed global wealth in 2002 and 2010, the value rose from US$24 trillion (2002) to US$44 trillion (2010). We are left with a familiar conclusion: our austerity agenda does not arise from a problem of scarcity or fiscal debt, but from a situation of inequality and under-taxation.

Forty years of neoliberal messaging, and thirty years of tax reductions and global tax competition, make it difficult politically to argue for progressive tax increases. Yet opinion polls around the world consistently find that people are willing to pay more taxes once the public services bought by taxes are made clear. The American jurist, Oliver Wendell Holmes, a century ago said, 'Taxes are the price we pay for civilization.' They are also the price we pay for decent and equitable health. That is the health activists' take-home message.

*Close tax havens* This progressive-tax message also needs to become global. Unless all countries begin to ratchet up their tax rates, uncontrolled capital will continue to 'fly' into lower-tax nations. Many of these lower-tax nations operate as tax havens (more formally known as 'offshore financial centres'), where the wealthy and transnational corporations can avoid taxation almost altogether. Banks in these tax-haven nations that are largely under British, American and European aegis shelter an estimated US$21–32 trillion in personal wealth. The forgone annual tax revenues on the investment growth of this principal alone range between US$180 and US$250 billion (Henry 2012; Oxfam 2013).

While capital flight and tax evasion have a negative effect on the revenues of high-income countries affected by the GFC, they have been fiscally devastating for many low-income countries. The African continent has lost more wealth over the past forty years in illicit capital flight, owing partly to criminality and corruption, but most of it involving commercial tax evasion, than it has received in foreign aid (African Development Bank and Global Financial Integrity 2013). This tax evasion (or, when legally 'grey', tax avoidance) occurs when companies route one step of their global production chain through a tax haven, 'transfer pricing' the cost of the goods leaving that country for their final market destination at exorbitantly high rates, thereby retaining most of the profit in the tax-haven subsidiary.

In the immediate aftermath of the 2008 GFC, many of the G20 countries began to talk tough about tax havens, with some successes in prising open the private Swiss bank accounts of tax dodgers. But the requirements for tax-haven reform were so lax that nothing has changed. In fact the top ten investment banks (all operating in tax-haven countries) saw their 'wealth management' jump from US$2.3 trillion to US$6 trillion post-GFC (Johannesen and Zucman 2012). Following more recent reports of high-profile tax avoidance by multinational corporations, the G20 in September 2013 committed, more ambitiously, to developing a global system of automatic exchange of tax information by 2015 to avoid transfer-pricing practices and to ensure that taxes are paid in the jurisdictions where economic profits and value are created (Curry 2013). Whether this latest initiative will be successful remains to be seen.

*Support global tax systems* Globalized financial markets require systems of global taxation, and the GFC has reinvigorated the debate over the implementation of a financial transaction tax (FTT), previously known as a 'Tobin tax' (named for the economist who first proposed it). The theory behind the original Tobin tax was that it would dampen destabilizing speculative capital flows, although evidence to date indicates that this may not be the case, as the rate suggested (0.05 or 0.005 per cent) may be too low to affect speculators. Some have called for an additional Spahn tax, with rapidly escalating rates should there develop panic outflows or if there is evidence of significant capital flight. The 2008 GFC has created new FTT adherents, no longer necessarily with a view to dampening speculation or to financing global development. The current concern is with raising funds to recapitalize central banks weakened by private-bank bailouts or to provide emergency relief for countries at risk of sovereign default. The potential revenues of an FTT could be large. A low rate of 0.05 per cent (5 cents for every 100 dollars) if applied to bond and share sales globally could raise US$410 billion. A much lower tax rate of 0.005 per cent (5 cents for every 1,000 dollars), if applied globally to all foreign exchanges, including derivatives and over-the-counter trading, would raise US$863 billion annually; this means that at the 0.05 per cent rate, it would total US$8.63 trillion (McCulloch and Pacillo 2011).

By late 2011, forty countries had some form of an FTT, raising about US$28 billion (Griffith-Jones and Persaud 2012). In January 2013, eleven EU countries agreed to implement an FTT, albeit at a low level that would raise about €35 billion annually (Inman 2013). The UK government remains fiercely opposed to this EU initiative, fearing that it will dampen the financial sector operating out of the City of London, a sector that contributes relatively little to the country's GDP, employment or taxation revenue, but which creates enormous wealth for elite global investors and investment bankers. Several countries have expressed public support for a global FTT, including the

**Image A1.5** Climate change discussions consigned to the dustbin of conventional growth rhetoric (Indranil Mukhopadhyay)

sixty-three member nations of the Leading Group on Innovative Financing for Development. There is also general agreement on a distribution formula for the revenues raised by an FTT, with half going into public deficit and debt reduction and the other half going into funds to help developing countries meet development goals and adapt to and mitigate the impacts of climate change. But powerful countries are opposed to a global FTT, including the USA, the UK, China and India.

*Confront the limits to growth* This is not a new issue. Economists and eco-logists have been warning about the limits to growth for decades. Despite the dramatic evidence of climate change, the GFC and GR consigned concerns over a probable and imminent environmental catastrophe into the dustbin of conventional growth rhetoric. Early in the recession, the World Bank argued that 'the financial system should be fixed, and countercyclical spending should be increased', in order 'to increase consumption to re-energize production to recreate growth' (World Bank 2009b). In the same year, the UK Department for International Development (DfID) was more critical, noting that 'Climate change, state fragility, violent conflict, population growth and urbanization are all rising up the agenda [and] throw into sharp relief questions about the long term viability of aspects of the market-economy model.' Its conclusion, nonetheless, was simple: 'Maintaining growth is a priority' (DfID 2009).

Even if we succeed in constraining what David Harvey (2003) described as neoliberalism's predatory 'capital accumulation through dispossession', by reining in 'casino capitalism' and subordinating the global economy to social purposes, there is an environmental limit to any 'business as usual' approach to the 'real economy' of production and consumption. As Tim Jackson, Economics Commissioner, Sustainable Development Commission, pointed out in 2009: 'There is as yet no credible, socially just, ecologically sustainable scenario of continually growing incomes for a world of nine billion people' (Jackson 2009: 8). The growth model of the economy must be displaced if environmental sustainability is to be achieved. The Commission modelled two scenarios for such a displacement to show that it could be done. The first scenario (low growth and sustainability) would require substantial forms of national and global wealth redistribution; a small redistributive tax on the richest quintile of the world would have a far more dramatic impact on poverty and inequality reductions than conventional 'trickle-down' growth. It further assumes a large downward shift in work-time so that more people work less for reasonable incomes to avoid massive unemployment, increased social protection spending, and a reversal of the consumer culture. The second scenario (to complement the first) demands a shift into a non-fossil-fuel economy. This would require consensus to be built on a global scale around the achievement of a 'green' future as a global public good.

A carbon taxation scheme is also an unavoidably urgent tool. Without a carbon tax to accompany such global measures as an FTT, historic, geographic and intergenerational ecological imbalance will persist. Moreover, a carbon tax can be inherently redistributive, since it is the wealthier few who have disproportionately large carbon footprints. And as a colleague recently pointed out: the two most powerful private corporate actors in the world today (often enwrapped in each other) are banks and oil companies. It would be dangerous to tax one into regulatory submission without doing likewise for the other.

*Reclaim public discourse* There remains the need to continue advancing policy and programmatic alternatives to the world we inhabit, not with naive presumptions about the exercise of power, yet with a level of detail that demands engagement by the powerful. Our neoliberal nemesis knows this necessity better than we do, with its short, sharp, simple messaging that taps into a moral and emotive state. Blaming government for undermining the nobility of the individual, and equating less government with more personal power, is a message that sells well across social classes. It may be empirically fatuous, but if veracity were a criterion for marketing, we would not have the multibillion-dollar advertising industry. In one of the presentations at the third People's

Health Assembly in Cape Town in 2012, four similarly short, sharp, simple messages were suggested:

- a life with security;
- opportunities that are fair;
- a planet that is habitable;
- governance that is just.

The first reclaims the security agenda by connecting it to employment, social protection, the environment and safety and freedom from the necessity of gated communities designed to protect the fabulously wealthy from the rest of us. The demand for equal opportunities links to how a fair taxation regime combined with high social spending can level our grossly uneven playing fields. The need for a habitable planet needs little explanation; ecology will sustain and direct the radical politics of the future. Governance – the space where states, markets and civil society attempt to manage the crises of capitalist modernity – taps into the issue of social rights and political participation to decide where public investment should be made. People mobilize in anger, for a time, but it takes a larger and more inclusive vision of how we might live to sustain organized movements that can take us forward from there.

Another simple statement of purpose is the vision from the *People's Charter for Health*, which commits activists to achieving equity, ecologically sustainable development and peace ... a world in which a healthy life for all is a reality; a world that respects, appreciates and celebrates all life and diversity; a world that enables the flowering of people's talents and abilities to enrich each other; a world in which people's voices guide the decisions that shape our lives. There are more than enough resources to achieve this vision (People's Health Movement 2000).

There is a further challenge. Forty years of a dominant discourse of individualism, coupled with attacks on the state by the right (aided as well by attacks from the left) and fused with media-hyped stories of corruption, have bred a cynicism about organized politics that only strengthens the neoliberal agenda. Even as political participation is thriving in many low- and middle-income countries (at least where it is not violently suppressed), it is waning in most of the democratic high-income countries. Writing about the Republican Party's efforts in 2013 to make the US political system ungovernable by forcing the federal government into bankruptcy, Robert Reich argues that this is the intent of right-wing conservatives: 'to make us all so cynical about government that we give up ... making it easier for the moneyed interests to get whatever they want' (Reich 2013).

Activists in the progressive health movement need to revalorize the role of the state: not the competitive state of Neoliberalism 1.0, the investment state of Neoliberalism 2.0 or the austerity state of Neoliberalism 3.0, but the regulatory and redistributive state that provides the goods and services essential to public health. Revalorizing (or simply valorizing) the role of the state will require different arguments and claims in different countries, depending on the levels of democratic accountability, fiscal transparency and existing levels of taxation and public spending. But freeing governments from their neoliberal prison is one of the most important political tasks for social activists, regardless of the mobilizing issue.

As we engage with this task, we need finally to reclaim public discourse. We do not have a fiscal crisis. We have a crisis of inadequate taxation. We are not living in conditions of scarcity. We are living in conditions of inequality. Our voices of opposition to neoliberal globalization need to be louder and stronger. Evidence and ethics are both on our side.

**Where should health activists start?**

Tackling the underlying global (political and economic) determinants of health and injustice can seem an impossible task. Capitalism (neoliberal or otherwise) has proved incredibly resilient to crises. But there are several ways in which health activists can participate in mounting a challenge.

1 Recognize that the health sector is not alone in seeking a globe that is just and sustainable. Peasants' movements, labour organizations, environmental groups, women's groups and many others are also critiquing the predatory inequities of neoliberal globalization and pressuring their governments for reforms.

2 Globalization, and particularly its suite of binding trade and investment treaties, has put restraints on the abilities of governments to manage economies for socially useful purposes. But national governments can push back from such agreements or can otherwise ensure that they have much stronger and legally binding language protecting their rights to regulate in any way they deem necessary to protect public health, the environment and other public goods. National governments ultimately are responsible for the shape globalization takes; they are the first targets for health advocacy aimed at securing a healthy, equitable and environmentally sustainable future.

3 Most countries have social movement groups engaged in some form of advocacy work at the national level on one or another of the key globalization-related determinants of health within their borders. This work could be around improving or reasserting labour rights, expanding social protection coverage, increasing and improving the fairness of domestic taxation to finance public goods, ensuring access to quality healthcare without financial barriers, strengthening gender rights and those for marginalized or discriminated groups, protecting the environment and reducing fossil-fuel dependency, and so on. Such groups need to continue to 'act locally', but to link up with their international counterparts to not only 'think globally', but also to 'advocate globally'. They also need volunteer resources. Pick

a group that comes closest to supporting your local passion, and support its work nationally while ensuring the globalization dimension is never lost sight of.

4 Keep abreast of globalization-related developments, and of useful critiques of neoliberal globalization and its reform and more revolutionary alternatives. Social media, blogs and online discussion groups have become important tools in maintaining a 'watching brief' on these developments.

5 Avoid pessimism of the intellect, and practise optimism of the will. Consider optimism as a purposeful act of political resistance.

## Note

1 There should be another area on this list: ensure that new trade and investment treaties fully protect the policy space of governments for public health regulation and do not further empower corporations over states and citizens. But any reasonable discussion of this issue falls beyond the scope of this chapter.

## References

African Development Bank and Global Financial Integrity (2013) *Illicit Financial Flows and the Problem of Net Resource Transfers from Africa: 1980–2009*, Tunis-Belvedère, Tunisia/Washington, DC: African Development Bank/Global Financial Integrity.

Altvater, E. and B. Mahnkopf (2012) 'European integration at the crossroads: deepening or disintegration?', in N. Pons-Vignon and P. Ncube (eds), *Confronting Finance: Mobilizing the 99 per cent for economic and social progress*, Geneva: International Labour Organization.

Bárcena, A. (2012) 'Financiamiento para el desarrollo sostenible', United Nations Economic Commission for Latin America and the Caribbean (ECLAC), www.bndes.gov.br/SiteBNDES/export/sites/default/bndes_pt/Galerias/Arquivos/conhecimento/seminario/economiaverde_60ANOS_alicia.pdf.

Baxter, J. (2011) 'The glossary of greed', *Pambazuka News*, www.pambazuka.org/en/category/features/72112.

Bech, M. (2012) 'FX volume during the financial crisis and now', *BIS Quarterly Review*, March, pp. 33–43, www.bis.org/publ/qtrpdf/r_qt1203f.pdf.

Benach, J. and C. Muntaner (2007) 'Precarious employment and health: developing a research agenda', *Journal of Epidemiological Community Health*, 61(4): 276–7.

Bezruchka, S. (2009) 'The effect of economic recession on population health', *Canadian Medical Association Journal*, 181(5): 281–5.

Blanchard, O. and D. Leigh (2013) *Growth Forecast Errors and Fiscal Multipliers*, New York: International Monetary Fund, www.imf.org/external/pubs/ft/wp/2013/wp1301.pdf.

Bond, P. (2008) *Global Political Economic and Geopolitical Trends, Structures and Implications for Public Health*, Globalization Knowledge Network, WHO Commission on the Social Determinants of Health, Institute of Population Health, Globalization and Health Equity, University of Ottawa, www.globalhealthequity.ca/webfm_send/18.

Breman, A. and C. Shelton (2001) 'Structural adjustment and health: a literature review of the debate, its role-players and presented empirical evidence', CMH Working Paper Series no. WG6:6, Geneva: Commission on Macroeconomics and Health, WHO, library.cphs.chula.ac.th/Ebooks/HealthCareFinancing/WorkingPaper_WG6/WG6_6.pdf.

Brunsden, J., G. Broom and B. Moshinsky (2013) 'Banks win 4-year delay as Basel liquidity rule loosened', *Bloomberg Personal Finance*, 7 January, www.bloomberg.com/news/2013-01-06/banks-win-watered-down-liquidity-rule-after-basel-group-deal.html.

Chan, J. (2012) 'Labour unrest and a slowing economy in China: unpaid wages spark strikes', Global Research, www.globalresearch.ca/labour-unrest-and-a-slowing-economy-in-china-unpaid-wages-spark-strikes/5317380.

Chapman, D. (2013) 'The Fed and rising interest

rates!', Gold-Eagle, 14 November, www. gold-eagle.com/article/fed-and-rising-interest-rates.

Chappell, B. (2013) 'JPMorgan Chase will pay US$13 billion in record settlement', National Public Radio, 19 November, www.npr.org/blogs/thetwo-way/2013/11/19/246143595/j-p-morgan-chase-will-pay-13-billion-in-record-settlement.

CIDP (Canadian International Development Platform) (2013) Foreign Aid and Crises, by A. Bhushan, cidpnsi.ca/blog/foreign-aid-and-crises/.

Connolly, K. and L. Osborne (2013) 'Low-paid Germans mind rich–poor gap as elections approach', Guardian, 30 August, www.theguardian.com/world/2013/aug/30/low-paid-germans-mini-jobs.

Cornia, G. A., S. Rosignoli and L. Tiberti (2008) Globalisation and Health: Pathways of transmission and evidence of impact, Ottawa: Institute of Population Health.

Curry, B. (2013) 'G20 countries to share tax records to crack down on cheats', Globe and Mail, 6 September, www.theglobeandmail.com/news/politics/g20-countries-to-share-tax-records-to-crack-down-on-cheats/article14158136/.

Devarakonda, R. K. (2012) 'The battle over development-led globalisation', Inter Press Service News Agency, 6 April, www.ipsnews.net/2012/04/the-battle-over-development-led-globalisation/.

DfID (Department for International Development) (2009) Eliminating World Poverty: Building our common future, London: Stationery Office.

Elliott, L. (2013) 'IMF eyes tax potential of the world's super-rich', Guardian, 3 October, www.theguardian.com/business/2013/oct/13/imf-meeting-united-states-debt-ceiling.

Engler, Y. (2013) 'Harper's global austerity agenda', The Tyee, 25 May, thetyee.ca/Opinion/2013/05/25/Harpers-Global-Austerity-Agenda/.

Fieldhouse, A. (2013) A Review of the Economic Research on the Effects of Raising Ordinary Income Tax Rates, Washington, DC: Economic Policy Institute, 2 April, www.epi.org/publication/raising-income-taxes/.

Floro, M. and G. Dymski (2000) 'Financial crisis, gender, and power: an analytical frame-work', World Development, 28(7): 1269–83, dx.doi.org/10.1016/S0305-750X(00)00025-5.

Forbes (2010) 'The world's billionaires', Forbes, 10 October, www.forbes.com/lists/2010/10/billionaires-2010_The-Worlds-Billionaires_Rank.html.

— (2013) 'Inside the 2013 billionaires list: facts and figures', by L. Kroll, Forbes, 25 March, www.forbes.com/sites/luisakroll/2013/03/04/inside-the-2013-billionaires-list-facts-and-figures/.

— (2014) 'The 67 people as wealthy as the world's poorest 3.5 billion', by K. Moreno, Forbes, 25 March, www.forbes.com/sites/forbesinsights/2014/03/25/the-67-people-as-wealthy-as-the-worlds-poorest-3-5-billion/.

George, S. (2008) 'Susan George on the financial crisis', Global Sociology Blog, 17 October, globalsociology.com/2008/10/17/susan-george-on-the-financial-crisis/.

Goodley, S. and P. Inman (2013) 'Zero-hours contracts cover more than 1m UK workers', Guardian, 5 August, www.theguardian.com/uk-news/2013/aug/05/zero-hours-contracts-cover-1m-uk-workers.

Griffith-Jones, S. and A. Persaud (2012) 'Why critics are wrong about a financial-transaction tax', European Voice, www.europeanvoice.com/article/2012/march/why-critics-are-wrong-about-a-financial-transaction-tax/73843.aspx.

Haldane, A., S. Brennan and V. Madouros (2010) 'What is the contribution of the financial sector – miracle or mirage?', in A. Turner et al. (eds), The Future of Finance: The LSE report, London: London School of Economics and Political Science, pp. 87–120, harr123et.files.wordpress.com/2010/07/futureoffinance5.pdf.

Harvey, D. (2003) The New Imperialism, Oxford: Oxford University Press.

Helm, T. (2013) 'Two-tier workforce condemning millions to low-paid jobs, study warns', Guardian, 31 August, www.theguardian.com/money/2013/aug/31/two-tier-work force-low-paid-jobs.

Helmore, E. (2013) 'US fast-food workers in vanguard of growing protests at "starvation" wages', Guardian, 10 August, www.theguardian.com/world/2013/aug/10/us-fast-food-protests-wages.

Hendrikse, R. P. and J. D. Sidaway (2010) 'Neo-liberalism 3.0', *Environment and Planning*, 42(9): 2037–42.

Henry, J. S. (2012) *The Price of Offshore Revisited: New estimates for 'missing' global private wealth, income, inequality, and lost taxes*, Tax Justice Network, www.taxjustice. net/cms/upload/pdf/Price_of_Offshore_ Revisited_120722.pdf.

Hudson, M. (2010) *US 'Quantitative Easing' is Fracturing the Global Economy*, Annandale-on-Hudson, New York: Levy Economics Institute.

IADB (Inter-American Development Bank) (2011) *Urban Sustainability in Latin America and the Caribbean*, Washington, DC: Inter-American Development Bank.

ILO (International Labour Organization) (2011) *Global Employment Trends 2011: The challenge of a jobs recovery*, Geneva: International Labour Office, www.ilo.org/ wcmsp5/groups/public/---dgreports/--- dcomm/---publ/documents/publication/ wcms_150440.pdf.

— (2013) *Global Employment Trends 2013: Recovering from a second jobs dip*, Geneva: International Labour Office, www.ilo.org/ wcmsp5/groups/public/---dgreports/--- dcomm/---publ/documents/publication/ wcms_202326.pdf.

IMF (International Monetary Fund) (2012) *World Economic Outlook, October 2012: Coping with high debt and sluggish growth*, Washington, DC: International Monetary Fund, www.imf.org/external/pubs/ft/ weo/2012/02/pdf/text.pdf.

Inman, R. (2013) 'Managing country debts in the European monetary union: stronger rules or stronger union?', in F. Allen, E. Carletti and J. A. Gray (eds), *Political, Fiscal, and Banking Union in the Eurozone?*, Philadelphia: FIC Press, pp. 79–102.

Jackson, T. (2009) *Prosperity without Growth? The transition to a sustainable economy*, London: Sustainable Development Commission, 30 March, www.sd-commission. org.uk/data/files/publications/prosperity_ without_growth_report.pdf.

Johannesen, N. and G. Zucman (2012) 'The end of bank secrecy? An evaluation of the G20 tax haven crackdown', 12 October, www. parisschoolofeconomics.eu/docs/zucman-gabriel/revised_october12.pdf.

Karanikolos, M. et al. (2013) 'Financial crisis, austerity, and health in Europe', *The Lancet*, 381(9874), pp. 1323–31.

Keating, G., M. O'Sullivan, A. Shorrocks, J. B. Davies, R. Lluberas and A. Koutsoukis (2012) *Global Wealth Report 2012*, Zurich: Credit Suisse, economics.uwo.ca/news/ davies_creditsuisse_oct12.pdf.

Kentikelenis, A. et al. (2011) 'Health effects of financial crisis: omens of a Greek tragedy', *The Lancet*, 378(9801): 1457–8.

Kiladze, T. (2014) 'Canada's bank watchdog adopting Basel-style soundness meas-ure', *Globe and Mail*, 14 January, www. theglobeandmail.com/report-on-business/ bank-watchdog-moves-to-comply-with-global-standard-swaps-key-calculation/ article16324818/.

Koivusalo, M., T. Schrecker and R. Labonté (2008) 'Globalization and policy space for health and social determinants of health', Globalization Knowledge Network, World Health Organization Commission on the Social Determinants of Health, www. academia.edu/242100/Globalization_ and_Policy_Space_for_Health_and_Social_ Determinants_of_Health.

Korten, D. C. (2001) *When Corporations Rule the World*, San Francisco, CA/Bloomfield, CT: Berrett-Koehler Publishers/Kumarian Press.

Lee, Y. S. (2006) *Reclaiming Development in the World Trading System*, New York: Cambridge University Press.

Lewis, P. (2014) 'US economy losing "up to $1bn a week" after jobless benefits cut', *Guardian*, 3 January, www.theguardian.com/ business/2014/jan/03/us-economy-losing-1bn-jobless-benefits-cuts.

Marmot, M. G. and R. Bell (2009) 'How will the financial crisis affect health?', *British Medi-cal Journal*, 338: b1314.

McCulloch, N. and G. Pacillo (2011) *The Tobin Tax: A review of the evidence*, Brighton: Institute of Development Studies.

Micossi, S. (2013) 'A viable alternative to Basel III prudential rules', *VOX*, 9 June, www. voxeu.org/article/viable-alternative-basel-iii-prudential-rules.

Mooney, G. H. (2012) *The Health of Nations: Towards a new political economy*, London: Zed Books.

ODI (Overseas Development Institute) (2009a) *ODI Annual Report 2009*, London: ODI

Publications, www.odi.org.uk/sites/odi.org.uk/files/odi-assets/publications-opinion-files/4910.pdf.

— (2009b) 'The global financial crisis: poverty and social protection', Briefing Paper 51, www.odi.org.uk/sites/odi.org.uk/files/odi-assets/publications-opinion-files/4285.pdf.

Ortiz, I. and M. Cummins (2013) 'The age of austerity: a review of public expenditures and adjustment measures in 181 countries', Working paper, New York/Geneva: Initiative for Policy Dialogue/South Centre, 24 March, ssrn.com/abstract=2260771.

Ortiz, I., J. Chai and M. Cummins (2011) *Austerity Measures Threaten Children and Poor Households: Recent evidence in public expenditures from 128 developing countries*, New York: UNICEF, webcache.googleusercontent.com/search?q=cache:http://www.unicef.org/socialpolicy/files/Austerity_Measures_Threaten_Children.pdf.

Osborne, H. (2014) 'The combined fortune of the ultra-wealthy has doubled since 2009', *Guardian*, 31 March, www.theguardian.com/money/2014/mar/31/london-billionaire-preferred-residence.

Oxfam (2013) 'Tax on the "private" billions now stashed away in havens enough to end extreme world poverty twice over', 27 May, www.oxfam.org/en/eu/pressroom/pressrelease/2013-05-22/tax-havens-private-billions-could-end-extreme-poverty-twice-over.

Parrado, E. A. and R. M. Zenteno (2001) 'Economic restructuring, financial crises, and women's work in Mexico', *Social Problems*, 48(4): 456–77.

People's Health Movement (2000) *People's Figureer for Health*, People's Health Movement, www.phmovement.org/sites/www.phmovement.org/files/phm-pch-english.pdf.

Quintana, C. D. D. and B. G. Lopez-Valcarcel (2009) 'Economic crisis and health', *Gaceta Sanitaria*, 23(4): 261–5.

Reeves, A., S. Basu, M. McKee, C. Meissner and D. Stuckler (2013) 'Does investment in the health sector promote or inhibit economic growth?', *Globalization and Health*, 9(1): 43, doi:10.1186/1744-8603-9-43.

Reich, R. (2013) 'Their real goal: to make us all so cynical about government, we give up', 7 October, robertreich.org/post/63417612450.

Reinhart, C. M. and K. S. Rogoff (2010) *Growth in a Time of Debt*, Cambridge, MA: National Bureau of Economic Research, 100(2): 573–8.

Robinson, E. A. G. and C. W. Guillebaud (1941) *Monopoly*, Cambridge Economic Handbooks 11, Cambridge/London: Cambridge University Press/Nisbet & Co.

Ruckert, A. and R. Labonté (2012) 'The global financial crisis and health equity: toward a conceptual framework', *Critical Public Health*, 22(3): 267–79.

SAPRIN (Structural Adjustment Participatory Review Initiative Network) (2004) *Structural Adjustment: The SAPRI report: The policy roots of economic crisis, poverty, and inequality*, London and New York/Penang/Manila/Bangalore: Zed Books/Third World Network/IBON Foundation/Books for Change.

Shin, J. S. and H. J. Chang (2005) 'Globalization and East Asian economies: an introduction', *Global Economic Review*, 34(4): 355–62.

Standing, G. (2011) *The Precariat: The new dangerous class*, London: Bloomsbury Academic.

Stanford, J. (2013a) 'The myth of Canadian exceptionalism: crisis, non-recovery, and austerity', *Alternate Routes: A Journal of Critical Social Research*, 24: 19–32.

— (2013b) 'The failure of corporate tax cuts to stimulate business investment', in R. Swift (ed.), *The Great Revenue Robbery: How to stop the tax cut scam and save Canada*, Toronto: Canadians for Tax Fairness, Between the Lines.

Stewart, H. (2010) 'The greatest trade ever: how John Paulson bet against the markets and made $20 billion by Gregory Zuckerman', *Guardian*, 7 March, www.theguardian.com/books/2010/mar/07/the-greatest-trade-ever-by-gregory-zuckerman-review-heather-stewart.

Stuckler, D., S. Basu and M. McKee (2011) 'Commentary: UN high level meeting on non-communicable diseases: an opportunity for whom?', *British Medical Journal*, 343: d5336.

Talley, I. (2013) 'IMF details errors in calling for austerity', *Wall Street Journal*, 3 January, blogs.wsj.com/economics/2013/01/03/imf-details-errors-in-calling-for-austerity/.

Treanor, J. (2012) 'John Vickers says George Osborne's banking reforms don't go far enough', *Guardian*, 14 June, www.the

guardian.com/business/2012/jun/14/
vickers-george-osborne-banking-reforms.

UN (United Nations) Habitat (2003) *The
Challenge of Slums: Global report on human
settlements, 2003*, London: Earthscan,
www.aq.upm.es/habitabilidadbasica/docs/
recursos/monografias/the_challenge_of_
slums-(2003).pdf.

UNCTAD (United Nations Conference on
Trade and Development) (2011) *Trade and
Development Report 2011; post-crisis policy
challenges in the world economy*, New York
and Geneva: United Nations, unctad.org/
en/docs/tdr2011_en.pdf.

UN DESA (United Nations Department of
Economic and Social Affairs) (2006) *World
Economic and Social Survey 2006: Diverging
growth and development*, Geneva: United Nations, www.un.org/en/development/desa/
policy/wess/wess_archive/2006wess.pdf.

— (2010) *World Economic Situation and Prospects 2010*, Geneva: United Nations, www.
un.org/en/development/desa/policy/wesp/
wesp_archive/2010wesp.pdf.

UNICEF (United Nations Children's Fund)
(2012) *The State of the World's Children 2012;
children in an urban world*, Geneva and
New York: United Nations, www.unicef.
org/sowc2012/pdfs/SOWC-2012-Main-
Report_EN_21Dec2011.pdf.

Wade, R. (2009) 'From global imbalances to
global reorganisations', *Cambridge Journal
of Economics*, 33(4): 539–62, doi:10.1093/cje/
bep032.

Wall Street Watch (2009) *Sold Out: How Wall
Street and Washington betrayed America*,
Washington, DC: Wall Street Watch.

War on Want (2011) *Stitched Up: Women workers
in the Bangladeshi garment sector*, London:
War on Want.

WHO (World Health Organization) (2014)
'Greek crisis fallout is an opportunity
for health', *Bulletin World Health Organ*,
92: 8–9, doi: http://dx.doi.org/10.2471/
BLT.14.030114; www.who.int/bulletin/
volumes/92/1/14-030114.pdf.

World Bank (2005) *Economic Growth in the
1990's: Learning from a decade of reform*,
Washington, DC: World Bank, www1.world
bank.org/prem/lessons1990s/.

— (2009a) *The Global Economic Crisis: Assessing vulnerability with a poverty lens*,
Washington, DC: World Bank, siteresources.
worldbank.org/NEWS/Resources/WBG-
VulnerableCountriesBrief.pdf.

— (2009b) *Swimming against the Tide: How
developing countries are coping with the
global crisis*, Washington, DC: World Bank,
www.un.org/ga/president/63/PDFs/World
Bankreport.pdf.

— (2010) *Foreign Direct Investment – the
China Story*, www.worldbank.org/en/
news/feature/2010/07/16/foreign-direct-
investment-china-story.

— (2014) *World DataBank: World Development Indicators*, Washington, DC: World
Bank, databank.worldbank.org/data/
views/variableSelection/selectvariables.
aspx?source=world-development-indicators.

Zero Hedge (2011) 'Total over the counter
outstanding derivatives', Zero Hedge, www.
zerohedge.com/sites/default/files/images/
user5/imageroot/2011/10/BIS%20OTC%20
Gross%20Notional_0.jpg.

## A2 | FISCAL POLICIES IN EUROPE IN THE WAKE OF THE ECONOMIC CRISIS: IMPLICATIONS FOR HEALTH

Those opposed to the welfare state never waste a good crisis. (McKee and Stuckler 2011)

### Genesis of the economic crisis in Europe

Until recently, Europe was exemplified by a combination of robust economies and strong social protection systems. After the Second World War, a combination of domestic and international compulsions promoted the development of social security systems and national health systems that had been at the centre of workers' struggles over most of the continent.

But from the early 1970s, things started to change. Markets became saturated and profit rates decreased. The first signs of a crisis of overproduction appeared. The OPEC's (Organization of Oil Exporting Countries) decision to increase oil prices exacerbated economic tensions, leading to a full-blown crisis (Cottenier and Houben 2008). This was no cyclical recession, as is 'normal' in a capitalist economy. The general economic trend became one of long-term decline (Shutt 1998). (See Figure A2.1.)

As the saturation of industrialized markets became a constraint on further growth, fierce competition forced transnational corporations to cut costs and to seek new markets. Over time this was done through different strategies. During the 1980s, there was a major thrust in exploitation of the markets of the global South, in order to dump excess capacity. This led to a huge rise in Third World debt and, for decades, the interest on this debt ensured an important source of income for the developed capitalist economies of the

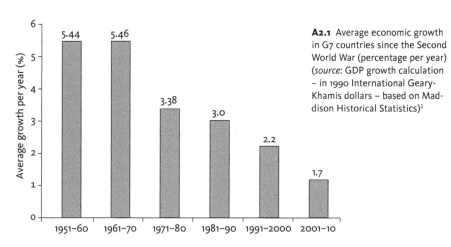

**A2.1** Average economic growth in G7 countries since the Second World War (percentage per year) (*source*: GDP growth calculation – in 1990 International Geary-Khamis dollars – based on Maddison Historical Statistics)[1]

**Image A2.1** Dismantling the 'welfare state' in Europe (Indranil Mukhopadhyay)

North (for a detailed analysis, see GHW 1, ch. A, www.ghwatch.org/sites/www.ghwatch.org/files/A.pdf).

The second strategy employed was the restructuring of transnational companies. These companies were supported through tax reductions and privatization programmes. Concurrently, developing countries were forced to accept further liberalization, deregulation and privatization of their economies, thereby providing transnational corporations with an outlet for their excess capital. The health sector was not an exception; its profitable parts were increasingly privatized (Ginzberg and Ostow 1997; Armada et al. 2001; Iriart et al. 2001).

These strategies effectively masked the decline in the purchasing power of the developed capitalist economies, mainly the United States (consumption in the USA accounts for 25–30 per cent of the globe's GDP). Consumption needed to be maintained by increasing credits and debts in different ways, of which the most well known focused on real estate – the infamous 'sub-prime debts' (see GHW 3, ch. A1, www.ghwatch.org/sites/www.ghwatch.org/files/A1.pdf). This third strategy was based on 'fictive capital' – creation of money that exceeded the capacities of the real economy to produce the wealth needed to ensure its material basis.

Since 1985, important measures for integration were taken at the European level. A common market was set up in 1990 and the Maastricht Treaty (which created the European Union and led to the creation of the single European currency) was signed in 1992. In 2002, the euro was introduced as a common currency across Europe. The Lisbon Strategy (an economic plan for the European Union between 2000 and 2010) was developed in the first decade of the twenty-first century, although it faced fierce popular resistance.

### Influence of policies in Germany

Policies pursued in Europe today are deeply influenced by those in Germany – the largest economy in Europe. Germany is the exporting nation par excellence, and the strongest driver of the monetary unification of Europe. Through its exports to the rest of Europe, Germany became the biggest beneficiary of the euro. Its profits were made mainly at the expense of the peoples in the south of Europe. The crisis in countries such as Greece, Italy and Portugal and the trade surplus enjoyed by Germany are clearly linked. In Portugal, Greece and Italy, national industries were wiped out, German products were imported, and these countries amassed substantial debts (Mertens et al. 2012). Germany's export-led economy is predicated on domestic wage reductions and retrogressive polices towards the unemployed and other socio-economically disadvantaged groups. Now this policy is presented as an example to be emulated by the rest of Europe. European integration shuns the possibility of countries in Europe developing sovereign financial policies, especially those in a crisis. Loans are being offered to bail out the economies in crisis in Europe on the condition that they are used to pay the interest on accumulated debts, but not to protect the populations of the affected countries (e.g. in Greece) (Bricmont 2012). Today's crisis is used as an opportunity to impose an even more radical process calling for the same neoliberal 'solutions' as employed in Germany.

It needs to be understood that the recession in Europe is linked to the functioning of the capitalist system itself, based on the need of continued growth while the consumption possibilities of the population are increasingly limited (Houben 2011). When overproduction occurs, a capital surplus follows. This excess capital cannot be used to increase production because it collides with the limits of the market. This capital constantly searches for high returns. Conditions enabling the emergence of this situation were created by financial deregulation and the invention of new financial instruments. The entire bubble was inflated even further through excessive credit stimulus, as granting credit is a way of creating money out of nothing (see GHW 3, ch. A1, www.ghwatch. org/sites/www.ghwatch.org/files/A1.pdf).

### Crisis in the US and its aftermath

In 2006, the United States was hit by an economic recession (which still continues) and in February 2007 the first banks providing mortgage loans went bankrupt. In spite of attempts by the US government to continue bailing out the failing banks, in September 2008 the bubble finally burst and over two million house owners lost their homes in the USA. The crisis in the largest global economy had a cascading effect throughout the world. Across the world, over US$1,000 billion worth of junk bonds had been sold (i.e. bonds which the banks were unable to buy back), and – one after the other – banks declared losses. Almost every country come to the swift rescue of their banks – governments from London to Berlin took over or bailed out faltering banks (Landler 2008). Consequently, the (private) bank debt became a problem of the state (that is, of all of us), combined with a worsening economic crisis. As we discussed earlier, the rapid creation of 'fictive capital' (money that exceeds the capacities of the real economy) has now come to haunt the developed capitalist economies of the world.

Fears of a serious debt crisis grew from late 2009. In several countries private debts arose from a property bubble, but were transferred to sovereign debt as a result of banking-system bailouts. The overall slowdown in the economy also implied a decrease in tax incomes, further adding to national debts (Lewis 2011). In addition, the downgrading of government debt on international markets led to a dramatic increase of interest on debt. To tide them over the crisis, several countries in Europe have effected cuts in public and social expenditures, which in turn have led to a further decrease in the purchasing power of a large majority (Plumer 2012).

### Greece and Spain: acute manifestations of the crisis

Greece, which has attracted attention since 2010 for the country's growing economic instability, is a typical example of the unfolding crisis in Europe. Leaders of the EU and sections of the media have tried to place the blame for the crisis on Greece itself. They claim that Greece's misfortune has been brought about by a 'way of living beyond its means', as the country allegedly created a 'ballooned welfare state' and offered (over-)'generous payments' to its civil servants and 'low retirement age pensioners' (Armitstead 2012; BBC News 2012). Uncontrolled government spending combined with inefficient state-owned enterprises and cumbersome business regulations are claimed to be the key factors for Greece's public debt crisis (OECD 2011).

Greece's predicament, however, is much more clearly linked to the structure

**Image A2.2** A deserted street in Barcelona as the city is closed down by pro-testers (Eddie Dep)

and policies of the European Union. The economic contraction in Greece is an outcome of Greece's unequal development within the EU and the pressure exerted on the national economy by the global structural crisis (Mavroudeas 2012b). The participation of Greece in the EU and in the Eurozone weakened the country's economic competitiveness. EU regulations forced Greece to open its doors to cheap imports (from Germany, for example), thus destroying domestic manufacturing capacity and leading to a deteriorating trade balance since the late 1980s in favour of the more industrialized countries of Europe (Mavroudeas 2012a; Lapavitsas 2010). With the onset of the global crisis in 2007, Greece was one of the worst affected, given its already unstable economic foundation.

While Greece is being blamed for its 'overdeveloped and overspending public sector', actually the Greek welfare state – when compared to those of many other European countries – was always poorly funded and had a relatively limited outreach (Navarro 2012). While there have been issues about efficiency in the public sector in Greece, the much bigger issue is that the public deficit in the country was a result of declining state revenues rather than expanding public expenditures (ibid.). On the other hand, huge amounts of public revenue were forgone owing to tax-relief measures for the flourishing Greek shipping industry and billions of euros of untaxed money have flowed into Swiss banks.

In Spain, the crisis immediately translated into massive job losses. The unemployment rate reached an unprecedented 25.1 per cent in August 2012, with more than 50 per cent of the youth being denied employment. Just like that of Greece, the Spanish economy had already been destabilized as a consequence of cheap imports from within the EU and the recession further aggravated the situation. A surplus budget of 20.2 billion euros in 2007 quickly turned into a deficit of 98.2 billion euros as consequence of declining tax revenues (accounting for 43 per cent of the total decrease in the government budget). Similar trends were seen in many other European states, but the weakness of the industrial structure in Spain and the collapse of its housing market aggravated the situation.

There have been attempts to link the crisis in Spain to its public debt. However, facts indicate an entirely different picture (Figure A2.2). At the onset of the global economic crisis, Spain's public debt was 36.2 per cent of GDP (down from 65 per cent in 1995) and the budget deficit was 1.9 per cent of GDP. By 2011 the public debt had increased to almost 70 per cent of GDP. On the other hand the budget deficit was converted into a surplus by new austerity measures that imposed savage cuts on public expenditure. Thus the 1.9 per cent budget deficit in 2007 was quickly transformed into a surplus of more than 11 per cent by 2009. We see two important trends here – a sharp increase in public debt *after* the crisis hit Spain, and a sharp contraction in public spending leading to a high budget *surplus*. The austerity measures have, thus, led to decreased economic activity. In contrast, what is required is an

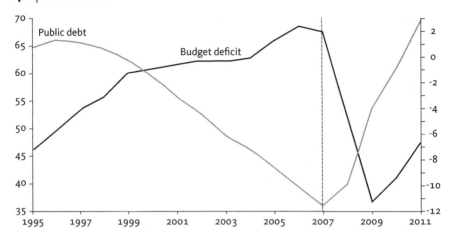

*Note*: left scale = figures for public debt; right scale = figures for budget deficit

**A2.2** Public debt and the budget deficit in Spain (as a percentage of GDP) (*source*: AMECO database)[2]

economic recovery programme to increase economic activity which is driven by higher government spending. However, the neoliberal agenda, which is being driven by German capital and by some European business leaders, is very different. They see an opportunity in the crisis to impose austerity measures across Europe and thereby decrease costs in manufacturing (essentially by reduction in salaries), so as to make European exports more 'competitive' in the global market. The crisis is also an opportunity for them to dismantle social protection measures across Europe.

### Social consequences

The responses to the global economic crisis, in Europe, are based on strengthening of market mechanisms, combined with the encouragement of competition between countries through reduced production costs (by lowering labour costs), fiscal policies and social dumping. The inevitable consequences of these measures are decreasing purchasing power of the population, declining public investment, and a steady breakdown of social protection mechanisms.

In October 2012, the unemployment rate for the EU was 10.7 per cent, an increase of 3.6 per cent over the rate in 2008. Young people have been badly affected – in September 2012, of the economically active population in the EU in the age group fifteen to twenty-four years, at least 22.8 per cent were unemployed (Alatalo et al. 2013). In 2011, more than 24.2 per cent of the EU's population (nearly 120 million people) were at risk of poverty, with women having a 2 per cent higher risk than men. Having a job was no longer an insurance against poverty; 8.7 per cent of workers in 2011 were below the poverty line and one third of the poor were the 'working poor' (ABVV 2012).

The dramatic increase in public debt and thus the alleged 'unsustainability' of health and social security systems is used as an argument to push for further privatization. While the social consequences of the crisis (joblessness, housing problems, poverty, etc.) are the determinants of dramatically increasing health needs, healthcare is being progressively transformed into a marketable commodity.

## Greece: the face of the health crisis in Europe

While the Greek government still argues that the economic crisis in Greece does not constitute a threat to the population's health (Liaropoulos 2012; Polyzos 2012) a World Health Organization report stated in January 2009 that 'some countries are at particular risk ... and these include developed countries that have required emergency assistance from the IMF, where spending restrictions may be imposed during loan repayment' (WHO 2009). Today, in Greece, the toxic combination of protracted economic recession and neoclassical adjustment policies constitutes a double threat to the population's health and well-being.

The economic recession and the austerity measures imposed in the country by the troika – European Commission, International Monetary Fund (IMF) and European Central Bank – have triggered a sharp deterioration in the socio-economic conditions of the working class and even sections of the middle class. It is estimated that 3.9 million Greeks (out of a total population of 11 million) were living below the official poverty line by the end of 2013 (Stevens 2013) and the unemployment rate stood at 27.3 per cent in 2013 (Dabilis 2013). The inability to pay mortgages is increasing evictions and steadily increasing the number of homeless people; 28 per cent of the Greek population (compared to 22 per cent of the population in 2008) stated that they were living in conditions of severe material deprivation, not being able to meet basic needs such as paying rent, eating a meal with meat, chicken

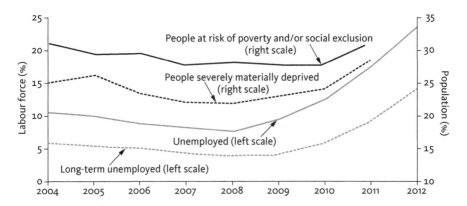

**A2.3** Basic social indicators, Greece, 2004–September 2012 (*sources*: Calculations based on data derived from (a) Hellenic Statistical Authority (ELSTAT), *Quarterly Labour Force Survey*, www.statistics.gr; (b) ELSTAT, *Survey on Income and Living Conditions 2011: Indicators of change 2003–2011*, www.statistics.gr)

or fish every second day, and keeping their home adequately warm (Kondilis, Bodini et al. 2013). (See Figure A2.3.)

Greece's mortality and morbidity data reflect the deep impact of the crisis on people's lives. For example, the Infant Mortality Rate (IMR) in Greece increased by 51 per cent between 2008 and 2011. Further, suicide and homicide mortality increased by 11.5 and 40 per cent respectively between 2007 and 2010 (ibid. 2013). Concurrently, private health expenditure started decreasing sharply from 2009, and total private health expenditure in Greece (calculated on 2009 constant prices) decreased by 16.2 per cent between 2008 and 2010 (Table A2.1) This reflects the inability of households, in times of crisis, to purchase health services even in a situation where the public system is crumbling.

TABLE A2.1 Private health expenditure in Greece, 1998–2010

| Type of service/survey year | 1998/99 | 2004/05 | 2008 | 2009 | 2010 |
|---|---|---|---|---|---|
| Pharmaceuticals | 1,031.72 | 1,369.77 | 1,633.09 | 1,542.80 | 1,525.89 |
| Medicines | n/a | 1,128.96 | 1,353.16 | 1,275.22 | 1,299.11 |
| Therapeutic devices | n/a | 240.8 | 279.93 | 267.09 | 226.30 |
| Outpatient care | 3,811.95 | 4,515.30 | 4,329.52 | 3,923.91 | 3,186.24 |
| Medical care | 1,311.93 | 1,600.92 | 1,487.19 | 1,331.01 | 1,062.87 |
| Dental care | 1,878.19 | 2,140.46 | 2,092.06 | 1,947.64 | 1,574.18 |
| Other outpatient | 621.82 | 1,547.83 | 1,501.04 | 1,290.53 | 1,097.43 |
| Inpatient care | 683.23 | 988.98 | 1,065.32 | 1,162.65 | 1,178.86 |
| Public hospitals | 167.88 | 278.351 | 293.28 | 299.18 | 336.61 |
| Private hospitals | 515.35 | 710.63 | 772.53 | 862.98 | 841.77 |
| TOTAL | 5,527.07 | 6,874.04 | 7,027.93 | 6,628.88 | 5,890.99 |

*Notes:* 1. Private health expenditure expressed in million euros (€), 2009 constant market prices; 2. n/a = data not available

*Sources:* Calculations based on data derived from (1) ELSTAT, *Households' Budget Surveys for the Years 1998/99, 2004/5, 2008, 2009, 2010*, www.statistics.gr; (2) ELSTAT, *Consumer Price Index 1959–2012*, www.statistics.gr

At the same time, the demand for public healthcare services has increased since the advent of the crisis. The growing demand on healthcare facilities is reflected in an increase of 36 per cent, between 2008 and 2012, in the number of hospitalized patients (Greek Ministry of Health 2012). Paradoxically, austerity measures imposed by the Greek government on the directive of the troika are restricting free access to healthcare services. In a situation of increased healthcare needs, the Greek government has responded by adopting restrictive policies: a decrease in funding and a downsizing of public health services, higher user fees, and cost-sharing. Between 2009 and 2011, the total expenditure of the Greek Ministry of Health decreased by €1.8 billion. On the other hand, in 2011, patients spent €25.7 million on out-of-pocket-payments for outpatient services in public hospitals – services that had been free at the point of use before the crisis (Kondilis, Giannakopoulos et al. 2013). Further, from 2009

ΔΗΜΟΨΗΦΙΣΜΑ

18 ΜΑΪΟΥ 2014

σώστε το νερό

ΣΤΗ ΘΕΣΣΑΛΟΝΙΚΗ
ΨΗΦΙΖΟΥΜΕ
ΟΧΙ στην ιδιωτικοποίηση του νερού
στην πώληση της ΕΥΑΘ

**Image A2.3** Poster for the plebiscite against water privatization in Greece (Alexis Benos)

to 2011, the number of people reporting inability to visit a doctor owing to economic hardship or high waiting lists increased by almost 50 per cent.[3]

Health insurance coverage is available only to those who work for more than fifty days per year. This leaves out major sections of the population, including the unemployed, casual workers and irregular immigrants; 2.5 million people in Greece are without any form of health insurance coverage (according to 2014 data from the Greek Ministry of Labour). The current situation points to a fundamental flaw in the way public healthcare services have traditionally been funded. Historically, the social insurance funds were linked to employment, and this worked fairly well when unemployment rates were low. Faced with the present crisis and the huge rise in unemployment, the system is on the verge of collapse and the assets of social insurance schemes have decreased dramatically. Clearly, there is a need to organize public health services and their financing in a manner that doesn't entirely link access to healthcare with conditions of employment.

The crisis in financing of the public healthcare system has had a cascading effect. To tide over this crisis the government has introduced co-payments, which further increase the burden of out-of-pockets costs. Cost containment policies and expenditure cuts are being imposed, leading to the virtual dismantling of the public services infrastructure. Staff shortages abound and health professionals are facing a huge increase in workload.

The restructuring of public health services is being driven by conditionalities imposed on Greece, as part of the austerity programme. From 2010 to 2013, 170 conditionalities related to healthcare were included in the memorandums of understanding signed by the Greek government and the troika. These include budget caps, introduction of multiple user fees, freezing recruitment of staff, and substantial reductions in health workers' wages and in the social security funds' healthcare benefit packages (Kondilis, Giannakopoulos et al. 2013). Also included are various measures on healthcare reforms that promote the establishment of an internal market in public health services, and ultimately lead to the privatization of these services. By virtue of a vicious cycle of increasing demand and decreasing capacity, the collapse of Greece's public health system has triggered a humanitarian crisis of unprecedented proportions. In sharp contrast to the current reforms in Greece's health system, what is urgently necessary is the construction of a tax-funded national and public healthcare system that provides high-quality care that is free and accessible to all.

### Manifestations of the crisis on healthcare in different parts of Europe

In the UK, the government has allowed corporations to enter the arena of healthcare by implementing a series of incremental and far-reaching legal changes designed to allow the entry of capital (see Chapter B2 for a detailed analysis of the NHS reforms in the UK).

In Portugal, public spending declined by 8 per cent in 2011, after having remained stable between 2009 and 2010.[4] Measures imposed by the troika have led to decreasing salaries, pensions and unemployment benefits, with overall tax increases. The national health service is under siege; important parts of the public sector have been privatized and many health workers are losing their jobs (Augusto 2012). Co-payments for healthcare have gone up drastically, causing a decrease of 900,000 first-line consultations and half a million emergency consultations between January and October 2012 compared to the year before, while 'rationalization' of medicine use has led to significant increases in cost to patients (Campos 2013). A study conducted in May 2012 of 980 Portuguese families showed that 22.2 per cent had reduced their health expenditures. In families where one or more members were unemployed (20 per cent of those interviewed), the figure was 39.9 per cent. The crisis is having its most dramatic impact on mental health. Between 2011 and 2012, diagnosis of depression increased by 30 per cent in the north of the country. In the same period, suicide attempts grew by 47 per cent among women, and by 35 per cent among men. The monthly average admissions to mental health hospitals have increased by 76 per cent. In a recent study of family health centres, basic equipment for routine activities had been out of stock more than ten times during 2012 in 34.3 per cent of the centres (OPSS 2013).

In Italy, the growth in health expenditure between 2000 and 2010 was the lowest among the thirty-four OECD countries; yet savage health budget cuts have been imposed (projected to be 25–30 billion euros during 2012–15). This is resulting in increased user fees, removal of healthcare benefits, reduction in specialist care and decreased access to care – particularly for vulnerable socio-economic groups (Costa et al. 2012).[5] In 2011/12, the overall expenditure for drugs decreased by 5.6 per cent. While public healthcare expenditure decreased by 8 per cent, private expenditure increased by 12.3 per cent. A sharp increase in user fees for drugs (117.3 per cent between 2008 and 2012) has contributed to this (ISTAT 2013). In a recent survey, 10 per cent had postponed surgical treatment for financial reasons and 26 per cent reported increased expenditure for medical emergencies due to higher co-payments (Freni Ricerche Sociali e di Marketing 2011). Given that government officials claim that the National Health System (NHS) is no longer sustainable, reforms to achieve more 'efficiency' may well lead to even greater privatization of the healthcare system (Maciocco 2012). A national survey showed that for the first time 40.9 per cent of Italians are dissatisfied with the NHS (ranging from 21 per cent in the north-east to 57.6 per cent in the south of the country). People are shifting increasingly to the private sector, which is not surprising considering that 27 per cent of those interviewed said that they have paid higher fees in the public sector compared to the fees charged by the private sector for the same service. Even more worryingly, 41.2 per cent of Italians now consider the NHS as a safety net for essential services, and believe that all the rest should be purchased privately, and 11 million are covered by private insurance schemes (ISTAT 2013).

In Spain, the healthcare budget has declined by 18.21 per cent since 2009 (Economist 2013). Healthcare services have been cut, 53,000 health professionals have been removed from the public health system in the last three years, and user fees have been increased (including co-payments for medicines). The earlier universal entitlement to access to the public health system has been replaced by employment-based entitlement, thus excluding large population groups (e.g. approximately 900,000 undocumented migrants, who are now entitled only to emergency care and maternal and childcare). As a consequence quality of services has declined and out-of-pocket expenditure on healthcare has increased. There is a rise in waiting lists for patients who require major procedures – in 2010, 50,705 patients were on the waiting list for surgical interventions, while in 2013 their number had increased to 89,000. National and regional governments are using budget cuts targets to force the privatization of the Spanish healthcare system – 236 out of 550 acute care hospitals are now private (European Network 2014). While public–private partnerships (PPPs) are promoted (Quercioli et al. 2012; Peiró and Meneu 2012; Benach et al. 2012), there are widespread reports about conflicts of interest, nepotism, monopolistic practices and 'revolving doors' between government officials and private sector healthcare managers (Abril et al. 2012; Jara 2010; Güell and Castedo 2012).

While the German economic model is presented as a success story, 16 per cent of the German population live in poverty and almost five million workers have 'mini-jobs' with a monthly salary of 400 euros. The 8 per cent increase in employment between 1996 and 2011 is due to an increase in working hours and also related to an increase in part-time employment without social security rights (ABVV 2012); 26 per cent of jobs in Germany are precarious (temporary contracts, part-time jobs, etc.); 8 million workers (23 per cent of the country's workforce) lived in poverty in 2010, and this included 50 per cent of workers with full-time jobs (Bosch 2012). In 1998, the poorest 50 per cent of the population possessed only 4 per cent of Germany's wealth and this plummeted to 1 per cent in 2008. Germany has also seen one of the largest waves of hospital privatization in Europe. Between 1995 and 2010, the proportion of private hospitals doubled while at the same time the total number of hospitals fell by 11 per cent (Destatis 2013). The share of cases treated in private hospitals grew from 5.2 per cent in 1995 to 9.1 per cent in 2003, and further to 16.1 per cent in 2010.

In Belgium, the social security system still functions better than in Germany, in spite of attacks against it by proponents of neoliberal policies (terming the system 'wasteful'). Though 15 per cent of the population are poor and their numbers are growing, compared to Germany, Belgium had a higher rate of increase in employment between 2006 and 2011 (ABVV 2012). The number of working poor did not increase, while the figure almost doubled in Germany and increased even more sharply in Spain and Greece. However, since the 1990s, Belgium too has cut back on investments in public healthcare infrastructure and social security. Healthcare provision is evolving to favour for-profit, private care provision. While, currently, 140,000 elderly people reside in retirement homes, the proportion of commercial retirement homes rose from 45 per cent to 57 per cent between 2009 and 2010 (European Network 2014). From 1997 to 2005, out-of-pocket payments for healthcare rose from 23 per cent to 28 per cent and this has had catastrophic effects. In 2007, about 14 per cent of the Belgian population reported having postponed necessary care because of financial problems (compared to 8 per cent in 1997 and 10 per cent in 2004) (OECD 2007). Data from 2009 suggest that almost 30 per cent of the population regularly has trouble paying medical bills. In 2010, 8 per cent of Belgian families stopped an ongoing treatment and 26 per cent postponed it for financial reasons (Test-Aankoop 2012).

### Solidarity in the midst of a crisis

The evidence from post-crisis Europe, especially as regards the major changes that have taken place in healthcare services, is a clear reminder of the need to defend public services. It is precisely at this juncture – when the economic crisis in Europe is eroding the livelihoods of millions of people – that public investment in education, healthcare and infrastructure needs to be ramped up.

The question may be asked, who would pay for enhanced investment in social protection measures? In large parts of Europe the public debt is extremely high and mounting. Yet there remain islands of extreme affluence within Europe – 3.2 million families have a combined wealth of 7,800 billion euros (Waitzkin 2011). A tax on the financial wealth of the richest 2 per cent could yield 100 billion euros every year. There is a need for European solidarity, and it is only through solidarity that problems can be solved, differences narrowed, and conditions ameliorated.

There are moments in history when social logic must take precedence over other considerations. In the late nineteenth century, the British parliament was opposed to the prohibition of child labour on the grounds that children were the perfect size to work in the mines. The labour movement imposed a social logic, and child labour was abolished. It is high time that we followed the elementary logic that collective solidarity and actions lead to collective prosperity and improved living conditions for all. We need an economy that is not driven by maximizing profits for the few, but by the fulfilment of the needs of the many.

To argue for a health 'commons' is to guide health workers and activists towards new ways of engagement and resistance, of participation in the struggle to protect and animate the public sphere. As noted by Stuckler and McKee: 'There is an alternative: public health professionals must not remain silent at a time of financial crisis' (Stuckler and McKee 2012). Mass mobilization by civil society that encourages public debate and raises political consciousness will demystify the given orthodoxy and counteract the received wisdom. The challenge is to develop strategies for activism that can lead to broader social change (Waitzkin 2011).

## Notes

1 See Maddison Historical Statistics, Groningen Growth and Development Centre, www.rug.nl/research/ggdc/data/maddison-historical-statistics.

2 See Annual Macro-Economic database (AMECO), European Commission's Directorate General for Economic and Financial Affairs, ec.europa.eu/economy_finance/ameco/user/serie/SelectSerie.cfm.

3 See Hellenic Statistical Authority (ELSTAT), www.statistics.gr.

4 See OECD Health Statistics, OECD iLibrary, www.oecd-ilibrary.org/statistics.

5 See ibid.

## References

Abril, G., E. G. Sevillano and J. Prats (2012) 'De la pública a la privada y al revés', El País, 2 December, sociedad.elpais.com/sociedad/2012/12/01/actualidad/1354393366_194247.html, accessed 5 May 2014.

ABVV (Algemeen Belgisch Vakverbond) (2012) 'Sociaal-economische barometer 2013', December, www.abvv.be/web/guest/news-nl/-/article/1217527/;jsessionid=dM7Cpw Pe3M967AoY5UYlqT9&p_l_id=10187, accessed 5 May 2014.

Alatalo, J., J. Furuberg, H. Gustavsson et al. (2013) 'A sketch of youth unemployment in selected countries', Nuremberg: Institute for Employment Research, 30 July 2013, doku.iab.de/aktuell/2013/aktueller_bericht_1303.pdf, accessed 23 June 2014.

Armada, F., C. Muntaner and V. Navarro (2001) 'Health and social security reforms in Latin America: the convergence of the World Health Organization, the World Bank, and transnational corporations', *International Journal of Health Services*, 31(4): 729–68.

Armitstead, L. (2012) 'What's the Greek debt crisis all about?', *Daily Telegraph*, 23 February, www.telegraph.co.uk/finance/financialcrisis/9098559/Whats-the-Greek-debt-crisis-all-about.html, accessed 5 May 2014.

Augusto, G. F. (2012) 'Cuts in Portugal's NHS could compromise care', *The Lancet*, 379(9814): 400.

BBC News (2012) 'Eurozone crisis explained', 27 November, www.bbc.co.uk/news/business-13798000, accessed 4 May 2014.

Benach, J., G. Tarafa and C. Muntaner (2012) 'El copago sanitario y la desigualdad: ciencia y política', *Gaceta Sanitaria*, 26(1): 80–2.

Bosch, G. (2012) *Prekäre Beschäftigung und Neuordnung am Arbeitsmarkt: Expertise im Auftrag der Industriegewerkschaft Metall*, IAQ-Standpunkt, Institut Arbeit und Qualifikation, Universität Duisburg-Essen, September, www.iaq.uni-due.de/iaq-standpunkte/2012/sp2012-02.pdf, accessed 5 May 2014.

Bricmont, J. (2012) 'How dare they? A best-seller on the Belgian and European crisis', *Revolting Europe*, 24 April, revolting-europe.com/2012/04/24/how-dare-they-a-best seller-on-the-belgian-and-european-crisis/, accessed 5 May 2014.

Campos, A. (2013) 'Taxas moderadoras nas urgências podem subir para 40 euros', *Publico*, 9 January, www.publico.pt/sociedade/noticia/taxas-moderadoras-nas-urgencias-podem-subir-para-40-euros-1580129, accessed 5 May 2014.

Costa, G., M. Marra and S. Salmaso (2012) 'Health indicators in the time of crisis in Italy', Gruppo AIE su crisi e salute, *Epidemiologia & Prevenzione*, 36(6): 337–66.

Cottenier, J. and H. Houben (2008) 'De systeemcrisis', in H. Lerouge (ed.), *De sys-teemcrisis*, Brussels: Marxistische Studies, vol. 84, pp. 11–33.

Dabilis, A. (2013) 'Greece unemployment stays at 27.3%', *Greek Reporter*, 14 November, greece.greekreporter.com/2013/11/14/greece-unemployment-stays-at-27-3/, accessed 5 May 2014.

Destatis (2013) *Annual Report 2012*, Wiesbaden: Federal Statistical Office, www.destatis.de/EN/AboutUs/OurMission/AnnualReport/AnnualReport2012.pdf, accessed 5 May 2014.

Economist (2013) 'Is Spain on the verge of a public health-care crisis?', 16 December, www.economist.com/blogs/charlemagne/2013/12/health-care-spain, accessed 5 May 2014.

European Network (European Network against Privatization and Commercialization of Health and Social Protection) (2014) *Health and Social Protection are Not for Sale!: Manifest of the European Network against Privatization and Commercialization of Health and Social Protection*, Brussels, 7 February, www.sante-solidarite.be/sites/default/files/manifest_english.pdf, accessed 5 May 2014.

Freni Ricerche Sociali e di Marketing (2011) 'Comportamenti in materia di spese sanitarie davanti alla crisi economica', Florence.

Ginzberg, E. and M. Ostow (1997) 'Managed care: a look back and a look ahead', *New England Journal of Medicine*, 336(14): 1018–20.

Greek Ministry of Health (2012) 'ESY.net NHS financial and operational data 2012', www.moh.gov.gr/articles/esynet, accessed 15 May 2013.

Güell, O. and A. Castedo (2012) 'La acumulación de escándalos agita la sanidad pública catalana', *El País*, 11 June, ccaa.elpais.com/ccaa/2012/06/10/catalunya/1339355699_069772.html, accessed 5 May 2014.

Houben, H. (2011) *La crise de 30 ans*, Brussels: Editions Aden.

Iriart, C., E. Merhy and H. Waitzkin (2001) 'Managed care in Latin America: the new common sense in health policy reform', *Social Science and Medicine*, 52(8): 1243–53.

ISTAT (Instituto Nazionale di Statistica) (2013) *The Annual Report 2013: The State of the Nation*, Rome, 22 May.

Jara, M. (2010) 'Las puertas giratorias', 17 May,

www.migueljara.com/2010/05/17/las-puertas-giratorias, accessed 5 May 2014.

Kondilis, E., C. Bodini, P. de Vos et al. (2013) 'Fiscal policies in Europe in the wake of the economic crisis: implications for "health" and "healthcare" access', Background paper for *The Lancet*, University of Oslo Commission on Global Governance for Health, www.med.uio.no/helsam/english/research/global-governance-health/background-papers/fiscal-policies-eu.pdf, accessed 5 May 2014.

Kondilis, E., S. Giannakopoulos, M. Gavana et al. (2013) 'Economic crisis, restrictive policies, and the population's health and health care: the Greek case', *American Journal of Public Health*, 103(6): 973–9.

Landler, M. (2008) 'The U.S. financial crisis is spreading to Europe', *New York Times*, 30 September, www.nytimes.com/2008/10/01/business/worl business/01global.html, accessed 5 May 2014.

Lapavitsas, C. (2010) 'The structural crisis of Eurozone's periphery', in L. Vatikiotis, C. Vergopoulos, M. Givalos et al. (eds), *The Map of the Crisis: The End of Illusion*, 2nd edn, Athens: Topos, pp. 57–79.

Lewis, M. (2011) *Boomerang: Travels in the New Third World*, New York: W. W. Norton & Co.

Liaropoulos, L. (2012) 'Greek economic crisis: not a tragedy for health', *British Medical Journal*, 345: e7988.

Maciocco, G. (2012) 'SSN. Allarme rosso', 28 November, www.saluteinternazionale.info/2012/11/ssn-allarme-rosso/, accessed 5 May 2014.

Mavroudeas, S. (2012a) 'Development and crises: the troubled paths of Greek capitalism', in L. Vatikiotis, C. Vergopoulos, M. Givalos et al. (eds), *The Map of the Crisis: The End of Illusion*, 2nd edn, Athens: Topos, pp. 81–113.

— (2012b) 'The Greek crisis, the European Union and the inter-imperialist rivalries', *Utopia*, 92: 12–14.

McKee, M. and D. Stuckler (2011) 'The assault on universalism: how to destroy the welfare state', *British Medical Journal*, 343(7837): d7973, www.bmj.com/content/343/bmj.d7973, accessed 5 May 2014.

Mertens, P., D. Pestieau, D. Verhulst et al. (2012) *Comment Osent-Ils? L'Euro, la Crise et le Grand Hold-up*, Brussels: Editions Aden.

Navarro, V. (2012) 'The crisis and fiscal policies in the peripheral countries of the Eurozone', *International Journal of Health Services*, 42(1): 1–7.

OECD (Organisation for Economic Co-operation and Development) (2007) *Health at a Glance 2007: OECD Indicators*, Paris: OECD Publishing.

— (2011) *OECD Economic Surveys: Greece 2011*, Paris: OECD Publishing, August, www.mindev.gov.gr/wp-content/uploads/2011/08/Ekthesi_OACD_-Economic-Surveys-GR.pdf, accessed 5 May 2014.

OPSS (Observatório Português dos Sistemas de Saúde) (2013) *Duas Faces da Saúde*, Relatório de Primavera 2013, Coimbra: Mar da Palavra Ed.

Peiró, S. and R. Meneu (2012) 'Eficiencia en la gestión hospitalaria pública: directa vs privada por concesión', *Nada es Gratis*, 27 December, www.fedeablogs.net/economia/?p=27263, accessed 5 May 2014.

Plumer, B. (2012) 'IMF: austerity is much worse for the economy than we thought', *Washington Post*, 12 October, www.washingtonpost.com/blogs/wonkblog/wp/2012/10/12/imf-austerity-is-much-worse-for-the-economy-than-we-thought/, accessed 5 May 2014.

Polyzos, N. (2012) 'Health and the financial crisis in Greece', *The Lancet*, 379(9820): 1000.

Quercioli, C., G. Messina, S. Basu et al. (2012) 'The effect of healthcare delivery privatisation on avoidable mortality: longitudinal cross-regional results from Italy, 1993–2003', *Journal of Epidemiology and Community Health*, 67(2): 132–8.

Shutt, H. (1998) *The Trouble with Capitalism: An Enquiry into the Causes of Global Economic Failure*, London: Zed Books.

Stevens, R. (2013) 'Greek strikes continue as unemployment, poverty hit record levels', World Socialist website, 16 February, www.wsws.org/en/articles/2013/02/16/gree-f16.html, accessed 5 May 2014.

Stuckler, D. and M. McKee (2012) 'There is an alternative: public health professionals must not remain silent at a time of financial crisis', *European Journal of Public Health*, 22(1): 2–3.

Test-Aankoop (2012) *Test Gezondheid*, 107, Belgium, February.

Waitzkin, H. (2011) *Medicine and Public Health*

*at the End of Empire*, Boulder, CO: Paradigm Publishers.

WHO (World Health Organization) (2009) *The Financial Crisis and Global Health: Report of a High-Level Consultation, World Health Organization, Geneva, 19 January 2009,* Information Note/2009/1, 21 January, www.who.int/mediacentre/events/meetings/2009_financial_crisis_report_en_.pdf, accessed 5 May 2014.

# A3 | SOCIAL STRUGGLE, PROGRESSIVE GOVERNMENTS, AND HEALTH IN LATIN AMERICA

The 1980s witnessed major protests against military dictatorships in several countries of Latin America. Some of these culminated in revolutions, and a new wave of organizations replaced those destroyed by the dirty wars waged by the dictatorships during the 1960s and 1970s (Petras 1997). Faced with the prospect of armed uprisings, civilian governments (with the tacit support of the United States) 'preventively' replaced dictatorships in several other countries. Many of these civilian governments followed an explicit neoliberal agenda – such as the governments headed by Collor de Melo in Brazil, Alfonsín and Menem in Argentina, Fujimori in Peru, Caldera in Venezuela, and Aylwin in Chile.

By the late 1990s, economic crises gripped these countries, and were accompanied by major corruption scandals. The period also saw a rise in social struggles and movements, leading to the formation of a second wave of organizations. These included the Caracazo of 1989 (a protest movement against price hikes that was brutally repressed by the Venezuelan army); the struggles in Cochabamba and El Alto in Bolivia against privatization of water and gas, which overthrew the Sánchez de Lozada government; the Landless Workers' Movement in Brazil, which took over land from large plantation owners; the indigenous peasant uprising by the Zapatista National Liberation Army in Mexico; and large indigenous struggles in Ecuador (Colussi 2008). New political and social movements grew out of these struggles.

Since the beginning of this millennium several progressive governments have replaced neoliberal governments in Latin America. Among such governments were those led by Hugo Chávez in Venezuela, Evo Morales in Bolivia (the country's first indigenous president), Luiz Inácio da Silva (Lula) and his Workers' Party in Brazil, Néstor Kirchner in Argentina, Rafael Correa in Ecuador, Fernando Lugo in Paraguay and Mauricio Funes of the FMLN (Farabundo Martí National Liberation Front) in El Salvador. In Mexico, the oligarchy had been forced to commit electoral fraud in 2006 to prevent the election of Andrés Obrador.

All these governments share some common characteristics: they stand in opposition to the local capitalist elite and the United States, both of whom continue to seek ways to 'restore' the traditional oligarchies. Their attempts were successful with the coup in Paraguay, but failed in attempted coups in Venezuela and Bolivia. The new governments are comprised of heterogeneous blocs that also include some sectors of the capitalist class that were earlier

**Image A3.1** Valparaíso in Chile: while inequities persist, new forms of the welfare state have started emerging (Carolina Ibacache)

marginalized by more hard-line oligarchs (Sader 2008), along with more popular forces. In each country, different power groups have emerged, giving rise to new contradictions and tensions. Such contradictions are typified by the dual nature of criticisms against Dilma Rousseff's government in Brazil – while sections of the media and the elite press for neoliberal reforms, grassroots movements are mobilizing to demand more progressive reforms (García Linea n.d.).

In many of these countries new forms of the 'welfare state' have started emerging, based on social rights and citizenship. Transformations are occurring in types of ownership of national assets ('national' and 'state' ownership, co-operatives of different forms, etc.), linked to new ideas about building socialism. New ways of defining social inequalities and what 'is socially good' are also emerging. Noteworthy, in this context, has been the rise of the idea of 'living well' as a new paradigm, geared towards new forms of communal socialism (see Chapter E1). These transformations are just starting to make inroads into economies where capitalist forms of production continue to be the norm.

### Social changes and the health sector

The changes in the landscape of politics and economics in Latin America, which we talk about earlier, have had a profound influence on health and healthcare. Shifts in healthcare models, throughout the twentieth century, had been the result of two contradictory processes: on one hand, the attempt by capital to make it into an opportunity for accumulation and investment, and on the other social struggles to demand healthcare primarily through public institutions with equal access.

By the end of the twentieth century, the countries of Latin America had health systems that reflected the contradiction between these two processes. Struggles by salaried workers had achieved the creation of their own health-care institutions as part of social security systems. These existed alongside a more deficient healthcare network for people in rural areas and informal urban workers. The systems – in part – developed as a result of struggles by workers, but were also created as a way of legitimizing the existing social order (Offe 2007). The relative importance of private participation in provision of healthcare continued and grew. Thus, the enormous social inequalities that characterize Latin America were also expressed in inequality in access to and in the quality of medical services.

The economic crisis at the end of the twentieth century triggered reforms aimed at weakening a wide variety of public institutions and favouring private models and market relationships. Policies in the 1980s tended to dismantle the relationships and institutions created to provide some elements of welfare. For those who could not obtain care through the market, 'targeted' and temporary programmes were conceived, with the understanding that the beneficiaries of such programmes would eventually join the market (González and Alcalá 2008). The dismantling of public institutions and their replacement by private businesses and the market took the form of strategies that promoted 'managed competition' or 'structured pluralism'. These were aimed at separating the functions of regulation, financing, insurance and service delivery, opening the door for private insurance and medical care consortia to possibly get their hands on health funds.

Neoliberal governments adopted the recommendations of the World Bank's

**Image A3.2** Delegates from Latin America at the People's Health Assembly in 2012 (People's Health Movement)

1993 report *Investing in Health* (World Bank 1993), which called for large-scale dismantling of public health institutions, development of targeted programmes, reduction in health spending, and promotion of a basic package of services (rather than comprehensive provision) for the poor (López Arrellano et al. 2009). These policies paved the legal and financial road to privatization. In Chile and Colombia, this process progressed rapidly (Agudelo 2009). Based on the experiments in these two countries, a second phase of reforms was instituted in the rest of Latin America (and in other low- and middle-income countries in the world) under the broad framework of what has come to be called Universal Health Coverage (UHC). As we discuss in Chapter B.1, while UHC appears to respond to people's priorities, it is actually being utilized in many settings to further neoliberal policy (Laurell 2013).

### Advances towards universal public health systems

Latin America's health policy map is being redrawn, and neoliberal reforms – which promote segmented, unequal and inequitable health systems – are being questioned and remodelled to differing extents. The new direction foreshadows an unfinished agenda to institutionalize alternatives opposed to neoliberalism and linked to a public, free, single health system (SHS). This new direction, in different countries, is driven in different proportions from the 'bottom up' and from the 'top down', which also influence the form of health systems that are being built. While in Sections B and E of this volume the emerging health systems in many Latin American countries are discussed, we present below a political analysis of the trends that are visible in different regions of the continent.

*Cuba, Brazil, Costa Rica – more advanced experiences* Of all the experiences with developing an SHS, the Cuban experience continues to be the most complete and advanced. Even with the very difficult conditions created by the blockade and later during the 'Special Period' (after the fall of the Berlin Wall in 1990), the Cuban health system has survived and grown. Cuba has also continued to expand its international support and cooperation, sending tens of thousands of doctors to different Latin American and other developing countries (see GHW 3, ch. E3, www.ghwatch.org).

In Brazil (see Chapter B4) the struggle for democracy in the 1980s incorporated demands for expansion of social rights, which include the right to health. This led to the creation of the Unified Health System (*Sistema Único de Saúde* – SUS) – a single unified, public and free system. However, unlike in Cuba, the SUS coexists with a large private sector that perpetuates social inequality in health and is persistently pushing for public funds through contracts and by offering private medical insurance for certain groups of employees.

In Costa Rica (see GHW 3, ch. B3, www.ghwatch.org), the move towards a unified system has been led by the government rather than by direct popular pressure.

*Recent attempts at advancing towards SHS* All the progressive Latin American governments inherited segmented and deteriorating public health systems. These systems were generally iniquitous, plagued with the problem of an inadequate health workforce, and insensitive towards traditional cultures and practices. While attempting to remodel healthcare services the 'new' governments face resistance from leading medical organizations and from traditional social security systems that opposed an equitable SHS. Faced with these challenges, progress towards SHS has been partial and uneven. Venezuela, El Salvador, Bolivia and Uruguay fall into this group. In countries such as Argentina and Ecuador, much less progress is evident.

The new constitution in Venezuela, drawn up in 1999, defines health as a human and social right. It requires the state to guarantee this right through the formation of a state-owned National Public Health System that is intersectoral, decentralized and participatory, and governed by the principles of universality, comprehensiveness, equity and solidarity, merging the social security and ministry of health systems, primarily tax funded, and free of charge to individuals for its use (Feo and Curcio 2004). Progress towards a new system, which incorporates these principles, has been opposed by a large proportion of physicians and economically powerful groups interested in keeping the system segmented and maintaining opportunities for the involvement of the private sector in financing and in healthcare provision. There has also been resistance from a section of workers who have private medical insurance paid

---

**Box A3.1 Heard from a community worker**

I remember when the doctors came to Caracas, the first ones ... 63 doctors, the communities started calling me ... 'We're going to divvy them up.' The doctors had to be divided amongst the health committees that had been set up, can you imagine? 'Where are the cars?' 'There aren't any cars!' 'Well, there's my car and there are two others.' And we had to distribute 63 doctors at five in the morning. They hadn't eaten breakfast, or dinner; there was no water, there was nothing, no money either. [The doctors said,] 'well, it doesn't matter, let's go!' And when we got to the communities, it was like, 'so, he's going to stay in so-and-so's house.' We went to so-and-so's house, and many already had their ... they were making welcome signs with their own hands: 'Welcome Cuban Doctor.' So when the doctors would see that, it would make them happy.

*Source:* Briggs and Mantini-Briggs (2007)

for by their employers. Venezuela's health system as a whole, however, remains segmented and continues to perpetuate inequality in access and in quality (see Chapter E3). Reforming it from the inside has proved to be extremely difficult and plagued by opposition. People's struggles have had to force the development of a parallel system that offers universal primary care from the grass roots (see Box A3.1).

In El Salvador (see Chapter E2), following the victory of the FMLN in 2009, public spending on health has increased considerably. Direct charges in health centres were immediately eliminated, and this increased demand for care by 25–40 per cent. To the displeasure of pharmaceutical companies, drug costs were reduced and shortages considerably eased. Efforts were made to extend public services to the poorest areas of the country, seeking to counteract the greatest inequalities in healthcare. These changes have led to improved care, manifested in the rise in the proportion of pregnancies and births cared for in the system, an increase in hospital beds, and reduced maternal mortality and hospital mortality (ibid.). Much remains to be done, but significant progress is clearly evident.

Bolivia inherited a privatized health system (see Chapter E1) and is now developing 'a single public system that is integrated, decentralised, participatory, has autonomous management and a unified social security system' (Offe 2007). Central to this model is the concept of the development of Intercultural Family and Community Health (Ministerio de Salud y Deportes 2006). Greater resources are being injected into the system, prioritizing socio-economically disadvantaged areas. Progress is slowly being made, with civic engagement through community meetings.

Uruguay too inherited an underfunded health system with enormous disparities in the distribution of resources, with 75 per cent of health spending going to the private sector (Borgia 2008). One of the first tasks of the new government has been to increase funding. A National Integrated Health System is being developed, which brings together public and non-profit private providers. This is financed by a National Health Insurance Plan with funds from a National Health Fund, which remunerates public and private providers using a risk-based capitation system. People pay according to their income; their contributions go into a single fund and the government ensures that everyone gets the care they need (Olesker 2013). Consumers who choose private providers have to make co-payments. The Ministry of Health is making progress towards closing the gap between the care provided by the social security system for employed workers and care from the Ministry of Health (which is traditionally poorer).

### Countries where neoliberal reforms dominate

Colombia's neoliberal health reform (see Chapter E4) has been used as an example in other countries seeking to introduce market-oriented reforms

**Image A3.3** Movements in Latin America use different forms for social mobilization: street theatre activists in Argentina (Marcela Bobatto)

in their health systems. Begun in 1993, the reforms led to visible negative impacts on health. Public systems were weakened, medical care deteriorated and there was a negative impact on other public health activities and disease surveillance. Working conditions for health personnel also deteriorated. Additionally, barriers to services increased because private providers rejected patients with increased risk factors or because of limits to coverage in insurance policies. In response, various protest movements arose, and attempts were made to unite several of the disparate groups on a common platform. Bogotá city elected a non-neoliberal government in 2003 which tried to change the situation, but it has had to face the many difficulties and constraints created by the national model. In 2013, the national government introduced a new Bill that sought to further deepen the neoliberal reforms (Agudelo 2013). A National Alliance for a New Health Model is fighting in the streets and in the senate against the new proposal and for a complete overhaul in the model (Hernández Álvarez n.d.).

Peru's health system is segmented (see Chapter E5) and there is gross inequality between services available through social security (for salaried employees) and those provided by the Ministry of Health (for the general, often poorer, population) (FMP et al. 2013). Consumer out-of-pocket spending on healthcare is high and has been increasing in recent years, both in absolute terms and as a proportion of the GDP. Peru's health expenditure as a proportion of the GDP is very low (5.1 per cent) and a considerable portion is private (2.1 per cent) (Ríos Barrientos 2013). Reforms promoted by the government favour insurance mechanisms and the participation of private insurers and healthcare providers, with limited benefits packages (and as in Mexico, there is insufficient funding to pay for these packages) (Laurell 2013).

In Mexico (see Chapter B3) social security institutions, particularly the IMSS (Instituto Mexicano de Solidaridad Social), cover over half the population, and the Ministry of Health (MoH) covers a part of the population outside the social security system. However, unlike in Colombia and Chile, successive neoliberal governments were not able to dismantle and rapidly privatize public institutions in the face of popular resistance. Instead public institutions were starved of funds so that they could be discredited, pensions were removed from the system and transferred to private banks, and laws were amended to permit the purchase of private services. A second phase in the early 2000s overhauled care provided by the MoH and created an individual insurance mechanism that covers a basic package of services much smaller than that provided by the social security system and which permits the purchase of services from public and private providers (ibid.). The next step in the reform announced by the government, based on the structured pluralism model of Frenk and Londoño (Londoño and Frenk 1997), will be the creation of Universal Health Insurance, with a basic package of services that reduces social security benefits and permits the creation of financial intermediaries to manage health funds and private companies to provide healthcare.

### Conclusions

Today in Latin America, healthcare is one of the major areas of contestations between the neoliberal offensive mounted by multinational corporations and local ruling classes on one side and progressive movements and governments on the other. Some regions are resisting the introduction of neoliberal policies and governments are promoting policies geared to developing single, public, free and universal systems. However, a variety of obstacles that may not be resolved immediately are hampering progress. These include the need to reconstruct public healthcare systems following a decade of deliberate dismantling. There is also resistance from the upper echelons of physicians who control the medical societies and medical schools and who oppose moves to strengthen public services and who also oppose multiculturalism. Resistance from the medical-pharmaceutical-insurance complex is also playing a role in blocking grassroots progress. Nevertheless, partial models that embody health as an equal right for all are making inroads. These experiences must be disseminated, supported and nurtured as seeds of what could be the future health system grounded in the concept of *living well*, to counteract those who would see healthcare as the big transnational business opportunity of the twenty-first century.

# References

Agudelo, S. F. (2009) 'La salud al final del milenio', in *ALAMES en la Memoria: Seleccion de Lecturas*, Havana: Ed. Caminos.

— (2013) 'Otro remedio peor que la enfermedad: a propósito de los proyectos en curso de reforma a la salud', Bogotá, 27 September, www.alames.org/documentos/remedio.pdf.

Borgia, F. (2008) 'La salud en Uruguay: avances y desafíos por el derecho a la salud a tres años del primer gobierno progresista', *Medicina Social*, 3(2), May, www.medicinasocial.info.

Briggs, C. L. and C. Mantini-Briggs (2007) *Salud Colectiva*, Buenos Aires, May–August, 3(2): 159–76.

Colussi, M. (2008) '¿Latinoamérica va hacia la izquierda?', *Rebelión*, August, www.rebelion.org/noticia.php?id=40951.

Feo, O. and P. Curcio (2004) 'La salud en el proceso constituyente venezolano', *Revista Cubana de Salud Pública*, 30(2), April–June.

FMP (Federación Médica Peruana), FSP (Foro Salud Perú) and APS (Academia Peruana de Salud) (2013) *En Defensa del Derecho Fundamental a la Salud*, Lima, 3 August, www.alames.org.

García Linea, A. (n.d.) *Las Tensiones Creativas de la Revolución: La Quinta Fase del Proceso de Cambio*, Presidencia de la Asamblea Legislativa Plurinacional, Vicepresidencia del Estado Plurinacional, La Paz.

González, R. and J. Alcalá (2008) 'La dimensión ética en políticas de salud en América Latina', MA thesis, Universidad Autónoma Metropolitana, Mexico City, December.

Hernández Álvarez, M. (n.d.) 'Un sistema universal para enfrentar la crisis de la salud', Alianza Nacional por un Nuevo Modelo de Salud (ANSA), Comisión de Seguimiento de la Sentencia T-760/08 y de Reforma Estructural del Sistema de Salud y Seguridad Social (CSR), www.alames.org.

Laurell, A. C. (2013) 'Impacto del seguro popular en el sistema de salud mexicano', CLACSO, biblioteca.clacso.org.ar/clacso/clacso-crop/20130807020931/Impactodel SeguroPopular.pdf.

Londoño, J. L. and J. Frenk (1997) 'Structured pluralism: towards an innovative model for health system reform in Latin America', *Health Policy*, 41(1): 1–36.

López Arellano, O., J. Blanco Gil and J. A. Rivera Márquez (2009) 'Descentralización y paquetes básicos de salud. ¿"Nuevas" propuestas incluyentes?', in *ALAMES en la Memoria: Selección de Lecturas*, Havana: Ed. Caminos, pp. 437–8.

Ministerio de Salud y Deportes (2006) *Modelo de Salud Familiar y Comunitaria Intercultural*, Government of Bolivia, www.sns.gob.bo/index.php?ID=SAFCI.

Offe, C. (2007) 'Some contradictions of the modern welfare state', in C. Pierson and G. Francis, *The Welfare State Reader*, Cambridge: Polity Press.

Olesker, D. (2013) 'Social reform and health: advances in a socializing sense', *Divulgação em Saúde para Debate*, 49, Rio de Janeiro: CEBES.

Petras, J. (1997) 'Latin America: the resurgence of the left', *New Left Review*, 1(223), May/June.

Ríos Barrientos, M. (2013) 'Luz verde a reforma de la salud mercantilista', *Revista Ideele*, 231, June, www.revistaideele.com/ideele/content/luz-verde-reforma-de-la-salud-mercantilista.

Sader, E. (2008) 'The weakest link? Neoliberalism in Latin America', *New Left Review*, 52, July/August.

World Bank (1993) *World Development Report 1993: Investing in Health*, Washington, DC.

## A4 | AFTER THE ARAB SPRING

The uprisings of 2011 (described widely as the 'Arab Spring') have had a decisive impact on the Arab world. The scale of these changes was not predictable even a decade ago, when the neoliberal security state, exemplified by the Mubarak regime in Egypt, appeared to be deeply entrenched in the entire region. The 'Arab Spring' of 2011 was not a sudden development, as it is often made out to be. It was the culmination of festering discontent in the region against authoritarian regimes – and the discontent exploded into active rebellion, fuelled by declining conditions of living and growing unemployment (especially among the youth). The resistance included different political and social strands. These different social and political forces, in different ways – at times working in tandem and often in antagonism to each other – contributed to the final upsurge that washed away the visible faces of the old regimes.

### Neoliberal policies and the decline of the welfare state

There has been a singular failure to appreciate (at least in the mainstream discourse) that the revolutions represented a rebellion not just against local dictators, but against many elements of the global neoliberal project (Mackell 2011). The huge mobilizations in Egypt and Tunisia, in 2011, did want to bring down the regimes of Mubarak and Ben Ali. But that was not all; they were also mobilized against rising unemployment (approximately 25 per cent of the young people in the Middle East and North African region officially lack a job) and skyrocketing food and fuel prices (Jannin and Forontini 2013).

To make better sense of what is happening today, it would be useful to begin by tracing the history of the Arab region from the immediate post-colonial period (from the 1950s and 1960s).

A number of regimes in the Arab region, in this period, combined authoritarianism with a redistributive welfare state. The development of nascent welfare systems within an authoritarian framework of governance was an important feature, in the post-colonial period, in many countries of the region (Coutts et al. 2013: 52). Egypt, Tunisia and Libya are all examples of this trend. These states consolidated power under what were essentially dictatorships, by trading development for the political loyalty of key social forces (Dahi 2011). In a way, these regimes 'bought' legitimacy for themselves through the promotion of a range of welfare measures. Many of these states developed fairly strong social protection systems that guaranteed access to education, health, housing, food, etc. to significant sections of the popula-

**Image A4.1** Tahrir Square, Egypt: demands of the revolution (Bert de Belder)

tion. Also, as a consequence, they developed a strong public-sector-driven infrastructure.

The relatively stable equilibrium began to unravel after a couple of decades. GDP growth rates generally rose till the late 1970s and then began declining in the 1980s. An important contributory factor was the growing repressive character of the regimes, which attempted to suppress popular discontent against the corrupt practices of those who were closely allied to the power structures of the regimes. Importantly the decline in economic conditions of the vast majority of the people coincided with the incorporation of this region into the global neoliberal system. Neoliberal prescriptions were applied, leading to the privatization of public goods like water, electricity, housing, health and education. By steadily retracting redistributive policies while maintaining authoritarian governance, the regimes started losing the veneer of legitimacy. Paradoxically, for a brief period after the onset of the neoliberal reforms, aggregate economic indicators improved, but at the expense of equity (Erakat 2013).

The neoliberal agenda was promoted in all countries of the region, at the behest of international financial institutions. Combined with declining oil revenues from the mid-1980s, this led to the dismantling of the welfare state apparatus in the region. In Egypt, for example, liberalization and structural adjustment policies severely undermined what was once a highly developed social protection system. Social protection provided by the government to vulnerable segments of the population shrank. Equitable access to education and healthcare was severely affected. Concurrently, people faced increased economic hardships as a consequence of the continuous rise in the cost of basic services such as water, electricity and transportation as a result of increases in fees levied on services provided by the government (Majdo 2007).

Structural adjustment programmes imposed in the region did not stop at just the dismantling of public services. They led to wide-ranging reforms of the economic systems. Many countries in the region had started building self-reliant capacity in vital sectors of the economy, including industry and agriculture. The path to self-reliance was facilitated by technological aid from the then Soviet bloc. After the fall of the Soviet Union, countries of the region – as was the case for low- and middle-income countries (LMICs) in many other regions – lost their bargaining power vis-à-vis global capital and were forced to unequivocally follow the prescriptions doled out by agencies such as the World Bank and the International Monetary Fund (IMF).

For example, beginning in the 1990s, IMF-led structural adjustment programmes saw the privatization of the bulk of the Egyptian textile industry and the slashing of its workforce from half a million to a quarter-million. Further, wages stagnated while the price of living escalated owing to the dismantling of social security measures (Mackell 2011).

### Praise from the IMF

The IMF pressed for a clear policy shift in the region, thus dismantling vestiges of the welfare state. The IMF's prescriptions for the region can be understood from an excerpt of a speech delivered in 1996 by the then managing director of the IMF, Michael Camdessus, at the annual meeting of the Union of Arab Banks:

> To begin with, we tell them [governments in the Arab region] that they must pursue disciplined and predictable fiscal and monetary policies. In particular, government deficits must be reduced to a point where they can be financed in a non-inflationary way and do not crowd out private investment or require the drawdown of foreign assets. For many countries in the region, this will require strengthening the tax base – by reducing import duty exemptions, replacing high trade taxes with broad-based consumption taxes, and improving tax administration. It will also require reducing expenditure – by curbing the growth of the government wage bill, and cutting such unproductive expenditures as subsidies and defence spending. Privatization has an important role to play in this regard. At the same time, governments need to improve the quality of expenditure – by redirecting spending toward education, health, and well-targeted social safety nets. (Camdessus 1996)

These prescriptions were followed avidly by virtually all countries in the region and the IMF acknowledged such compliance with fulsome praise. In 2008, Ben Ali in Tunisia received praise from the then IMF chief, Dominique

Strauss-Kahn: 'Economic policy adopted here is a sound policy and is the best model for many emerging countries.' In 2010 (a mere few weeks before Mohamed Bouazizi's self-immolation in Tunisia sparked the beginning of the Arab Spring) the IMF again commended Ben Ali's commitment to 'reduce tax rates on businesses and to offset those reductions by increasing the standard Value Added Tax (VAT) rate' (the most regressive form of taxation). The IMF also continued to advise Tunisia to 'contain subsidies of food and fuel products' (Bond and Sharife 2012).

## Change and continuity

A political analysis of the different social and political actors that forced the downfall of the old regimes (at least their visible faces) is beyond the remit of this chapter. Suffice it to say that they inhaled their own power and potential and exhaled to overthrow leaders who hitherto had seemed invincible. But their exhalation was not sufficient to knock down the entire regime in one blow (Prashad 2013). In Egypt, the bulk of the neo-authoritarian regime has survived the end of the Mubarak era, not only in terms of the military taking over but also as far as the ruling elites (with the exception of the Mubarak clan and the top echelons of the regime) (Pioppi et al. 2011: 4). The situation is more fluid in other countries such as Tunisia and Libya. It would not be wrong to say, however, that even in places where the old regimes have not been able to claw back power, they remain a powerful force.

States are not built only above ground, but grow deep roots that are often

**Image A4.2** Demanding the end of the old regime; Tahrir Square, Egypt (Bert de Belder)

as hard to identify as they are to unearth. Old social classes with ties to all political branches find themselves standing upright regardless of who takes power, as long as it is not the working class and its working-poor ally. The bourgeoisie is intimately linked to the military through family ties and through close business arrangements, and it is the bourgeoisie as well which has been able to incorporate itself into the moderate (elite) sections of political Islam. Its interests are held intact despite the transformation. The bourgeoisie's view of the world is helped along by its intellectual and political allies on the international stage (the bankers, the IMF, the ratings agencies and of course the governments of the North and the Gulf Arab monarchies). They urge the new regimes to follow older policies poured into new concepts to sweeten them for political consumption, thus ensuring that there are unchanging elements that maintain power regardless of who is now in charge.[1]

### Rebuilding the neoliberal agenda

Gathering around the new regimes, aggravating their limitations, are forces of global capital and of Northern imperialism who have objectives in mind other than the needs of the Arab people. The revolts of 2011 rattled the USA, whose main pillars of stability – the Gulf Arab monarchies and Israel – had been threatened by the power shifts. The NATO–GCC (Gulf Coordination Council) intervention in Libya allowed the North to hoist its own social forces back into the saddle. In fact, not long after the coalition of domestic rebels and NATO forces toppled Gaddafi's regime in Libya, multinational corporations in security, construction and infrastructure turned their sights from Iraq and Afghanistan to Libya (Coutts et al. 2013: 55).

The popular unrest seemed likely to spread via Bahrain into the other Gulf monarchies. The removal of Mubarak and the potential threats to Assad in Syria and Hussein in Jordan would have encircled Israel with 'untested' Islamic regimes. This had to be forestalled, which provided the urgency of the NATO intervention. Now the North could re-establish itself as the friend of freedom after the ignominy of seeing its allies (France's Ben Ali and the USA's Mubarak) being ousted.

Via the IMF and through its military subvention, the USA has been able to re-enter the everyday management of Egypt and Tunisia – despite the continued antipathy of the people to US meddling (as the chants against US ambassador Anne Patterson in 2013 and the attacks on US consular facilities in Libya and Egypt in 2012 establish). It is these imperialist manoeuvres which enable the old social classes to comfort themselves about their immortality.

The IMF and the World Bank continue to exert influence in the region. Despite protests, they persist in pushing a neoliberal agenda on the population. An IMF working paper that studied the turbulence of the Arab Spring notes that the situation is bleak for the population. Nonetheless, it suggested the need to implement 'a growth-friendly fiscal adjustment to reduce generalized subsidies, bolster investment, and strengthen targeted social safety nets' – everything that the IMF has pushed for in the past several decades (Khandelwal and Roitman 2013: 10). A more recent paper reiterates: 'Countries need prudent economic management, paired with bold reforms to create an enabling environment for private sector-led growth, to safeguard the promise of the Arab transitions for better living conditions and job creation on a meaningful scale'; and further that: 'Expenditure-side reforms should include redirecting social protection from expensive and inefficient generalized subsidies to transfers that better target the poor and vulnerable' (Ahmed 2014).

Political Islam is incapable of challenging these old social classes (and unwilling to do so). It has links to them, and it does not sufficiently grasp the enormity of the economic challenge that it has so cavalierly claimed it can solve. Between the Ennahda party led by Rached Ghannouchi in Tunisia and the now deposed presidency of the Brotherhood's Mohamed Morsi there is no difference in terms of their solicitude to the IMF and their inability to craft a pro-people alternative. There is no social democratic agenda even: demanding an annulment or a radically renegotiated odious debt and crafting proposals for capital controls to harness foreign direct investment rather than allow it to run riot in the real estate and financial sectors. It did not help Morsi's government that it chose to emphasize the creation of a socially conservative state through sectarian means, rather than stand up for what the people wanted – a more democratic civil society and a more just economy. Social policies driven by religious rhetoric did not resonate well with a population that had united to depose a long-standing authoritarian leader. Rather than lead the people against the policies of the old regime, the Morsi government attacked the people, only to make it easier for the military to return. It was a missed opportunity because the Islamists had a narrow vision for their rule, and they misread the situation and reversed the tide of history as a result.

### Conclusions

The spectacular fall of major Arab leaders in 2011 created impatience among the population. But revolutionary waves work at a different pace. They do not work in the short term alone. The Mexican Revolution, for instance, began in 1910 and lasted for two decades. Only when Lazardo Cardenas took power in 1934 did the dust settle. The Soviet Revolution began in 1917, but did not find its feet (and then only barely) before 1928. The overthrow of the autocratic government occurs in the short term, the consolidation of the new regime takes place in the medium term and then the economic and cultural changes required to set up a new dispensation take place in the long term.

The totality of the Arab Revolution is a 'civilizational' uprising against the dispensation that they have had to live under: a two-headed force, with one head representing neoliberal economic policies and the other the security state. It was an uprising for a political voice, certainly, but not for a political voice alone. This was a revolutionary process against economic deprivation and political suffocation.

## Note

1 The term deep state comes from Turkish – *derin devlet*. The term has now travelled; see, for example, E. Woertz, 'Egypt: return of the deep state', *Open Democracy*, 20 January 2014.

## References

Ahmed, M. (2014) 'Arab economic transformation amid political transitions', IMFdirect, 11 April, blog-imfdirect.imf.org/2014/04/11/arab-economic-transformation-amid-political-transitions/#more-7229, accessed 5 May 2014.

Bond, P. and K. Sharife (2012) 'IMF and the Arab spring: will neoliberalism make a come back in Africa?', NAI Forum, 14 February, naiforum.org/2012/02/imf-and-the-arab-spring/, accessed 5 May 2014.

Camdessus, M. (1996) 'The challenges for the Arab world in the global economy: stability and structural adjustment', Address at the Annual Meeting of the Union of Arab Banks, New York, 20 May, www.imf.org/external/np/sec/mds/1996/mds9608.htm, accessed 5 May 2014.

Coutts, A., D. Stuckler, R. Batniji et al. (2013) 'The Arab spring and health: two years on', *International Journal of Health Services*, 43(1): 49–60.

Dahi, O. S. (2011) 'Understanding the political economy of the Arab revolts', *Middle East Report*, 41(259): 2–6, relooney.info/SI_ME-Crisis/0-Important_342.pdf, accessed 5 May 2014.

Erakat, N. (2013) 'On neoliberal development, human rights & the Arab uprisings', 9 October, www.nouraerakat.com/1/post/2013/10/on-neoliberal-development-human-rights-the-arab-uprisings.html, accessed 5 May 2014.

Jannin, J. and A. Forontini (2013) 'Unfulfilled promises: an assessment of the Arab spring, its challenges and prospects', *SIAK-Journal*, 1, July, pp. 4–18, www.bmi.gv.at/cms/BMI_SIAK/4/2/1/2013/ausgabe_1/files/Janning_1_2013.pdf, accessed 5 May 2014.

Khandelwal, P. and A. Roitman (2013) 'The economics of political transitions: implications for the Arab Spring', IMF Working Paper WP/13/69, Washington, DC, www.imf.org/external/pubs/ft/wp/2013/wp1369.pdf, accessed 5 May 2014.

Mackell, A. (2011) 'The IMF versus the Arab spring', *Guardian*, 25 May, www.theguardian.com/commentisfree/2011/may/25/imf-arab-spring-loans-egypt-tunisia, accessed 5 May 2014.

Majdo, A.-H. (2007) 'Shrinking state role undermines social protection', Social Watch, www.socialwatch.org/node/11020, accessed 5 May 2014.

Pioppi, D., M. C. Paciello, I. El Amrani et al. (2011) 'Transition to what: Egypt's unclear departure from neo-authoritarianism', Mediterranean Paper Series 2011, German Marshall Fund of the United States, Washington, DC, www.iai.it/pdf/mediterraneo/GMF-IAI/Mediterranean-paper_11.pdf, accessed 5 May 2014.

Prashad, V. (2013) 'The state of the arable revolution', *The Marxist*, 29(2), New Delhi, cpim.org/sites/default/files/marxist/201302-Prashad-Arab-Revolution.pdf, accessed 5 May 2014.

# HEALTH SYSTEMS: CURRENT ISSUES AND DEBATES

# B1 | THE CURRENT DISCOURSE ON UNIVERSAL HEALTH COVERAGE (UHC)[1]

The current discourse on Universal Health Coverage (UHC) dominates most international discussions on healthcare. UHC is presented as *the* solution to pressing healthcare needs in low- and middle-income countries (LMICs) and enthusiastic proponents have termed it the 'third great transition' in health, changing how services are financed and how systems are organized (Rodin and De Ferranti 2012).

On the international stage, one of the earliest mentions of UHC was at the 58th World Health Assembly in 2005, in a resolution calling on member states to: 'ensure that health-financing systems include a method for prepayment of financial contributions for health care, with a view to sharing risk among the population and avoiding catastrophic health-care expenditure and impoverishment of individuals as a result of seeking care' (WHA 2005). Thus, from its early days, the emphasis was on 'sustainable health financing'. The use of the term 'coverage' rather than 'care' symbolizes the move away from concerns of health-systems design towards financing.

International agencies quickly rallied behind UHC as a response to the precipitous rise in catastrophic out-of-pocket expenditure on healthcare. As a consequence of a prolonged period of neglect of public healthcare and privatization of health systems, by the turn of the millennium healthcare in most LMICs was characterized by:

1 A crumbling public health system, with poor infrastructure, falling morale among health workers and diminishing resources.
2 Increased penetration of the private sector, especially for secondary and tertiary care.
3 A consequent rise in catastrophic health expenditures by households, a large proportion of which was 'out-of-pocket'.

To remedy the situation, there could have been efforts to prioritize the rebuilding and strengthening of public systems. Instead, the emphasis shifted from how services should be provided to how services should be financed, under the rubric of UHC. The underlying belief appeared to be that if the finances were secured, provisioning of health services could be taken care of by a variety of mixes that involved both the private and the public sector. Such an assumption completely missed the point that a health *system* is not a mere aggregate of dispersed facilities and service providers, but is an integrated

**Image B1.1** A woman from Malawi with her health card: reforms in the 1980s led to crumbling health systems (David Sanders)

network of facilities and services that are appropriately situated at primary, secondary and tertiary levels.

The contours of UHC that began to take shape were based on some early initiatives in the late 1990s and early 2000s – especially in parts of Latin America, where reforms were based on universal insurance schemes (see Chapter A3). These reforms led to increases in national healthcare expenditures, both public and private; and promoted a market logic centred on 'individual care' conceived as a 'private' good. There was no clear evidence that the reforms improved public health outcomes. In fact, evidence from Colombia and Chile suggested that quality of care did not improve, equity and efficiency were negatively influenced, and transnational corporations and consultancy firms accrued significant benefits (Homedes and Ugalde 2005). Worse, the market logic destroyed the institutional scaffolding of public and collective health. The result was the re-emergence of previously controlled diseases and the reduction of preventive interventions (Laurell 2010). However, these reforms were given a positive spin to justify the push for a certain model of UHC.[2] The World Bank played a key role in consensus-building around reforms that were to become precursors to UHC, before the World Health Organization (WHO) formally adopted it as part of its policy.[3]

**Image B1.2** Massive demonstrations against health-system reforms in Bogotá, Colombia (Mauricio Torres)

### The ideological foundations of UHC

The 2010 *World Health Report* illustrated the concept as a diagram, reproduced in Figure B1.1.

In the cube UHC is conceived as a system that would progressively move towards: i) the coverage of the entire population by a package of services, ii) inclusion of an increasing range of services, and iii) a rising share of pooled funds as the main source of funding for healthcare, and thereby a decrease in co-payments. Julio Frenk, the architect of the Mexican health insurance system,

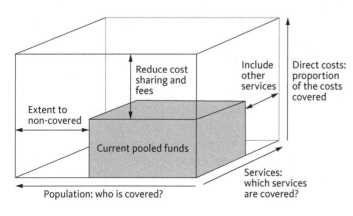

**B1.1** The UHC cube (source: World Health Organization, World Health Report, WHO, Geneva, 2010)

suggests that stewardship (including deployment of equitable policies) and fair financing are essential public responsibilities, whereas delivery of services is best served through a pluralistic mix that includes the private sector and civil society (Frenk and De Ferranti 2012). Such a model of UHC requires a clear 'provider–purchaser' split, the issues of financing and management being entirely divorced from provisioning. The importance of public healthcare services is not a part of this narrative and the state is confined to the role of manager of this system. The split between the state as a provider and as purchaser of services means that health services can be entirely provided by private enterprises while the state mediates to secure the funding for such services and regulates their quality and range. A provider–purchaser split puts a price on services; that is, it commodifies them, which is the precondition for their transaction in the marketplace (Laurell 2007).

The retreat of the state as a provider of public services has been accompanied by a clear reform push in public services, often referred to as 'new public management' (Vabø 2009). The UHC proposal is no stranger to this trend. The strategy has been to introduce private sector management, organization and labour market ethos and practices into the public sector, with a push to introduce 'internal markets' within the domain of public provision. While public funding is retained (and in some cases expanded), mechanisms are introduced to isolate the purchasers from the providers. The intention is that individual 'units' should compete for consumers and patients should be able to move between providers with relative ease. This reorganization along the lines of new public management is crucial to subsequent privatization of public services, as erstwhile public services in their classical form were not marketable commodities (Pierson 2001: 157). The current discourse on UHC accomplishes the almost seamless transition in the role of the government from provider of services to purchaser of services. For example, an issue of the WHO *Bulletin* argues: 'To sustain progress, efficiency and accountability must be ensured. The main health financing instrument for promoting efficiency in the use of funds is purchasing, and more specifically, strategic purchasing' (Kutzin 2012).

This reconceptualized role of governments is defined in the 2010 *World Health Report*: 'Governments have a responsibility to ensure that all providers, public and private, operate appropriately and attend to patients' needs cost effectively and efficiently.' This 'impartial' role of governments can be interpreted in many ways. With most public health systems in a state of disarray, it is an appealing option for governments to choose not to rebuild public systems but to rely increasingly on private providers. The logic is that the catastrophic impact of out-of-pocket expenditures needs an immediate remedy, and as the public system is too weak to respond, it is more strategic to turn to the private sector. The UHC model, thus, provides the opportunity to make the choice to open up a country's health system to private providers rather than consider public provision of services as the mainstay of its healthcare system.

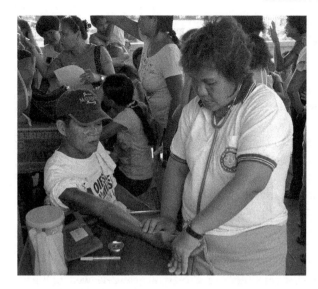

**Image B1.3** A health worker in the Philippines: basic and not comprehensive public services was the message from the World Bank (Third World Health Aid)

Further, under the UHC model, governments can choose more progressive options for financing – such as tax-based funding in a progressive regime of taxation. However, in situations where the state itself is committed to pursuing neoliberal policies, such progressive options may not be adopted.

This current discourse on UHC is in sharp contrast with the vision of Primary Health Care envisaged in the Alma Ata declaration of 1978, which called for the building of health systems that would provide comprehensive care, would be integrated, organized to promote equity, and driven by community needs (GHW 1 2005: 56). Instead, UHC envisages healthcare as bits and pieces of a jigsaw puzzle, connected only by a common financing pool and by regulation of an array of private and public providers. What is also glossed over is that universal health 'coverage' is only one aspect of universal health 'care'. Coverage as a strategy focuses primarily on the achievement of a wide network of health providers and health institutions extending access to health services to the population. The components that are 'sufficient' to be considered for adequate coverage remain highly contested, however (Stuckler et al. 2010).

Nonetheless, UHC is a step forward to the extent that it represents an explicit recognition of two important aspects of public health. First, by prescribing a central role to the state in securing funding for healthcare and in regulating the quality and range of services, UHC recognizes that 'market failures' are a feature of private healthcare. Secondly, UHC also recognizes that health is a 'public good' with externalities, and that the state has a responsibility to ensure access to health services. Thus, UHC provides the possibility of exercising a choice, and progressive governments can try to privilege public systems and examine funding mechanisms that promote equity. Financial pooling through

UHC (a 'single payer' system) makes it easier to develop comprehensive public systems, but whether that will happen is a political choice.

### The ambiguities of UHC

The dominant concept of UHC proposes that funding for health should be pooled; it does not propose the same for the provision of services – that is, it does not propose a unified system of public provision. Neither does it define the 'depth' of coverage and hence allows an interpretation that coverage can mean a very basic package, akin to the World Bank's prescriptions of the previous decades. This latter point is captured by the UHC proposition that the exact mechanisms for pooling will depend on social processes and political action that establish the parameters for an acceptable public role in healthcare. In some cases, the result will be a government that primarily regulates the healthcare sector, while in other cases a government that finances and directly provides care (Savedoff et al. 2012). These obscurities were clearly captured by a recent literature survey of peer-reviewed publications on UHC. Of 100 papers analysed only twenty-one provided an explicit definition of UHC. Among these twenty-one, there was little consensus on the concept, and its meanings were often unclear. The majority referred to UHC as universal coverage, but differed in regard to whether they meant a comprehensive set of healthcare services or a limited initiative (Stuckler et al. 2010).

The UHC model provides choices in a particular political and economic environment that is not neutral. The dominant neoliberal environment can exploit the ambiguities inherent in the UHC model and promote a model that is market-driven. Such a model, through a combination of pooling of funds and private provision, becomes an efficient way for private capital to extract profits. With the state intervening to pool healthcare funds in one basket (the locus of collection may range from primarily tax-based to a combination of employee, employer and government contributions), new avenues for profit-making are opened up through the medium of insurance companies and health management organizations.

Pooling of funds provides an effective demand (i.e. purchasing power) for the healthcare industry in settings where most people live in extreme poverty. It also opens up a new and lucrative private market: the administration of health insurance funds. In an insurance-based model, although more public funds are earmarked for health, this is done through demand subsidization (putting money in the hands of the users) rather than subsidizing supply by increasing the budget of public institutions. As a result, a new layer of competition is added to the system. Not only do public and private service providers compete, we also see competition between public and private insurance plans. Furthermore, private companies are offered a series of advantages in order to break the 'monopoly' of public institutions (Laurell 2010).

## Where is the evidence?

The unquestioning faith in the 'efficiency' of private healthcare services in the mainstream UHC model is related to the complexity in measuring the quality and efficacy of integrated public health services (see Box B1.1). Usual measures of health outcomes – e.g. child mortality, life expectancy, etc. – cannot be linked directly to healthcare services, as they often depend more fundamentally on other determinants of health (poverty, housing, nutrition, employment, environment, gender roles, etc.). In fact, only 10–15 per cent of gains in life expectancy are estimated to be attributable to healthcare (Leys 2009: 6). Yet existing measures of health coverage tend to focus on quantitative assessments of access to particularly high healthcare expenses (Moreno-Serra and Smith 2011). Another common method of measuring 'efficiency' in healthcare services is by looking at subjective perceptions such as 'patient satisfaction', 'behaviour of health workers' and crude criteria such as waiting times at clinics and hospitals. The use of such metrics often places public health services at a disadvantage as private care providers are likely to be more adept at addressing these concerns, although they may not be relevant as regards the actual quality of care. Patients are rarely in a position to correctly judge the quality of services, given the huge information asymmetry that exists in the case of medical care.

Finding evidence to assess the impact of newly implemented UHC schemes

---

### Box B1.1 The World Bank's attempt at generating 'evidence'

A recent World Bank Publication, *The Impact of Universal Coverage Schemes in the Developing World: A Review of the Existing Evidence* (Giedion et al. 2013), examines all the possible meanings of and approaches to UHC and then details its final conclusions.

The review analyses 309 papers identified by searching known web-based databases of biomedical and social science publications using a few chosen keywords. Of these, 204 are excluded for not being relevant to LMICs or because they are not based on primary data – leaving 105 in the final review. The review then scores the papers for quality of the work and finds that only 41 make it to a minimum necessary score. Of these 41 papers, 29 papers are able to correlate UHC with outcomes of access and utilization, 21 with financial protection and 13 with health status. Only three studies are able to comment on all three outcomes.

The introductory section on conceptual framework does not adequately clarify what can be considered a 'UHC effort'. It implies that virtually every health system, programme or intervention could potentially be classified as a UHC scheme as long as it claims to pursue the goals of

UHC. It explicitly states that the report goes beyond the consideration of insurance schemes, but of the final 41 papers, all except 3 papers discuss insurance-based systems. Even in the first shortlist of 105 papers, there are almost no examples of budget-based resource allocation to public provisioning of services. Clearly, a filter has been applied to privilege insurance-based approaches to UHC.

Much of the public support for UHC is mobilized on the expectation that it would contribute to a significant increase in access to a wide range of services – going beyond the narrow package of Reproductive and Child Health (RCH) services that many public health systems in LMICs restrict themselves to. It therefore comes as a surprise that most of the schemes studies are insurance schemes, and that the packages covered by insurance are very limited. The entire methodology, thus, virtually accepts that UHC can often (or usually) mean coverage by an extremely narrow package of services. Thus, of the 17 studies in the evidence base that assessed impact of UHC on access, 6 studies only discuss care during pregnancy and one of these only measures the number of visits for prenatal care! The remaining 11 studies in the review that examine impact of UHC on access simply enumerate number of visits or admissions, without any reference to the type of care sought and what proportion of health needs was met.

The conclusions of the review border on the bizarre. The evidence base for 'impact of UHC on health status' is provided by 19 papers and the authors conclude from the evidence that: '... it is hard to achieve and show such impacts'. The authors also conclude that: '... while an earlier section provided convincing evidence on the positive impact of UHC schemes on access and utilization, this is much less so with regard to financial protection'. In other words: i) no convincing evidence of any impact of UHC on financial protection; and ii) claimed impact of UHC on access based on evidence generated regarding provision of a very narrow and selective set of packages, and by the use of indicators that provide no real analysis of the quality of services. The review finds reason to further hedge its bets by saying: '... the lack of impact on out of pocket expenditures does not necessarily imply a failure of the programme given that this result might be explained – at least partly – by a desirable effect (increased utilization)'. This is indeed circular logic at its best (or worst!) – first provide no real evidence regarding 'better utilization' and then assert that lack of evidence for financial protection is explained by 'increased utilization'! It is worth noting that only 15 of the 41 papers that qualified for the evidence base had even measured for impact on financial protection.

is particularly challenging (ibid.) and methodologies designed to collect good evidence are singularly lacking. Many evaluations of UHC schemes end up measuring the impact on 'out-of-pocket' expenses incurred (ibid.: 101) but do not measure the quality and depth of services offered. As a consequence, the 'proof' of positive impact on health outcomes remains extremely thin, with huge methodological challenges. For example, some evaluations of the much-acclaimed '*Seguro Popular*' scheme in Mexico reported no effect on self-reported health indicators and did not report change in general patterns of service use (Moreno-Serra and Smith 2012).

The basic argument for pooled financing and insurance (the hallmark of UHC) is that it reduces financial risk. However, insurance also opens up new opportunities for consuming expensive high-technology care that permits health improvements that are valued by the patient – especially since the private provider is able to exploit its informational advantage; it is an open question, however, whether insurance (of any form) will in practice reduce financial risk. A large 2005 study of China's health insurance schemes indicates that it may, to the contrary, be associated with increased risk of large out-of-pocket payments (Wagstaff and Lindelow 2005).

There is even less evidence available about what strategies within the UHC approach are more promising. And there are virtually no data that compare the relative merits of approaches that are premised on predominant public delivery of services versus those that follow a private–public mix with predominant private sector delivery of services.

### Public systems efficiencies

There are, however, clear structural reasons why market-driven healthcare and competition do not in fact promote efficiency[4] or quality (Rice 1997). Commercialized healthcare systems have higher transaction costs, required to manage or regulate the market. A study of long-term care facilities in the USA estimated that in 1999 as much as $294.3 billion was used for administrative costs, representing 31.0 per cent of healthcare expenditures in the country. Transaction costs tend to be much lower in more public systems; for example, the transaction costs in the National Health Service in the UK in the mid-1970s, before it began to be converted into a market, were estimated at between 5 and 6 per cent of total expenditure (Leys 2009: 18).

Public systems are more efficient also because they ensure economies of scale in the purchasing, supply and distribution of drugs and equipment (Robinson and White 2001). They are also best placed to avoid wasteful capital investment, duplication of equipment and services, and an emphasis on frills that are endemic to hospitals in a competitive market environment (Ramesh et al. 2013). Public systems perform a broad range of public health tasks that are not directly linked to providing care. It can be argued that an array of private providers could offer these services if robust regulatory mechanisms imposed conditions that mandated private providers to do so. In practice, however, public goods such as mass coverage, public awareness, community outreach and emergency services are more effectively provided through public programmes rather than the sum of regulated private programmes (Sachs 2012).

Further, there are significant marginal costs involved in delivery of care to the most inaccessible or the most disadvantaged sections of the population. Health services for those with pre-existing chronic conditions are often relatively more expensive, as is the treatment of rare diseases (Allotey et al. 2012). In rapidly ageing societies a very high proportion of healthcare needs are concentrated in the last few months or years of life. Public systems can absorb these marginal costs and spread them across an entire population. Private systems, on the other hand, would typically attempt to exclude those who have special needs or are otherwise disadvantaged. Finally, competition harms collaboration between different providers, often an important ingredient of good-quality care, especially in relation to referrals between different kinds of specialists or between different levels of the healthcare system.

The argument that health systems in LMICs should leverage the already dominant private sector is clearly misplaced. The large out-of-pocket expenditures and private provision in low-income countries are mainly a reflection of the paucity of public services, especially for the poor, forcing the middle and upper classes to go directly to private providers, while the poor are left without reliable services. This reality is unfortunate, and not a convincing case for private provision, but rather should serve as a call to action to bolster the deeply underfinanced public sector (Sachs 2012: 945).

## UHC in advanced capitalist countries

Variants of the UHC model that is being proposed today have existed in parts of the globe for over 130 years, starting with Germany under Bismarck in the second half of the nineteenth century. Such models inform the design of health systems in most developed countries to this day (with the notable exception of the USA).

*Health and the negotiating power of labour* The introduction of universal health coverage schemes in Europe and elsewhere has its roots in attempts to quell rising discontent among the working class. Initially, they were designed as welfare payments during sickness and later integrated into entitlements to healthcare. The primary reason for the emergence of these programmes in Europe was income stabilization and protection against the wage loss of sickness, rather than payment for medical expenses, which came later. Programmes were originally conceived as a means to maintain incomes and buy the political allegiance of workers (Palmer 1999). The impetus came from a need to offer concessions to the working poor, and not from a coherent view of how health services were to be organized. As we discuss later, all developed capitalist countries shied away from adopting an entirely public system, though there was enormous variation in the public–private mix that was implemented. The fact that social health insurance systems in western Europe are still largely functioning is not a commentary on their viability and efficiency. Rather, it reflects the ability of the ruling classes, when forced to respond to popular mobilization against poor healthcare access, to offer ideological resistance to the introduction of entirely public-funded care provided through a single, publicly run system.

*Internal contradictions* The current strains facing universal health systems in the North – in the form of rising costs and the inability of the systems to keep pace with the health needs of the population – are a function of the reluctance to build truly comprehensive public systems for the delivery of healthcare. Such challenges have led to health-system reforms in many of these countries. Paradoxically, almost without fail, the prescription offered is to introduce more pronounced market mechanisms.

The European experience is important to our discussion because health systems on the continent tended to be built around the notion of social solidarity. Irrespective of the forces that led to their inception, this principle of social solidarity is inherent to the two principal models present in Europe: the so-called Bismarck model that exists in large parts of continental Europe (a similar model was also extended to other countries such as Australia, Canada, Japan and, more recently, Singapore and South Korea) and the Beveridge model in the UK, which emerged post-Second World War. A third model that was prevalent in the erstwhile socialist states in the Soviet Union and eastern Europe (the Semashko model)[5] has virtually disappeared.

The Bismarck model, nowadays typically known as social health insurance, pooled health funds contributed by the state, employers and employees in a common fund, while healthcare was provided by a mix of public and private facilities. The organization of care delivery differed by country, but in situations where private facilities were involved, they were tightly controlled. Across the English Channel, the Beveridge model's financing was tax-based and primary care was provided by a network of general practitioners, and secondary and tertiary services by public institutions. The general practitioners, while not technically government employees, were tightly bound to the system through contracts with the National Health Service. The Semashko system, which existed in the Soviet Union and eastern Europe, was state-funded and care provision was the sole prerogative of state-run facilities.

Both the Bismarck and the Beveridge models explicitly recognized the role of social solidarity, while devising ways to fund healthcare. They were, however, built around fundamental contradictions. The first was the contradiction (especially in the Bismarck model) between the solidarity character of the financing and the private appropriation of the collectively financed funds by care providers, including industries such as pharmaceutical enterprises and producers of medical equipment. The second was the contradiction between the interests of individuals and the society as a whole in safe, efficient and cheap healthcare on one hand, and the interests of private providers and producers in selling more products, performing more operations, etc., on the other (Pato 2011). Thus, for example, European patients contribute to the super-profits of pharmaceutical manufacturers through solidarity funding (either through tax contributions or contributions to health funds).

*The demise of solidarity-based systems* The private sector never ceased to exist in western Europe, in spite of solidarity-based health systems being introduced, and it re-emerged in eastern Europe after the 1980s. This private healthcare sector has made new inroads into the public sector (ibid.: 20), especially in the last two decades. While there are several factors at play in the transformation of solidarity-based health systems into market-based ones, a major enabling factor has been the weakened bargaining power of labour post-1970s.

A combination of tax cuts and budget austerity (well before the 2008 financial crisis broke) heralded the European health system reforms in the 1980s (see Chapter A2). This not only affected the tax-based systems but also countries with social health insurance. In the latter case, hospital infrastructure was typically funded by local government funds, which came under strain. Social insurance was also affected because of the difficulty in raising premiums paid by workers already suffering from stagnation in wages (Hermann 2009: 127). Reforms of a particularly brutal egregious nature are ripping apart the National Health Service (NHS) in the UK (see Chapter B2). The NHS represented what was anathema to capital – a well-functioning tax-funded and predominantly public health system in a developed capitalist economy. The ideological underpinnings of health reforms in Europe lie at the very foundation of the UHC model that is being promoted in LMICs today.

## UHC in low- and middle-income countries

Low- and middle-income countries face a series of challenges that high-income countries did not confront when they began to develop universal health coverage systems. The demands on healthcare systems were fewer in the early twentieth century because the available medical technologies were less developed. Epidemiological challenges facing LMICs today are more serious because they have faster-growing populations, a higher prevalence of infectious diseases, and a growing burden of non-communicable illnesses compared with countries that attained universal health coverage in the past century (Savedoff et al. 2012).

We turn to three countries – Brazil, Thailand and India – to highlight current challenges faced by LMICs while trying to secure universal healthcare. The examples are illustrative and should not be seen as entirely representative of UHC models being implemented elsewhere in the world. Brazil and Thailand are interesting cases given that they are cited (often correctly) as successful models of universal care. As for India, global attention has been devoted to its health-system reforms and the rapid rollout of social health insurance programmes, and these are useful to scrutinize because they typify some of the negative aspects of a health financing and insurance-based approach to healthcare.

Before we proceed, however, it is important to mention that beyond the confines of 'coverage', there are several alternative examples of how quality care has been, or is being, provided by public systems in the global South, such as in China, Costa Rica, Cuba, Malaysia, Sri Lanka, and in Rwanda and Venezuela much more recently. That there may have been a complete or partial reversal of the role of public systems in many of these countries is reflective of how neoliberal economics prevailed over evidence. We can nevertheless summarize the stories of Brazil, Thailand and India to understand how UHC is being interpreted in LMICs today, in contrast with such models of comprehensive, integrated healthcare systems, and how the approach is imbued with a neoliberal ethos.

*Thailand: high coverage, low public expenditure* In 2002 Thailand's National Health Insurance Bill was enacted, creating the Universal Health Care Coverage scheme, primarily funded by the government based on a per capita calculation, and administered by the National Health Security Office. The focus has been on providing primary healthcare services to Thais who were left out of the healthcare system prior to 2002. Within just over a decade, coverage has increased dramatically and now reaches almost the entire population (Sengupta 2012: 200). However, there is another part of the story that is generally not discussed. The Thai reform of 2002 was preceded by the 'Decade of Health Centre Development Policy (1986–1996)' which worked to establish primary health centres in rural areas. Public investment in health also increased quite dramatically towards the end of this period, and the government's share of total health expenditure increased from 47 per cent in 1995 to 55 per cent in 1998 (Ramesh et al. 2013: 8). Consequently, before the turn of the millennium there were few geographical barriers to healthcare access in the country. Thanks to massive infrastructure creation, 78 per cent of hospital beds were in the public sector by 1999 – a trend that has remained fairly constant, with 77 per cent of hospital beds continuing to be in the public sector in 2012.

The Thai reforms, thus, leveraged upon a newly built *public* health infrastructure. Under the UHC reforms, both public and private facilities can be providers of health services. However, in practice, private participation is low because it was made mandatory for private providers offering tertiary care to also provide primary-level care.

However, these genuine attempts to provide access to healthcare services are taking shape in an overall neoliberal climate in Thailand. This places strains on the health system and may well undermine its viability in the long term. Public financing (most of which is consumed by public services) remains fairly low: health expenditure increased from 1.7 per cent of GDP in 2001 to 2.7 per cent in 2008, but this remains lower than the global average for LMICs. The percentage of funds earmarked for the public system has increased from 50 to 67 per cent (Limwattananon et al. 2012), yet in terms of human resource development low expenditures have meant that there are just three physicians for every 10,000 patients, compared to 9.4 in Malaysia, 11.5 in the Philippines, 12.2 in Vietnam and 18.3 in Singapore, and barely 1.5 nurses for every 1,000 people, compared to 2.3 in Malaysia and 5.9 in Singapore. The shortage of health workers, especially nurses, is serious in many public facilities. Some are hired on temporary contracts, which must be renewed every year. Better wages in private hospitals (the private sector is still strong and draws further strength from a burgeoning medical tourism market) draws nurses away from the public sector, as does the lucrative market for nurses in nearby Singapore (Saengpassa and Sarnsamak 2012).

*Brazil: comprehensive primary care, private hospital care* Brazil is a different kind of enigma. It went against the neoliberal trend in vogue in the rest of Latin America by creating the tax-funded *Sistema Único de Saúde* (SUS, the Unified Health System) in 1986 and by proclaiming in its 1988 constitution the government's duty to provide free healthcare for all (see Chapter B4).

The creation of the SUS has resulted in the rollout of an impressive primary-care scheme, which covers almost the entire country (Paim et al. 2011). However, while most primary healthcare is provided by a vast network of public providers and facilities, hospital care is largely provided by private facilities. Based on an arrangement typical of the UHC approach,[6] the state purchases a bulk of secondary and tertiary care from the private sector and only a small percentage of such care is provided by public facilities.

This places several kinds of strain on the system. The private sector continues to ratchet up the cost of care it provides, and with health expenditure standing at 9 per cent of GDP, Brazil now has one of the most expensive health systems in the world. Such dominance of the private sector (in tertiary-care provision) introduces inequity in access and is further reinforced by the fact that most Brazilians who can afford it (including an influential and growing middle class) purchase private insurance to 'top up' services that they are able to access through the public system (ibid.).

*India: poor public care, ineffective health insurance* UHC as implemented in India exemplifies an entirely different set of issues and challenges, which have accompanied the introduction of social health insurance programmes elsewhere. The public sector in India is in a state of neglect and has traditionally been poorly funded. Public expenditure on health stood at around 1.04 per cent of

**Image B1.4** Delegates at the People's Health Assembly in 2012 (Louis Reynolds)

GDP in 2012, one of the lowest rates in the world (Planning Commission of India 2013: 3). With private healthcare accounting for 80 per cent of outpatient and 60 per cent of inpatient care, India is one of the most privatized systems in the world (NSSO 2006).

Out-of-pocket expenditure on healthcare (approximately 70 per cent of households' healthcare expenses) contributes to widespread poverty in India (HLEG 2011: 43). In an attempt to protect patients from 'catastrophic' health expenses, publicly funded social health insurance schemes have been rolled out in recent years. The Rashtriya Swasthya Bima Yojana (RSBY), a national, entirely public-funded scheme, was launched in 2009 and has been hailed as a major achievement by the government, and in the current 12th Five-Year Plan similar insurance schemes have received even greater attention and support. The RSBY is supplemented by several state-level health insurance schemes that have been launched or are in the pipeline. Scaling up of the social health insurance schemes has been impressive: by the end of 2010 an estimated 247 million people – a quarter of the population – were covered by one or more of these schemes, and coverage has since expanded (GHW 3 2011: 108).

The social health insurance schemes provide coverage only for hospital-based care for a specified list of procedures. Patients are provided with a choice of accredited institutions where they can receive treatment and be reimbursed for costs not surpassing a set ceiling. A large majority of accredited institutions are in the private sector (Yellaiah 2013: 14). The net impact of the publicly funded and largely private-provisioned social health insurance schemes has been to further distort the entire structure of the country's health system.

Public money is now being employed to strengthen an already dominant private sector. The schemes are also distorting the flow of resources to the hospital-based tertiary-care sector (largely private) and away from primary care services. In 2009/10, direct government expenditure on tertiary care was slightly over 20 per cent of total health expenditure, but if one adds spending on the insurance schemes that focus entirely on hospital-based care, total public expenditure on tertiary care would be closer to 37 per cent (Reddy et al. 2011: 13).

*A common trend* The three countries, taken together, represent some interesting similarities about UHC. While the settings are diverse, there is a similar persistence with private sector participation in provision of care. In all the cases, public funding does not match needs, and this opens space for the progressive creep of the private sector into the larger health system. Consequently all three countries have a powerful private sector that influences the functioning of the system as a whole, jeopardizing the integrity of the public sector and drawing away resources, both financial and human, from resource-starved public facilities. Several detailed country studies in the subsequent chapters of this section further highlight these issues.

## Conclusions

If health outcomes are to be improved the central question that needs to be asked is not how public systems are to be privatized but how existing public systems could be made truly universal. Public systems need to be reclaimed by citizens, reformed in the interests of the people and made accountable. People's movements and organizations have much to lose from the present drift, legitimized by a particular discourse in the name of UHC. Historically, healthcare systems worldwide have been shaped by labour's fight for better living conditions – either through transformation of the capitalist system itself or through the extraction of better terms from the ruling classes. The fight for a just and equitable health system has to be part of the broader struggle for comprehensive rights and entitlements. To take this struggle forward, the dominant interpretation of UHC today – weakening public systems and the pursuit of private profit – needs to be understood and questioned.

## Notes

1 A previous, longer version of the major contents of this chapter is available at: www.municipalservicesproject.org/publication/universal-health-coverage-beyond-rhetoric.

2 For example, an article in *The Lancet* in 2009 argues: 'The entire Latin American continent is on track to achieve universal health coverage within the next decade. The achievement of Latin America offers hope to Africa, the Middle East, and Asia – but success looms only because of years of hard work and innovation across the continent' (Garrett et al. 2009: 1297).

3 See, for example, Kutzin (2000).

4 Here we use the term 'efficiency' not in the way it would be used in a market environment, but in terms of the returns achieved through investment in a public good.

5 The 'Bismarck' model is so termed as it was introduced in Germany during the reign of Chancellor Otto von Bismarck, beginning with the introduction of a health insurance bill to mandatorily cover all workers, in 1883. The Semashko system was named after the first minister of health of the USSR. The Beveridge system was introduced (in the form of the National Health Service) by the government in the post-Second World War UK, based on the report of the Inter-Departmental Committee on Social Insurance and Allied Services, known commonly as the Beveridge Report (it was chaired by the British economist William Beveridge).

6 It should be noted that the Brazilian reforms started before UHC was developed as a model, and the Brazilian system has not been designated as being modelled on the concept of UHC. However, nomenclature notwithstanding, Brazil's problems are very similar to those being faced by UHC models elsewhere.

## References

Allotey, P., S. Yasin, S. Tang et al. (2012) 'Universal coverage in an era of privatisation: can we guarantee health for all?', *BMC Public Health*, 12(suppl. 1): S1.

Frenk, J. and D. de Ferranti (2012) 'Universal health coverage: good health, good economics', *The Lancet*, 380(9845): 862–4.

Garrett, L., A. M. R. Chowdhury and A. Pablos-Méndez (2009) 'All for universal health coverage', *The Lancet*, 374(9697): 1294–9.

GHW 1 (Global Health Watch 1) (2005) *Health Care Systems and Approaches to Health*, London: Zed Books.

GHW 3 (Global Health Watch 3) (2011) *Dysfunctional Health Systems: Case studies from China, India and the US*, London: Zed Books.

Giedion, U., E. A. Alfonso and Y. Díaz (2013) *The Impact of Universal Coverage Schemes in the Developing World: A Review of the Existing Evidence*, UNICO Study Series 25, Washington, DC: World Bank, January.

Hermann, C. (2009) 'The marketisation of healthcare in Europe', in L. Panitch and C. Leys (eds), *Morbid Symptoms: Health under Capitalism*, Pontypool: Merlin Press.

HLEG (High Level Expert Group on Universal Health Coverage for India) (2011) *High Level Expert Group Report on Universal Health Coverage for India*, Planning Commission of India, New Delhi, planningcommission. nic.in/reports/genrep/rep_uhc0812.pdf, accessed 7 May 2014.

Homedes, N. and A. Ugalde (2005) 'Why neo-liberal health reforms have failed in Latin America', *Health Policy*, 71(1): 83–96.

Kutzin, J. (2000) 'Towards universal health care coverage', Health, Nutrition and Population (HNP) Discussion Paper, Washington, DC: World Bank, July.

— (2012) 'Anything goes on the path to universal health coverage? No', *Bulletin of the World Health Organization*, 10 October.

Laurell, A. C. (2007) 'Health system reform in Mexico: a critical review', *International Journal of Health Services*, 37(3): 515–35.

— (2010) 'Can insurance guarantee universal access to health services?', *Social Medicine*, 137(3): 137–8.

Leys, C. (2009) 'Health, health care and capitalism', in L. Panitch and C. Leys (eds), *Morbid Symptoms: Health under Capitalism*, Pontypool: Merlin Press.

Limwattananon, S., V. Tangcharoensathien, K. Tisayaticomet et al. (2012) 'Why has the universal coverage scheme in Thailand achieved a pro-poor public subsidy for health care?', *BMC Public Health*, 12(suppl. 1): S6, www.biomedcentral.com/1471-2458/12/S1/S6, accessed 7 May 2014.

Moreno-Serra, R. and P. C. Smith (2011) 'Towards an index of health coverage', Discussion paper 2012/11, Imperial College Business School and Centre for Health Policy, December.

— (2012) 'Does progress towards universal health coverage improve population health?', *The Lancet*, 380(9845): 917–23.

NSSO (National Sample Survey Organisation) (2006) 'Morbidity, health care and the condition of the aged', Report no. 507, NSS 60th round (January–June 2004), New Delhi: Ministry of Statistics and Programme Implementation, Government of India, mospi.nic.in/rept%20_%20pubn/507_final. pdf, access 7 May 2014.

Paim, J., C. Travassos, C. Almeida et al. (2011) 'The Brazilian health system: history, advances, and challenges', *The Lancet*, 377: 1778–97.

Palmer, K. S. (1999) 'A brief history: universal health care efforts in the US', Transcribed from a talk given at a Physicians for a

National Health Program (PNHP) meeting, San Francisco, www.pnhp.org/facts/a-brief-history-universal-health-care-efforts-in-the-us, accessed 7 May 2014.

Pato, T. (2011) 'Health systems in Europe: changes and resistance', Opening report to health workers' conference, 4 July, internationalviewpoint.org/spip.php?article2180, accessed 7 May 2014.

Pierson, P. (2001) *The New Politics of the Welfare State*, Oxford: Oxford University Press, rszarf.ips.uw.edu.pl/welfare-state/pierson.pdf, accessed 7 May 2014.

Planning Commission of India (2013) *Twelfth Five Year Plan (2012–2017): Social Sectors*, vol. 3, New Delhi: Government of India, planningcommission.gov.in/plans/planrel/12thplan/pdf/vol_3.pdf, accessed 7 May 2014.

Ramesh, M., W. Xun and M. Howlett (2013) 'Second best governance? Governments and governance in the imperfect world of health care delivery in China, India and Thailand', Paper presented at the International Conference on Public Policy, Grenoble, 26–28 June, www.icpublicpolicy.org/IMG/pdf/panel_11_s3_ramesh.pdf, accessed 7 May 2014.

Reddy, K. S., S. Selvaraj, K. D. Rao et al. (2011) 'A critical assessment of the existing health insurance models in India', New Delhi: Public Health Foundation of India, planningcommission.nic.in/reports/sereport/ser/ser_heal1305.pdf, accessed 7 May 2014.

Rice, T. (1997) 'Can markets give us the health system we want?', *Journal of Health Politics, Policy and Law*, 22: 383–426.

Robinson, M. and G. White (2001) 'The role of civic organizations in the provision of social services: towards synergy', in G. Mwabu, C. Ugaz and G. White (eds), *Social Provision in Low-Income Countries – New Patterns and Emerging Trends*, Oxford: Oxford University Press.

Rodin, J. and D. de Ferranti (2012) 'Universal health coverage: the third global health transition?', Rockefeller Foundation, *The Lancet*, 380(9845): 861–2.

Sachs, J. D. (2012) 'Achieving universal health coverage in low-income settings', *The Lancet*, 380(9845): 944–7.

Saengpassa, C. and P. Sarnsamak (2012) 'Thailand public health service in critical condition', *The Nation*, 15 October.

Savedoff, W. D., D. de Ferranti, A. L. Smith et al. (2012) 'Political and economic aspects of the transition to universal health coverage', *The Lancet*, 380(9845): 924–32.

Sengupta, A. (2012) 'Creating, reclaiming, defending: non-commercialised alternatives in the health sector in Asia', in D. A. MacDonald and G. Ruiters (eds), *Alternatives to Privatisation*, New York: Routledge.

Stuckler, D., A. B. Feigl, S. Basu et al. (2010) 'The political economy of universal health coverage', Background paper for the global symposium on Health Systems Research, 16–19 November, Montreux, Switzerland.

Vabø, M. (2009) 'New public management the neoliberal way of governance', Working papers no. 4, thjodmalastofnun.hi.is/sites/thjodmalastofnun.hi.is/files/skrar/working_paper_4-2009.pdf, accessed 7 May 2014.

Wagstaff, A. and M. Lindelow (2005) 'Can insurance increase financial risk?: the curious case of health insurance in China', *Journal of Health Economics*, 27(4): 990–1005, repository.upenn.edu/gansu_papers/20/, accessed 7 May 2014.

WHA (World Health Assembly) (2005) 'Sustainable health financing, universal coverage and social health insurance', Resolution WHA58.33, Geneva.

Yellaiah, J. (2013) 'Health insurance in India: Rajiv Aarogyasri health insurance scheme in Andhra Pradesh', *IOSR Journal of Humanities and Social Science*, 8(1): 7–14.

## B2 | THE NATIONAL HEALTH SERVICE (NHS): PREY TO NEOLIBERAL LUST FOR MARKETS

For more than sixty years the National Health Service (NHS) of the UK has been the leading model of tax-financed, universal healthcare in Europe. But in 2012, the passage of the Health and Social Care Act (HSCA) (National Archives 2012) dealt a fatal blow by dismantling the constitutional basis of the NHS and paving the way for a market-driven system of healthcare. This chapter describes how the shift from NHS to 'National Healthcare Market' was made possible through various failures of democracy and professional leadership and reflects on the implications for the downfall of the NHS.

### The NHS as it was conceived

The NHS, established in 1948, grew out of recommendations in the Beveridge Report (Beveridge 1942), which proposed widespread reform to the existing system of social welfare to address 'Five Giant Evils' in society: Squalor, Ignorance, Want, Idleness and Disease. As health minister Aneurin Bevan famously remarked to the first ever NHS patient, thirteen-year-old

**Image B2.1** Aneurin Bevan, founder of the NHS, speaking to Sylvia Diggory, the first ever patient of the NHS, in 1948 (National Archive, UK)

Sylvia Diggory, the establishment of the NHS was 'the most civilized step any country had ever taken'. The three core principles of the original NHS were: it would be *universal, comprehensive* and *free at the point of delivery*.

For the first thirty years of its life, the NHS evolved on the basis of rational planning, aimed at redistributing healthcare resources and services across the country on the basis of need. Strong systems of bureaucracy and political accountability included much devolution of decision-making power to regional and district health authorities, facilitating fluid and responsive planning processes. Crucially, all NHS organizations were directly accountable to the Secretary of State for Health through the Department of Health (DoH).

Universal access to health in Britain since 1948 has helped improve the health of the nation: life expectancy has increased by just over ten years for men and by more than eight years for women, while children are five times less likely to die in infancy than they would have been sixty years ago (ONS 2012). Moreover, recent comparisons of health systems in seven industrialized countries rated the NHS very highly on quality of, and access to, care; it was top (above, for example, Australia and the Netherlands) on efficiency (Ingleby 2012). Simply put, publicly funded, publicly owned and publicly provided healthcare worked: it was fair, inclusive and good value for money.

### Thatcher and the attack on the NHS

Things began to change in the 1980s when Margaret Thatcher became prime minister, heralding the rapid ascendancy of neoliberal policy in the UK. Thatcher would not permit 'the nanny state' to 'interfere' in what she regarded as individual decisions about people's health.

Thatcher's government began the application of private sector management principles to healthcare. The two most important changes were linked: the NHS became subject to a particular form of *managerialism* that in turn led to marketization and the introduction of a *quasi-market and outsourcing in healthcare* centred around competition and 'choice' (Hunter 2008).

The introduction of 'new public management' (NPM) models in the 1980s and 1990s as part of an international trend in public administration introduced a new logic and culture into the NHS (Hood 1991). This new perspective resulted in a number of notable changes to the NHS. Among the most controversial was the policy of *outsourcing*, introduced in 1983, whereby health authorities were required to set up competitive tendering arrangements for their cleaning, catering and laundry services (Pollock and Talbot-Smith 2006: 5).

The encroachment of NPM advanced with the NHS and Community Care Act of 1990. Suddenly, NHS hospitals and other bodies such as ambulance and community health services were expected to operate as semi-independent 'trusts' – and thus behave like businesses in a marketplace. This introduced – for the first time – the *purchaser–provider split*. Health authorities were expected to act as 'commissioners' or 'purchasers' of health services, with trusts acting as the 'sellers'. The idea was to open up the provider side of the NHS to market forces – the so-called 'Internal Market' – as a stepping stone towards a full market system (ibid.: 6). NHS hospitals and other services could no longer rely on an annual block budget, and as a result they no longer had an incentive to give priority to patients' health. They focused instead on generating their own income, cutting costs and competing with each other for business.

Trusts were no longer given free support for capital planning, estates management and information technology from the DoH. Rather, they were expected to buy these services from private management consultancies. Thus began the slow decline of almost a third of newly formed trusts into financial difficulties, mergers and service closures.

The extension of market logic to health reached its height in 1992 with the inception of the Private Finance Initiative (PFI). Proposed as an alternative way of mobilizing capital for public investments, PFI was touted as the key to the 'biggest hospital-building programme in the history of the NHS'. The principle is this: the government goes to a consortium of bankers, builders and service operators, which raises the money on the government's behalf – in return for which they get the contract to not only design and build a hospital, but also to operate the supporting facilities for thirty or more years (Pollock 2005: 27). But there's a catch. The responsibility for paying back the debt – not to mention the interest and shareholders' profits – rests not with the DoH, but with the hospital itself. And this money must come out of its annual budget for patient care. Even worse, PFI rapidly turned out to be much more expensive than expected: the private sector cannot borrow as cheaply as governments can, and moreover, there are costs incurred in servicing the new bureaucracies, which are needed to make and monitor all the contracts and subcontracts involved – costs that would not be incurred under normal government procurement.

The now universally condemned PFI hospital programme made extraordinary profits for the PFI consortia involved and reduced many of the NHS trusts involved to near-bankruptcy, leaving them with the obligation to go on paying for thirty years or more for buildings which experts now say are not fit for purpose (Leys and Player 2011: 91).

By 2000, even clinical services were opened up to the market. The eventual model was one of the NHS as a sort of holding company '*franchising*' health services out to various public and private providers. Thus, the NHS was to be the government-funded payer, but less and less the direct provider of health services. This model enables for-profit companies to siphon wealth directly from public coffers supposedly set aside for national healthcare.

The DoH downsized as more and more of its functions were outsourced to the market. This was made possible when the NHS was forced to move to a system of '*payment by results*'. Each and every treatment was put up for sale in the private market at a price set by the DoH – the so-called '*national tariff*'; as in other sectors, the itemization and reduction of every service to

## The original NHS

| | | |
|---|---|---|
| **Public finance**<br>general taxation pays for healthcare in a progressive system | **Public budgets**<br>publicly managed | **Public providers**<br>acting in public interest |
| **Private finance**<br>paid by high-income people | **Private insurance**<br>and out-of-pocket payments | **Private providers**<br>acting for private interests |

This box represents the whole of the UK health system. The NHS comprises the unshaded portion – publicly financed, publicly provided and centrally planned. Only the small bottom portion (shaded) of the health system was private.

The transformation under Thatcher's policies until 2012

## The NHS from the 1980s until 2012

| | | |
|---|---|---|
| **Public finance** | **Public budgets** | **Public providers**<br>increasingly acting as market-based actors with self-interest in 'internal markets' |
| **Private finance** | **Private insurance** | **Private providers**<br>able to take over more activities in the internal market |

Enactment of the HSCA

The box is slightly bigger, reflecting increase in health system spending in the 1990s and 2000s

**B2.1** Progress of the NHS to a National Healthcare Market

## The national healthcare market

| Public finance decreasing in significance | Mixed insurance system a residual public budget for health protection alongside an increasing proportion of private and public insurance and co-payments, operated entirely by insurance companies | Mixed provider market in which the majority private providers and remaining public providers compete for contracts on an equal footing |
|---|---|---|
| Private finance further increases in the form of co-payments or top-ups on personal budgets, affecting even low-income families | | |

The overall size of the box has increased because health expenditure is expected to increase from 8.7% of GDP and approach US level of 16% of GDP. The public sector is now almost entirely privatized.

↑

Relentless commercialization in the future

## The NHS in 2012 following the HSCA

| Public finance decreased in an era of austerity but further shrunk by diversion to local authority budgets used for other public services | Public budgets though held by statutory Clinical Commissioning Groups (CCGs), managed by Commissioning Support Units (CSUs), which are soon to be privatized | Public providers still the majority of provision, but Foundation Trust operating enirely in self-interest in a market |
|---|---|---|
| Private finance increases in the form of co-payments within and outside the NHS | Private budgets increase as insurance companies expand services | Private providers able to take over more services under 'Any Qualified Provider' (AQP) |

Though the size of the box remains the same, the amount of private ownership and provision is gradually increasing

## Box B2.1 Implications of a market in health

*1. Reduced accountability* The HSCA controversially severs the duty of the Secretary of State for Health to secure comprehensive healthcare throughout England. Substantial powers will instead be extended to commissioners and providers of care. Public and private providers now compete with each other for customers, while legal contracts and commercial law have replaced direct political accountability for the health of the nation (Pollock and Price 2011).

*2. Fragmentation* The NHS is no longer a comprehensive and universal system. Instead it will be a reduced component within a larger system of a growing number of private providers, private management consultancies and private insurance companies.

*3. Increased costs* Competitive markets necessitate extra bureaucracy for individualized tracking of costs and compliance with competition legislation, pushing up costs. In addition, the service funding arrangements planned will almost certainly increase expense without improving outcomes. The new 'Any Qualified Provider' (AQP) system pays hospitals for what they do and allows them to keep any profits they make, incentivizing over treatment by for-profit hospitals. In the US system, which most closely approximates the model we are moving towards, up to 37 per cent of all healthcare expenditure goes on unnecessary treatment (Berwick and Hackbarth 2012).

*4. Regressive financing* Public financing for the NHS will not increase in an era of austerity. More and more private money will be necessary, much of this coming from individual users through co-payments and insurance, both within the NHS and with private corporations.

*5. Decreased efficiency* There is no evidence that the private sector is more efficient than the NHS; in fact competition between NHS providers has been shown to drive down productivity (Charlesworth and Jones 2013). The impact of efficiency gains differs between public and private sectors. Publicly provided health services exist only to provide healthcare, while the overriding goal of profit-making corporations is to generate profit. Efficiency gains in public services have the effect of increasing the value for money of the services they provide in exchange for the public funds they receive. In contrast, efforts to increase efficiency in the private sector are aimed at maximizing profit made for the money invested, i.e. maximizing the gap between what they receive for their healthcare efforts and what they spend on them.

*6. Decreased quality* Since the government demands higher productivity for the same budget, all this extra spending on unnecessary administration and profits can only come at the expense of the amount and quality of care provided. The most vulnerable groups in society will bear the worst effects of this, including the chronically ill, the elderly and young children. Furthermore, market reform will leave many patients exposed to the conflict of interest between the profit motives of medical service companies and the professional medical ethics of their staff (Caleb Alexander et al. 2006). Because most patients lack the technical understanding to judge medical quality, strict regulation is needed to ensure that only care of high medical quality can lead to high profits – but the government explicitly favours 'light touch' regulation.

7. *Decreased professional control* Through their involvement in Clinical Commissioning Groups (CCGs), GPs have acquired new financial and legal responsibilities for balancing budgets and deciding whose care can be paid for and whose cannot. However, the result has been *less* professional autonomy, not more. Rather than being able to help patients navigate through the system and arrange optimal care, GPs won't be allowed to advise patients on which provider to choose because it would 'distort' competition.

8. *Increased inequity* The sums for a comprehensive free-of-charge NHS don't add up for a marketized system, despite the much-heard phrase 'NHS care will continue to be free at the point of use' (Reynolds and McKee 2012). An increasing proportion of care will no longer be available on the NHS, and such care may then not be free of charge. This has already happened to chiropody and physiotherapy. There are now structures that permit the introduction of charging for services that were previously free under the NHS; the rollout of transferable *'personal health budgets'* in 2013 heralded the start of a transition to a contributory system for some types of care.

9. *Weaker public health* By devolving powers to disparate bodies the HSCA spelled the end of a coherent public health system in the UK. Public Health England (PHE) has now appropriated control over health protection issues such as environmental hazards and infectious outbreak control. However, as effective employees of the civil service, public health workers in PHE are under direct political control – essentially neutralizing their independence and ability to speak out in the public interest, especially on behalf of ordinary citizens and marginalized groups, and often against powerful or vested interests (Kmietowicz 2011). Marketizing the health system and dismantling of the geography-based architecture of the NHS weakens the ability of public health to: improve the uptake of screening and immunization programmes; coordinate multiple agencies for preventing and responding rapidly to public health emergencies; and conduct both population- and systems-based health surveillance and monitoring.

a cost figure allows private providers a way into the system. And since some treatments are more profitable than others, providers naturally want to do more of the former and fewer of the latter (Pollock and Talbot-Smith 2006: 9). The inevitable result: services for patients who need the less profitable services, such as chiropody and physiotherapy, have become unavailable.

### The Health and Social Care Act (HSCA) and the new 'National Healthcare Market'

As the latest key system change to the NHS, the HSCA goes even farther to promote neoliberal ideas such as competitive markets and mixed funding. From a *national health service* – publicly funded, publicly delivered and publicly accountable – the UK is steadily moving towards an increasingly privately provided '*National Healthcare Market*' (see Figure B2.1). This is not just a question of whether health is in public or private hands. The marketization of health has much more fundamental implications (see Box B2.1).

### The failure of democracy to save the NHS

The loss of the NHS signals a profound failure of democracy. The current government made no declaration that they would be dismantling the NHS; the British public was never asked to vote on reforming a healthcare system they were satisfied with and that was performing well. In place of the promise that there would be 'no more top-down reorganizations of the NHS', the government delivered the biggest restructuring of the NHS in its history. In short, they lied.

Thus the HSCA came into force on 1 April 2013 – with no democratic mandate and massive public opposition. How was this possible? Public interest and common sense were defeated by neoliberal ideology because of the combined failure of Britain's politicians, media, medical establishment, trade unions and even the public – the erstwhile defenders of healthcare – to resist.

*The politicians* Though initiated by Thatcher, the privatization of the NHS was always part of a broader move from a welfare state to a market state (Bobbitt 2003) – a process that continues today. The reforms would not have been passed without persistent, behind-the-scenes lobbying and fixing by a network of insiders. The permeation of NHS management by ex-McKinsey and ex-KPMG personnel reflects this proclivity (Leys and Player 2011). The DoH now has a fast-revolving door to business, and neoliberal ideologues hold prominent positions in government, including the current head of the NHS, Simon Stevens, the former president of the multinational United Health group. Even worse, many of the politicians who voted the HSCA through stood to gain financially from it.

The government misrepresented the HSCA, using feel-good labels like 'GP-led', 'diversity' and 'choice'. The DoH relentlessly drip-fed press releases

**Image B2.2** Student nurses demonstrate against NHS reforms in 2011 (Guddi Singh)

calling into question whether the NHS was 'sustainable' or 'affordable'. The public was repeatedly told that the public sector is bad at management; only the private sector is efficient and could manage services well.

*The media* The British Broadcasting Corporation (BBC) – the national public broadcaster – and other mainstream news outlets carried the government spin uncritically (Huitson 2013). They constantly referred to the reforms as 'handing power to GPs'. Moreover, the BBC never questioned the government's mistaken definition of privatization. The media fanned the flames by amplifying bogus research intended to promote the benefits of competition in healthcare. The government co-opted the media, using it to shake the public's faith in its favourite institution.

*The medical establishment* Worse still was the role of the leaders of the medical profession. The very people who should have been its defenders ended up betraying the NHS. In the run-up to the passing of the HSCA, surveys showed that doctors did not back the reforms, despite government claims that they did (Kmietowicz 2011). Silence, a lack of leadership and the absence of a timely opposition to the reforms by the medical establishment, however, meant that this opinion was never effectively projected.

Why would the nation's medical vanguard give up on health?

IGNORANCE Public health and the importance of socialized medicine are not paramount in medical curriculums, so medical students are susceptible to the claim that the NHS is inefficient and unwieldy and that healthcare should be privatized. A misleading media made the NHS look increasingly incompetent – even to its own workers – justifying dismantling it from the inside out (Singh 2013).

FEAR Bullying and scare tactics were employed to silence voices of discontent. With jobs on the line, it became especially difficult for individuals to speak out against the reforms. Doctors and nurses concerned about the impact of marketization on their patients were suspended, even dismissed or forced to accept gagging clauses. Money bought their silence. When individuals did speak up they received little or no organizational support.

Clare Gerada, then chair of the Royal College of General Practitioners (RCGP), was a prominent voice of dissent. Patronized and dismissed, Gerada was on the receiving end of misogynistic rhetoric from both ministers and the predominantly male medical establishment for her critique.

The British Medical Association (BMA) – Britain's foremost doctors' trade union with 150,000 members – claims to be the 'voice for doctors and medical students throughout the UK'. Yet when it came to the reforms it failed spectacularly: neither rising to the challenge of representing its members' wishes nor standing up for the healthcare system it belongs to. It was a full five months after the reforms became public that the BMA finally came out in opposition to the healthcare reform bill – and not once did it mention that it was against privatization.

GREED Politicians stymied much of the political resistance to the NHS reforms by co-opting a layer of the medical profession to give a veneer of clinical leadership to the marketization of health. In exchange for positions of power or entrepreneurial opportunities, notable doctors – some of whom were leaders of medical bodies such as the BMA or Royal Colleges – sold out. Rather than opposing the reforms, these figures, such as chair of the BMA Hamish Meldrum, pushed for 'critical engagement' with the government (Davis and Wrigley 2013). Drawn into a process that was designed to shape rather than stall, the medical establishment became distracted by concerns about *how* the reforms should be implemented and not *whether* they should be. Such involvement, time and again, lent legitimacy to an otherwise undemocratic process.

Just as the birth of the NHS required cooperation from the doctors, so too were they necessary accomplices in its murder.

*The trade unions* Rather than looking at the big picture and rising to the NHS's defence, the trade unions focused merely on aspects of pay and conditions. Their impotence raises questions about how the unions have become increasingly inward looking, sectoral and neutered – and suggests that market ideology has reached deep into the labour movement.

*The public* Misinformed and duped by their politicians and media, the public came to know about NHS privatization only too late. Even then, it is clear that a generation of diminishing political participation (Morgan and Connelly 2001) makes mobilization around issues such as health and social welfare increasingly difficult.

But the fight for democracy goes on. Corporate interests continue to be maintained by several pieces of legislation which are either currently being debated or were recently passed, reflecting further incursions on democracy. Greater protections for commercial secrecy, a clamp-down on protest and limits to civil society campaigning are all in the offing. And it is no surprise that private providers of care are subject to a less rigorous 'regulatory burden' than public ones, when Monitor, the lead regulator of the NHS, is run by ex-McKinsey and ex-KPMG management consultants and heavily lobbied by those same companies.

Finally, and most worrying, is the irreversible nature of the changes. International trade laws, such as the controversial Transatlantic Trade and Investment Partnership (TTIP) (see Chapter E6), would essentially lock the health system into a competitive market arrangement (Hilary 2014). If it goes ahead, it could see multinational health giants – already poised to snap up billions of pounds' worth of NHS contracts – file complaints directly to international tribunals should they perceive threats to their interests from government regulation, completely bypassing national courts. A future government would not be able to reverse the changes through new legislation without incurring the risk of trade sanctions and legal challenges, or having to pay out huge amounts of compensation.

### The moral of the story of the NHS

What will the downfall of the NHS mean, both nationally and globally?

Since 2012 alone, widespread hospital closures have been leading to increasing mortality rates and delayed care, while thousands of nursing jobs continue to be lost. Given also the 'unnecessary and unjust premature deaths of many British citizens caused by Thatcher's policies in the 1980s' (Scott-Samuel 2014), it is clear that the 'National Healthcare Market' harms patients, populations and professionals alike.

PFI illustrates how the increased financial costs of using private enterprise are linked to the human cost. PFI is projected to cost the UK taxpayer £300 billion (Campbell et al. 2012) by the time projects have been paid off over the coming decades – largely paid for by major cuts in clinical budgets and the largest service closure programme in the NHS's history. At the height of the financial crisis in 2008, PFI cost the taxpayer an additional £1.6 billion alone. What could this have paid for? Over 185,000 hip replacements, the salary for 78,000 more nurses or 5.2 million ambulance calls. Left with no alternative but to pare away services, hospitals sacrifice patient care in the interests of paying their creditors.

What has happened to the NHS is not unique: it is a story playing out across the world, where universal healthcare systems are being dismantled and privatized with disturbing rapidity and regularity. The global corporate takeover of health continues apace, guided and backed by the World Bank, the International Monetary Fund and the World Trade Organization – even the WHO is complicit. Just as we saw in the UK, catchphrases such as 'public–private partnerships', 'modernization' and 'local ownership' are being bandied around – all while the much-hailed '*Universal Health Coverage*' takes a prominent place on the global health agenda. Universal health *coverage* is not the same as universal health *care*. We cannot allow it to become a convenient smokescreen for privatization (Sengupta 2013).

Already the same neoliberal methods at work in the NHS have been exported from the UK to new playing fields. Take the introduction of PFI to Lesotho, for example, where a massive 100 per cent increase in costs at the Queen Mamohato Memorial Hospital in Maseru will likely have the same disastrous effects on healthcare as it has in the UK.

### The challenge for health professionals

Citizens' rights in democracies are underpinned not just by limitations on government powers but also by legal duties imposed on governments – such as those that guarantee citizens' access to healthcare. The HSCA and the loss of the NHS after a long process of privatization withdrew this legal underpinning.

Politics and health are inextricably linked. In the face of increasingly un-democratic governance, health professionals, alongside civil society, need to be prepared to confront power. In the UK, the aim now is to turn growing public dissatisfaction in the new 'National Healthcare Market' against the establishment, with the NHS acting as a political pressure point in the run-up to the 2015 general election.

In the meantime, it is the duty of doctors, scientists and academics to collate evidence of how political decisions affect people's lives. As the government privatizes healthcare, it is crucial to have complete and high-quality data to monitor the impact of these policies. This watchdog function is vital if we are to hold the marketizers of health to account for their decisions.

History is replete with examples of the failure of the professions to challenge or resist egregious policies to the detriment of all concerned. The scale of the threat to the NHS – coupled with the government's lack of a democratic mandate to end the NHS and its propensity to misinform the public – suggests that we are in a situation where professional dissent is not just appropriate, but urgently required.

# References

Berwick, D. and A. Hackbarth (2012) 'Eliminating waste in US health care', *Journal of the American Medical Association*, 307(14): 1513–16.

Bevan, A. (1952) *In Place of Fear*, New York: Simon and Schuster.

Beveridge, W. (1942) *Social Insurance and Allied Services*, New York: Macmillan.

Bobbitt, P. (2003) *The Shield of Achilles: War, Peace and the Course of History*, London: Penguin.

Caleb Alexander, G., M. Hall and J. Lantos (2006) 'Rethinking professional ethics in the cost-sharing era', *American Journal of Bioethics*, 6(4): 17–22.

Campbell, D., J. Ball and S. Rogers (2012) 'PFI will ultimately cost £300bn: repayments on contracts will grow to £10bn a year by 2017–18, say Guardian figures, and government is still striking new deals', *Guardian*, 5 July, www.theguardian.com/politics/2012/jul/05/pfi-cost-300bn.

Charlesworth, A. and N. Jones (2013) *The Anatomy of Health Spending: A Review of NHS Expenditure and Labour Productivity*, Nuffield Trust.

Davis, J. and D. Wrigley (2013) 'The silence of the lambs', in J. Davis and R. Tallis (eds), *NHS SOS: How the NHS was betrayed – and how we can save it*, London: One World.

Gamble, A. (1994) *The Free Economy and the Strong State*, London: Macmillan.

Hilary, J. (2014) 'Why this year's Davos could be bad for our health', openDemocracy, 4 September, www.opendemocracy.net/ournhs/john-hilary/why-this-year%E2%80%99s-davos-could-be-bad-for-our-health.

Hood, C. (1991) 'A public management for all seasons?', *Public Administration*, 69: 3–19.

Huitson, O. (2013) 'Hidden in plain sight', in J. Davis and R. Tallis (eds), *NHS SOS: How the NHS was betrayed – and how we can save it*, London: One World.

Hunter, D. J. (2008) *The Health Debate*, Bristol: Policy Press.

Ingleby, D. (2012) 'How the NHS measures up to other health systems', *British Medical Journal*, 344: e1079.

Kmietowicz, Z. (2011) 'Public health doctors call for House of Lords to reject health bill', *British Medical Journal*, 343: d6391.

Leys, C. and S. Player (2011) *The Plot against the NHS*, Pontypool: Merlin Press.

McKee, M. and D. Stuckler (2011) 'The assault on universalism: how to destroy the welfare state', *British Medical Journal*, 343, doi: 10.1136/bmj.d7973.

Morgan, B. and J. Connelly (2001) *UK Election Statistics: 1945–2000*, House of Commons Research Papers 01/37, House of Commons Library.

National Archives (2012) *Health and Social Care Act 2012*, www.legislation.gov.uk/ukpga/2012/7/pdfs/ukpga_20120007_en.pdf.

ONS (Office for National Statistics) (2012) *Mortality in England and Wales: Average Life Span, 2010*, www.ons.gov.uk/ons/dcp171776_292196.pdf.

Pollock, A. (2005) *NHS plc: The privatization of our health care*, 2nd edn, London: Verso.

Pollock, A. and D. Price (2011) 'The Health and Social Care Bill: how the secretary of state for health proposes to abolish the NHS in England', *British Medical Journal*, 342: 1695–7.

— (2013) 'From cradle to grave', in J. Davis and R. Tallis (eds), *NHS SOS: How the NHS was betrayed – and how we can save it*, London: One World.

Pollock, A. and A. Talbot-Smith (2006) *The New NHS: A Guide*, Oxford: Routledge.

Reynolds, L. and M. McKee (2012 ) '"Any qualified provider" in the NHS reforms: but who will qualify?', *The Lancet*, 379: 1083–4, doi: 101016/S0140-6736(11)61264-6.

Scott-Samuel, A. (2014) 'The impact of Thatcherism on health and well-being in Britain', *International Journal of Health Services*, 44(1): 53–71.

Sengupta, A. (2013) 'Universal Health Coverage: beyond rhetoric', in D. A. McDonald and G. Ruiters (eds), *Municipal Services Project*, Occasional Paper no. 20, November.

Singh, G. (2013) 'Asleep on the job: England's young doctors and the NHS reforms', openDemocracy, 4 September, www.opendemocracy.net/ournhs/guddi-singh/asleep-on-job-englands-young-doctors-and-nhs-reforms.

## B3 | REFORM OF THE MEXICAN HEALTHCARE SYSTEM: THE UNTOLD STORY

Currently, there appears to be a wide consensus regarding the importance of Universal Health Coverage (UHC). However, there are at least two different understandings of this notion. The hegemonic one is promoted by, among others, the World Bank, the Rockefeller Foundation, the World Economic Forum, *The Lancet*, and partially the World Health Organization (WHO). Their notion is of a health insurance model with a basic explicit service package, usually quite restricted, and with a plurality of privately and publicly funded administrators and/or service buyers and providers, with payments based on income. The second notion is that of a single public tax-financed system based on the principle of equal access for the same health need. What is at stake is the choice between the logic of a competitive and commoditized health system and the logic of a health system driven by health needs.

However, both notions apparently defend the same values, such as the right to health, equity, universalism and solidarity, but the words have different meanings according to who uses them. We are, then, playing a role in a battle over discourse or participating in a sort of 'ideological warfare'. The reason for this is that these are broadly held social values, and denying them openly is not a viable political strategy.

Countries in Latin America have been host to several 'experiments' in the arena of health reforms designed to promote UHC, beginning with the health and social security reforms in Chile in the mid-1970s, carried out by Pinochet. This trend has continued with a wave of neoliberal reforms in most countries in the continent during the 1990s[1] (ISAGS 2012). The most celebrated was the Colombian reform of 1993, which was recommended to other countries as a successful model. With the virtual collapse of the Colombian health system, a fact recognized even by the country's government (Franco 2013), its place on the international scene has been taken by the Mexican health reform and its 'Popular Health Insurance Programme' (*Seguro Popular*). However, the supposed success story of *Seguro Popular* does not correspond to reality. This official account has been challenged (Laurell 2007), but the research has been ignored or has been labelled 'grey literature'.

### The Mexican health system

In order to understand health system reform, it is essential to consider the structure of the health system that is being reformed, since this is what modulates the process. The Mexican health system is segmented and fragmented, but it is predominantly public. The thrust for universal coverage for four decades rested on a social security strategy. By 1982, about 70 per cent of the population was covered by public social security, including a large part of the rural population. This public social security system had its own infrastructure and salaried personnel. At this time, private insurance and private healthcare provision were marginal (Laurell 2001).

The turning point came with the debt crisis in 1983 when structural adjustment was imposed by the International Monetary Fund (IMF) and the World Bank, and was consented to by the government. From then on, Mexican society as a whole has been reorganized on the premises and principles of neoclassical economics and neoliberal ideology. This has had a deep impact on the health system, but the public system is still strong and remains the main health service insurer and provider, while private commercial insurance and large for-profit hospitals play a minor role. Although private doctors and pharmacies play a role in the provision of ambulatory care, public providers attend to more than half of the population and play a dominant role in the provision of hospital care and in public health activities (Laurell 2013).

### Reforms to promote a clear agenda

The fiscal adjustment carried out for political and economic reasons subjected the health system to an abrupt decline in financing. The Ministry of Health suffered a huge direct budget cut, and social security revenues dropped drastically as a result of the decline in wages and formal employment. The underfinancing persisted for two decades and severely undermined public health institutions,[2] paving the way for neoliberal reforms in the health system.

The structural reform of the health system began in 1995 and is not yet concluded. It has gone through various phases, but the underlying conception is the same. The basic proposal is to introduce Enthoven's 'managed competition' (1988) in its Latin American adaptation – 'structured pluralism', as elaborated by Juan Luis Londoño[3] and Julio Frenk (1997) while acting as consultants to the World Bank. The scheme aims to separate the tasks of regulation, administration of funds/purchase of services, and provision of services. This splitting of functions is essential because it permits the introduction of markets and competition, and consequently allows for the commodification of the health system (see also Chapter B1).

The first stage of the reform (Laurell 2001) took place in 1995–97 and its main target was the social security institute for private sector workers, IMSS,[4] which alone held about 60 per cent of the public health funds. The reform changed the financing of health insurance, reducing the employer premium and increasing the government contribution about fivefold. Even so, the result was a drop in IMSS's total health fund. Additionally, the IMF's 'bridging loan' was made on the condition that private fund administrators would be introduced.

This part of the reform failed, essentially because of strong public resistance and the imminent threat that the social security for healthcare, available to a majority of the population, might collapse.

The second part of the reform consisted of the decentralization of the facilities of the Ministry of Health to the state[5] level and the provision of the 'universal coverage' of a small health package that included just seventeen interventions.

### Health insurance: the fashionable 'success story'

The failure to establish a payer/provider split in the IMSS and the failure to introduce private health fund administrators led to a modification in the strategy when a conservative government won the presidential election in 2000. The new minister of health (Julio Frenk) set about achieving the conversion of the health system to fully fledged structured pluralism despite the severe problems faced by the twin reforms in Colombia after almost a decade of implementation. Accordingly, the National Health Law was modified in 2003 and the National System for Social Health Protection was established after some behind-the-scenes manoeuvring in parliament (Laurell 2007).

The *Seguro Popular* (SP) is the operative programme of the new system. It is a voluntary insurance scheme for people who are not covered by social security insurance and offers a basic explicit package of 274 interventions, including drugs and eight 'catastrophic cost' diseases for adults, while the medical coverage for children is broader. However, the SP excludes common high-cost diseases and conditions such as multiple trauma, cardiovascular disease, stroke, most cancers, and renal insufficiency. The SP package corresponds to 11 per cent of the package that social security provides for free. The SP is free for the lowest-income groups, and the rest pay a premium of about 3–4 per cent of their income (Laurell 2013).[6]

The SP is financed by federal tax funds, state tax funds and family premiums in amounts and proportions established by law. The organizational arrangements of the SP are administered by decentralized agencies at the federal and state levels (structured pluralism). The federal government collects, administers and transfers funds to state fund administrators based on the number of enrolled individuals, and also to a special fund for 'catastrophic cost' that buys personal health services for SP affiliates from public or private providers. Public health actions and collective health initiatives are financed by a special fund, and are the responsibility of the decentralized state health services.

The Ministry of Health claims that universal insurance coverage has been achieved in Mexico, thereby enhancing social security and strengthening SP. However, this claim is refuted by other official data sources such as the census and by health and income/expenditure surveys for 2012. These surveys demonstrate that 21–25 per cent of the population lack insurance coverage, corresponding to between 25 and 30 million people. Nor is it true that the main SP beneficiaries constitute the poorest section of the population: 37 per cent of the lowest-income quintile of the population are uninsured. Official health statistics also show that the SP is providing far fewer services to its beneficiaries than the public social security system (see Table B3.1).

TABLE B3.1 Comparison of service provision by type of insurance

| Type of service | Seguro Popular | IMSS |
| --- | --- | --- |
| Consultations* | 1.4 | 3.0 |
| Emergency room care* | 0.07 | 0.43 |
| Hospital care** | 2.7 | 4.8 |

*Notes:* * per person; ** per 1,000 insured persons
*Source:* Laurell (2013)

The data show that insurance coverage does not mean access in the presence of a restricted service package. In the Mexican case, the unequal distribution of health facilities and human resources further restricts access, given that the expansion of SP enrolment was not accompanied by a commensurate increase in service facilities.

So far, the SP has contracted private providers only marginally, which means that the population, both with and without the SP, is attended to at the same facilities, but with one crucial difference: the SP population is accorded preference when it comes to receiving care, while the non-SP population is discriminated against in public facilities. A comparison of the access to care available to those having health problems between the uninsured, those with the SP and those with social security reveals that 15.9 per cent of the uninsured, 12.5 per cent of those with the SP and 6.4 per cent of those with social security failed to receive care. According to both the uninsured and the SP beneficiaries, the main causes for this failure were economic barriers. In this context, it should be noted that for each peso spent by those enrolled for the SP, the SP spent 0.93 pesos, while the same datum for those enrolled for social security is one peso to 1.39 pesos. The SP provides only slight protection against 'catastrophic health costs' for the insured as compared to the uninsured, but SP's affiliates still have to bear considerable out-of-pocket expenditure. It should also be emphasized that the overall proportions of public and private spending have changed very little.

Another shortcoming of the SP is that the amount of financial resources meant to be provided per person and supposed to be transferred by the federal government to providers is much lower than stipulated. The SP budget has increased by almost 300 per cent since it was started, but the health expenditure for the population without social security is a little less than the stated objective of 1 per cent of gross domestic product (GDP). The Ministry of Health takes pride in the narrowing of the gap between per person expenditure for the SP and for social security, but does not note that per capita expenditure has been stationary with regard to social security beneficiaries.

### An uncertain future

The above provides a hint about the strategy for achieving complete structured pluralism. In 2015, the present government, it is understood, will announce the introduction of a 'Universal Health System'. Under this, all Mexicans will be covered by a basic insurance that will grant access to an explicit service package and they will be able to choose their public or private provider freely. However, a closer reading of the hidden agenda behind this proposal shows that the service package is that belonging to the SP, the free choice of provider means that private providers will be promoted, and the social security institutes will be obliged to attend to everybody despite their overcrowded facilities. Since the basic insurance provides access only to basic services, a large space is created for the role of complementary private insurance. This means that about 50 per cent of Mexicans will lose most of their present health benefits or will have to contract such complementary private insurance.

However, the last part of the story, as described above, is hypothetical. As we have seen, health insurance available at present is far from universal; there is a lack of health facilities that can provide even basic healthcare; private providers driven by the profit motive are unlikely to fill the service gap; the payer/provider split has been unviable and has been resisted by social security institutes. Further, any move to deprive 50 per cent of the population of the benefits of health insurance is a major cause of political conflict. Finally, not unexpectedly, nobody has as yet proved any positive health-related impact of the reform of the Mexican healthcare system, and even its creators recognize that public health activities have been increasingly neglected by the government (Knaul et al. 2012). Commenting on this fact, the World Bank has argued that a health-related impact was not an objective of this reform! (Giedion et al. 2013).

### Notes

1 Latin America has also been a showcase for health-needs-driven, single and public health systems – for instance, in Brazil, Venezuela, Bolivia, Ecuador and other countries after the victories of progressive governments in South and Central America.

2 Social security institutes and the Ministry of Health.

3 The minister responsible for the reform of social security in Colombia.

4 Instituto Mexicano de Seguridad Social.

5 Mexico is a federation of thirty-two states.

6 The rest of the text is based on this reference if not indicated otherwise.

### References

Enthoven, A. C. (1988) 'Managed competition: an agenda for action', *Health Affairs*, 7(3): 25–47.

Franco, S. (2013) 'Entre los negocios y los derechos' [Between business and rights], *Revista Cubana de Salud Pública*, 39(2): 268–84.

Giedion, U., E. A. Alfonso and Y. Díaz (2013) 'The impact of universal coverage schemes in the developing world: a review of the existing evidence', UNICO Studies Series 25, Washington, DC: World Bank.

ISAGS (2012) *Sistemas de salud en suramérica: desafíos para la universalidad, la integralidad y la equidad*, Rio de Janeiro: Instituto Suramericano de Gobierno en Salud.

Knaul, F. M. et al. (2012) 'The quest for universal health coverage: achieving social protection for all in Mexico', *The Lancet*, 380(9849): 1259–79.

Laurell, A. C. (2001) 'Health reform in Mexico: the promotion of inequality', *International Journal of Health Services*, 31(2): 291–321.

— (2007) 'Health system reform in Mexico: a critical review', *International Journal of Health Services*, 37(3): 515–35.

— (2013) *El impacto del Seguro Popular sobre el sistema de salud mexicano*, Buenos Aires: CLACSO, www.asacristinalaurell.com.mx.

Londoño, J. L. and J. Frenk (1997) 'Structured pluralism: towards an innovative model for health system reform in Latin America', *Health Policy*, 41(1): 1–36.

## B4 | BRAZIL: THE ROCKY ROAD TO A UNIVERSAL HEALTHCARE SYSTEM

Brazil's unified national health system, known as the *Sistema Único de Saúde* (SUS), was created by Article 198 of the Federal Constitution adopted in 1988 (Senado Federal 1988). It was the result of pressures generated by popular mobilizations against the dictatorship (1964–85) and as part of the broad struggles for democracy in the country. It represented a commitment to the universal right to social security and health, including a critical approach to the social determinants of health. It was deeply influenced by the Italian health reform of 1978, Catholic ecclesiastical community movements that inspired a popular movement for health, and many groups of university students, labour union activists and other political leaders (Paim et al. 2011).

Brazil's infant mortality rate (IMR) dropped from 58 per 1,000 births in 1990 to 36 in 2000 and 16 in 2011 (UNICEF 2011). As with many industrialized nations, cardiovascular diseases are the leading causes of death in Brazil, followed by cancer, as well as external causes such as homicides and traffic accidents (WHO 2008). As chronic diseases are increasingly contributing to the burden of disease (Schmidt et al. 2011), communicable diseases are decreasing, but they still affect a sizeable portion of the population (Barreto et al. 2011). Injuries are the third general cause of mortality and are increasing owing to homicides and traffic injuries, a direct reflection of urbanization, inequalities and drug trafficking (Reichenheim et al. 2011).

### The health system in Brazil

Although Brazil has the largest economy in South America, its government spends less on health (per capita) than those of Argentina, Chile and Uruguay (WHO 2008).

SUS includes more than 73,000 outpatient services, including 32,000 family health teams with a medical doctor, a nurse, one or two nurse technicians and four to six community health agents (Ministério da Saúde 2012). These teams are the basic module of a national strategy of primary healthcare, and each covers around 3,500 people, reaching more than 106 million people throughout the country. The impact of better primary care is evident in a 24 per cent decrease in hospitalization rates from 1999 to 2007 (NESCON 2012). SUS also provides a range of tertiary care services (nearly 24,000 transplantations, over 84,000 cardiac surgeries, 62,000 cancer surgeries, and care to over eleven million inpatients). However, there is a persistent unmet demand for such care (Ministério da Saúde 2008).

Approximately 144 million people depend exclusively on SUS, while the remaining 46 million are covered by private insurance (CFM/CREMESP 2011). Approximately 94 per cent of the privately insured (including a large proportion of civil servants) have insurance protection provided through agreements with employers. A majority of these insurance plans do not cover a number of services, such as transplantations, dialysis, expensive drugs, intensive care, etc.

*Human rights and accountability* Article 196 of the Brazilian Constitution of 1988 denotes health as a human right and its provision as a duty of the state. It faced strong resistance from politically conservative sections, who favoured the privatization of the healthcare system. Immediately following the adoption of the new Constitution, a neoliberal government was elected in 1989, which presented significant barriers for the implementation of the legislation and regulations necessary for the financing of the new universal health system. The implementation of SUS was therefore very slow until the end of 1992 (until the impeachment of President Collor de Mello).

*Decentralized financing of health services* Fiscal decentralization was implemented in 1993, facilitating the transfer of federal funds to municipal health funds. This provided the opportunity to local governments to fulfil their responsibilities regarding primary healthcare and health surveillance. This has led to the adoption of the 'family health' strategy as a cornerstone of primary healthcare since 1994 (Ministério da Saúde 1993, 1994).

A constitutional amendment permitted the restoration of a constitutional rule that had been eliminated by the Collor government, which guarantees a minimum amount of funds to finance public health services. Federal, state and municipal revenues were earmarked to jointly finance basic health services. It is mandated that, each year, federal government expenditures must increase by an amount equal to the nominal GDP growth rate. Municipal governments are required to spend 15 per cent and states and federal districts 12 per cent of their own net revenues on health services (Governo Federal 2000a). A long-standing demand of Brazilian civil society has been that the federal government should spend 10 per cent of the federal budget on health. In the face of reluctance by the government to guarantee this level of expenditure, a broad movement, initiated in September 2013, collected 2.2 million signatures demanding immediate compliance by the government.

In two decades, major progress has been made in Brazil as regards universal access to comprehensive healthcare services, but significant challenges remain. These relate to the continued presence of a strong private sector, the need to promote a more progressive taxation system to finance social security, and the need for a solidarity-based social protection system.

**Image B4.1** Rio de Janeiro, Brazil: inequity in society impacts on the health system (Janie Ewen)

*Social control* Federal Law No. 8.142/1990 mandates that the health system must be under social control. Health councils at different levels – national, state and municipality – have decision-making powers over health plans and budgets. Citizens' representatives compose half of the membership on these councils, and the other half is divided among representatives from government, health workers and health providers. In addition, a National Health Conference organized every four years and attended by representatives of the health council at all levels determines the strategic pathway of the system (Governo Federal 1990b).

The extensive system of social control has promoted consciousness regarding citizens' right to health. This has led to an increasing incidence of litigation claiming health rights, and courts are beginning to liberally interpret the constitutional guarantee on right to health (Cubillos et al. 2012).

*Accessibility* SUS is a single-payer system financed through general taxation. According to Federal Law No. 8.080/1990, healthcare must be: provided in all parts of the country, with the same universal coverage and quality, with no restrictions except on purely cosmetic procedures; provided free at the point of service; and egalitarian, with no restrictions to any person as regards access or kinds of treatment (Governo Federal 1990a). SUS integrates all government facilities as part of the universal system. In addition, many private service providers (mostly non-profit institutions) remain a substantial complementary part of the public system. Private providers account for 60 per cent of hospital beds under SUS.

Despite improved access to tertiary care through SUS, significant gaps remain. For instance, while there are 356,000 hospital beds (1.85 beds per 1,000 people) in the public system. In order to achieve a minimum of four beds per 1,000 inhabitants (the rate in Spain), Brazil would need 335,000 new hospital beds. Lack of sufficient tertiary-care services pushes people to the private sector, thus continuing to perpetuate a private market for healthcare. Improved and more equitable funding is necessary to break this dynamic, which continues to block the full development of SUS (DATASUS 2012).

*Acceptability and quality* When the 1988 Constitution was drafted, lobbyists successfully pushed for the exclusion from SUS of health services for the military, civil servants and employees of state-owned enterprises. Unfortunately, legislators and government employees who seldom use SUS continue to promote a widespread notion that high-quality care is available only in the private sector, while the public system is simply a solution for the more 'vulnerable'. Nevertheless, the government of Brazil has taken continuous steps to improve the quality of public services, including in traditionally deficient areas, such as for emergency services (Machado et al. 2011; Ministério da Saúde 2002, 2003a, 2003b, 2011).

### Challenges and limitations of SUS

Until 1988, only formal workers and their families were covered by social insurance, while 85 per cent of the population received care at charitable institutions and through inadequate public facilities in some cities and states. The main accomplishment of SUS has been to make health a right for all. However, public expenditure represents only 45 per cent of total health expenditure in Brazil, which accounts for 8.8 per cent of GDP. Private expenditure on health is still very high, at US$44,300 per capita per year (IBGE 2010). As health costs rise while public expenditures remain relatively constant, out-of-pocket payments are higher at present than in the late 1990s, though catastrophic impoverishment because of such payments remains relatively low, affecting 2 per cent of the population (Gragnolati et al. 2013).

About 46 million people are primarily serviced by the private sector, which operates in tandem with private insurance companies, including those that manage the funds of social security systems of large public sector enterprises. The private sector is regulated by the National Agency of Supplementary Health, under the aegis of the minister of health. Despite some advances in regulations to protect patients' rights, there are major gaps in effective regulation of the private system (CFM/CREMESP 2011).

The SUS, despite its accomplishments, remains in permanent conflict with unfavourable power structures embedded in the political and economic system in Brazil. It has been systemically underfinanced, posing a major barrier to the building of a truly universal system which is entirely public and provides comprehensive healthcare services to all citizens. Powerful politically conservative sections continue to obstruct the allocation of increased finances for SUS.

The SUS is also hamstrung in its ability to deploy adequate human resources for health, by a law on 'fiscal responsibility' approved in the 1990s. The law decrees that the total cost on personnel (wages, etc.) cannot exceed 53 per cent of the total budgets for public administration (Governo Federal 2000b). The law forces public authorities to contract personnel through intermediaries such as cooperatives or enterprises. This practice promotes discontinuity in the provision of public services and exacerbates corrupt practices.

The fact that a large section of the middle class and high-income employees remain outside SUS also acts as a barrier for SUS itself. Under Brazilian law, personal expenditures on private health and education are deductible from personal income tax (Nyman and Barleen 2005). In effect, this means that those who rely on public systems ultimately subsidize the rich, who save taxes while accessing private healthcare and education.

### Looking ahead

After twenty-five years of social participation through the health councils, it is time to reflect about the need to overcome the structural barriers that prevent the full implementation of SUS. In order for SUS to be truly universal and in a position to provide comprehensive services to all, government expenditure on health should increase from US$367 per capita/year to US$1,000, reaching around 10 per cent of GDP. Also needed are enhanced public management standards to eliminate gaps in access and quality. This will require the promotion of progressive tax reforms, political reforms that ensure participatory democracy, and a rights-based approach to state reform.

A clear plan and process are needed to ensure that public services provided by the state are progressively expanded so that they become the dominant form of healthcare provision in the Brazilian health system. Moreover, it is necessary to establish public regulation of private–public provider contracts that complement state-owned services, and contracted private providers need to be regulated to ensure that they promote public health goals.

### References

Barreto M. L., M. G. Teixeira, F. I. Bastos et al. (2011) 'Successes and failures in the control of infectious diseases in Brazil: social and environmental context, policies, interventions, and research needs', *The Lancet*, 377(9780): 1877–89.

CFM/CREMESP (2011) *Demografia médica no Brasil*, portal.cfm.org.br/images/stories/pdf/demografiamedicanobrasil.pdf, accessed 10 October 2012.

Cubillos, L., M. L. Escobar, S. Pavlovic and R. Iunes (2012) 'Universal health coverage and litigation in Latin America', www.ncbi.nlm. nih.gov/pubmed/22852461, accessed 10 October 2012.

DATASUS (2012) *CNES – Recursos Físicos – Hospitalar – Leitos de internação – Brasil*, tabnet.datasus.gov.br/cgi/tabcgi.exe?cnes/cnv/leiintbr.def, accessed 10 October 2012.

Governo Federal (1990a) *Lei Federal nº 8.080, de 19 de setembro de 1990*, www.planalto.gov.br/ccivil_03/leis/L8080.htm, accessed 10 October 2012.

— (1990b) *Lei Federal nº 8.142, de 28 de dezembro de 1990*, www.planalto.gov.br/ccivil_03/leis/L8142.htm, accessed 10 October 2012.

— (2000a) *Emenda Constitucional nº 29, de 13 de setembro de 2000*, www.planalto.gov.br/ccivil_03/constituicao/Emendas/Emc/emc29.htm, accessed 10 October 2012.

— (2000b) *Lei Complementar nº 101, de 4 de maio de 2000*, www.planalto.gov.br/ccivil_03/leis/LCP/Lcp101.htm, accessed 10 October 2012.

Gragnolati, M., M. Lindelow and B. Couttolenc (2013) *Twenty Years of Health System Reform in Brazil – an Assessment of the Sistema Único de Saúde*, World Bank, dx.doi.org/10.1596/978-0-8213-9843-2, accessed 10 April 2014.

IBGE (2010) *Censo Demográfico 2010*, www.ibge.gov.br, accessed 10 October 2012.

Machado, C. V., F. G. F. Salvador and G. O'Dwyer (2011) 'Serviço de atendimento móvel de urgência: análise da política brasileira', *Revista de Saúde Pública*, www.scielo.br/scielo.php?script=sci_arttext&pid=S0034-89102011000300010&lng=pt&nrm=iso&tlng=en.

Ministério da Saúde (1993) *Portaria nº 545, de 20 de maio de 1993*, siops.datasus.gov.br/Documentacao/Portaria%20545_20_05_1993.pdf, accessed 10 October 2012.

— (1994) *Programa Saúde da Família: dentro de casa*, Brasilia: Editora do Ministério da Saúde.

— (2002) *Portaria nº 2048, de 5 de novembro de 2002*, www.saude.mg.gov.br/atos_normativos/legislacao-sanitaria/estabelecimentos-de-saude/urgencia-e-emergencia/portaria_2048_B.pdf, accessed 10 October 2012.

— (2003a) *Portaria nº 1863, de 29 de setembro de 2003*, dtr2001.saude.gov.br/sas/PORTARIAS/Port2003/GM/GM-1863.htm, accessed 10 October 2012.

— (2003b) *Política Nacional de Atenção às Urgências*, Brasilia: Editora do Ministério da Saúde, bvsms.saude.gov.br/bvs/publicacoes/politica_nac_urgencias.pdf, accessed 10 October 2012.

— (2008) *Mais saúde: direito de todos: 2008 – 2011*, Brasilia: Editora do Ministério da Saúde, bvsms.saude.gov.br/bvs/publicacoes/mais_saude_direito_todos_2ed.pdf, accessed 10 October 2012.

— (2011) *Portaria nº 1.600, de 7 de julho de 2011*, bvsms.saude.gov.br/bvs/saudelegis/gm/2011/prt1600_07_07_2011.html, accessed 10 October 2012.

— (2012) *Saúde da Família*, dab.saude.gov.br/abnumeros.php, accessed 10 October 2012.

NESCON (2012) *Avaliação do impacto das ações do programa de saúde da família na redução das internações hospitalares por condições sensíveis à atenção básica em adultos e idosos*, www.nescon.medicina.ufmg.br/noticias/wpcontent/uploads/2012/05/Site-Nescon-ICSAP.pdf, accessed 8 November 2012.

Nyman, J. and N. Barleen (2005) *The effect of supplemental private health insurance on health care purchases, health, and welfare in Brazil*, Minneapolis: University of Minnesota.

Paim, J., C. Travassos, C. Almeida, L. Bahia and J. Macinko (2011) 'The Brazilian health system: history, advances, and challenges', *The Lancet*, 377(9779): 1778–97.

Reichenheim, M. E., E. R. de Souza, C. L. Moraes et al. (2011) 'Violence and injuries in Brazil: the effect, progress made, and challenges ahead', *The Lancet*, 377(9781): 1962–75.

Schmidt, M. I., B. B. Duncan, G. A. de Silva et al. (2011) 'Chronic non-communicable diseases in Brazil: burden and current challenges', *The Lancet*, 377(9781): 1949–61.

Senado Federal (1988) *Constituição da República Federativa do Brasil*, Brasilia: Senado Federal.

UNICEF (2011) *Situação mundial da infância 2011 – Adolescência uma fase de oportunidades*, www.unicef.org/brazil/pt/br_sowcr11web.pdf, accessed 10 October 2012.

WHO (2008) *World Health Statistics 2008*, www.who.int/gho/publications/world_health_statistics/2008/en/, accessed 10 October 2012.

South Africa has a deeply divided health system. About 17 per cent of the population, comprising the richest groups, have private health insurance (called medical schemes) and use private for-profit providers. While some who are not covered by medical schemes occasionally pay out of pocket to use a private GP or retail pharmacy, 83 per cent of the population are heavily dependent on tax-funded public sector services, particularly for specialist and hospital care (McIntyre et al. 2012). South Africa has the highest percentage of health expenditure funded by private health insurance in the world (Drechsler and Jutting 2005).

Funding for public sector health services declined in real per capita terms from the mid-1990s to the early part of the twenty-first century (McIntyre et al. 2012) owing to a self-imposed structural adjustment programme. This was precisely the time when the HIV epidemic was exploding, placing a growing burden on the under-resourced public health system and contributing to declining quality of care and staff morale. While there is no fee for care at public primary-level facilities, user fees are charged at public hospitals. Pregnant women and children under six years are exempt and the poor can apply for a fee exemption, but anyone outside of these categories and earning an income is faced with paying the not inconsiderable hospital fees on an out-of-pocket basis. Many South Africans, particularly those living in rural areas, face substantial barriers in accessing healthcare (Silal et al. 2012; Cleary et al. 2013).

The clearest indicator of the massive disparities in the health system is the differential in financial resources between the public and private sectors relative to the population they serve. While only 17 per cent of the population benefit from medical schemes, well over 40 per cent of total healthcare expenditure is attributable to these schemes. The effect of this is that while US$1,370 was spent per medical scheme beneficiary in 2008, less than $220 was spent on healthcare for those entirely dependent on tax-funded health services (McIntyre et al. 2012).

**Proposed reforms**

The South African government has committed itself to introducing a National Health Insurance (NHI) as a means of achieving a universal health system. Although termed NHI,[1] it is envisaged as a tax-funded system with universal entitlements to comprehensive health services for which there will be no user fees at the point of service delivery (Department of Health 2011). Key elements of the proposed NHI reforms are: to begin by rebuilding the public health system, with a particular emphasis on primary healthcare; to increase management authority in public hospitals and districts, accompanied by improved governance and accountability mechanisms; to increase tax funding for health services; and to introduce an NHI Fund (NHIF) as a strategic or active purchaser of services at a later stage. The NHIF would *not* be an insurance scheme; it is envisaged as a public institution with strong governance and accountability mechanisms tasked with allocating resources to equitably meet the needs of the population.

These reforms have the *potential* to move South Africa towards a universal health system.[2] The NHIF would create a single pool of tax funds that could be used to purchase services that benefit the entire population, promoting equity through maximizing cross-subsidies from the rich to the poor and from the healthy to those with greater healthcare needs. As an *active* purchaser, the NHIF would assess population needs for health services and allocate resources in line with these needs to ensure that quality services are available where and when needed. It could also use its financial power, as a single purchaser, to ensure that the cost of health services is affordable and sustainable and to pay providers in a way that promotes efficient delivery of quality care and an equitable distribution of services across the country.

The South African government has appropriately identified the starting point for these reforms as rebuilding the public healthcare *delivery* system.

Some of the current initiatives include: addressing infrastructure gaps and deficiencies (poor distribution of facilities and lack of equipment); improving the availability of essential medicines in facilities; increasing capacity for health worker training; appointing managers who meet specific criteria and embarking on extensive management training; and introducing mechanisms for quality assessment and improvement.

This is a mammoth undertaking, given the serious damage inflicted on the system during the period of neoliberal reforms by 'macroeconomic adjustment' policies. From 1994 to 1996, the broad policy agenda of the ANC government headed by Nelson Mandela was the Reconstruction and Development Programme (RDP). In 1996, the RDP was replaced by a neoliberal macroeconomic policy – GEAR (Growth, Employment and Redistribution) – favoured by the International Monetary Fund (IMF) and the World Bank (Mooney and McIntyre 2008).

Currently, primary healthcare is to be prioritized. However, there are some concerns about progress with the primary healthcare agenda. A key element of the 'PHC Re-engineering' initiative was to deploy 'primary healthcare agents' (i.e. community health workers, CHWs) in every municipal ward, to contribute to the delivery of population-oriented primary healthcare with extensive community- and home-based services to complement services at clinics and other primary-level facilities. While there was initially considerable enthusiasm about this programme, there now appears to be very slow progress in implementing it in some areas, with at least part of the reason reportedly being insufficient funds to cover the stipends of the primary healthcare agents (see also Chapter B7). Further, the number of CHWs in current policies is far too low for the work they are supposed to do, and completely neutralizes their activist role as catalysts of community mobilization around social determinants (People's Health Movement 2013).

### Obstacles posed by Treasury policy

Increased public funding is key to the success of these different initiatives. Although the health sector has received some budget increases in the last decade, given that human resources are the single largest expenditure item and that there is an urgent need to increase staffing in public facilities, more funds are required. Building new facilities, rehabilitating existing ones and maintaining this infrastructure also requires funding, as does procuring and maintaining essential equipment, improving medicine supplies and other efforts to improve the accessibility and quality of care in public sector facilities. Without these improvements, the NHIF will provide merely 'paper entitlements' without real access to quality care.

The National Treasury has been very circumspect in terms of increasing government spending in recent years, citing the impact of the global economic crisis as the key reason for this approach. However, it could create more fiscal space for increased spending on healthcare, and other social services that impact on the social determinants of health, if it chose to change its fiscal policy. The National Treasury is insistent on maintaining a tax-to-GDP ratio of 25 per cent (National Treasury 2012; Forslund 2012). To maintain this level, when tax revenue increased dramatically through improved tax collection efforts, the Treasury responded by systematically reducing personal income tax rates (e.g. the tax rate for the highest tax bracket has declined from 45 to 40 per cent) and corporate tax rates (from 35 to 28 per cent). Restricting the tax-to-GDP level is a policy choice; a change in this fiscal policy could translate into substantial increases in tax revenue and government expenditure. This could be achieved through reversing decreases in personal and corporate tax rates, but more importantly by addressing aggressive tax avoidance by multinational corporations and high-net-worth individuals. The South African Revenue Service (SARS) estimates that it was losing R48 billion in tax revenue annually as a result of tax avoidance by high-net-worth individuals, equivalent to about 7 per cent of total government revenue (Vanek 2012).

### Private sector challenges

A key concern relates to the role of private healthcare providers. The stated intention is that the NHIF could purchase services from both public and private providers. There are particular concerns about the power of private for-profit healthcare providers and the potential for them to drain the NHIF's public funds to provide high-tech, costly, curative services (particularly secondary and tertiary care) for the urban population, leaving few resources to meet the needs of the rest of the population. There are associated concerns that the NHI will become unaffordable and unsustainable. These are not unrealistic concerns, given the current experience of medical schemes in South Africa. While only 7 per cent of total medical scheme expenditure is devoted to general practitioners, about 3 per cent to dental health services and 8 per cent to allied health professionals (optometrists, physiotherapists, etc.), 23 per cent is allocated to specialists and over 36 per cent to private hospitals (Council for Medical Schemes 2013), highlighting the dominance of secondary and tertiary care in this sector. There is an imbalance of power between the hundred or so medical schemes and private providers, particularly hospitals, where three groups own more than three-quarters of all private hospital beds (McIntyre et al. 2012). This power imbalance has contributed to rapid increases in provider fees and provision of certain services and hence medical scheme expenditure, translating into large annual increases in contribution rates.

There are clearly potential risks in engaging with the private for-profit health sector, and its power should not be underestimated. The question is, how should low- and middle-income countries (LMICs) seeking to ensure access to quality health services and financial risk protection for their whole population deal with large existing private healthcare provision sectors, particularly given that the majority of the most highly skilled health professionals often work in the private sector?

One approach could be to see private providers as outside the universal health system and to attempt to limit the potential adverse impact on public health objectives (such as 'internal brain drain' from public to private sectors) through strong regulation. However, experience has shown that regulation of the private health sector is often ineffective in LMICs, owing largely to poor enforcement capacity (Kumaranayake 1997). In the South African context, the private health sector has repeatedly instituted court action to overturn government regulations.

### Strategic 'purchasing' of care?

Another approach is to purchase services from private providers, but strictly on terms that are in line with achieving public health objectives (i.e. strategic purchasing). In the South African context, this could *potentially* fast-track improved access to health services as the majority of most categories of healthcare professionals work in the private sector. The NHIF could draw on the human resources in both the public and private sectors to provide services for the entire population. However, this would undoubtedly require uncomfortable changes for private providers, who focus on curative care, seldom see some

**Image B5.1** Community health workers at a meeting in South Africa (Louis Reynolds)

of the conditions that are key contributors to the burden of disease for the majority of the population (such as tuberculosis), and are concentrated in the largest urban areas. The NHIF, as an institution that would have the major share of funds available for health services, would effectively 'hold the purse-strings' and be in a powerful position to influence the behaviour of providers (public and private).

In order for this strategic purchasing approach to dealing with the reality of the existence of a large private health sector to be successful, there are certain prerequisites or 'non-negotiables'. First, a strong, well-distributed public delivery system is essential and must be the backbone of the universal health system. Nothing would challenge the power of private service providers as much as quality, accessible public sector health services. Secondly, purchasing of services from private providers should occur where this would further the goals of the universal health system. For example, priority should be given to purchasing from private providers in geographic areas where there is inadequate public sector service delivery capacity and not in areas where there is an oversupply of service providers relative to the population to be served. Thirdly, the process of drawing on the human resources currently located in the private sector must be undertaken in a way that is subject to the public health system ethos (e.g. provision of comprehensive promotive, preventive, curative, rehabilitative and palliative services; working as a member of a team of health workers; etc.). Fourthly, the emphasis should be placed on purchasing services from primary healthcare providers (e.g. general practitioners, primary dental practitioners, physiotherapists, optometrists, pharmacists and pharmacy assistants, etc.). This is in line with the emphasis on strengthening primary healthcare services and ensuring primary-care gatekeeping to higher levels of care. Conversely, great caution should be exercised in purchasing high-technology diagnostic, specialist and inpatient services from private providers to ensure that the quantity of secondary and tertiary services available is in line with what is determined as being needed through appropriate referral practices.

Finally, the design of the NHIF must be such that it is empowered to undertake strategic purchasing and can be held accountable for its use of public funds. As a single purchaser, it can wield considerable power in determining how providers will be paid and payment levels; it can avoid the current pitfalls of the private health system of paying on a fee-for-service basis and having providers dictate their fee levels. The NHIF should also be empowered to ensure that service delivery by public and private providers from whom services are purchased is subject to standard treatment guidelines and other measures to promote efficiency and quality in services. There would also need to be routine monitoring of services provided to assess that they are in line with population needs, and not the result of supplier-induced demand, and adhere to standard treatment guidelines. Most importantly, there must be mechanisms for strong governance and public accountability, to ensure that public funds are used appropriately and that access to quality health services in line with the health care needs of the population is being achieved. Importantly, the NHIF must not be vulnerable to 'capture' by the private sector; its integrity in serving the public interest must be secured. (See also Chapter B1 regarding other issues related to the role of government as a 'purchaser' of healthcare services.)

A key assumption underlying this visualization of the role of strategic purchasing (including selective purchasing from private providers) is that an appropriate balance in the distribution of total healthcare expenditure between public funds and private voluntary insurance schemes is restored. The success of strategic purchasing in addressing challenges posed by the large private provision sector is critically dependent on the NHIF 'holding the purse-strings' for the majority of healthcare financing. There is clear evidence that many medical scheme members are concerned about the high and rapidly increasing cost of belonging to such schemes and would relinquish membership if the NHIF ensured access to quality services at lower cost (McIntyre et al. 2009).

There are considerable potential risks and obstacles to achieving a universal health system in South Africa. Nevertheless, the status quo cannot remain. The experience of South Africa in pursuing the proposed set of reforms will provide valuable lessons for other low- and middle-income countries that have large private health sectors.

## Notes

1 The use of the term NHI is a political artefact, in that the ruling party committed to introducing an NHI before detailed proposals on the most appropriate health system reforms had been developed, and has continued to use the terminology initially adopted. Unfortunately, the term NHI has created considerable public confusion about the nature of the

proposed reforms, and is contributing to international concerns that the drive for 'Universal Health Coverage' (UHC) is being equated with introducing or expanding the role of insurance schemes.

2 There is considerable debate at present about the concept of 'Universal Health Coverage' (UHC) and what it may or may not imply in terms of health system reform. This chapter, instead, uses the term universal health system, and interprets this to be founded on two fundamental principles: 1) Universalism, where everyone is entitled to the *same* health services (in terms of range, clinical quality of care and ability to access); 2) Social solidarity, where health services are funded on the basis of financial means (with cross-subsidies from the affluent to the impoverished) and accessed on the basis of need (with cross-subsidies from the healthy to the sick or those in need of preventive services).

## References

Cleary, S., S. Birch, N. Chimbindi, S. Silal and D. McIntyre (2013) 'Investigating the affordability of key health services in South Africa', *Social Science and Medicine*, 80: 37–46.

Council for Medical Schemes (2013) *Annual Report, 2012–13*, Pretoria: Council for Medical Schemes.

Department of Health (2011) *National Health Act (61/2003): Policy on National Health Insurance. Government Gazette 34523*, Pretoria: Department of Health.

Drechsler, D. and J. Jutting (2005) *Is there a role for private health insurance in developing countries?*, Berlin: German Institute for Economic Research.

Forslund, D. (2012) *Personal income taxation and the struggle against inequality and poverty: tax policy and personal income taxation in South Africa since 1994*, Observatory: Alternative Information Development Centre.

Kumaranayake, L. (1997) 'The role of regulation: influencing private sector activity within health sector reform', *Journal of International Development*, 9(4): 641–9.

McIntyre, D., J. Doherty and J. Ataguba (2012) 'Health care financing and expenditure', in H. van Rensburg (ed.), *Health and Health Care in South Africa*, Pretoria: Van Schaik Publishers.

McIntyre, D., J. Goudge, B. Harris, N. Nxumalo and M. Nkosi (2009) 'Pre-requisites for National Health Insurance in South Africa: results of a national household survey', *South African Medical Journal*, 99: 630–4.

Mooney, G. H. and D. E. McIntyre (2008) 'South Africa: a 21st century apartheid in health and health care?', *Medical Journal of Australia*, 189(11/12): 637–40.

National Treasury (2012) *2012 Budget Speech: Minister of Finance*, Pretoria: National Treasury.

People's Health Movement (2013) Testimonies from community care workers, meeting convened by People's Health Movement, Wellness Foundation, Community Care Workers' Forum, 25 May.

Silal, S., L. Penn-Kekana, B. Harris, S. Birch and D. McIntyre (2012) 'Exploring inequalities in access to and use of maternal health services in South Africa', *BMC Health Services Research*, 12(120).

Vanek, M. (2012) 'SARS uncovers 1000s of missing rich tax cheats', *Moneywebtax*, 13 January.

In a chilling reminder of the self-immolation of Mohamed Bouazizi in 2010 that sparked the 'Arab Spring', less than three years later (on 13 May 2013) a twenty-seven-year-old street vendor named Adel Khazri immolated himself in front of the National Theatre on Habib Bourguiba Avenue in Tunis. Adel, just like Mohamed earlier, was forced by the dismal condition of his life to take such a precipitate step. He used to earn about US$100 a month by selling smuggled cigarettes on the streets, but this was not enough to feed him and his old parents, who lived in the poor governorate of Jendouba, in north-western Tunisia.

Adel Khazri's family later revealed that he had been suffering from multiple health problems, and that most of his limited income had gone towards paying for healthcare and medicines in the private sector. He had not been able to get the indigence certificate, which could have allowed him to get free healthcare in public hospitals. This tragedy reveals the failure of successive governments that came to power in the period after the 17 December–14 January 'Freedom and Dignity Revolution' to address issues of social protection. It also reveals the gradual erosion of the right to health of the people of Tunisia, particularly since the implementation of structural adjustment reforms and neoliberal policies starting in the mid-1980s.

Measures to provide social security and accessible healthcare in Tunisia have evolved gradually and have seen many changes since the independence of Tunisia in 1956, in sync with changes in the political and economic environment of the country. Important political changes have influenced the nature and extent of the government's role in protecting the right to health and in determining the concrete policies that were implemented to protect this right.

### Social security in the pre-independence period

The ground for the creation of a social security system had been prepared during the colonial period, at a time when progressive forces were in power in France, particularly in the period between the two world wars. The first social security Act was institutionalized through a decree on 8 June 1944.[1] The Act created an inter-professional fund for family allowances, set up a family allowance fund for miners, and created a social compensation fund for workers engaged in construction, public works, and port and dock work. Early measures such as this paved the way for the development of social security, including social health insurance, after Tunisia gained independence.

**Image B6.1** Scene from the uprising in Tunisia that led to the overthrow of President Ben Ali (Chris Belsten)

Before independence, the healthcare system was not well developed, particularly in rural areas. General hospitals were established in big cities, particularly in Tunis, for specific populations, including for specific religious groups (Christians of French and Italian origin, and indigent Muslims). The latter were also catered to by charitable institutions such as the Aziza Othmana (named after a Muslim sponsor). Civil society organizations also provided free healthcare to the poor and the needy. However, there was no real system of organized social health protection in the form of social health insurance for Tunisians.

### Provision of free healthcare after independence

Tunisia achieved independence from France in 1956 after an armed nationalist struggle. The first constitution (adopted in 1959) recognized the right to health and education in its preamble. Important measures were taken to make education free and mandatory for both sexes, to outlaw polygamy, to promote gender equality, and to provide free healthcare for all citizens.

The ruling party in the post-revolution period until the late 1980s was the Socialist Destourian Party. Provision of healthcare services was principally through public services, organized by the state. The 'socialist' approach of the ruling party resulted in a welfare state, in which free healthcare and education were integral components.

In 1960, social security was strengthened through the creation of special funds for workers in the private and government sectors.[2] These funds dealt with pension funds, family allowances, work accidents and injuries, and health insurance. The adoption of progressive policies was not only dependent on a wise and visionary leadership, but also reflected the influence of the working classes on the liberation movement. The main workers' union, UGTT, played an important role during the independence struggle and was instrumental in shaping the social and economic programmes of the country.

For more than two decades after independence, health and education were high on the political agenda and the budgets allocated to these two sectors amounted to 33 per cent of the total government budget. Significant efforts were made to build public healthcare facilities all over the country, following a primary-healthcare-based service delivery model. Also, policies aimed at improving human resource development were implemented, and several nursing and paramedical schools were built in most governorates. The first medical school was established in Tunis in 1965 with technical support from the WHO (Akin et al. 1987). From the mid-1970s more medical schools, a school of dentistry and a school of pharmacy were built.

Social health protection was further improved by the strengthening of the two insurance funds covering workers in the government and private sectors and by providing various social security services, including health insurance. The gradual increase in insurance coverage through mandatory enrolment has led to the coverage of about 60 per cent of Tunisians by contributory health insurance schemes. Poor and deprived sections, representing nearly 30 per cent of the total population, were covered by the government through the medical assistance programme which allowed eligible citizens free or subsidized access to public healthcare facilities.

The improvement in the social determinants of health, including education, nutrition, housing, access to water and sanitation, and investment in human resource development, and the increased coverage by promotive and preventive programmes, led to important achievements in health outcomes, as reflected by an increase in life expectancy and a reduction of general mortality and morbidity rates in various age groups.

### Authoritarian rule and crisis

However, the political system based on one-party rule and limited freedom of speech and democracy led to several crises. The most important was the economic crisis of 1969 following the failure of top-down and poorly designed agrarian reforms aimed at establishing production cooperatives. Incidents such as this ended the socialist orientation of the government after the then responsible minister, Ahmed Ben Saleh, was sacked and his successor imprisoned.

The ruling party increased its interference in the workers' unions in order to get the working classes to support unpopular economic and political decisions. This situation led to a general strike in 1978 led by the workers' union.

President Bourguiba ordered a military general named Ben Ali to repress the general strike, leading to bloodshed and violence that resulted in the loss of more than two hundred lives.

In the mid-1980s, the government was almost bankrupted and turned to the International Monetary Fund (IMF) and the World Bank to borrow money in a bid to resolve its financial problems. These Bretton Woods institutions imposed macroeconomic reforms and a structural adjustment programme on Tunisia, with stringent reductions in public spending, particularly in the social sectors, including health and education.

## Structural adjustment programmes and the erosion of the right to health

The well-known recipe of a structural adjustment programme (Achour 2011) consisted of the introduction of user fees for publicly provided healthcare services to compensate for diminishing government spending in the social sectors, including health, reduction of food subsidies, and promotion of privatization in the area of service delivery.

Significant reduction in the subsidies for bread, pasta, sugar and oil, which are the main staples of Tunisians, led to the 'bread riots' in 1984. These were once again severely repressed by the government, leading to tens of deaths and injuries to many more. The magnitude of the riots throughout the country obliged the then president to reverse these measures. The measures were gradually reintroduced during the second dictatorship of President Ben Ali.

User charges were implemented for all publicly provided healthcare services with the exception of preventive and promotional services. The share of the government in total healthcare spending decreased from 45 per cent in the 1970s to nearly 26 per cent in 2008. At the same time, the share of households in total healthcare expenditure increased from 36 per cent in the 1970s to nearly 45 per cent in 2010. As public facilities became gradually underfunded, patients, including insured ones, sought healthcare in the private sector. Supplies of medicines in public facilities were often limited and skilled health workers migrated to work in the more lucrative and better-equipped private sector.

The increase in out-of-pocket healthcare expenditure is explained by several factors, including active and passive privatization resulting from a weak public sector, balanced billing for insured patients, and co-payments and provider-induced demand resulting from the dual practice promoted in public healthcare institutions. Equity studies, carried out with technical support from WHO (Chaoui et al. 2012), have shown that nearly 5 per cent of households faced catastrophic expenditure levels and that 2 per cent were pushed every year into poverty following ill health.

The landscape of service provision has also changed as a consequence of government policies aimed at promoting the role of the private sector in both healthcare financing and delivery. Between 1990 and 2008, the total number of private hospitals increased from thirty-three to ninety-nine, while private bed capacity increased during the same period from 1,142 to 2,578 (a 2.25-fold increase) (Achouri and Achour 2002). All of this has led to a two-tier system of service provision: one for the rich, who can afford to pay for quality private healthcare services, and one for the poor, who are served by a failing public sector. These changes have led to the *erosion of the Tunisians' constitutional right to health*.

### Neoliberal policies and healthcare for those who can afford it

The growing role of the private sector in service delivery and financing, which was initiated in the 1980s, further increased after 2000 with the adoption of neoliberal policies and the subsequent privatization of major sectors of the economy and the implementation of free trade agreements (FTAs) (Zogby 2011). At the same time, reduction in government spending led to the freezing of civil service recruitment, which increased the number of unemployed health professionals.

The pace of growth of private healthcare investments was higher than in previous decades. Several national medicine companies were established, as were joint ventures with international pharmaceutical firms. This has had a positive impact in terms of increasing self-reliance in medicine production and manufacturing to around 45 per cent.

Some private investors, aware of the strategic position of the country and the availability of its competent and trained healthcare workforce, have started developing health and medical tourism services to attract patients from the region and from Europe.

Outsourcing of clinical and non-clinical public services to private providers was aggressively promoted by the government. Therefore, several functions carried out previously in public hospitals were outsourced, leading to job losses for health workers in government healthcare facilities. Also, public–private partnerships (PPPs) were encouraged at the national, regional and international levels.

The deterioration of public health care facilities in general and of hospitals at various levels in particular has meant that the healthcare options available to middle-class citizens and insured patients are limited. Price inflation in the private sector, weak governance and regulatory mechanisms are forcing important segments of the patient population to seek healthcare privately, even at the risk of becoming indebted or impoverished. The marketization of healthcare has become an unacceptable reality.

The reform initiated by the government to establish a unique insurance fund covering civil servants and workers in the private sector was based on providing access for the insured to private healthcare providers. Since the implementation of the health insurance reform in 2008, reimbursement costs for services bought privately by insured patients have witnessed a significant increase, threatening in the medium term the financial viability of the national health insurance fund. The financial deficit of the insurance fund in 2011 was estimated to be around US$100 million.

National policies of privatization and practices of labour flexibility have exacerbated unemployment among young Tunisians and have increased social vulnerability. Increasing frustration and anger resulting from social unrest, political impasse, unemployment, exclusion and the erosion of human rights, including the right to health, led to the 17 December–14 January 'Freedom and Dignity Revolution', which ended half a century of political dictatorship in Tunisia (ANC 2014).

### The right to health in the aftermath of the 'Freedom and Dignity Revolution'

The defence of, and the importance accorded to, human rights, including the right to health, came to occupy a very high place on the political agenda following the Tunisian revolution. Most electoral campaign programmes of the major political parties have highlighted the importance of promoting and protecting the right to health in the country's future constitution. Most programmes have called for the introduction of a universal health system and for the rehabilitation of the public health sector as an important partner in service provision.

Civil society organizations (CSOs) are becoming very active in advocacy of the right to health in a democratic and free society. Several associations are defending the rights of patients to access quality care services without the financial burdens being placed on individuals and families, including access to quality and affordable medicines, particularly for patients with chronic diseases and cancers.

The Tunisian Association Defending the Right to Health (ATDDS) has played an active role in facilitating networking among CSOs that defend the right to health and in advocating and promoting the right to health in the new constitution (ibid.). Thanks to media coverage and interaction with members of the constitutional assembly, the statement on the right to health in the draft constitution has been improved and expanded, and this has in turn promoted the forging of links with social determinants of health, such as employment, housing and education.

However, it has not been possible to introduce into the new constitution explicit reference to the government's responsibility in protecting the right to health and in securing mechanisms for the monitoring and evaluation of such a right. Also, concerns have been raised about the 'charity-based' approach promoted by some influential members of the governing Islamist party, which does not recognize health as a right, but rather regards it as an act of charity that could be provided through a network of faith-based associations.

The ATDDS plans to conduct studies on equity in healthcare financing and on social health protection in collaboration with other public health professionals and researchers. Non-governmental organizations (NGOs) have also contributed to a societal dialogue on health reforms supporting the promotion of the right to health at the national, regional and local levels.

## Conclusion

The self-immolation of the young unemployed Tunisian man deprived of his constitutionally guaranteed human right to health has shaken CSOs and political activists. His death, seen as an unacceptable tragedy, has led CSOs and human rights activists to strongly advocate the inclusion of economic and social rights in the future constitution.

The values of social justice and equity upheld by the Tunisian revolution, which has opened the way for freedom and democracy in some Arab countries, need also to be used to support the struggle for the rights-based approach for universal health coverage nationally, regionally and globally.

## Notes

1 See Centre des Liaisons Européennes et Internationales de Sécurité Sociale (CLEISS), 'Le régime tunisien de sécurité sociale', www.cleiss.fr/docs/regimes/regime_tunisie.html.

2 See ibid.

## References

Achour, N. (2011) *Le Système de Santé Tunisien: Etat des Lieux et Défis*, September, www.unfpa-tunisie.org/usp/images/modules/modules2013/module2_5_5/Le_syst%C3%A8me_de_sant%C3%A9_tunisien_NAchour.pdf, accessed 5 May 2014.

Achouri, H. and N. Achour (2002) 'Health services in Tunisia in the light of world trade organization agreements', in *Trade in Health Services: Global, regional, and country perspectives*, Washington, DC/Geneva: Pan American Health Organization/World Health Organization, Strategy Unit, pp. 207–20, www.who.int/trade/en/THpart3chap16.pdf, accessed 5 May 2014.

Akin, J. S., N. Birdsall and D. M. de Ferranti (1987) 'Financing health services in developing countries: an agenda for reform', Washington, DC: World Bank.

ANC (Assemblée Nationale Constituante) (2014) *Constitution Tunisienne*, 26 January.

Chaoui, F., M. Legros, N. Achour et al. (2012) 'Les Systèmes de santé en Algérie, Maroc et Tunisie: défis nationaux et enjeux partagés', *Les Notes IPEMED*, 13, April, www.ipemed.coop/adminIpemed/media/fich_article/1336128563_LesNotes IPEMED_13_Sante_avril2012.pdf, accessed 5 May 2014.

Zogby, J. (2011) 'The "Arab spring" effect', *Huffington Post*, 17 December, www.huffingtonpost.com/james-zogby/the-arab-spring-effect_b_1155359.html, accessed 5 May 2014.

## B7 | THE REVIVAL OF COMMUNITY HEALTH WORKERS IN NATIONAL HEALTH SYSTEMS

### Introduction

The generic designation of 'community health worker' (CHW) is used to refer to a variety of types of community workers, with different modes and areas of activity, with a scope of practice that may extend to comprehensive actions or be limited to specific interventions depending on the context. Nonetheless, the special relationship CHWs share simultaneously with both the community and the health system, regardless of setting or location, can be considered their defining characteristic (Lavor et al. 2004). A common feature of the numerous and diverse experiences with CHWs is their role in both improving access to healthcare of the most vulnerable populations and involving community members in this role (Walt 1990). Equally, the use of CHWs is recognized as an important strategy for health systems' development (Haines et al. 2007; Lehmann and Sanders 2007).

One of the most inspiring early experiences of CHWs was that of barefoot doctors, introduced as a national policy in China in 1968. This and other community-based experiences that were being developed around the world attracted the attention of the World Health Organization (Brown et al. 2006). Experiences such as that of the Chimaltenango development project in Guatemala, the comprehensive rural health project in Jamkhed, India, the community development approach to raising health standards in Solo, Central Java, Indonesia, among others, were documented by the WHO as examples in the global effort to strengthen health systems and ensure positive health outcomes for the rural majority (Newell 1975). These experiences contributed to the adoption of a primary healthcare (PHC) perspective that included CHWs as a core component.

In 1978, the outcome document of the International Conference on Primary Health Care in Alma-Ata, the Alma-Ata Declaration, highlighted the role of a properly trained CHW in responding to community health needs (WHO 1978). In 1989, the WHO defined CHWs as follows:

CHW's should be members of the community where they work, should be selected by the communities; should be answerable to the communities for their activities; should be supported by the health system but not necessarily as a part of its organisation; and have a shorter training than professional workers. (WHO Study Group 1989)

**Image B7.1** CHW: lackey or liberator? CHWs as social mobilizers (Indranil Mukhopadhyay)

The 1980s saw great interest and investment in CHWs but this declined in the 1990s as national programmes often experienced difficulties that had been less visible in NGO-driven initiatives and a few selected countries. Changes in priorities and funding availability were major factors, but the collapse was aggravated by conceptual and implementation problems of several large programmes, such as 'unrealistic expectations, poor initial planning, problems of sustainability, and the difficulties of maintaining quality' (Gilson et al. 1989).

The demands of the HIV/AIDS pandemic, especially in sub-Saharan Africa, and the crisis in human resources for health (see Chapter B9) have contributed to the revival of CHW programmes, which are currently being implemented in many low- and middle-income countries (LMICs). The initial conceptualization of CHWs took place in the context of the then dominant 'basic needs' approach to development, and of struggles of communities for political power and transformative change. Examples include Village Health Workers in Tanzania and Zimbabwe (in the wake of the decolonization struggle in Zimbabwe and the Ujamaa movement in Tanzania), which both focused on self-reliance, rural development and the eradication of poverty and societal inequities.

These contexts fuelled a vigorous debate regarding the potential dual role of CHWs: provision of basic healthcare (preventive and curative) to communities, and their social mobilizing role. This dichotomy was encapsulated in David Werner's seminal paper that posed the CHW as lackey (of the health system) or liberator (of the community's potential) (Werner 1981). The idea that community health workers can catalyse the active involvement of community members in transforming the circumstances in which they live, and that members of the community can themselves be transformed in this process, was a key element in conceiving community health workers as transformative agents. The early literature emphasized the role of the CHWs as not only (and possibly not even primarily) a healthcare provider, but also as an advocate for the community and an agent of social change.

However, more recent experiences, initially in HIV programmes, but now

**Image B7.2** CHW: lackey or liberator? CHWs as extensions of health services (Indranil Mukhopadhyay)

generalized to many national initiatives, emphasize the healthcare provision activities of CHWs, characterizing the process that defines their role as one of 'task shifting'. Task shifting is the name now given to a process of delegation whereby tasks are moved, where appropriate, to less specialized health workers. This implies that CHWs act solely as extensions of health services, with a restricted set of tasks delegated by 'superior' health workers.

This concentration on service 'delivery' has focused attention on several important technical aspects and the need for integration of community-level healthcare with the health system. Key technical factors that have received attention are adequate and appropriate training, supportive supervision and professional development opportunities. Past experience has spurred experimentation with different forms of financing and new communication technologies have spawned a number of interesting initiatives that use mobile phone technology (see Chapter B10) in support for and monitoring of CHW performance.

However, key questions remain for government CHW programmes, including the issue of their dual accountability (to the community and to the health system), and the accompanying conundrum of ensuring their secure employment and safe working conditions. Through four case studies, from four parts of the world, we discuss some of the issues outlined above in current programmes and conclude with reflections for the reconceptualization of the 'community health worker' in the current context.

### *Programa de Agentes Comunitários de Saúde* in Brazil

The CHW programme in Brazil is rooted in a comprehensive PHC strategy (Lehmann and Sanders 2007; WHO 2008; Bhutta et al. 2010). The Brazilian Community Health Worker Programme (*Programa de Agentes Comunitários de Saúde*, PACS) was created in 1991 by the Brazilian Ministry of Health. It was motivated by the positive results achieved in an earlier state-wide programme, involving 'community health agents', in the north-eastern state of Ceará. The Ceará programme was introduced after the drought of 1987. The programme was designed to address a broad range of health-related functions, such as prenatal care, vaccinations, health screening, breastfeeding promotion and oral rehydration (McGuire 2001).

In 1994, the Family Health Programme (PSF) was established and is the core component of Brazil's primary healthcare initiative. CHWs under the PACS became part of a health team created by the PSF, comprising at least a physician and a nurse, as well as nurse technicians and dentists. The team is responsible for the primary care of the population living in a geographically defined area. This ensures that CHWs are not working in an isolated fashion, but are supported by a health team, adequately remunerated and formally part of the health system.

A Unified Health System (*Sistema Único de Saúde*, SUS) was established in Brazil in 1990 (see Chapter B4). The inclusion of the PACS in a national health system based on universality, equity and social participation enabled it to expand geographically and extend the reach of the activities of CHWs.

Currently, there are over 32,000 Family Health Teams and 248,000 CHWs working across Brazil, covering 121 million people (DAB 2012) (each CHW, thus, covers about 500–750 people). Each team works with up to twelve CHWs, who build and strengthen links between the health team and the community. CHWs monitor the health conditions in the community and monitor high-risk patients, contribute to preventive public health interventions, provide health education, and maintain records. CHWs must be residents of the area and should have at least primary school education.

CHWs in the Brazilian system are full-time salaried workers and since 2002 have been legally recognized as health professionals affiliated with the SUS. Thus, technically, the CHWs are not 'volunteers' supported by the community. However, issues of community engagement are addressed in the SUS through an extensive and decentralized system of health councils (with statutory powers in determining budgets and monitoring performance) that have strong community ownership and participation (Cornwall and Shankland 2008; see also Chapter B4). However, successful community engagement depends on both an institutionalized system and the level of mobilization of the community (Lehmann and Sanders 2007).

## South Africa: still seeking a clear role for CHWs

South Africa has a long history of CHWs, going back as far as the 1940s. During the 1980s, while South Africa was still under the system of apartheid, CHWs in many NGO programmes became agents of social change and played a role in the liberation struggle for democracy and social justice. After liberation in 1994, the new government introduced a health system that was professional-driven, in which CHWs did not have a significant role. The influence of international trends in the 1990s, which promoted 'vertical' disease control programmes (e.g. HIV/AIDS control programmes), contributed to CHWs being deployed as 'single-purpose' workers. The concept of CHWs, thus, became far removed from the earlier concept of CHWs as community mobilizers and agents of change (Van Ginneken et al. 2010).

In an apparent policy shift, a Community Health Workers Policy Framework was adopted in 2004 (NDoH 2004). Unfortunately, the 2004 framework continued to promote fragmented vertical programmes, in lieu of comprehensive community health initiatives (Van Ginneken et al. 2010). As dictated by the policy, civil society organizations employ and coordinate 'community care givers' (CCGs), who could be 'multi-purpose' or 'single-purpose' workers. As a bulk of the CHWs focus on care (e.g. TB Direct Observed Treatment workers, HIV adherence counsellors, home-based care givers, etc.), they are referred to as 'community care givers'. In 2009, over 1,600 NGOs had a contractual relationship with the government under this programme, which accounted for around 65,000 CCGs, mainly involved in HIV/TB-related work (Lloyd et al. 2010).

CCGs, mainly women from poor communities, were often paid very low stipends – ranging from ZAR 500 (less than US$50) to ZAR 2,500 (more than US$200) per month. Many organizations employing CCGs complained of irregular and inadequate payments, while the poor remuneration that CCGs received had serious impacts on health service delivery. The programme lacks coherence because a number of organizations act as implementing agencies. While statutory structures exist for community participation (clinic committees, etc.), these are usually dysfunctional, owing in part to limited financial and technical support. As a consequence of the number of deficiencies in the programme, CCGs remain peripheral to the public health system (ibid.).

In 2009, the South African government proposed the implementation of a publicly funded National Health Insurance (NHI) scheme (ANC 2009). The NHI proposes the establishment of at least one PHC outreach team in each municipal ward. These teams are to be composed of professional nurses and environmental health and health promotion practitioners as well as CHWs, and the main function of these teams will be to promote good health; CHWs are expected to play a crucial role at the community level (Matsoso and Fryatt 2013). However, CHWs are not allowed to undertake any significant curative role, unlike in an increasing number of African countries, where CHWs now manage cases of childhood diarrhoea, pneumonia and malaria. In addition, the ratio of CHWs to population of approximately 1:1500 is less than half that of Brazil and a fraction of that in countries such as Rwanda and Thailand. Sufficient numbers of health workers and professionals, and an appropriate skills mix of personnel, remain a key challenge for the implementation of a NHI scheme that will improve healthcare for all in South Africa (Lloyd et al. 2010).

### India's 'ASHA' programme

In 2005, the government of India's Ministry of Health and Family Welfare (MoHFW) launched the National Rural Health Mission (NRHM) as a flagship health programme, with the aim of improving healthcare delivery in rural areas. Under this, new mechanisms for healthcare delivery were proposed, including a large-scale community health worker component – namely, the Accredited Social Health Activist (ASHA) Scheme.[1] In 2013, there were more than 860,000 ASHAs active in the country (MoHFW 2013), each covering up to 1,000 people in the eighteen high-focus states envisaged by the scheme (NHSRC 2011).

ASHAs are envisaged as health activists from and based in their community. Guidelines for the scheme mandate involvement of the community in the selection of ASHAs (MoHFW 2005). Evaluations of the scheme indicate that in states where these guidelines were followed, ASHAs performed better in carrying out their defined tasks (NHSRC 2011).

**Image B7.3** Indian CHWs (ASHA workers) at a convention for secure employment conditions, in Ranchi, India (Amit Sengupta)

ASHAs are required to facilitate access to health services, mobilize communities to realize healthcare access, entitlements and rights, provide community-level care for priority health conditions, make referrals and accompany people to health facilities when needed (MoHFW 2005). Experience with the scheme, as regards performance, is varied. An evaluation of the ASHA programme found that: (a) the role of ASHAs as facilitators in linking community members to public health services has successfully developed; (b) their role as a service provider is developing; and (c) their role as community mobilizers and activists is still very limited (NHSRC 2011).

The ASHA programme's design incorporates several key elements of the 'Mitanin programme', a decade-old initiative to provide health support at the village level through community health volunteers in the newly created Indian state of Chhattisgarh.[2] The genesis of the Mitanin programme was marked by collaboration between the state government and civil society organizations, based on the civil society proposition of promoting community action in health mainly through the activity of a village health worker, belonging to and selected by the local population (PHFI 2012). The ASHA scheme, however, does not incorporate a similar level of engagement with civil society groups and community-based organizations, and poor community participation and ownership have been a major shortcoming of the ASHA programme.

Except in a couple of states, the ASHAs have no fixed salary, but receive performance-based incentives for activities related to priority health programmes (such as institutional deliveries, Pulse Polio Day, immunization days, etc.). A large majority of ASHAs have demanded a regular salary, status and corresponding employee rights (Bajpai and Dholakia 2011). The government has continued to resist demands that ASHAs be treated as regular workers, on the ground that this would negatively impact on the community. However, as the responsibility of disbursement of incentives is given to the healthcare system, ASHAs are generally perceived anyway as part of the healthcare system, and not as community representatives (ibid.). As most ASHAs are from indigent backgrounds and are dependent on the programme for their livelihood, their actions centre on activities with monetary incentives rather than the critical activities without allocated incentives, such as community mobilization (Joshi and George 2012).

Other key issues have been those of training, monitoring and supervision, and institutional support. The MoHFW has developed a seven-round training plan for ASHAs, which includes a twenty-three-day induction training, added to which is skill training for home-based newborn care of similar length, with dedicated training personnel and structures. However, states are ultimately responsible for implementing and revising the training curriculum. Though training is undertaken in all states, rates of training completion are uneven across states. Tellingly, activism and leadership were missing in the training until the fifth ASHA training module was introduced (NHSRC 2011).

The annual allocation for the ASHA programme in 2013 was close to INR 20,000 (around US$330) per ASHA per annum (MoHFW 2013). While this allocation is seen as inadequate, the actual spending by the states has been found to be even lower (NHSRC 2011). Capacity and motivation of ASHA workers are uneven and low in many areas (Bajpai and Dholakia 2011; Joshi and George 2012), indicative of inadequate support provided through training and continuing education.

Finally, while supervision and constant mentoring support have been identified as critical components of the ASHA programme, there are major gaps in these areas (NHSRC 2011; Bajpai and Dholakia 2011). Further, poor institutional support and the rigid hierarchical structure of the health system continue to be challenges (Scott and Shanker 2010).

However, while ASHAs were meant to be the first contact with the health sector, in practice they have become the only contact with the health system for many poor people in difficult areas of India, as a result of the inadequate public health infrastructure, poor outreach of health systems and higher costs to access the next levels of public or private healthcare facilities. This underscores the importance of ensuring overall development of the entire health system, to optimize the potential of CHW programmes.

### *Behvarz* in Iran: linchpin of primary healthcare

The Iranian healthcare delivery system expanded quickly after the Iranian Revolution in 1979. The ensuing reforms aimed at ensuring the right of all citizens to enjoy the highest attainable level of health and access to healthcare (Article 29 of the Constitution of the Islamic Republic of Iran) (IHRDC 1979). In practice, this resulted in a strong focus on a public healthcare system financed from the public budget and delivered through a strong public primary-care delivery system.[3]

A particular feature of the healthcare reforms was the introduction of a national CHW programme, based on pilot projects that had begun decades earlier (Amini et al. 1983; Ronaghy et al. 1983). Iranian CHWs, called *behvarz* – derived from *beh* (good) and *varz* (skill) in the Farsi language – are permanent employees and they receive specialized training on the health needs of rural populations. Primary-care facilities in rural areas are called 'health houses', and the *behvarz* function from these facilities. Each health house is designed to cover a population of about 1,500. There are now over 17,000 health houses in Iran, covering most of Iran's 65,000 villages, with almost 31,000 *behvarz* working in these facilities. All health houses have at least one female *behvarz* and almost two-thirds of the *behvarz* are female (each health house has at least one female *behvarz*) (Javanparast, Heidari and Baum 2011). Today, in Iran, almost all rural people have easy access to basic healthcare via a trained and community-friendly *behvarz*.

The responsibility of recruiting the *behvarz* lies with a committee consisting of representatives of the *behvarz* training centre and local rural councils. A *behvarz* should preferably be a native of the village where the health house is situated. The *behvarz* training centres (BTCs) provide pre-service as well as in-service training. *Behvarz* need to have completed the secondary level of schooling, and they undergo a two-year training course (including clinical placement in rural areas during training). The content of training is reviewed regularly and adjusted according to changing patterns of illness and population needs (ibid.). The training covers a broad range of topics from healthcare services to communication skills and social determinants of health (Javanparast et al. 2012).

The inclusion of topics on social determinants of health, inter-sectoral collaboration and community engagement in the curriculum and job profile of the *behvarz* demonstrates a welcome move towards a comprehensive approach to primary healthcare. However, given that the *behvarz* are engaged in multiple tasks aimed at providing basic healthcare, they have little time to adequately serve as agents for community development and change. The workload of the *behvarz* (which has increased over time) needs further review. Further, the amount of time the *behvarz* spend in meeting the 'cultural expectations' of local communities is not sufficiently appreciated (Javanparast, Baum and Sanders 2011).

Studies indicate significant improvements in a range of health indicators in Iran (Movahedi et al. 2008; Mehryar et al. 2005). Dramatic improvements in some indicators such as infant, maternal and neonatal mortality rate, population growth, immunization and child malnutrition have been attributed (at least in part) to the performance of the *behvarz* (Asadi-Lari et al. 2004).

**Conclusion**

The case studies range from well-established programmes integrated into robust and well-resourced health systems (Brazil and Iran) to more recent initiatives with several weaknesses (South Africa and India). CHWs in Brazil and Iran are salaried employees of the health services, while in India they are paid for performance, which appears to distort their practice in favour of certain 'incentivized' activities. South Africa has a 'mixed' system, with CCGs paid stipends by NGOs and newer government-employed CHWs receiving salaries, resulting in significant unhappiness on the part of CCGs. Community participation is institutionalized in both Brazil and Iran, although its extent and depth are unclear and likely to be variable in different settings, while in India and South Africa community participation is weak, reflecting not only the relative newness of these initiatives, but also the genesis of the former programmes during periods of widespread political and social mobilization in these countries.

These programmes do, however, demonstrate a number of commonalities: they all exhibit a relatively weak focus on and arrangements for inter-sectoral

**Image B7.4** CHW delegates at a People's Health Assembly, 2012 (Louis Reynolds)

action on social and environmental determinants of health. Within the perspective of comprehensive PHC, national health systems should bring healthcare as close as possible to where people live and work. CHWs constitute the first and most important element of this process. However, CHWs are much more than 'task-shifting' agents, i.e. cheaper providers of primary-level care directly located in the community. As they are themselves members of the community, they have the potential to bridge the perspective of the health team and that of the community. In doing so, they can contribute to shaping healthcare to the expectations and reality of the community the health team serves.

In addition, in order for the CHW to claim a place in the community, the relationship between the CHW and the community has to be a two-way process. The community should, ideally, be involved in the selection of CHWs, and in decisions on what they are taught and the tasks they are given, and CHWs should be accountable to the community, which guides their work.

The role of a CHW has to be understood to go beyond basic healthcare, or essential healthcare, and extend to what can be described as community development (Lehmann and Sanders 2007). By community development, we understand a process by which social conditions improve and good conditions are available for and accessible to all community members (ibid.). In this conception, the CHW's role is to contribute to a just distribution of health resources and, ultimately, power. The narrowing of their role in currently dominant health discourse to that of agents to whom tasks should be shifted reflects a broader depoliticization of health (and development) policy, one consonant with the hegemonic paradigm which sees healthcare as a commodity to be 'delivered' as cost-efficiently as possible. This emphasis, which is the core feature of a technocratic and 'selective' PHC, neglects the important 'demand' side of an organized population and its potential to serve both as an active contributor to health service coverage and quality, and also as a key factor in securing government responsiveness in addressing the social determinants of health.

In summary, then, community health workers' role is to:

1 Ensure improved coverage of first-contact care. This entails providing essential healthcare, including basic treatment of acute conditions, as well as facilitating referral to primary-level facilities (clinics and health centres), and receiving back referrals for continuing care.
2 Take action on all dimensions of health comprehensively, including addressing the broader social and environmental determinants through advocacy and social mobilization.
3 Engage communities and their structures in dialogue and action concerning their health situation and its causes, including issues of social, economic and political inequity.

Clearly, the capacity of CHWs to undertake these related actions will depend both on such key technical factors as their training, support and working conditions and also, fundamentally, on the local and national political context – in short, the extent to which participatory democracy operates and power is shared.

## Notes

1 The term 'ASHA' in Hindi translates to 'hope' in English.

2 See www.shsrc.org/mitanin-programme. htm.

3 The private health sector, through private hospitals and clinics, mainly focuses on secondary and tertiary care and on urban areas.

## References

Amini, F., M. Barzgar, A. Khosroshahi et al. (1983) *An Iranian Experience in Primary Health Care: The West Azerbaijan Project*, New York: Oxford University Press.

ANC (African National Congress) (2009) *National Health Insurance Policy Proposal*, Pretoria, 22 June.

Asadi-Lari, M., A. A. Sayyari, M. E. Akbari et al. (2004) 'Public health improvement in Iran – lessons from the last 20 years', *Public Health*, 118(6): 395–402.

Bajpai, N. and R. H. Dholakia (2011) 'Improving the performance of accredited social health activists in India', Working Paper no. 1, May.

Bhutta, Z., Z. S. Lassi, J. Pariyo et al. (2010) *Global Experience of Community Health Workers for Delivery of Health Related Millennium Development Goals: A Systematic Review, Country Case Studies, and Recommendations for Integration into National Health Systems*, Geneva: World Health Organization, Global Health Workforce Alliance.

Brown, T. M., M. Cueto and E. Fee (2006) 'The World Health Organization and the transition from "international" to "global" public health', *American Journal of Public Health*, 96(1): 62–72.

Cornwall, A. and A. Shankland (2008) 'Engaging citizens: lessons from building Brazil's national health system', *Social Science & Medicine*, 66, 11 March, pp. 2173–84.

DAB (Departamento de Atenção Básica) (2012) 'Atenção básica e a Saúde da Família: os números', Saúde da Familia, dab.saude. gov.br/abnumeros.php#numeros, accessed 26 April 2013.

Gilson, L., G. Walt, K. Heggenhougen et al. (1989) 'National community health worker

programs: how can they be strengthened?',
*Journal of Public Health Policy*, 10(4): 518–32.

Haines, A., D. Sanders, U. Lehmann et al.
(2007) 'Achieving child survival goals:
potential contribution of community health
workers', *The Lancet*, 369(9579): 2121–31.

IHRDC (Iran Human Rights Documentation
Centre) (1979) *Constitution of the Islamic
Republic of Iran*, Tehran.

Javanparast, S., F. Baum and D. Sanders (2011)
'Community health workers' perspectives
on their contribution to rural health and
well-being in Iran', *American Journal of
Public Health*, 101(12): 2287–92.

Javanparast, S., G. Heidari and F. Baum (2011)
'Contribution of community health workers
to the implementation of comprehensive
primary health care in rural settings, Iran',
Teasdale-Corti Global Health Research
Partnership Program, April, www.global
healthequity.ca/electronic%20library/
Iran%20Final%20Project%20Report.pdf,
accessed 25 April 2014.

Javanparast, S., F. Baum, R. Labonte et al.
(2012) 'The experience of community health
workers training in Iran: a qualitative
study', *BMC Health Services Research*, www.
biomedcentral.com/1427-6963/12/291,
accessed 25 April 2014.

Joshi, S. R. and M. George (2012) 'Healthcare
through community participation: role
of ASHAs', *Economic and Political Weekly*,
47(10): 70–6.

Lavor, A. C. H., M. C. Lavor and I. C. Lavor
(2004) 'Agente comunitário de saúde: um
novo profissional para novas necessidades
de saúde', *Sanare*, 5(1): 121–8.

Lehmann, U. and D. Sanders (2007) *Community
Health Workers: What do we know about
them?*, Geneva: Department of Human
Resources for Health, World Health Organization, January.

Lloyd, B., D. Sanders and U. Lehmann (2010)
'Human resource requirement for national
health insurance', *South African Health
Review*, ch. 17, Durban: Health Systems
Trust, www.hst.org.za/sites/default/files/
sahr10_17.pdf, accessed 26 April 2014.

Matsoso, M. P. and R. Fryatt (2013) 'NHI 1st
eighteen months', *South African Health
Review*, ch. 2, Durban: Health Systems
Trust, www.hst.org.za/sites/default/
files/Chapter2_National%20Health%20

Insurance-The%20first%2018%20months.
pdf, accessed 26 April 2014.

McGuire, J. W. (2001) 'Democracy, social policy,
and mortality decline in Brazil', Department
of Government Wesleyan University, Paper
prepared for delivery at the 23rd International Congress of the Latin American
Studies Association, Washington, DC,
6–8 September.

Mehryar, A. H., A. Aghajanian, S. Ahmad-Nia
et al. (2005) 'Primary health care system,
narrowing of rural–urban gap in health
indicators, and rural poverty reduction: the
experience of Iran', XXV General Population
Conference of the International Union for
the Scientific Study of Population, Tours,
France, 18–23 July, iussp2005.princeton.
edu/papers/50790, accessed 25 April 2014.

MoHFW (Ministry of Health and Family Welfare) (2005) *Guidelines on Accredited Social
Health Activists (ASHA)*, New Delhi.

— (2013) *2011–2013: Update(s) on the ASHA
Programme*, New Delhi.

Movahedi, M., B. Hajarizadh, A. Rahimi et al.
(2008) 'Trend and geographical inequality
pattern of main health indicators in rural
population of Iran', *Hakim Research Journal*,
10: 1–10.

NDoH (National Department of Health) (2004)
*Community Health Workers Policy Frame-
work*, Pretoria.

Newell, K. (1975) *Health by the People*, Geneva:
World Health Organization.

NHSRC (National Health Systems Resource
Centre) (2011) *Asha which way forward …?:
Evaluation of ASHA Programme*, New Delhi.

PHFI (Public Health Foundation of India) (2012)
*Understanding 'Scaling-Up' of Community
Action in Health: A Pilot Realist Exploration
in Chhattisgarh State, India*, New Delhi.

Ronaghy, H. A., J. Mehrabanpour, B. Zeighami
et al. (1983) 'The middle level auxiliary
health worker school: the Behdar project',
*Journal of Tropical Pediatrics*, 29(5): 260–4.

Scott, K. and S. Shanker (2010) 'Tying their
hands?: institutional obstacles to the success of the ASHA community health worker
programme in rural north India', *AIDS Care*,
22(suppl. 2): 1606–12.

Van Ginneken, A., S. Lewin and V. Berridge
(2010) 'The emergence of community
health worker programs in the late apartheid era in South Africa: an historical

analysis', *Social Science & Medicine*, 71(6): 1110–18.

Walt, G. (1990) *Community Health Workers in National Programmes: Just another pair of hands?*, Milton Keynes: Open University Press.

Werner, D. (1981) 'The village health worker: lackey or liberator?', *World Health Forum*, 2(1): 46–68, whqlibdoc.who.int/whf/1981/vol2-no1/WHF_1981_2(1)_(p46-68).pdf, accessed 26 April 2014.

WHO (World Health Organization) (1978) *Primary Helath Care: Report of the International Conference on Primary Health Care, Alma Ata, USSR, 6–12 September 1978*, Geneva: World Health Organization, United Nations Children's Fund, whqlibdoc.who.int/publications/9241800011.pdf, accessed 26 April 2014.

— (2008) *Primary Health Care Now More Than Ever: The World Health Report*, Geneva.

WHO Study Group (WHO Study Group on Community Health Workers) (1989) *Strengthening the Performance of Community Health Workers in Primary Health Care: Report of a WHO Study Group*, World Health Organization, apps.who.int/iris/ handle/10665/39568, accessed 24 April 2014.

# B8 | THE CRISIS OF MATERNAL AND REPRODUCTIVE HEALTH

Motherhood is unsafe for many women in the world, especially those in low- and middle-income countries (LMICs). In this chapter we look at the different factors which contribute to this continuing human tragedy, with a particular focus on Africa (which has the highest rates of maternal mortality in the world).

Of the Millennium Development Goals, MDG 5 aimed at reducing maternal mortality by 75 per cent between 1990 and 2015 (United Nations 2003). In 2007, a part (b) was added to MDG 5: universal coverage of reproductive health. This addition was an important gain for women's health since it challenged the notion of pregnancy only being linked to motherhood and instead embraced the goal of reproductive choice for women. Universal access to reproductive and sexual health includes access to effective contraception, safe abortion, and treatment of sexually transmitted infections, and incorporates a focus on adolescents and adolescent-related issues around sexuality. The paradigm shift to viewing contraceptive provision as part of women's freedom of choice and of exercising control over their own fertility, from embracing the population control ideology of the 1960s, was another important gain that needs to be closely guarded. This goal was accepted at the International Conference on Population and Development (ICPD) in Cairo in 1994 (UNFPA 1995).

Progress in achieving the MDG 5 goal has been extremely uneven – a progress report in 2005 identified sixty-eight priority countries that were farthest from meeting their MDG target. They included all the countries of sub-Saharan Africa (SSA) (UNICEF 2008).

Women's sexual and reproductive rights, which include the right to survive childbirth and the right to be treated with dignity, are clearly enunciated in the technical guidance document produced by the UN Human Rights Council in July 2012 (United Nations 2012). Within this framework, accountability for maternal deaths extends beyond families and health workers to government institutions and leaders. Item no. 65 states: 'A rights-based approach requires simultaneous attention to immediate health interventions and the longer-term social transformation required to reduce maternal mortality and morbidity.'

## Global progress in reducing maternal mortality rates, 1990–2010

Maternal Mortality Rate (MMR) is the health indicator that shows the greatest disparity between rich and poor countries, with women in high-income

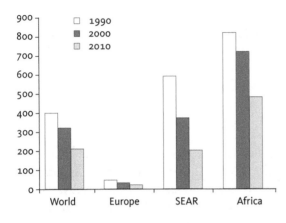

**B8.1** Progress in reducing maternal mortality, 1990–2010 (source: WHO, *World Health Statistics*, May 2012)

countries having a one in 3,800 lifetime chance of dying of a cause related to childbirth and women in low-income countries having a one in 39 chance (WHO et al. 2012). These disparities have not improved since 1987, though the absolute numbers of maternal deaths per year (global) have declined from 543,000 in 1990 to 287,000 in 2010. One third of all maternal deaths occur in two countries: India (56,000 deaths per year) and Nigeria (40,000) and the slowest reduction in maternal mortality is in SSA. Importantly, 10 per cent of maternal deaths in Africa were due to the aggravating effects of HIV.

Figure B8.1 presents trends regarding maternal deaths in different areas of the world.

However, within the African continent there are considerable differences between the countries of northern Africa, which have the lowest MMRs and show the greatest percentage decline (Table B8.1). Several countries in southern Africa showed an increase in MMR from 1990 onwards, and some countries in conflict-affected areas have MMRs in excess of 1,000.

TABLE B8.1 Progress in reducing maternal mortality rates in selected African countries, 1990–2010

|              | 1990  | 2000 | 2010 |
| ------------ | ----- | ---- | ---- |
| Egypt        | 230   | 100  | 66   |
| Malawi       | 1,100 | 840  | 460  |
| Mozambique   | 910   | 710  | 490  |
| Botswana     | 140   | 350  | 460  |
| Zimbabwe     | 450   | 640  | 570  |
| South Africa | 250   | 330  | 300  |

*Source*: WHO, *World Health Statistics*, May 2012

**Why pregnancy kills women in Africa**

The potential answers to why so many women die during childbirth in Africa (as well as in many LMICs) are examined in the following section.

---

**Box B8.1  Beyond the numbers**

Personal stories of bereaved families show us what it really means to have a mother who dies in childbirth, as in the following vignette from a rural village in southern Africa (Fawcus et al. 1996).

Ms Z, forty years old and into her fifth pregnancy, was told to deliver at a district hospital (50 kilometres away). Her labour pains started during the night. No transport was available and she was worried about leaving her children alone at home. She delivered at home but then suffered massive bleeding. Her eleven-year-old daughter went to alert neighbours to inform the hospital to send an ambulance. She returned home and found her mother dead in a pool of blood surrounded by other younger children.

Although this incident occurred twenty years ago, it still reflects the reality of many remote rural communities in the African continent.

---

*Lack of reproductive health choices* The unmet need for contraception is estimated to be experienced by one in four eligible women in SSA. This has roots in patriarchal values, cultural norms and high levels of infant mortality, resulting in the lack of provision of contraceptive services for many women in SSA (Singh and Darroch 2012). Other important indicators are access to safe abortion care and services that promote sexual health in women and adolescents.

It is estimated that if contraceptive needs were fully met for all women throughout the globe, it would reduce MMR by one third (Cleland et al. 2012). While it is a priority to expand and diversify the contraceptive choices offered to women, it is important that the debate around safe abortion and associated legislative changes is not dropped from the agenda. Post-abortion care programmes have improved safety, but have not tackled the related and relevant legislative issues. Unsafe abortions affect 6.2 million women annually (2008) and SSA accounted for 29 per cent of this total (Shah and Ahman 2009). The US 'gagging rule' under which USAID (US Agency for International Aid) set conditions that foreign aid to women's health programmes must not be linked to abortion care services limited the effectiveness of such programmes (Cohen 2011).

*Untreatable childbirth complications* The childbirth (obstetric) complications that result in maternal death can all be treated and some can be prevented. These include: excessive bleeding after birth, high blood pressure (eclampsia), infection after childbirth, unsafe abortion, medical disorders such as rheumatic heart disease, infections such as AIDS, TB and malaria.

**Image B8.1** Young mothers at a health centre in Malawi (David Sanders)

It is important to note that these conditions cause maternal deaths, but even more frequently result in severe morbidity rates among survivors, a notable example being women who survive sepsis and haemorrhage associated with prolonged labour but are left with urinary incontinence from a vesico-vaginal fistula (Wall 2006).

*Untreated medical conditions* The majority of medical conditions indirectly associated with maternal deaths can be treated. In most southern African countries, AIDS-related respiratory infections are the most common cause of maternal death, accounting for 40 per cent of all maternal deaths (Department of Health, Pretoria 2012).

One of the reasons that countries in SSA initially showed an increase in MMR after 1990, and why they are so far from meeting their target for achieving the MDG 5 goal, is the HIV epidemic.

*Inadequate functioning of health systems* In several African countries, local and national enquiries into maternal deaths show that many deaths could have been prevented if 'the health system had functioned better'. The South African Confidential Enquiry into Maternal Deaths (2008–10) showed that in 35 per cent of maternal deaths, there was an administrative problem such as lack of blood, lack of functioning operating theatres, or lack of transport that contributed to the death. Further, in 14–38 per cent of maternal deaths (depending on the level of care), there was inadequate care provided by the health worker (ibid.).

Problems with health personnel can be quantitative, relating to inadequate numbers and inequitable distribution between private and public sectors, between rural and urban areas, and between low-income women and higher-income women. The problems can also be qualitative, relating to the competence of health providers in terms of knowledge, skills and attitudes. They also include deficiencies in life-saving emergency obstetric skills among health providers.

*Poor access to and utilization of health facilities* It is estimated that in SSA only 69 per cent of pregnant women had at least one antenatal care visit, only 42 per cent gave birth with a skilled birth attendant present and only 45 per cent received postnatal care. In addition, the average Caesarean section (CS) rate was 3 per cent, which is well below the minimum of 10 per cent set by WHO, and required to save the lives of mothers and newborns (Adegboyega et al. 2006). Access to CS is a marker of access to emergency obstetric care, and when CS rates are too low, it reflects inadequate coverage. Many women and newborns in SSA die from conditions such as ruptured uterus and uterine infection because they did not have access to a CS for complicated labour. In addition, many women in SSA suffer from obstetric vesico-vaginal fistulae, which may cause lifelong disability owing to lack of access to timely CS for obstructed labour.

Coverage rates are usually presented as averages to hide inequities within and between population groups. They also give no indication of the quality of care, which, as suggested earlier, may be substandard, with considerable inequities between rural/urban and different socio-economic quintiles of the population (see Box B8.2, which throws up very similar issues).

What are the implications of overcrowded hospitals?

1 Many children continue to be delivered by midwives, but the official system ignores traditional birth attendants (TBAs).
2 Primary-care centres are not equipped to attend to deliveries that can be handled at this level with proper training and facilities.
3 Hospitals are overwhelmed by cases that could be handled by midwives at the primary level of care, thus making it difficult for them to attend women who truly need care at secondary or tertiary levels.
4 In hospitals, women are less likely to receive socially and culturally appropriate care.

In Chiapas, fewer than one third of women are indigenous. Yet, of women who die from maternity-related causes, half are indigenous (OMM 2014). In Chiapas, indigenous women's greater risk of death is evidence of how inequality and discrimination are a persistent cause of preventable deaths.

One of the World Health Organization's recommendations for attaining MDGs 4 and 5 is for all deliveries to be attended by skilled personnel (WHO 2004). However, places like Chiapas do not have enough professional midwives. Yet the response has not been a coordinated effort to improve the technical skills of existing TBAs. Instead midwives were explicitly banned from attending births.

**Box B8.2 Maternal death in Chiapas: an unfinished story**

One of the strategies Mexico adopted to reduce maternal mortality was to encourage institutional delivery (Secretaria de Salud 2007). In practice, this decision has resulted in growing overcrowding in hospitals. It has created a collateral problem: a decline in the quality of emergency obstetric care. The problem is more serious in regions with high levels of poverty and marginalization, such as the state of Chiapas.

A policy of dismantling obstetric services at the primary-care level and a tacit ban on traditional birth attendants (TBAs) delivering babies, in the interests of having deliveries attended by 'skilled personnel', has resulted in overcrowding of referral hospitals. The hospital in San Cristóbal de Las Casas is illustrative, receiving numerous obstetrical emergency referrals from the Altos de Chiapas region (home to a largely indigenous population, plagued by poverty and social exclusion). However, the hospital also receives deliveries that do not necessarily need this level of care.

In October 2013, Susana, a Tzotzil Indian woman aged twenty-six, from the community of Cruztón, died in the Women's Hospital in San Cristóbal de Las Casas, Chiapas. She was misdiagnosed, gave birth via

Several structural reasons contribute to poor access to care, including:

- Unavailable or inequitably distributed services.
- Natural disasters, wars, and conflicts.
- Serious transport problems.
- Unfriendly facilities: this includes unkind and harsh attitudes of health workers towards women in labour at a time when the latter are at their most vulnerable. This, together with some culturally insensitive practices such as a supine position for delivery, can be a deterrent to seeking care (Jewkes et al. 1998; Human Rights Watch 2011).
- Unaffordable services: this is a problem of *user fees*. The majority of African countries rely on user fees to fund part of their healthcare systems (Dzakpasu et al. 2014). This is because public healthcare systems are seriously underfunded. Some countries, such as Ghana, are trying to radically change the financing of their health system by introducing fee exemption for delivery care (Blanchet et al. 2012).

Several community-based studies have explored the reasons for poor access to care. When families in rural Masvingo province in Zimbabwe were asked why their relative had died in childbirth, the common responses were 'no money' and 'no transport' (Fawcus et al. 1996). In India, the verbal autopsy approach a delayed Caesarean section, and then her gall bladder was removed. Later, inadequate post-operative care led to her death (Sinembargo 2013).

Susana's family, with support from civil society organizations, filed a lawsuit, not only because of the medical errors, but also because both Susana and her family were subjected to mistreatment that demonstrated a lack of cultural sensitivity in a healthcare facility that primarily treats indigenous women. This lawsuit has spurred discussions on several important issues: the need for development of technical and physical capacity to attend normal births at the primary-care level; improvement of training of medical personnel and use of treatment protocols; the development of technical standards for intercultural healthcare; and installation of an intensive care unit in the hospital. However, at another level, this case should also lead to a review of public policies that are causing overcrowding in hospitals (largely to attend to normal deliveries), an increase in unnecessary CS (while needed CS are delayed, as in Susana's case), and the marginalization of TBAs in official health services.

In 2012, there were at least sixty-eight maternal deaths in Chiapas. Of these, 44 per cent were indigenous women, 71 per cent died in a public clinic or hospital, and another 10 per cent in a social security clinic or hospital (OMM 2014).

looks at delays in accessing care from the family's perspective and uses the symbolism of the Rashomon phenomenon (contradictory interpretations by different people of the same event) to show that there are many different ways of looking at a problem (Iyer et al. 2013). What health providers frequently label as 'delay in seeking care' would, from the community's perspective, have many very different explanations.

*Socio-economic determinants* Inequitable distribution of wealth, poverty and associated lack of transport are all linked with increasing MMR. Studies show that the poorest quintiles have the highest MMR (Ronsmans and Graham 2006). Poverty is associated with higher levels of MMR owing to food insecurity, lack of transport and lack of female educational or work opportunities.

*Gender discrimination and oppression* Owing to their gender, women lack power to control their own fertility, to engage with health services, and to exercise their right to good healthcare. Women are frequently disadvantaged owing to prevailing patriarchal values, cultural practices that are harmful, and sometimes religious prescripts. Female literacy is only 50 per cent in one third of the countries that are not on track to meet their MDG 5 target. Access to secondary education for girls is less than 20 per cent in some African countries

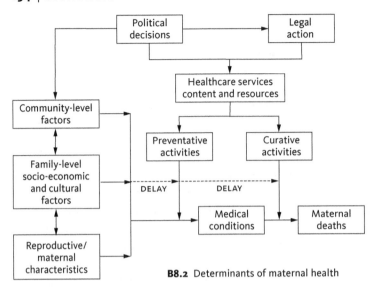

**B8.2** Determinants of maternal health

and less than the rate for boys (African Union 2013). Practices such as child marriage, which may be a cultural norm, are not in the interests of the health of young women. Patriarchal values and patriarchal systems mean that some women are not able to take decisions about their own health or the need to access care. Delays in seeking care occur because the woman is forced to await male permission to do so.

Further, violence experienced by women both in the domestic environment and in the context of armed civil conflict negatively affects their reproductive health outcomes as well as their utilization of health facilities (see Chapter C4). Female genital mutilation is a practice that is dangerous for maternal health and is an abuse of women's sexuality (Banks et al. 2006). Maternal death on its own can be viewed as a form of gender-based violence, since it is specific to women and dependent on their gender.

Women are dying because they lack the power to control their own fertility and because they lack access to safe contraception and abortion. Women are dying because maternity services are of poor quality, and there are multiple reasons for poor access to care. In addition, various socio-economic determinants contribute to poor reproductive health outcomes for women. Women are denied the right to safe childbirth because of failures of the health system, but these, in turn, may be determined by legislation, political decisions and cultural practices. The model above (Figure B8.2) illustrates all the determinants of maternal health (Fawcus et al. 1996).

### Interventions that could make a difference

The 'three delays' model is a useful framework around which to identify interventions (Thaddeus and Maine 1994).

- Delay in the decision to seek care
- Delay in reaching the place of care
- Delay in receiving appropriate-quality care after arriving at the health facility.

However, the model does have some limitations. The first two delays can be interpreted too narrowly as indicating poor knowledge and poor transport, whereas a much broader interpretation would look at all the socio-economic determinants that shape decision-making and influence access to care. In addition, the third delay does not distinguish the administrative aspects of the health system, such as lack of supplies, poor infrastructure and absence of medication, from the actions (or lack thereof) of the health workers themselves.

*Monitoring and analysis* Local and national processes for Maternal Death Surveillance and Response (MDSR) can promote accountability as well as monitoring of information (Commission on Information and Accountability for Women's and Children's Health 2011). The WHO is facilitating the development of these processes that encourage improved surveillance and measurement and perform a root-cause analysis of the causes and systems failures associated with the death (WHO et al. 2013). Verbal autopsy is a tool for identifying the sequence of events in the community by interviewing family and community members (WHO 2007). The 'r' in MDSR is the 'response' to the death at the national or local level. This includes identifying the remedial actions taken to prevent a similar recurrence of problems and their implementation. This aspect is the most important and challenging of any audit, but is often the weakest link in the audit loop.

### Conclusion

In spite of some recent progress, the levels of maternal mortality and morbidity remain unacceptably high and there are major inequities between and within countries. Universal access to reproductive and sexual health is the cornerstone of programmes aimed at improving both maternal and women's health, and there has been a renewed focus on contraceptive provision, but safe abortion and care programmes must not be marginalized.

The strengthening of health systems and improvement of human resources to provide equitable access to quality emergency obstetric care and to prevent maternal health complications are vital for reducing maternal mortality. However, this has political implications in terms of health financing and budgetary allocations, which are, in turn, determined by national and global economic policies and recessionary trends. The prevailing political systems entrench the perpetuation of poverty for the majority of women in Africa, resulting in both poor health outcomes and the lack of mechanisms that allow women to demand their right to health.

## References

Adegboyega, T., E. ba-Nguz, R. Bahl et al. (2006) *Opportunities for Africa's newborns: practical data, policy and programmatic support for newborn care in Africa, Cape Town*, Geneva: WHO, www.who.int/pmnch/media/publications/oanfullreport.pdf, accessed 21 March 2014.

African Union (2013) *Status report on maternal newborn and child health in Africa*, Addis Ababa: African Union.

Banks, E., O. Meirik, T. Farley, O. Akande, H. Bathija and M. Ali (2006) 'Female genital mutilation and obstetric outcome: WHO collaborative prospective study in six African countries', *The Lancet*, 367(9525): 1835–41.

Blanchet, N. J., G. Fink and I. Osei-Akoto (2012) 'The effect of Ghana's National Health Insurance Scheme on health care utilisation', *Ghana Medical Journal*, 46(2): 76–84.

Cleland, J., A. Conde-Agudelo, H. Peterson, J. Ross and A. Tsui (2012) 'Contraception and health', *The Lancet*, 380(9837): 149–56.

Cohen, S. A. (2011) 'U.S. overseas family planning program, perennial victim of abortion politics, is once again under siege', *Guttmacher Policy Review*, 14(4): 7–13, www.guttmacher.org/pubs/gpr/14/4/gpr140407.pdf, accessed 23 March 2014.

Commission on Information and Accountability for Women's and Children's Health (2011) *Keeping promises, measuring results*, Geneva: WHO, www.who.int/topics/millennium_development_goals/accountability_commission/Commission_Report_advance_copy.pdf, accessed 21 March 2014.

Department of Health, Pretoria (2012) *Saving mothers, 2008–2010: fifth report on the confidential enquiries into maternal deaths in South Africa*, doi: 10.1093/heapol/czs142.

Dzakpasu, S., T. Powell-Jackson and O. M. Campbell (2014) 'Impact of user fees on maternal health service utilization and related health outcomes: a systematic review', *Health Policy and Planning*, 29(2): 137–50.

Fawcus, S., M. Mbizvo, G. Lindmark and L. Nyström (1996) 'A community-based investigation of avoidable factors for maternal mortality in Zimbabwe', *Studies in Family Planning*, 27(6): 319–27.

Human Rights Watch (2011) '*Stop making excuses': accountability for maternal health care in South Africa*, New York: Human Rights Watch, www.hrw.org/sites/default/files/reports/sawrd0811webwcover.pdf, accessed 23 March 2014.

Iyer, A., G. Sen and A. Sreevathsa (2013) 'Deciphering Rashomon: an approach to verbal autopsies of maternal deaths', *Global Public Health*, 8(4): 389–404, doi: 10.1080/17441692.2013.772219.

Jewkes, R., N. Abrahams and Z. Mvo (1998) 'Why do nurses abuse patients? Reflections from South African obstetric services', *Social Science and Medicine*, 47(11): 1781–95.

OMM (Observatorio de Mortalidad Materna en México) (2014) *Numeralia 2012: Mortalidad Materna en México*, www.omm.org.mx/omm/images/stories/Documentos%20grandes/Numeralia%202012%20marzo19.pdf, accessed 26 April 2014.

Ronsmans, C. and W. J. Graham (2006) 'Maternal mortality: who, when, where, and why', *The Lancet*, 368(9542): 13–24.

Secretaria de Salud (2007) *Programa de Acción Específico 2007–2012: Promoción de la Salud: Una Nueva Cultura*, Mexico DF.

Shah, I. and E. Ahman (2009) 'Unsafe abortion: global and regional incidence, trends, consequences, and challenges', *Journal of Obstetrics and Gynaecology of Canada*, 31(12): 1149–58.

Sinembargo (2013) 'Ahora en Chiapas: una mujer indígena muere en labores de parto; familia y ONGs dicen que hubo negligencia médica', Sinembargo, 10 October, www.sinembargo.mx/10-10-2013/780786, accessed 26 April 2014.

Singh, S. and J. E. Darroch (2012) *Adding it up: costs and benefits of contraceptive services – estimates for 2012*, New York: Guttmacher Institute and UNFPA, www.guttmacher.org/pubs/AIU-2012-estimates.pdf, accessed 24 March 2014.

Thaddeus, S. and D. Maine (1994) 'Too far to walk: maternal mortality in context', *Social Science and Medicine*, 38(8): 1091–1110.

UNFPA (1995) *Report of the International Conference on Population and Development, Cairo, Egypt, September 1994*, A/CONF.171/13/Rev.1, www.unfpa.org/webdav/site/global/shared/documents/publications/2004/icpd_eng.pdf, accessed 27 April 2014.

UNICEF (2008) *Countdown to 2015: maternal, newborn and child survival: tracking progress in maternal, newborn and child survival,* New York: UNICEF, www.who.int/pmnch/ Countdownto2015FINALREPORT-apr7.pdf, accessed 21 March 2014.

United Nations (2003) *Millennium development indicators: world and regional groupings,* New York: United Nations, mdgs.un.org/ unsd/mdg/Host.aspx?Content=Data/ RegionalGroupings, accessed 23 March 2014.

— (2012) *United Nations General Assembly, Human Rights Council, Twentieth session, Agenda items 2 and 3, Annual report of the United Nations High Commissioner for Human Rights and reports of the Office of the High Commissioner and the Secretary-General,* A/HRC/21/22, 2 July, www2. ohchr.org/english/issues/women/docs/A. HRC.21.22_en.pdf, accessed 23 April 2014.

Wall, L. L. (2006) 'Obstetric vesicovaginal fistula as an international public-health problem', *The Lancet,* 368(9542): 1201–9.

WHO (World Health Organization) (2004) *Skilled Care for Every Birth,* Geneva: WHO.

— (2007) *Verbal autopsy standards: ascertaining and attributing causes of death,* Geneva: WHO, www.who.int/healthinfo/statistics/ verbal_autopsy_standards_intro.pdf?ua=1, accessed 21 March 2014.

WHO et al. (2013) *Maternal death surveillance and response: technical guidance: information for action to prevent maternal death,* Geneva: WHO, apps.who.int/iris/bitstream/ 10665/87340/1/9789241506083_eng. pdf?ua=1, accessed 21 March 2014.

WHO, UNICEF, UNFPA and World Bank (2012) *Trends in maternal mortality, 1990–2010,* Geneva: WHO, UNICEF, UNFPA and the World Bank, whqlibdoc.who.int/ publications/2012/9789241503631_eng.pdf, accessed 23 March 2014.

## B9 | THE GLOBAL HEALTH WORKFORCE CRISIS

In its analysis of the global health workforce published in 2004 (JLI 2004), the Joint Learning Initiative on Human Resources for Health and Development (JLI) called for mobilization and strengthening of human resources for health (HRH) as a key strategy to combat the health crises in the world's poorest countries and to build sustainable health systems everywhere.

The JLI report marked the beginning of a short period when, at a global level and in the WHO, the health workforce crisis enjoyed considerable attention. The *World Health Report 2006: Working together for health* (WHO 2006) and the first Global Forum on Human Resources for Health in 2008 (GHWA n.d. a) with its Kampala Declaration and Agenda for Global Action ('All people, everywhere, shall have access to a skilled, motivated and supported health worker within a robust health system') were milestones in this development. In 2006, the *World Health Report* also led to the launch of a 'decade of action' and the creation of the Global Health Workforce Alliance (GHWA).

In 2010, the World Health Assembly unanimously adopted the WHO Global Code of Practice on the International Recruitment of Health Personnel (WHO 2010). The Code is non-binding and can only suggest voluntary standards of behaviour. The WHO has recommended that the Code be incorporated into national policies and laws so that it can become legally binding. However, some states have suggested that a more formal system for monitoring and implementing the Code is necessary for it to become a meaningful response to global HRH recruitment. The adoption of the Code, unfortunately, marked the end of a few 'good years for HRH' in global health policy. The health workforce crisis should be looked at in a systemic way instead of placing it in its own thematic 'silo'. Unfortunately we are far from there. What we see is a desperate attempt to keep HRH on the global agenda by linking it to the current 'big' global issues – such as universal health coverage and the post-2015 agenda. But are these manoeuvres substantively addressing the problem?

### The 'big picture' challenges for human resources for health

Current global initiatives on 'overcoming the health workforce crisis', such as presented in the recent Third Global Forum (GHWA n.d. b) in Recife, Brazil, mainly address technical issues within the health sector, propose 'multi-stakeholder' alliances and renew calls for political engagement and financial commitment. But there are no easy 'quick-fix' solutions ahead. The health workforce crisis is part – and mirror – of a deeper health sector and health financing crisis as well as rapidly changing labour migration patterns related to the global fiscal crisis.

Since the 2006 *World Health Report* and the 2008 Kampala Forum and Declaration, there has not been much new analysis of the political and economic determinants of the health workforce crisis and, at least at a global level, sound proposals for addressing these determinants are still lacking.

However, the scarcity of health workers and the scarcity of funds to be invested in the production, equitable distribution and retention of health workers cannot simply be assumed as a given (Van de Pas 2013). In an interconnected world, globalization and scarcity are closely linked. The fiscal realities that frame available public financing for health systems and health workforce salaries are shaped by such issues as untaxed wealth, capital flight, wealth inequalities, etc. This fiscal crisis (including former 'ceilings' on expenditure of the health workforce public wage bill, imposed by the IMF in a number of African countries until 2007) has contributed to external migration, which, in turn, has caused significant savings in training costs to importing countries. For instance, in nine African source countries, the estimated government-subsidized cost of a doctor's education ranged from US$21,000 in Uganda to US$58,700 in South Africa. The overall estimated loss of returns from investment for all doctors currently working in the destination countries was US$2.17 billion, ranging from US$2.16 million for Malawi to US$1.41 billion for South Africa. The benefit to destination countries of recruiting trained doctors was largest for the United Kingdom (US$2.7 billion) and the United States (US$846 million) (Mills et al. 2011).

Ninety-six per cent of the additional 1.4 billion people in low- and middle-income countries in 2030 will live in urban areas and by 2050 one in three births will take place in Africa. Giving priority to and delivering equitable health services, responsive to population change, will create new dynamics. Both public and private services will have to respond to demand, but there is an inherent doubt about whether the health market, if left to its own commercial interests, will favour equitable access on the basis of need and universality (WHO and GHWA 2014).

By 2035, an additional 1.9 billion people will be seeking to access and obtain high-quality healthcare. Under this assumption, 107 countries would be affected by gaps by 2035: this would lead to a global deficit of about 12.9 million skilled health professionals. The two WHO regions where the absolute deficit would be highest are South-East Asia (5.0 million), representing 39 per cent of the global total, and the African region (4.3 million), representing 34 per cent of the global total (ibid.).

### Flawed analysis and proposals

The analysis provided by WHO and GHWA on future workforce strategies indicates an inherit ambivalence. On one hand we read: 'The costs of producing and retaining a workforce fit for purpose and fit to practice will influence the cost-effectiveness of health services. This is a recurrent cost, and investment in public-sector education is required to maintain the capacity, faculty and quality of training institutions. The education sector cannot be left entirely to market forces, as these can put the quality of public sector education at risk.' In the same analysis we can read that the HRH deficit (in Africa) is related to labour 'market' failure. 'The interaction of health workers as economic agents with institutional employers and patient consumers is an exciting and growing area of work related to results-based funding and incentive systems for performance' (ibid.).

The latter position is strongly promoted by the World Bank, which argues that we should better understand the health labour market forces in low- and middle-income countries (LMICs). It is argued that instead of looking at sup-ply factors, we should look more at demand-side factors, or the 'willingness to pay' on the part of government, private sector and international actors. The Bank further states:

A widely promoted solution for increasing the availability of human resources for health is to expand training and increase funding for public sector employ-ment. But this requires funds, largely from the public purse. Countries such as Ethiopia and Niger, whose macroeconomic conditions prevented them from implementing this approach, chose to invest in community-based health workers, who undergo shorter training and require less pay. In early experi-ences, these cadres have played a significant role in improving service coverage and health outcomes in underserved communities. Similarly, experiences in Mozambique and elsewhere show that mid-level cadres respond differently to health labour market conditions and are more easily retained in rural areas than physicians. (McPake et al. 2013)

From a human-rights-based approach, it would be relevant to learn from HRH strategies implemented in several LMICs, such as Brazil, Ecuador, Thailand and Sri Lanka. These examples tell us that the building of a public health workforce is a more sustainable path to a strong health system, rather than the commodification and privatization of a scarce common good, as the World Bank suggests.

The health worker crisis is now starting to affect Europe as well. In many European countries, austerity measures (including reduction of public spending and strict ceilings on wage bills for public sector employees – see Chapter A2) have led to a reduction in the public sector workforce. Employee wages, salaries and allowances account for 42.3 per cent of public spending on health and austerity measures have focused on wage cuts for health workers in many countries (Mladovsky et al. 2012). Austerity in Europe is also beginning to spur health workers' mobility and migration within the region (Wismar et al. 2011), and to negatively affect the availability of qualified health providers in countries worst affected by the fiscal crisis (Aiken et al. 2014). In Romania, for example, after wage cuts were imposed in 2011, more than two thousand doctors registered for international recognition of their credentials in order to be able to migrate and work in western Europe (Mans 2013).

The recent developments in Europe clearly illustrate the interdependence among health systems: in the context of the economic crisis in Europe, for example, countries have to compete to attract scarce health professionals. It is precisely this recognition – that the health systems of low- and middle-income countries (LMICs) are undermined by the recruitment of their health workers by high-income countries – which led to the adoption of the WHO Global Code of Practice on the International Recruitment of Health Personnel (Code) in 2010 (ibid.; WHO 2013).

### WHO's Global Code of Practice: fatally deficient

At the 2013 World Health Assembly, when Code implementation was reported for the first time, a WHO assistant director general admitted that progress was 'painfully slow' (Schwarz 2013). While the fact that progress in implementation has been slow is a matter of concern, it is important to underline that the Code is also fatally deficient in one very important aspect. The Code provides guidance on ethical recruitment, the rights of health workers and strengthening of health systems. But one obvious element is missing: that of financial compensation (HPA 2013).

During the elaboration of the Code in 2010 the language was diluted to make it acceptable to all WHO member states (including the powerful countries of the North which gain from health worker migration). As a consequence, the mention of compensation to source countries for the costs incurred in training migrant health workers was removed. It is time to repoliticize the discussion and much stronger instruments need to be developed to address countries' lost investment due to external migration. The feasibility of compensation, e.g. by repatriating taxes paid by 'imported' health workers to their countries of origin, should be raised again. Such measures need to be complemented by strategies that can make available significantly enhanced resources to fund health services in LMICs. Health systems are grossly underfunded in most LMICs, in part because of domestic policies, but also in large measure because of power imbalances at the global level and the imposition of neoliberal policies by global institutions such as the World Bank, the IMF and the WTO. Discussions on these aspects must be integrated in the public discourse on the health workforce crisis.

### Who is a health worker?

We now turn to a blind spot regarding the health workforce crisis. The *World Health Report 2006* accepts that data available on health worker numbers are generally limited to people engaged in paid activities. It further classifies two

**Image B9.1** A health worker examining a patient in the Philippines; a very large proportion of health workers in the Philippines migrate to Northern countries (Patricio Matute)

types of health workers: 'health service providers' and 'health management and support workers'. Thus, only medical doctors, nurses and midwives are counted as professional service providers. When WHO talks about shortage of health workers, it talks mainly about these professional categories.

Community health workers (CHWs) are, in many countries, a crucial element of a people-centred health system, but are not generally counted as part of the health workforce (see Chapter B7). Despite local successes, uptake by governments to have CHWs integrated in sustainable national programmes with proper remuneration and education has remained limited.

Proposed solutions such as the recent 'One million community health workers' campaign need to be carefully assessed (One Million n.d.). This initiative proposes the deployment of health workers equipped with high-tech point-of-care diagnostic tools, communicating with national supervisors via broadband access and smartphones, providing standardized care based on consistent supplies of life-saving medicines and easy-to-follow treatment protocols, and trained in short-term intensive courses. The obvious questions are:

- How will this be financed? And what are the plans for a sustainable integration of these CHWs in national health systems? How will exploitation of this 'cheap' workforce be prevented?
- What will the scope of work of these CHWs be? How will they be linked with the communities they are intended to serve?
- How will such CHWs function optimally without substantial strengthening of national health systems?

### Steps forward in mitigating the crisis

Norway and Ireland (AGHD 2013) – the two recent European winners of the Health Worker Migration Policy Council award – have nevertheless demonstrated that the Code can provide an anchor for a coherent health workforce policy. Both countries have implemented national measures to ascertain how many doctors and nurses need to be trained and in which specialities. In making these countries less dependent on foreign health personnel, these measures also ensure they will not exacerbate the global and regional brain drain. Alongside this audit and focus on education and training, these countries are also looking at how to retain their own health personnel, for example through education programmes and salary provisions. And if foreign health personnel are needed, they make agreements with the countries of origin regarding the duration of stay, employment conditions, training options and workers' return. Additionally, Norway and Ireland have both adopted foreign policies that aim to help low-income countries strengthen their own health systems, including measures and investments focused on health personnel.

Extending such policies to other importing countries is unlikely to occur without civil society pressure. In order to address the global health migration issue, new alliances are required: between social movements fighting for the right to health, global health advocates and health workers' organizations at all levels. In the HW4ALL project (HW4ALL n.d.), organizations from eight European countries have partnered to raise awareness about the WHO Code of Practice for the International Recruitment of Health Personnel. Efforts include translation of the WHO Code for practitioners and the facilitation of dialogue between the actors involved in training, recruiting, and retaining and deploying health workers.

## Scaling up transformative education

The health worker crisis clearly demands rapid scaling up and transformation of the education of health professionals in order to close the widening quantitative and qualitative deficit in health worker requirements. In the following section we briefly present three current proposals and initiatives and discuss their coherence, feasibility and sustainability.

*Lancet Commission report on health professionals for a new century* The Lancet Commission report published in 2010 highlighted the importance of a competency-based curriculum integrating education systems with health systems, at local, national, regional and global levels (Frenk et al. 2010). In this new model, 'populations', which previously may have been viewed as clients or consumers of a health system, are seen as fundamental stakeholders and contributors to the design of an integrated education and health system that addresses real needs in the workforce.

Although this report is welcome in drawing attention to the global need for reform of health professions education, unfortunately the report's analysis is quite narrow in conception.

The Commission's report starts with a set of global health challenges which (it argues) are not being addressed because of weaknesses in the global health workforce which (it argues) are due to inappropriate curricula in health professional education. The report calls for competency-based education (in part as a strategy for addressing the divisive effects of professional tribalism); inter-professional education (to promote teamwork); and international accreditation of health professional training (to promote quality). The report envisages conditional funding from large US philanthropies as the principal driver to promote reform globally, which risks entrenching rather than challenging inequity in global health.

The report, thus, treats health professional education without reference to the wider social forces which shape public health, healthcare and practitioner education. There is no reference to the global economic regime in explaining the contemporary health crisis, or to the impact of neoliberal policies on cutting public expenditure on healthcare and higher education and on driving universities as well as hospitals towards increased dependency on user fees. Indeed, the report welcomes private funding (student fees), despite the access barriers such fees impose. This implies an acceptance that public funding of excellent health professional training is not a prerequisite to resolving the crisis.

*Initiatives in the World Health Organization* At the request of its member states (World Health Assembly resolution WHA59.23), the World Health Organization has been developing, over the last years, evidence-based policy guidelines (WHO 2011) to assist countries, development partners and other stakeholders in efforts to expand the health workforce and improve the alignment between the education of health workers and population health needs. The guidelines were formally launched at the Third Global Forum in Recife, in 2013, but are currently not yet publicly available.

The 2013 World Health Assembly, in an ad hoc exercise led by Thailand and supported by many countries suffering from a health workforce crisis, passed a resolution (WHO 2013) on 'Transforming health workforce education in support of universal health coverage' (Resolution WHA66/23). The resolution, also referring to the WHO Global Code, urges WHO member states 'to further strengthen policies, strategies and plans as appropriate, through intersectoral policy dialogue among the relevant ministries that may include ministries of education, health and finance, in order to ensure that health workforce education and training contribute to achieving universal health coverage'.

While these initiatives are to be welcomed, it is unlikely that most member states of WHO will be able to implement such guidelines vigorously or at scale unless their fiscal constraints are addressed, and, for many of them, their continuing losses of health personnel through migration are stemmed, or they are compensated for this 'brain robbery' (Patel 2003). Indeed, while the expansion of medical school places in public sector institutions has stagnated in most African countries – with some exceptions such as Ethiopia – there has been a rapid growth of private medical schools in the past decade. The Sub-Saharan Medical School Study in 2009 found 168 medical schools of which thirty-three had been created in the previous decade. At that time approximately 26 per cent of medical schools in sub-Saharan Africa were private schools. The first private schools opened in the 1990s and their number keeps increasing, but reports suggest that several of them are of dubious quality.

*PEPFAR Medical and Nursing Education Partnership* In 2010 an initiative intended to achieve rapid scaling up of the African health workforce was launched by PEPFAR (PEPFAR n.d.). The Medical Education Partnership Initiative (MEPI) supports 'foreign institutions in Sub-Saharan African countries that receive funding from PEPFAR and its partners to develop or expand and enhance models of medical education'. These models are intended to support PEPFAR's goal of increasing the number of new healthcare workers by 140,000, strengthen medical education systems in the countries in which they exist, and build clinical and research capacity in Africa as part of a retention strategy for faculty of medical schools and clinical professors. The Nursing Education Partnership Initiative (NEPI) is an allied initiative, developed to strengthen the quality and capacity of nurses and midwives throughout Africa. NEPI intends to strengthen the quality and capacity of nursing and midwifery education institutions, increase the number of highly skilled nurses and midwives, and support innovative nursing retention strategies in African countries.

The MEPI partnership involves medical schools in twelve African countries and is coordinated by George Washington University in the USA with an African coordinating partner, ACHEST, based in Uganda. The respective financial allocations to African and US partner institutions are difficult to find, but there are suggestions that the US coordinating partner receives a disproportionate slice of total MEPI funding.

## Conclusion

The availability of a strong health workforce, supported by public funds, is a prerequisite for strong, universal and quality health systems. The current focus on UHC carries the potential threat of reducing the role of health workers to undertaking selective diagnosis and treatment, rather than addressing the health of people and communities in a comprehensive and integrated way, combining public health as well as individual clinical approaches. The concept of comprehensive primary healthcare, as enunciated in the Alma Ata declaration, envisages the latter. However, there is a growing imperative for health workers' role to be guided primarily by concerns of economic efficiency. This approach inevitably emphasizes treating diseases rather than promoting health and reduces the health worker to a mere production unit. We not only need many more health workers, we require professionals working towards a society oriented to greater equity in health and wellbeing.

# References

AGHD (Aspen Global Health and Development) (2012) 'Health worker migration global policy council announces 2012 innovation award winners', Aspen Institute, 24 May.

— (2013) 'The health worker migration policy council celebrates Ireland and Rwanda for their innovation and leadership', Aspen Institute, 13 November.

Aiken, L. H., D. M. Sloane, L. Bruyneel et al. (2014) 'Nurse staffing and education and hospital mortality in nine European countries: a retrospective observational study', *The Lancet*, 26 February.

Frenk, J., L. Chen, Z. A. Bhutta et al. (2010) 'Health professionals for a new century: transforming education to strengthen health systems in an interdependent world', *The Lancet*, 376(9756): 1923–58.

GHWA (Global Health Workforce Alliance) (n.d. a) 'First global forum on human resource for health', www.who.int/workforce alliance/forum/2008/en/, accessed 8 May 2014.

— (n.d. b) 'Third global forum on human resource for health', www.who.int/workforce alliance/forum/2013/en/, accessed 8 May 2014.

HPA (Health Poverty Action) (2013) 'The health worker crisis: Natalie Sharples blogs from the third global forum on human resources for health', 15 November.

HW4ALL (Health Workers 4 All) (n.d.) www.healthworkers4all.eu/eu/home/, accessed 8 May 2014.

JLI (Joint Learning Initiative) (2004) *Human Resources for Health: Overcoming the Crisis*, The President and Fellows of Harvard College, www.who.int/hrh/documents/JLi_hrh_report.pdf, accessed 8 May 2014.

Mans, L. (2013) 'Europe concerned about the mobility of health personnel', *Get Involved in Global Health*, 16 September.

McPake, B., A. Maeda, E. Correia Araújo et al. (2013) 'Why do health labour market forces matter?', *Bulletin of the World Health Organization*, 91(11): 841–6.

Mills, E. J., S. Kanters, A. Hagopian et al. (2011) 'The financial cost of doctors emigrating from sub-Saharan Africa: human capital analysis', *British Medical Journal*, 343(d7031).

Mladovsky, P., D. Srivastava, J. Cylus et al. (2012) *Health Policy Responses to the Financial Crisis in Europe*, Policy Summary 5, World Health Organization, www.euro.who.int/__data/assets/pdf_file/0009/170865/e96643.pdf, accessed 8 May 2014.

One Million (One Million Community Health Workers Campaign) (n.d.) 1millionhealthworkers.org/about-us/, accessed 8 May 2014.

Patel, V. (2003) 'Recruiting doctors from poor countries: the great brain robbery?', *British Medical Journal*, 327(7420): 926–8.

PEPFAR (US President's Emergency Plan for AIDS Relief) (n.d.) www.pepfar.gov/partnerships/initiatives/index.htm, accessed 8 May 2014.

Schwarz, T. (2013) 'WHO global code of practice – lost in translation?', *Get Involved in Global Health*, 12 June.

Van de Pas, R. (2013) 'Human resources for health – a bottleneck for primary health care?', *Get Involved in Global Health*.

WHO (World Health Organization) (2006) *The World Health Report 2006: Working Together for Health*, Geneva, www.who.int/whr/2006/whro6_en.pdf?ua=1, accessed 8 May 2014.

— (2010) *WHO Global Code of Practice on the International Recruitment of Health Personnel*, Resolution WHA63.16, May, www.who.int/hrh/migration/code/code_en.pdf?ua=1, accessed 8 May 2014.

— (2011) *Transformative Scale Up of Health Professional Education: An Effort to Increase the Numbers of Health Professionals and to Strengthen Their Impact on Population Health*, US President's Emergency Plan for AIDS Relief (PEPFAR), Geneva.

— (2013) *Transforming Health Workforce Education in Support of Universal Health Coverage*, Resolution WHA66.23, 27 May, apps.who.int/gb/ebwha/pdf_files/WHA66/A66_R23-en.pdf, accessed 8 May 2014.

WHO (World Health Organization) and GHWA (Global Health Workforce Alliance) (2014) *A Universal Truth: No Health without a Workforce*, Geneva.

Wismar, M., C. B. Maier, I. A. Glinos et al. (eds) (2011) *Health Professional Mobility and Health Systems: Evidence from 17 European Countries*, Observatory Study Series no. 23, European Observatory on Health Systems and Policies, WHO Regional Office for Europe, Copenhagen, www.euro.who.int/__data/assets/pdf_file/0017/152324/e95812.pdf, accessed 8 May 2014.

# B10 | THE POLITICS AND LANDSCAPE OF MEDICAL DEVICES IN A GLOBAL MARKET

The size of the medical device sector as a commercial enterprise is frequently underestimated, as is its importance to the contemporary practice of medicine. The innovation of medical device technologies in the healthcare system, as with pharmaceuticals, is a process in which a variety of social, economic and medical interests and visions meet. Government officials and healthcare policy-makers espouse a policy of modernization that promotes continual innovation in medical technology and practice. However, the pursuit of medical device innovation is often controversial, and modes of evaluation of the benefits and costs associated with new medical technologies are far more difficult than the standard approaches for testing and conducting clinical trials for pharmaceuticals.

Contemporary healthcare is characterized by the use of a multitude of medical devices, ranging from the bandage to the endoscope, from the thermometer to magnetic resonance imaging (MRI), from the portable blood pressure monitor to the condom, from the cancer screening test to the heart pacemaker, from the human cell and tissue therapies now termed 'regenerative' medicine to the diagnostic technologies of the much-heralded genomic medicine. These technologies are hugely different from each other as artefacts in their clinical modes of use, in their clinical significance, and in their impact on society.

Medical devices encompass therapeutic, diagnostic, screening, inert and powered technologies. The contemporary trends affecting the development of device technologies include the incorporation of information and telecommunications technologies (ITCs) – the increasing embedding of software into devices, and the increasing use of electronic communication between devices in use and 'servers' and their host organizations; miniaturization in general, especially that which enables 'point of care' tests and 'near patient' medicine and therapeutic intervention; and many developments associated with the advance of biomaterials and biotechnology. The latter include the development of 'combination products' in which elements of devices are combined with pharmaceutical or biological technologies, resulting in technological convergences called combination products (for example, 'companion diagnostics', in which a genetics-based diagnostic test is combined with a particular drug therapy, or a drug-delivery system using software-programmable infusion pumps).

The global market for medical devices includes a massive range of products. The fastest-growing sub-sectors include in-vitro diagnostics, orthopaedics and

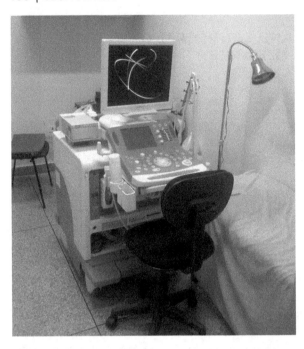

**Image B10.1** The size of
the medical device sector is
frequently underestimated
(Jose Leon Uzcátegui)

wound management, where there is a vast proliferation of different kinds of devices. Estimates of 10,000 device families and 400,000 different devices are not uncommon. The value of the global market was estimated at US$105 billion in 2001, but it has also been reported to be close to US$200 billion, about half the size of the global pharmaceutical market, and growing steadily (DTI 2005). The USA accounts for about 43 per cent of the total market, Europe for over 20 per cent, and the Asia-Pacific region for over 15 per cent. China's market is in the region of US$20 billion for medical devices, and India's in 2011 was estimated as worth US$3 billion.

The leading companies in the sector include enterprises such as Johnson & Johnson (specializes in the multi-product health sector), the 3M Group, Baxter International (specializes in devices related to the blood and circulatory system), Tyco International, GE Healthcare, Medtronic, Alcon, and specialists in other sectors such as the electronics company Siemens. The largest companies are highly specialized in their areas of focus. Medtronic is sometimes referred to as the world's leading medical-technology company. However, many companies in the sector are small and medium-sized enterprises (SMEs). For example, the UK sector has over two thousand companies, of which around 85 per cent are small firms. Roughly 75 per cent of medical device activity in the UK is in the supply of medical and surgical equipment, with diagnostics product suppliers accounting for most of the rest. China's main medical devices industry association reports some three thousand company organization members.

## Medical device innovation, safety and regulation

*Innovation* The structure of the medical technology industry contrasts with that of the pharmaceuticals industry in that the majority of technological innovation occurs in SME companies. Major device companies frequently acquire early-stage companies once a business model for their technologies has been stabilized. They improve the efficiency of producing the technology and use distribution networks for trading. Typically also, the large companies have a strategic aim of undertaking the iterative improvement of a given product through several product generations, thereby promoting a long-term contractual commitment from purchasers. Technological innovation is endemic, ranging from slight variants or modifications to existing devices to some breakthrough technologies. Some single-device types, heart pacemakers, for example, may have hundreds of different models available to the end-user.

*Regulation* The regulation of medical devices depends to some extent on the claims that manufacturers make about a device regarding its functionality and in particular its 'mode of action', which in some combination products is not always clear even from a scientific point of view. Compared to pharmaceutical regulation, medical device regulation is generally considered to be less onerous for manufacturers. Safety concerns are often less pronounced in device assessment at the point of application for entry to the market, because many devices have less extensive physiological effects than pharmaceuticals, and those that do (for example, implants) tend to have long-term physiological effects which cannot be assessed in short-term trials. This means that 'post-marketing surveillance' in the form of clinical studies, registers and incident-reporting systems ('vigilance') is incredibly important for devices. For medical devices and related technologies, the extent and nature of technical standardization achieved through specific regulatory regimes are crucial to understanding both the industrial economy of production and the system of public health protection for ensuring the safety, quality and efficacy of devices entering the healthcare system.

Across the globe, medical device regulation is patchy. The more developed regulatory regimes, expectedly, are in the USA and the EU. These are constituted in quite different ways, the US system being more centralized in its regulatory agency and highly prescriptive about the material composition and production of device technologies, and the EU system, established in the 1990s, relying on adherence by producers to 'essential requirements' defined by technical (ISO and other) standards, and policed by mandated commercial and technical organizations known as 'notified bodies'. The latter have been one of the main targets of the recent 'recast' of the European medical device laws (directives) that have been debated in the European Commission and Parliament during 2012/13, fuelled partly, although not initially, by the PIP breast implant scandal (BBC 2013; European Commission 2012). At the international level, a Global Harmonization Task Force (GHTF) bringing together the dominant regulators was recently replaced by the International Medical Device Regulatory Forum (IMDRF) in 2011 with similar goals, although excluding trade associations from representation.

Regulatory regimes are still at a relatively less advanced stage in LMICs. The China Food and Drug Administration (CFDA) has been developing regulations for some time, and in 2013 released a proposed regulatory framework for public comments. Conversely, while India has been debating the adoption of a formal regulatory framework for several years, it has so far only introduced a special category under the jurisdiction of the Drug Controller General. Brazil's system combines elements of the US and EU systems. Most established formal regulatory systems distinguish different classes of devices on a 'proportionate' system according to the health risk deemed to be associated with their use (HIV test equipment, for example, being in the highest class).

In line with World Health Assembly resolution WHA60.29, the WHO aims to ensure improved access, quality and use of safe and appropriate medical devices (WHO 2013). As part of this initiative, WHO is producing an expanding set of information based on the monitoring of levels of diffusion of devices across low- and middle-income countries (LMICs).

*Safety and regulatory enforcement* As with pharmaceuticals, the poor quality of devices is a commonly reported problem, along with alleged and sometimes proven corruption. As is the case in the medicines market, the problem of quality in the medical devices sector is far too often conflated with alleged counterfeiting. In 2010, the WHO reported that 8 per cent of the medical devices in circulation globally were potentially counterfeit (News Medical 2010). Regulatory authorities such as the UK's Medicines and Healthcare Products Regulatory Agency (MHRA) and the USA's Food and Drug Administration (FDA) are now actively engaging with this issue and global initiatives have begun to appear. The Australian Therapeutic Goods Administration reported in 2011 that contact lenses, condoms, blood glucose test strips and surgical mesh were subject to counterfeiting. The MHRA has acted in the matter of the selling of devices through eBay or other internet portals, and has identified, and confiscated, fake or non-safety-certificated devices such as dental equipment, including unsafe X-ray technology, and fake digital thermometers. The fact remains, however, that there is a paucity of reliable data on the quality of devices, particularly in LMICs, and conflation and confusion over the use of the terms spurious/falsely labelled/falsified/counterfeit (SFFC) that are preferred by WHO.

Another notable safety issue is that of the improper reuse of single-use devices. Historically, a majority of devices were intended for reuse because of the cleanable materials used (glass, ceramic, etc.), but as awareness of the infectiousness of diseases such as HIV and hepatitis increased, the policy has changed. The Western regulatory agencies now issue warning notices against this practice, and the EU's Medical Device Directives, for example, make a clear distinction between those intended and those not intended for reuse. The regulatory position varies nationally: in France, the practice is illegal; Germany and the UK have guidelines of different types in place. While there are supported regimes for reprocessing certain devices for reuse (cleaning, sterilizing, etc.), the unregulated use of this practice appears widespread. Surgical technologies are among those devices that are deemed single-use only, but these, too, are frequently reused in different parts of the world. For example, a survey in Brazil has reported that angiographic, diagnostic and therapeutic cardiac catheters were widely reused with limited protocol guidance in many Brazilian hospitals (Amarante et al. 2008).

The quality of medical devices in the global marketplace may also be regulated by agreements on mutual inspection regimes. Exporters of medical devices may be registered with the regulatory agency of the importing country, which may then inspect the producer's premises and processes. The extent to which this inspection is actually carried out is low; the FDA, for example, inspects around 5 per cent of registered device exporters to the United States in a year (GAO 2008).

*Nexus between the device industry and healthcare systems* As with the pharmaceutical industry, there is a conspicuous interdependence of healthcare delivery systems and medical device industries and their respective market strategies, captured by notions of 'corporate health' and of a 'medical–industrial complex'. Many devices are developed with the direct collaboration, if not the initial conception, of practising physicians. In the advanced industrial health systems, this situation has attracted criticism, including from within the medical professions themselves – for example, in the case of artificial hips, which are mostly produced by a global US-dominated orthopaedic industry consisting of fewer than ten multinational companies. Commentators in the orthopaedic profession have criticized the apparent dependency of the profession upon industry (Sarmiento 2003).

## Access and organization

The introduction of new or novel medical devices into a healthcare system inevitably requires the reorganization of infrastructure, the redesign of 'patient pathways', the frequent retraining of staff, and the reassignment of organizational roles, quite apart from the initial handling of resource issues.

Tuberculosis is an example of a lethal disease that is widespread in LMICs and which has become even more of a problem because of the development of multi-drug resistant (MDR) strains. TB detection and diagnosis have been upgraded in the higher-income national health systems. However, India, the country with the highest number of TB and MDR-TB cases, for example, is unable to cope with the scale of the problem given its existing laboratory facilities. It is clear that upgrading and the adoption of a new test regime, as recommended by WHO, will not occur without funding external to the public healthcare system. Innovation of diagnostics in this field has been shown to be inextricably bound with a need for product standardization at levels acceptable to governments: 'the way a diagnostic test is standardized as a product in a box can lead to challenges in the field if the test requires different laboratory control practices than are locally available' (Engel 2012). Thus, the 'roll-out' of even accepted technologies confronts a wide range of issues of expertise, working practices, physical facilities, organization, modes of standardization, patient acceptability, competing technologies and practices, all of which require adaptations before they can be incorporated into routine healthcare systems. Such considerations enter into the use of many other types of technology in LMICs, such as advanced molecular diagnostics that can be applied for the treatment of many infectious diseases.

*Health system oversight* The other side of the coin of social access and system adaptation to needed technologies relates to issues of safety, efficacy and cost-effectiveness. In high-income countries (HICs), the major government-endorsed mechanism that has been developed for this function is known as Health Technology Assessment (HTA) (Faulkner 2009; Lehoux 2006). This is a set of highly technical methodologies for assessing and comparing the potential benefits and risks of technological interventions. The assessment of risks pertaining to the technical performance, safety and efficacy of medical devices is a key part of the evolving regimes of evidence-related governance. Healthcare system procurement organizations may be less concerned about the cost-effectiveness of medical devices, since new devices often have less impact on healthcare budgets than new pharmaceuticals. Nevertheless, there are movements in the advanced healthcare systems to tie scientific evidence and procurement processes closer together in 'evidence-based purchasing' and similar schemes.

Unlike for medicines, there is not really a 'rational use' movement in the case of medical devices, although support for this might gather force among policy-makers if they were to bracket medicines and technologies together as 'medical products' (e.g. WHO 2011). What constitutes the 'user base' of devices is difficult to define, let alone monitor. Local and clinical factors are far more influential in determining or influencing patterns of uptake of devices, and, unlike with medicines, high-level global or national health policy cannot easily ascertain or draw up a shortlist of 'essential devices' to parallel 'essential medicines'. Thus, evaluations and interventions to improve the rational deployment of devices in a healthcare system are more piecemeal in the case of devices, and this applies to advanced healthcare economies as well as LMIC healthcare economies, although clearly not to the same extent.

Equally, the academic study of device adoption and diffusion is significantly less extensive than the study of the uptake of and compliance with medicines regimes. There have been movements in HICs, in the last decade or so, that are beginning to tackle this. However, with some exceptions (Yamey 2011), there are as yet only a few examples of this.

## The politics of medical technology and global health

As the importance and potential benefits of the range of existing and developing medical devices is increasingly recognized, as the number of scandals in the field receive wide global publicity, and as regulatory regimes are tightened up, it is becoming clear that there is a growing need and a timely opportunity for further advocacy and activism to promote public health goals worldwide related to the use of medical devices. Technological innovation creates pressure for innovation in clinical use, but the way this manifests itself varies across different health systems. Seductive visions of technological progress are used to influence healthcare policy-makers. This creates pressure on healthcare policy-makers and creates demand among patients and citizens through media exposure and the publicizing of innovative technologies. At the same time, medical device policy must address emerging technologies, which hold many uncertainties (e.g. nanotechnology).

Many medical devices have attracted controversy, although relatively few of these have emerged into the public sphere. Expertise in the evaluation of the performance of medical devices is often disputed. This has been the case for many years – for example, the controversy over the materials used in breast implants (Kent 2003), promoted by an industry which is largely shaped by commercial enterprise in plastic surgery (except in the case of breast reconstruction following surgery for cancer or congenital malformations). In the United States and Europe, consumer and support groups for women have emerged and are mounting legal class action cases against certain manufacturers. Aside from safety issues, there have been some cases where the intended users or recipients have actively resisted the innovation in question. This has been the case in Europe, for example, with cochlear implants, capable of restoring some sound signals to people who are profoundly deaf. There have been public disputes between deaf communities and parents of deaf children, on the one hand, and device developers, clinicians and public health professionals, on the other. Refusal to accept the device has been engendered by resistance from deaf language-signing communities, who fear disruption of family communication styles (Blume 2010).

In most LMICs, the penetration of devices used routinely in HICs is very low. Thus, for example, access to computer tomography (CT) is one per 64,900 people in high-income countries and one per 3.5 million people in low-income countries (WHO 2010). The first MRI scanner in a public hospital in Botswana was not introduced until 2011. In 2012, Ghana became the first

West African country to introduce advanced MRI scanning technology in public hospitals. The challenge in LMICs is to judiciously promote access to devices, while keeping in mind local medical, economic and cultural conditions. Unfortunately there is scarce research to guide the use of (often) expensive medical technologies in resource-poor settings. There are concerns in India, for example, that unrestricted access to imaging technologies has prompted doctors with inadequate training in radiology to set up imaging centres, leading to wrong diagnosis (Chakravarthi 2013).

Medical device multinational companies (MNCs) are now developing business strategies geared to the capacities and to the medical needs of the populations of emerging economies. For example, GE Healthcare, which holds the largest share of China's medical equipment market, has announced that it will develop middle- and low-end products targeting China's rural market. MNCs are adopting a similar strategy in India, to overcome constraints to expansion of their markets – currently restricted to major cities (Deloitte and Confederation of Indian Industry 2010).

We are witnessing new forms of inter-industry collaboration in the areas of mobile and electronic health (mHealth and eHealth). While these have been used for some time for the simple dissemination of public health messages in LMICs, future technological developments are of public health significance in both the developed countries and the LMICs, especially given the massive penetration of mobile communication and smartphone devices among rural populations. Remote medical monitoring is one area in which partnerships between medical device companies and telecommunications companies are being forged – for example, to produce systems for remote monitoring for patients implanted with cardiac rhythm management devices.

Portable devices clearly represent an attractive opportunity for companies seeking markets in LMICs. An example is the development of a handheld ultrasound device, launched by a major multinational with a global marketing strategy encompassing both high-tech hospitals in the developed healthcare systems and rural healthcare providers in the LMICs – although recent research indicates that the role for such a device is by no means straightforward, as it requires clear definition of use, revision of clinical pathways for acceptance, and involves issues of ultrasound image-reading expertise (Faulkner et al. 2013). Another example of miniaturization is an ultra-portable electrocardiogram (ECG) machine produced and priced for the Indian market by GE.

Medical tourism is one of the indirect forces shaping demand for medical technologies in some LMICs. Medical tourism is a growing industry in developing economies such as India and China, where entire 'medicities' are being set up, with consequent demands on technologies and techniques acceptable to patients, many (although by no means all) of whom travel from abroad for treatment.

## Conclusion

The global health community is beginning to start engaging with issues related to access to medical devices. Public health issues concerning medical devices are beginning to attract attention. Many difficult issues at the international political level still need to be addressed, not least of which are those related to intellectual property and global trade regimes (WTO–WIPO–WHO 2012).

An area for future scrutiny relates to the public health role and value of medical technologies, especially where challenges clearly outstrip resources. While the medical device industry, for obvious reasons, makes claims about how new devices (and technologies) can 'revolutionize' healthcare, there are too few independent studies that examine such claims. Technology can also drive the way health systems are organized – for example, the installation of expensive equipment requires scales that promote setting up of more tertiary-care facilities. Clearly those making choices need to bear in mind economic, social and political considerations. Regulatory regimens need much better evidence as regards the cost-effectiveness of a range of medical technologies, so as to prioritize adoption of such technologies in national health systems.

Another area for further work relates to the dominance of MNCs in LMIC markets for a range of medical devices. Challenges for self-reliant production of medical devices straddle issues of technology development and transfer, research, IP (intellectual property)-related barriers, etc. Public health practitioners need to start engaging with the complexities that are linked to the development of medical devices, their use in health systems and their regulation.

## References

Amarante, J. M., C. M. Toscano, M. L. Pearson et al. (2008) 'Reprocessing and reuse of single-use medical devices used during hemodynamic procedures in Brazil: a widespread and largely overlooked problem', *Infection Control and Hospital Epidemiology*, 29(9): 854–8, doi: 10.1086/590357.

BBC (British Broadcasting Corporation) (2013) 'Breast implants: PIP's Jean-Claude Mas gets jail sentence', 10 December, www.bbc.co.uk/news/world-europe-25315627, accessed 21 January 2014.

Blume, S. S. (2010) *The Artificial Ear: Cochlear implants and the culture of deafness*, New Brunswick, NJ: Rutgers University Press.

Chakravarthi, I. (2013) 'Medical equipment industry in India: production, procurement and utilization', *Indian Journal of Public Health*, 57(4): 203–7.

Deloitte and Confederation of Indian Industry (2010) *Medical technology industry in India: riding the growth curve*, Gurgaon, India: Deloitte Touche Tohmatsu India Private Ltd, www.deloitte.com/assets/Dcom-India/Local%20Assets/Documents/Lifesciences/Medical_technology_Industry_in_India.pdf, accessed 21 January 2014.

DTI (Department of Trade and Industry) (2005) *UK sector competitiveness: analysis of six healthcare equipment segments*, Report prepared by Arthur D. Little Ltd, London: Department of Trade and Industry, www.berr.gov.uk/files/file10462.pdf, accessed 21 January 2014.

Engel, N. (2012) 'New diagnostics for multi-drug resistant tuberculosis in India: innovating control and controlling innovation', *BioSocieties*, 7(1): 50–71.

European Commission (2012) *Revision of the medical device directives*, Brussels: European

Commission, ec.europa.eu/health/medical-devices/documents/revision/index_en.htm, accessed 21 January 2014.

Faulkner, A. (2009) *Medical Technology into Healthcare and Society: A sociology of devices, innovation and governance*, Basingstoke and New York: Palgrave Macmillan.

Faulkner, A., G. Elwyn and Z. Tomlin (2013) 'The adoption space of early-emerging technologies: evaluation, innovation, gatekeeping', Pathways to Adoption of Technologies in Healthcare (PATH), final research report to UK Department of Health/ NIHR Service Delivery and Organization Technology Adoption research programme, www.netscc.ac.uk/hsdr/projdetails. php?ref=08-1820-253, accessed 21 January 2014.

GAO (United States Government Accountability Office) (2008) *Medical devices: challenges for FDA in conducting manufacturer inspections: testimony before the Subcommittee on Oversight and Investigations, Committee on Energy and Commerce, House of Representatives: statement of Marcia Crosse, Director Health Care*, GAO-08-428T, Washington, DC, www.gao.gov/new.items/do8428t.pdf, accessed 21 January 2014.

Kent, J. (2003) 'Lay experts and the politics of breast implants', *Public Understanding of Science*, 12(4): 403–21.

Lehoux, P. (2006) *The Problem of Health Technology: Policy implications for modern health care systems*, New York and London: Routledge.

News Medical (2010) 'Over 8% of medical devices in circulation are counterfeit: WHO', www.news-medical.net/news/20100128/ Over-825-of-medical-devices-in-circulation-are-counterfeit-WHO.aspx, accessed 27 April 2014.

Sarmiento, A. (2003) 'The relationship between orthopaedics and industry must be reformed', *Clinical Orthopaedics and Related Research*, 412: 38–44.

WHO (World Health Organization) (2010) *Medical devices: fact sheet no. 346*, Geneva: WHO, www.who.int/mediacentre/factsheets/fs 346/en/, accessed 24 January 2014.

— (2011) *Local production for access to medical products: developing a framework to improve public health*, Geneva: WHO, www.who.int/ phi/publications/Local_Production_Policy_ Framework.pdf, accessed 23 February 2014.

— (2013) *Medical devices: compendium of innovative health technologies for low-resource settings: assistive devices | eHealth solutions | medical devices*, Geneva: WHO, www. who.int/medical_devices/en/, accessed 24 February 2014.

WTO–WIPO–WHO (World Trade Organization–World Intellectual Property Organization–World Health Organization) (2012) *Promoting access to medical technologies and innovation: intersections between public health, intellectual property and trade*, Geneva: WTO–WIPO–WHO, www.wto.org/english/res_e/booksp_e/ pamtiwhowipowtoweb13_e.pdf, accessed 23 February 2014.

Yamey, G. (2011) 'Scaling up global health interventions: a proposed framework for success', *PLoS Medicine*, 8(6), doi:10.1371/ journal.pmed.1001049.

SECTION C

**BEYOND HEALTHCARE**

# C1 | SOCIAL PROTECTION: REIMAGINING DEVELOPMENT

After twenty years of espousing 'poverty reduction' policies, international organizations are now proposing 'social protection' policies. The International Labour Organization (ILO) has adopted a recommendation on 'social protection floors'. This chapter discusses the merits of the new proposals on 'social protection' and whether they represent a break from neoliberal policies.

## History of the debate on 'development'

In 1969, the General Assembly of the United Nations (UN) adopted a Declaration on Social Progress and Development (United Nations 1969). The Declaration, akin to a programme of national modernization, included:

- confirmation of national sovereignty and the right to self-determination;
- assertion of the right and responsibility of states to pursue their own objectives of social development; and
- planning of social progress within the framework of comprehensive development plans, equitable distribution of national income, transformation of social structures, the right to work, sufficiently high minimum wages to ensure a decent standard of living, social security systems, and social services.

The fiscal crisis of the 1970s stalled all meaningful discussions on social development as neoliberal economics and its reliance on the 'market' came to dominate the development debate. In 1990 the World Bank woke up to the reality of the existence of poverty at a global scale. In that same year, the United Nations Development Programme (UNDP) published its first report on 'human development'. Discussions on 'social development' were now part of strategies for 'poverty reduction'. Ten years later, two parallel strategies for reducing extreme poverty were put into place: first, the poverty reduction strategy papers (PRSPs) introduced by the World Bank and the International Monetary Fund (IMF); and secondly, the Millennium Development Goals (MDGs) of the UN.

Today, it is clear that both strategies have failed (see Box C1.1). Neoliberal policies are not the only ones to be blamed for this state of affairs. Erroneous policies in the North and the South, lack and inefficiencies of development aid, capital flight and tax evasion are all equally responsible for poverty and hunger plaguing many regions of the world. Yet one should note that poverty reduction policies, as proposed at the turn of the millennium, were not designed to challenge the neoliberal agenda and, in fact, were totally compatible with neoliberal policies.

---

**Box C1.1 MDGs and the post-2015 development agenda**

In the Millennium Summit in September 2000 a set of eight global 'Millennium Development Goals' (MDGs) were adopted by the UN (UN General Assembly 2000), with twenty targets and corresponding indicators. Several of these goals dealt with major health issues: maternal health, infant mortality, sanitation and water supply, and access to preventive programmes and treatment for AIDS, malaria and other diseases.

*The 'charity' model of development* Over the next decade there was a dramatic increase in the flow of 'development assistance for health' (Ravishankar et al. 2009). *The central contradiction of the MDGs* is that while the Millennium Summit Declaration (MSD) contains some admirable, even inspiring, language, the goals that were adopted were largely about North–South charity; mobilizing funds from the rich world to assist poorer countries to ameliorate the nutrition, health, education, infrastructure and environmental burdens they were facing. It is not plausible that international charity, directed at ameliorating such burdens, is the most appropriate pathway to the goals of human development, social development and sustainable development. But if the MDGs were not designed to achieve 'development', what were they designed to achieve?

*The central myth of the MDGs* was that the dramatic increases in charitable funding which flowed after September 2000 were due to the intrinsic persuasive power of the MSD and its goals. It has been widely assumed, at least in the official rhetoric, that the adoption of the MDGs somehow propelled this increased flow of funding. However, two of the major sources of new funding were the Gates Foundation and the President's Emergency Fund for AIDS Relief (PEPFAR). It is hardly plausible that the adoption in the UN of a set of 'development goals' would somehow be sufficient to motivate Bill Gates and George W. Bush to redirect billions of dollars to the treatment of AIDS and TB and control of malaria. But if the expansion in 'development assistance' funding was not driven by the inspirational power of the MDGs, what was it driven by?

*Legitimation of neoliberal globalization* The key to answering both questions lies in the idea of 'legitimation': the increases in charitable funding transfers would serve to reaffirm the 'legitimacy' of the contemporary regime of neoliberal globalization against the threat of 'delegitimation', which was increasingly salient in the late 1990s.

The goals and targets which were adopted were overwhelmingly about charity and amelioration. It is necessary to ask: if the 'central challenge' was inequitable, unstable and unsustainable globalization, what was the relationship between the MDGs with their associated funding flows and the central challenge of moving towards a fully inclusive and equitable globalization?

This question points towards a structured hypocrisy on the part of the governments of the rich countries, in particular the USA and those of the European Union. During the fourteen years to date of the MDGs the USA and Europe have developed and implemented policies in the fields of trade, investment and finance designed to shore up the regime of globalization which Article 5 of the Millennium Summit Declaration identifies as the 'central challenge'. A raft of policies have been introduced which have exacerbated the inequities, instabilities and catastrophic environmental impacts of contemporary globalization, even while diverting a relatively small portion of the rents received to 'development assistance'.

The financial outflows from low- and middle-income countries associated with capital flight, tax evasion through transfer pricing and corrupt invoicing far outweigh the flow of 'development assistance'. However, 'development assistance' gives legitimacy to the governance structures which reproduce such outflows. If such 'development assistance' is not accompanied by structural changes in global finance, trade and investment, the claim to be assisting in 'development' is truly Orwellian.

*Post-2015 development agenda* The contradictions and myths and the hypocrisy of the rich-world elites in relation to the MDGs provide important warnings regarding the treatment of health in the post-2015 'development agenda'.

Among health officials it is widely repeated that the MDGs 'brought massive new funding into health' and there is fear that the post-2015 sustainable development goals might bypass 'health'. ('Health' in this context refers to institutions and programmes rather than population health outcomes.) A recent report by the WHO Secretariat (January 2014) stated that 'the prime concern for WHO at this stage is to support an approach that allows a wide variety of interests within the health sector to be accommodated as part of a single framework. This strategy reduces competition between different health conditions, different health interventions and different population groups' (WHO 2013).

Building better health systems is certainly part of development.

However, there are limits to the extent to which health systems can promote healthy populations, as opposed to providing preventive, diagnostic and therapeutic services to individuals. Health is created before and beyond the health system; it is created in the social conditions in which we grow, live, learn, work and play (Commission on Social Determinants of Health 2008). The primary healthcare (PHC) model recognized the social determination of health and argued for healthcare practitioners to work with their communities to recognize, consider and take action on the social determinants of health. This transformative dynamic of PHC is now passé within WHO, as is concern for the social determination of health, in both cases because of WHO's financial crisis. WHO is so dependent on its donors that it cannot afford to challenge their ideological and policy assumptions.

However, real progress in population health will depend on a rigorous and robust analysis of the links between health and development. This will involve:

- relating population health challenges to the wider economic and political environment and the economic, institutional and cultural dimensions of development;
- developing an explicit analysis of dynamics of the global economy which promote widening inequality and the unsustainable use of the earth's resources and capacities; and
- undertaking an explicit analysis of the regulatory settings, power relations and decision loci through which the global economy is regulated and through which it can be transformed.

While the UN is trying to develop a framework of global goals for sustainable development for the years following 2015, neoliberal economic policies currently being implemented are leading to widening inequalities and ecological destabilization. Provisions being included in trade agreements to further extend patent durations are going to maintain high prices for medicines; the 'free trade' agreements now being debated are going to protect the interests of transnational corporations at the cost of reducing the regulatory and policy space of sovereign governments. New economic relations and new forms of regulation are therefore critical prerequisites for addressing the challenges of today and the post-2015 era.

## Poverty reduction and social development

Poverty reduction policies were never meant to improve social protection, but were supposed to be an alternative to it. The goal that had to be achieved was enhancing poor people's capacity to manage and cope with risks (to which they were exposed to as a result of neoliberal policies) on their own.

Nor did poverty reduction policies, proposed by the World Bank and UNDP, have anything to do with a 'correction' of the negative outcomes of neoliberal policies. Rather, they were an integral part of these policies. The notion of social security was abandoned and 'Market-*inhibiting policies*' were claimed to be actually harming the poor (World Bank 1993). It was said that labour market regulations and minimum wages raised the cost of labour and prevented some groups of people from competing for jobs. Social insurances could exist, but should be provided by markets and not by public authorities (World Bank 1997).

The UNDP argued: 'The chronically deprived and dispossessed must be brought up to a threshold of human development to enter the mainstream of economic growth. But then it is time for governments to step aside ... if human development is the outer shell, freedom is its priceless pearl' (UNDP 1990). Old prescriptions that sought to tackle the problem of poverty through social expenditures and safety nets were seen to be erroneous diagnoses (PNUD 2000).

Thus, the tension between pressures from below to address socio-economic inequities and the need to maintain the integrity of the neoliberal agenda has informed debates on social development. However, criticisms of the 'poverty reduction' model for social development have now started surfacing.

In 2004, an independent report from the International Labour Organization (ILO) on the 'social dimension of globalization' asked for a 'certain minimum level of social protection ... to be accepted and undisputed as part of the socio-economic floor of the global economy' (ILO 2004). In 2009, in the early stages of the current fiscal crisis, different UN agencies published a report in which it is said that 'a social protection floor' could be useful in protecting people 'during the crisis and thereafter' (UN System Chief Executive Board for Coordination 2009). In 2010, several reports from the UN Research Institutes on Social Development (UNRISD) (Bangura et al. 2010) and the UN Department of Social and Economic Affairs (UN DESA) (United Nations 2010) were published with an implicit criticism of neoliberal policies, and also of poverty reduction policies: '... the narrow preoccupation with poverty may actually work against the broad and long term efforts that are required to eradicate poverty' (Bangura et al. 2010: 16). Many of these reports instead propose a transformative system of universal social protection. Given that the idea of social protection had been quickly buried with the emergence of the poverty discourse, this ideological turn is noteworthy.

### Universal social protection

Proposals on social protection have been put forward by several agencies: the World Bank, the European Commission (EC), the ILO, the UN Economic Commission for Latin America (ECLAC), etc.

The World Bank published a 'theoretical framework' for social protection in

2000, and confirmed and updated its strategy in 2013. For the World Bank, social protection is all about 'risk management'; risks and shocks – from economic downturns to epidemics and natural catastrophes – are inevitable and people have to be prepared to cope with them. This is called 'resilience'. The new element in the World Bank's strategy is labour. Jobs are seen as 'opportunities' that people have to seize and for which they need the necessary skills, all within the framework of 'improved' labour markets.

The best-developed proposals are those of the ILO for 'national social protection floors'. After the end of the Cold War, and with globalization gaining strength at the beginning of the 1990s, the ILO slowly became marginalized. The first step towards the reclaiming of its mission and relevance was the adoption of the 'Declaration of fundamental principles and rights at work', a compilation of basic conventions, with the right to unionize and the right to collective bargaining, the prohibition of forced labour and child labour, and the prohibition of discrimination at work (ILO 1998). In 1999, the ILO adopted a 'decent work' agenda, which consists of the fundamental rights to work, social protection, social dialogue, and employment (ILO 1999).

The International Labour Conference (ILC) of 2001 also gave the highest priority to policies and initiatives that aimed to provide social security to those not covered by existing schemes. Following this, in 2003, the ILO launched a global campaign on social security and coverage for all. In 2008, the ILC adopted a Declaration on Social Justice for a Fair Globalization (ILO 2008).

*ILO's proposal on social protection floors (SPFs)* Subsequently, a new initiative was taken for launching a 'social protection floor' (SPF). A preparatory report was written by an Advisory Group chaired by Michelle Bachelet and a recommendation was finally adopted on 'national social protection floors' at the ILC of 2012 (ILO Advisory Group 2011; ILO 2012).

The recommendation emphasizes that social security is a human right, and that it is 'an important tool to prevent and reduce poverty, inequality, social exclusion and social insecurity, to promote equal opportunity and gender and racial equality, and to support the transition from informal to formal employment' (ILO 2012). The economic objectives are seen as 'an investment in people that empowers them to adjust to changes in the economy and in the labour market, and that social security systems act as automatic social and economic stabilizers, help stimulate aggregate demand in times of crisis and help support a transition to a more sustainable economy' (ibid.).

Implementation of the recommendation is the overall and primary responsibility of the state (ibid.: 3) and 'Universality of protection' is mentioned as the first principle to be applied (ibid.: 3). The ILO recommendation explicitly states the types of benefits or guarantees that should be provided under national SPFs: '... a nationally defined set of goods and services, constituting essential health care, including maternity care ..., basic income security for children ..., for persons in active age who are unable to earn sufficient income, in particular in cases of sickness, unemployment, maternity and disability, and for older persons' (ibid.: 5, 9).

The recommendation is, however, ambiguous regarding coverage. It says that social protection has to be universal, but then goes on to say that it is mainly meant for those who are 'in need' (ibid.: 4). Thus, while guarantees are universal, benefits will go only to selected groups – which clearly implies targeting. The recommendation refers to a variety of methods to fund the proposal, including 'effective enforcement of tax and contribution obligations, reprioritizing expenditure, or a broader and sufficiently progressive revenue base' (ibid.: 11).

## Conclusion

ILO's proposal on 'social protection floors', while a step forward in the debate on development and social security, suffers from serious flaws. There is no unequivocal commitment to the achievement of universalism, social development and a shift away from neoliberalism. Ambiguities are also embedded in terminologies used. As the ILO itself points out, the terms social protection and social security are not used in consistent ways, their meaning differing widely across countries and international organizations, and also across time (ILO 2010).

Finally, no matter how positively the plans for SPFs are assessed, what

**Image C1.1** Women in India at a shelter for the homeless; 'social commons' can allow for a new conceptualization and broadening of social protection (Simon de Trey White/ActionAid)

the documents do not tell us should not be ignored. They do not speak of a redistribution of incomes. They do not speak of a 'transformative' agenda whereby 'development' implies an end to dual societies. There is no proposal to change the economic paradigm taking into account the ecological constraints, marking a shift away from productivism and an exclusively growth-oriented economy. If the SPF is limited to its minimal requirements, it will be compatible with neoliberal policies. Obviously, how these plans are implemented (if at all) will depend on the political will of governments. It will also depend on the strength of social movements to put pressure on governments and political leaders.

*The social commons* At the same time, it might be argued that social protection, however broadly it is defined, cannot be enough to 'build another world'. Social assistance can help poor people and universal social protection can help prevent poverty and reduce inequality. But they do not bring about political, economic and social change.

Therefore, the demand for a 'social commons' is fully legitimate. This would not only help prevent the erosion of the concept of 'social protection', but would also allow us to focus on the collective dimension of the protection that needs to be provided. 'Commons' refers to that which we all share as human beings – that is, our need for protection, food, shelter, healthcare and resources, so that we can lead a decent life and maintain a decent standard of living. Furthermore, as neoliberalism has focused exclusively on competition and flexibility, it has destroyed social relations and communities. This means that not only do individuals have to be protected, but so do societies. This collective dimension is particularly important when poverty is seen not as an individual problem of poor people but rather as a social relationship. It can never be eradicated if the whole of society is not involved. This demands solidarity and the participation of all.

The basic idea of 'social commons' is that social relationships are not purely contractual, but are constitutive of each person's individuality. Society is necessary for the survival of individuals. The notion of social commons can allow for a new conceptualization and broadening of social protection. It is based on the idea that people can master their present and shape their future, while mutually respecting each other and respecting nature. This can be a truly transformative project, leading to systemic change in the economy, polity and society, and ushering in wider democracy. It can contribute to building 'another world' (Mestrum 2014).

### References

Bangura, Y. et al. (2010) *Combating Poverty and Inequality: Structural change, social policy and politics*, Geneva: UNRISD (United Nations Research Institute for Social Development).

Commission on Social Determinants of Health

(2008) *Closing the Gap in a Generation: Health equity through action on the social determinants of health*, Geneva: WHO.

ILO (1998) *Declaration on Fundamental Principles and Rights at Work*, Geneva: ILO.

— (1999) *Decent Work: Report of the director-general*, International Labour Conference, 87th session, Geneva: ILC, June, www.ilo.org/public/libdoc/ilo/P/09605/09605(1999-87).pdf, accessed 23 April 2013.

— (2004) *A Fair Globalization: The role of the ILO: report of the director-general on the World Commission on the Social Dimension of Globalization*, Geneva: ILO.

— (2008) *ILO Declaration on Social Justice for a Fair Globalization*, Adopted by the International Labour Conference at its 97th session, Geneva, 10 June, www.ilo.org/wcmsp5/groups/public/---dgreports/---cabinet/documents/genericdocument/wcms_099766.pdf, accessed 23 March 2014.

— (2010) *World Social Security Report 2010/11: Covering people in times of crisis*, Geneva: ILO.

— (2012) *Text of the Recommendation concerning national floors of social protection*, Provisional Record no. 14A, Geneva: ILC, 14 June, www.ilo.org/wcmsp5/groups/public/---ed_norm/---relconf/documents/meetingdocument/wcms_183326.pdf, accessed 24 April 2014.

ILO Advisory Group (2011) *Social protection floor for a fair and inclusive globalization*, Report of the Social Protection Floor Advisory Group chaired by Michelle Bachelet, Geneva: ILO, www.ilo.org/wcmsp5/groups/public/---dgreports/---dcomm/---publ/documents/publication/wcms_165750.pdf, accessed 24 March 2014.

Mestrum, F. (2014) *Promoting the social commons*, www.globalsocialjustice.eu/index.php?option=com_content&view=article&id=463:promoting-the-social-commons&catid=10:research&Itemid=13, accessed 21 April 2014.

PNUD (2000) 'Vaincre la pauvreté humaine', New York: United Nations, www.who.int/hdp/publications/4ai.pdf, accessed 26 April 2014.

Ravishankar, N., P. Gubbins, R. J. Cooley, K. Leach-Kemon, C. M. Michaud, D. T. Jamison and C. J. L. Murray (2009) 'Financing of global health: tracking development assistance for health from 1990 to 2007', *The Lancet*, 373: 2113–24.

UN General Assembly (2000) *United Nations Millennium Declaration*, New York, www.un.org/millennium/declaration/ares552e.htm, accessed 23 April 2014.

UN System Chief Executive Board for Co-ordination [Conseil des chefs de secrétariat des organismes des Nations Unies pour la coordination] (2009) *The global financial crisis and its impact on the work of the UN system*, New York: United Nations.

UNDP (1990) *Human Development Report 1990*, New York: United Nations and Oxford University Press, hdr.undp.org/sites/default/files/reports/219/hdr_1990_en_complete_nostats.pdf, accessed 23 April 2014.

United Nations (1969) *Declaration on Social Progress and Development*, Res. GA 2542 (XXIV), 11 December.

— (2010) *Rethinking Poverty: Report on the world social situation 2010*, ST/ESA/324, New York: United Nations, www.un.org/esa/socdev/rwss/docs/2010/fullreport.pdf, accessed 26 April 2014.

WHO (2013) *Monitoring the achievement of the health-related Millennium Development Goals: Health in the post-2015 United Nations development agenda*, Geneva, apps.who.int/gb/ebwha/pdf_files/EB134/B134_18-en.pdf, accessed 26 April 2014.

World Bank (1993) *Poverty Reduction Handbook*, Washington, DC: World Bank.

— (1997) *World Development Report 1997: The state in a changing world*, Washington, DC/New York: World Bank/Oxford Univeristy Press, doi: 10.1596/978-0-19-521114-6.

## C2 | NON-COMMUNICABLE DISEASES: IS BIG BUSINESS HIJACKING THE DEBATE?

Non-communicable diseases (NCDs) have been promoted as a global health priority for the past ten years, culminating in a UN High Level Meeting in September 2011 on this subject. There is evidence that the incidence and prevalence of NCDs has increased over the past decades, and this has happened in both high-income countries (HICs) and low- and middle-income countries (LMICs). At the same time, available 'burden of disease' data shows that infectious diseases, maternal conditions, perinatal conditions and nutritional diseases (clubbed together as Type I diseases[1] and traditionally termed 'diseases of poverty') continue to be the priority in low-income countries, as well as in many middle-income countries.

This chapter explores the various issues involved in what has been called the 'epidemic of NCD diseases'. We first examine the evidence regarding various claims about the increase in NCD incidence. We then turn to the causal factors driving the rise of NCDs. We also discuss the role of various actors in the current attempt to project NCDs as a priority issue, including in LMICs. Finally we take a critical look at the strategies being promoted to tackle NCDs.

### Evidence as a marketing tool

Non-communicable diseases are described as the biggest killers worldwide. The focus is on four diseases (cardiovascular diseases, cancers, chronic respiratory diseases and diabetes) and on four risk factors (tobacco use, unhealthy diet, physical inactivity and harmful use of alcohol), embodied in a neat four-by-four matrix. Recently mental disorders have been included as a fifth priority condition.

Unfortunately, the debate on NCDs is being conducted virtually in the form of a corporate advertisement campaign, rather than as a reasoned scientific debate. The four diseases and four risk factors approach is in sync with such a format. In the process evidence is often presented to confuse rather than to educate. UN agencies, including the World Health Organization (WHO), often in partnership with philanthropic foundations and organizations such as the World Economic Forum, project strategies for combating NCDs as a market opportunity. In a typical promotional brochure (WHO 2005), the WHO urges national leaders to 'Invest now!', alerting them to 'substantial gains in countries' economic growth' and 'appreciable economic dividends for countries' (ibid.: 26).

**Image C2.1** Living conditions still determine the dominance of Type I diseases in poor countries (Roger Ciza)

The style and tone of these 'promotional' documents are remarkably similar to articles in business magazines, thus projecting an impression that NCDs are being 'sold' by the international health community to the private sector because health, as the reader is constantly reminded, represents a trillion-dollar market. This is unfortunate as it skews the terms of the debate and deflects attention away from NCDs as real public health priorities in many countries (including all high-income countries and a significant number of middle-income countries), and as future potential priority in many other countries. It is also unfortunate because this manner of 'hard sell' appears to create hierarchies between NCDs and traditional health priorities in LMICs – triggering discussions regarding which is a 'higher' priority.

From the standpoint of public health *all* morbid conditions that compromise health need to be addressed. The setting of priorities needs to be based on evidence regarding local conditions. Let us examine the evidence, with a view, not to minimize the importance of NCDs as a public health issue, but to scientifically analyse their impact on public health.

### A fresh look at mortality and 'burden of disease' data

The brochure (referred to earlier) claims that: 'Globally, of the 58 million deaths in 2005, approximately 35 million will be as a result of chronic

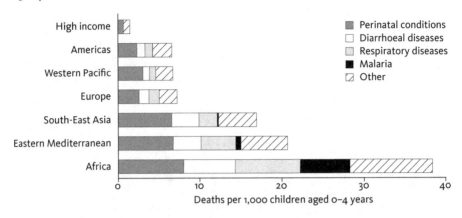

**C2.1** Child mortality rates by cause and region, 2004 (*source*: WHO 2008: 15)

diseases. They are currently the major cause of death among adults in almost all countries and the toll is projected to increase by a further 17% in the next 10 years' (ibid.: vii). The first part of the claim is correct, the second part is a projection that may or may not be borne out by future dynamics. The problem, however, is that such statements present a picture that conceals more than it reveals. The statement, by failing to specify age at death (that is, five, twenty, fifty or eighty years of age) ignores the very high rates of premature mortality that continue to prevail in many parts of the world. Further, it does not convey the fact that because most NCDs (except mental disorders like unipolar depression) are diseases of ageing (true, for example, for all the four priority conditions identified by the WHO), more people would be expected to die of NCDs when they get older. The fact that more people still die of Type I diseases in poorer regions of the world is an indication of gross inequity that persists between countries and within countries – it is a barometer of the unjust world that we live in. This does not mean, of course, that preventing premature deaths due to NCDs is not a public health issue.

Instead of looking at overall data on mortality, it is much more important to examine data regarding premature mortality. It is not as if such data is not available – WHO continues to produce reports on the global burden of diseases (GBD) (WHO 2008) that present a more nuanced picture of morbidity, mortality and major risk factors worldwide (see Figure C2.1 showing the causes of deaths in the 0–4 age group).

If we examine age-specific and region data on mortality (ibid.) we see a very different picture:

- More than seven out of ten child deaths globally take place in Africa and South-East Asia.
- In the African region, 46 per cent of all deaths were of children aged less than fifteen, whereas only 20 per cent were people aged sixty and over.

- In low-income countries, the dominant causes (of death) are infectious and parasitic diseases (including malaria) and perinatal conditions.
- Six causes of death account for 73 per cent of the 10.4 million deaths annually among children under five. Four communicable diseases (acute respiratory infections, diarrhoeal disease, neonatal infections such as sepsis, and malaria) account for one half of these deaths.
- An estimated 35 per cent of child deaths are due to undernutrition and 5 per cent are associated with HIV.
- The two leading causes of burden of disease in the world are infectious diseases – lower respiratory infections and diarrhoeal disease. HIV/AIDS is now the fifth cause of burden of disease globally and three other infectious diseases also appear in the top fifteen causes. In low-income countries, of the top ten causes, eight were Type I (communicable, maternal, perinatal and nutritional causes).

The above contradicts blithe assurances in NCD documents about 'successes against infectious disease' and 'health risks [which] have become globalized'.

As the WHO's GBD document explains, 'the contribution of premature death varied dramatically across regions' (ibid.: 40), with Years of Life Lost being seven times higher in Africa than in high-income countries. Most of the NCD documents, including those prepared for the UN Summit,[2] are addressed to national leaders who are not epidemiologists or even health experts. As the international health authority, WHO has a duty to present facts and figures to the public and to governments, in context, with careful explanations and cautionary notes. It does this in its GBD documents, but not in the documents that it produces in collaboration with various partners, notably the private sector.

The GBD data incorporates a methodology – using a computation method called 'Disability Adjusted Life Years' (DALYs) (Arnesen and Kapiriri 2004) – to calculate the total impact of both mortality and morbidity. It calculates the impact by setting a global standard life expectancy (currently taken as eighty years for males and 82.5 years for females) and then calculating 'Years of Life Lost' (YLL for deaths) and partial life years lost as a result of morbidity ('years lived with disease' – YLD). For the latter, different weights are assigned to different levels of 'disability' caused by a disease that leads to long-term morbidity. This method of calculating health impact assigns greater weight to deaths (or long-lasting morbidity) at a young age. YLL are calculated from the number of deaths at each age multiplied by a global standard life expectancy for the age at which death occurs. In this calculation, a female child dying at 5 years of age is calculated to have lost 77.5 years while a male dying at 78 years of age is calculated to have lost 2 years (so the burden of disease ratio is 77.5:2). In calculations that use only mortality data, both deaths are assumed to have equal impact.

What we have presented is a very simple explanation of how GBD is calculated using DALYs. There are other complexities that are part of the calculations which we shall only indicate here. While calculating YLL and YLD, different weights are given for different ages. Use of such an 'age weighted' calculation assumes a value (for each year) that rises from infancy to a peak at early adulthood and then gradually declines till old age.

GBD calculated using DALYs has been critiqued for several reasons, and is not a perfect methodology. For example, 'age weighting' has been critiqued as not valuing life equally across a person's life cycle (the logic for 'age weights' is that it assumes that a person is more 'productive' at a certain period of her/his life cycle). Disability adjustment has also been critiqued for the need to assign weights for different kinds of disability which may not be universally acceptable.

However, in spite of the imperfections, GBD data still remains much more useful to examine. The first reason for this relates to the purpose of examining data on mortality and morbidity. If we assume that the purpose is to use data as a tool to set priorities, then the 'burden of disease data' is far superior because it assigns a greater burden to premature deaths. Further GBD data captures the burden of both mortality and morbidity.

### What does the GBD data show?

The GBD reports show that if premature mortality (that is, in children and young adults rather than in mature adults over fifty years of age) is a criterion, then NCDs have a relatively lower impact in low-income countries and notably in three WHO regions (Africa, South-East Asia and the eastern Mediterranean). Very high levels of avoidable disease and premature death due to infectious disease, maternal, perinatal and nutritional conditions (Type I causes) persist in low-income countries. If we look at the global burden, then Type I conditions still continue to be the major contributors to the global burden of disease (see Table C2.1). The top two conditions (respiratory infections and diarrhoeal diseases) are Type I conditions, as are six of the top ten.

Overall the GBD report projects that the burden of non-communicable diseases accounts for nearly half of the global burden of disease (all ages), and that almost 45 per cent of the *adult* disease burden in low- and middle-income countries globally is now attributable to non-communicable disease. The report further predicts that 'the proportional contribution of the three major cause groups to the total disease burden is projected to change substantially. Group I causes are projected to account for 20% of total DALYs lost in 2030, compared with just under 40% in 2004. The non-communicable disease (Group II) burden is projected to increase to 66% in 2030, and to represent a greater burden of disease than Group I conditions in all income groups, including low-income countries' (WHO 2008: 50).

The GBD report does not minimize the risk of NCDs, but is a much

TABLE C2.1 Leading causes of burden of disease (DALYs), all ages, 2004

| Disease or injury | DALYs (millions) | Percentage of total DALYs |
| --- | --- | --- |
| Lower respiratory infections | 94.5 | 6.2 |
| Diarrhoeal diseases | 72.8 | 4.8 |
| Unipolar depressive disorders | 65.5 | 4.3 |
| Ischaemic heart disease | 62.6 | 4.1 |
| HIV/AIDS | 58.5 | 3.8 |
| Cerebrovascular disease | 46.6 | 3.1 |
| Premature and low birth weight | 44.3 | 2.9 |
| Birth asphyxia and birth trauma | 41.7 | 2.7 |
| Road traffic accidents | 41.2 | 2.7 |
| Neonatal infections | 40.4 | 2.7 |

*Source*: WHO (2008: 43)

more sober articulation of the present situation. Also to be kept in mind is that the projections for 2030 are based on assumptions of a certain rate of economic growth. The GBD report cautions: 'If economic growth is slower than in recent World Bank projections, or risk factor trends in low- and middle-income regions are adverse, then the global burden of disease will fall more slowly than projected' (ibid.: 50). We need to remember that the latest comprehensive data available is for 2004 (the update published in 2008 doesn't use later data, only refines the data from 2004). Since then, the global economic meltdown has halted, or even reversed, economic progress in many parts of the world. Moreover, a reduction in emphasis on Type I diseases in a period of economic slowdown (the burden of which is now being passed on to LMICs by the rich countries) can further skew the 2030 projections.

We now turn to another important issue – the distinction between Type I and Type II conditions. Traditionally, the former have been characterized as 'diseases of poverty' while the latter have been believed to be 'lifestyle' diseases, brought on by relative affluence. However, the GBD report indicates that 'non-communicable disease risks, as measured by age-standardized DALY rates, are higher in low- and middle-income countries than in high-income countries (LMICs)'. What this means is that many NCDs are affecting people at a younger age in LMICs. This is happening for a number of reasons, and blurs the distinction between Type I and Type II diseases. NCDs are killing people earlier and faster for the same reasons as Type I diseases – the conditions of living and poor access to healthcare services.

For most NCDs, obesity is a major risk factor. We now have evidence that children who are undernourished have higher risks of being obese during adulthood, if they get access to sufficient food (in calorific terms) (see Chapter C3). We also know that obesity in many LMICs is a consequence of the dumping of obesogenic foods by the global food industry (see Chapter C3). LMICs also have a higher incidence of risk factors that contribute to a number of cancers: exposure to harmful chemicals, low-fibre diets, smoking and alcohol abuse, exposure to some infectious diseases (viz. hepatitis C infections linked to liver cancers), etc. Poor primary-level care also contributes to development of NCDs in LMICs – for example, untreated hypertension and diabetes lead to early onset of cardiovascular complications. Finally, when affected by NCDs, patients tend to die early because of poor access to healthcare and because treatments are unaffordable. Most of the new anti-cancer drugs, for example, are protected by patents and are priced at levels that few in LMICs can afford.

## A critical look at the GBD

The GBD data is an important tool for estimating burden of diseases at a global scale. However, it has several limitations that need to be understood while using the data to set priorities.

The first limitation is the global span of the data. Because the data collected is *projected for the entire globe* there are certain assumptions that are made. The most important assumption underlying burden of data calculations is that of 'standard life expectancy'. As we have discussed earlier, this is set at 80 years for males and 82.5 years for females. However, if we look at the existing situation, such a level of life expectancy is far removed from the reality in all LMICs, which have an average life expectancy ranging from approximately 50 to 70 years (with some LMICs being outside this range). Consequently calculations of burden of disease for individual countries based on a global standard life expectancy have obvious limitations. It would be fairly obvious that when the standard life expectancy is set high it will overestimate the burden of NCDs (where a majority of the mortality and morbidity burden occurs in a relatively older age group) as against that of Type I diseases, where most deaths occur in the early years of life. This is only partly accounted for by factoring in 'age weights' (where the value of life is not the same across the entire lifespan, as explained earlier). However, the practice of assigning age weights has come in for criticism, as we have discussed earlier.

It has been argued that the 'value choices currently used, tend at under-estimating the burden of young populations and diseases that are predominant among poor populations. This contrasts the efforts of the WHO towards reducing the health gap between the rich and the poor countries' (Arnesen and Kapiriri 2004). As a consequence of this limitation of the GBD data, it is generally recommended that in order to set priorities in countries (or farther down at local levels), it is more reliable to set expected life expectancy closer to the national (or local) average while calculating the national or local burden of disease and while evaluating different interventions (Fox-Rushby and Hanson 2001). If this were done, in almost all LMICs the burden of Type I diseases would be consistently higher than what shows up in the GBD data.

## Promoting NCDs as a profit-making arena

In 2011, the WEF produced a report on NCDs (WEF and Harvard School of Public Health 2011: 1) to 'strengthen the economic case for action'. Readers were told that 'a large portion of health spending is appropriately viewed as investment – one that yields a handsome rate of return' (ibid.: 15).

The 'values' of NCDs in terms of direct and indirect costs of illness are set out in the WEF's report. The figures for cancer are US$290 billion rising to US$458 billion in 2030; cardiovascular disease: US$863 billion rising to US$1.04 trillion; chronic obstructive pulmonary disease: US$2.1 trillion rising to US$4.8 trillion; diabetes: US$500 billion rising to US$745 billion; and, finally, mental illness: US$2.5 trillion rising to US$6 trillion (ibid.: 35).

The WEF not only alerts the business community to a tremendous market opportunity but also makes clear its ambition and intention of influencing the spending decisions of national governments. 'It is our hope that the report informs the resource allocation decisions of the world's economic leaders – top government officials, including finance ministers and their economic advisers – who control large amounts of spending at the national level.' WEF Executive Chairman, Klaus Schwab boasts that 'practically all G20 governments – at the highest level – are now involved in working together with the Forum' (WEF 2012).

It is necessary to ponder the reasons that drive this 'hard sell' by industry. Clearly, industry (especially big pharmaceutical manufacturers) sees a booming market for their products in the midst of the NCD debate. Interestingly, while the tobacco, alcohol and (to some extent) food and beverages industry has been at the receiving end of criticisms for contributing to the NCD 'epidemic', 'big pharma' is routinely seen as a reliable partner. Big pharma has latched on to this opportunity and it has been quick to grab the 'pole position' in all NCD-related platforms.

The NCD Alliance is ubiquitous in all global platforms on NCDs. Its website (www.ncdalliance.org/who-we-are) claims: 'The NCD Alliance was founded by four international NGO federations representing the four main NCDs – cardiovascular disease, diabetes, cancer, and chronic respiratory disease. Together with other major international NGO partners, the NCD Alliance unites a network of over 2,000 civil society organizations in more than 170 countries. The mission of the NCD Alliance is to combat the NCD epidemic by putting health at the centre of all policies.' Even a cursory look at some of the people who lead the alliance provides insights regarding the deep penetration of the private sector. The alliance has five 'steering group' members. Among them is Cary Adams, CEO of the International Union against Cancer. In his previous assignment he worked as chief operating officer of Lloyds TSB Group International Banking.[3] Petra Wilson, as CEO of the International Diabetes Federation, also sits in the group. In her previous incarnation she was a director in the European Health Management Association.[4]

On its website the NCD Alliance lists 'private sector partners that have made financial contributions to the work of the Alliance'. Listed as 'current supporters' are twelve organizations – of these five (Bristol-Myers Squibb, Eli Lilly & Company, Merck, Novo Nordisk and Sanofi) are pharmaceutical MNCs.

Big pharma (pharmaceutical MNCs) has been particularly innovative in getting on to the NCD bandwagon. For decades it has prepared the ground by insidiously working to ratchet up standards of 'normalcy' in NCD patients. Pharma has consistently lobbied to set treatment thresholds so low that people with mild problems or modest risks are exposed to the harms and costs of treatment with little or no benefit (Moynihan 2011). For example, among the twelve members of the panel that created the controversial diagnostic category 'pre-hypertension' in 2003, eleven received money from drug companies, and half of those people declared extensive ties to more than ten companies each (ibid.). Further evidence of pharma influence on widening disease definitions comes from the *Diagnostic and Statistical Manual of Mental Disorders*. An examination of those who produced its fourth edition found that 56 per cent of panel members had financial ties to drug companies, although for some panels, including that for mood disorders, the figure was 100 per cent (ibid.). Again, eleven of the twelve authors of a 2009 statement on Type 2 diabetes were heavily conflicted, with authors working as consultants, speakers or researchers for an average of nine companies each. That panel advocated a contentiously low blood sugar target (ibid.). These are just a small sample of how the pharmaceutical industry is setting standards of treatments for NCDs, in a clear ploy to sell their medicines.

Pharmaceutical companies also use front organizations to promote apparently useful causes. Underlying their 'charity' are attempts to hijack the agenda on how treatments should be scientifically evaluated. (See Chapter D1 on the way pharma hijacked the observance of 'World Psoriasis Day'.)

If pharmaceutical companies are setting the terms of the debate on NCDs, the blame squarely lies with the World Health Organization (WHO). The WHO has 'dumbed down' the debate on NCDs through its four-by-four approach (see earlier). The approach is 'victim blaming' in its conception, placing the burden of action on individuals. There has been very little coordinated action to address the structural reasons for NCDs (many of them very similar to the underlying causes of the high incidence of Type I diseases, as we discuss earlier) and too little attention on real strategies to combat the rise in NCDs. The latter would need to include a scrutiny of the food and beverage industry, the erosion of food sovereignty in LMICs, deterioration of environmental conditions, and the role of strengthened public health services.

### Conclusions

The rise in the incidence and prevalence of non-communicable diseases poses a complex challenge. Vigilance is necessary to ensure that the agenda is not hijacked by very powerful interests which seek to profit from disease and suffering. At the same time it is necessary to carefully scrutinize data and trends, to arrive at a balanced view of the problems posed by NCDs. A motivated reading of the situation should not allow a deflection of focus away from the existing threats that Type I diseases continue to pose in a large number of LMICs. The creation of a false hierarchy between communicable diseases and NCDs does not serve the interests of public health.

## Notes

1 WHO categories: Type I causes: communicable, maternal, perinatal and nutritional conditions; Type II causes: non-communicable diseases; Type III causes: injuries.

2 It is interesting that WHO's GBD report was omitted from the UN Summit documents.

3 www.uicc.org/uicc-appoints-new-chief-executive-officer.

4 www.idf.org/news/idf-appoints-new-ceo.

## References

Arnesen, T. and L. Kapiriri (2004) 'Can the value choices in DALYs influence global priority-setting?', *Health Policy*, 70: 137–49.

Fox-Rushby, J. and K. Hanson (2001) 'Calculating and presenting DALYs in cost-effectiveness analysis', *Health Policy and Planning*, 16(3): 326–31, Oxford University Press, www.who.int/healthinfo/global_burden_disease/GBD_report_2004update_full.pdf, accessed 10 May 2014.

Moynihan, R. (2011) 'A new deal on disease definition', *British Medical Journal*, 342: d2548, doi: 10.1136/bmj.d2548.

WEF (World Economic Forum) (2012) *World Economic Forum annual report 2011–2012, Executive Chairman's statement*, Geneva: WEF, www3.weforum.org/docs/WEF_Annual Report_2011-12.pdf, accessed 10 May 2014.

WEF (World Economic Forum) and the Harvard School of Public Health (2011) *The Global Economic Burden of Non-communicable Diseases*, September, www3.weforum.org/docs/WEF_Harvard_HE_GlobalEconomic BurdenNonCommunicableDiseases_2011.pdf, accessed 10 May 2014.

WHO (World Health Organization) (2005) *Preventing chronic diseases: a vital investment*, Geneva: WHO, www.who.int/chp/chronic_disease_report/full_report.pdf, accessed 3 May 2014.

— (2008) *The global burden of disease: 2004 update*, Geneva: WHO, www.who.int/healthinfo/global_burden_disease/GBD_report_2004update_full.pdf accessed 10 May 2014.

# C3 | NUTRITION AND FOOD SOVEREIGNTY[1]

A quarter of all children in the world are undernourished today. This increases their chance of death, undermines their potential to learn in school, and reduces their future capacity to earn a living. Simultaneously, there is a rapidly growing global epidemic of overweight and obesity, with over two billion adults expected to be overweight or obese by 2015, and therefore increasingly susceptible to the early onset of diabetes, heart disease and certain cancers.

There are structural issues that affect the availability, affordability and acceptability of food, which, along with everyday living and working conditions, ultimately affect what people eat. This erosion of food sovereignty has been linked to poorer availability, accessibility and affordability of healthy foods, more unhealthy diets, and high levels of food insecurity and chronic diseases (UNICEF 2010). 'Food sovereignty includes the right to food – the right of peoples to healthy and culturally appropriate food produced through socially just and ecologically sensitive methods. It entails peoples' right to participate in decision making and define their own food, agriculture, livestock and fisheries systems' (Via Campesina 2007).

The means of, and the control over, the production of food are shifting from the farmers in the South to big agri-food businesses and transnational retail

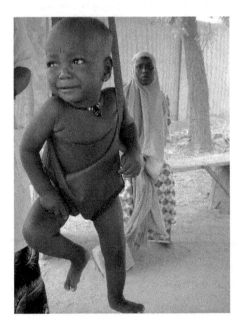

**Image C3.1** Growth monitoring in Niger; a quarter of all children in the world are undernourished today (David Sanders)

**Image C3.2** 'Hunger free' campaign in Burundi; control over food is shifting from farmers to agri-food businesses (Stephen Wandera/ActionAid)

companies based mainly in the North, removing power from local producers, consumers and, in many instances, policy-makers. Liberalized trade regimes, food price speculation in the global market and land grabs are contributing to this shift. The Agreements of the World Trade Organization (WTO) have moved control over the right to food and food security to the global market (Friel et al. 2013; Ghosh 2010). Human-induced climate change plus other forms of environmental degradation are also affecting the food system, contributing to the impaired quantity, quality and affordability of food in many countries (UNDP 2007).

The complex and often linked processes that erode food security and sovereignty in large parts of the globe are discussed in this chapter through two case studies. These case studies, located in India and the Pacific Islands, illustrate the (ill-) health effects of the macroeconomic and political dispensation of the past three decades that has resulted in the unprecedented creation of aggregate wealth, but has also resulted in sharp and increasing inequalities between North and South, and between rich and poor. Declining food sovereignty and poor nutritional status, the greatest contributors to the global burden of disease, are critical manifestations of this situation.

### Erosion of food sovereignty and impact on nutritional status in India

India is home to a quarter of the undernourished people in the world (Food and Agriculture Organization et al. 2012). Almost half of the children under

**Image C3.3** Food stocks rise in India while people are hungry (Indranil Mukhopadhyay)

five are stunted (low height due to sustained under-nutrition), and wasting (associated with recent starvation or disease) affects 20 per cent of children under five (MoHFW, GOI 2007).

While a third of the adult population is underweight and suffers multiple deficiencies related to inadequate food intake, such as high levels of anaemia (ibid.), overweight/obesity, diabetes and cardiovascular diseases among Indians are occurring in epidemic proportions (Shatrugna 2012). Childhood under-nutrition is often linked to a higher incidence of obesity, diabetes and cardiovascular diseases, as children without adequate muscle mass put on weight faster during adulthood when exposed to calorie-rich foods, but do so through fat accumulation and not through increase in muscle mass (ibid.).

The proportion of the population with inadequate food intake has increased in the past two decades (Table C3.1).[2]

TABLE C3.1 Calorie intake based on expenditure group

|  | Rural |  |  | Urban |
|---|---|---|---|---|
| Levels of calorie intake per day | 2,400 | 2,200 | 1,800 | 2,100 |
| Percentage of persons below specified levels, 2004–05 | 87 | 69.5 | 25 | 64.5 |
| Percentage of persons below specified levels, 1993–94 | 74.5 | 58.5 | 20 | 57 |
| Percentage of persons below specified levels, 1983 | 70 |  |  | 58.5 |

*Source*: Patnaik (2007a)

Paradoxically, the per capita availability of foodgrains has decreased in a period when there has been a steep increase in food stocks (see Box C3.1). Further, precisely in the period when food availability has decreased, India has become a net exporter of foodgrains (Patnaik 2007b).

---

### Box C3.1 Increase in food stocks and exports amid hunger

India produced 257.44 million tonnes of foodgrains during 2011/12, or close to 186 kilograms per capita. However, against a buffer norm of 21 million tonnes (that is, the minimum buffer required to be stocked to take care of emergencies), the Food Corporation of India had a stock of more than 66.5 million tonnes (as of 1 October 2012). Around the same period, 7.73 million tonnes of rice and 3.59 million tonnes of wheat were exported (PIB 2012).

---

The fall in per capita consumption of foodgrains can be explained only by a decline in income and purchasing power for a majority of the population, and is a symptom of general rural distress, combined with acute distress in specific regions. Rural distress is apparent from the recurrent and widespread incidence of farmers' suicides. Over 270,000 farmers are estimated to have committed suicide between 1995 and 2011 (Sainath 2012).

### Factors responsible for the erosion of food sovereignty

*Decline in public expenditure* Public expenditure on rural development is vital for maintaining rural productivity, for ensuring employment, and for sustaining wage levels. There has been a sharp decline in this (both as a percentage of total government expenditure and as a percentage of GDP). In the period 1985–90 (just prior to the initiation of neoliberal reforms in India), rural development expenditure was 14.5 per cent of GDP, but fell precipitously to 6 per cent of GDP in 2001 (Down to Earth 2005), and has fallen further since then.

This decline is linked with the policies recommended by the World Bank and the International Monetary Fund (IMF). While these institutions do not specifically tell governments to cut particular expenditures, studies show that countries implementing structural adjustment programmes[3] tend to implement similar policies, including imposing restraints on central government

TABLE C3.2 Growth rate of population and employment (per cent)

| Period | Population growth | Total | Employment growth Urban | Rural | Agriculture sector |
|--------|-------------------|-------|-------------------------|-------|--------------------|
| 1983–1993/94 | 2.10 | 2.43 | | | 1.51 |
| 1987/88–1993/94 | | | 3.39 | 2.03 | |
| 1993/94–1999/2000 | 1.93 | 1.51 | 2.27 | 0.58 | -0.34 |

*Source*: Patnaik (2003)

expenditure. Reforms of the financial sector in India also include curtailment of central bank credit to the government, which limits government expenditure (Chandrasekhar 2010).

The reduction in rural development expenditure has also adversely affected rural incomes and employment. The growth rate of employment in rural India was an abysmal 0.58 per cent in the period 1993/94–1999/2000 (far below the rate of growth of the rural population) (Table C3.2), thus curtailing the purchasing power of the rural poor.

*Changes in trade policy* As part of the 1991 reforms, wide-ranging changes were made in India's agricultural trade policy, resulting in reductions in taxes on imports and removal of restrictions on the quantum of imports. India's accession to the World Trade Organization's Agreement on Agriculture led to further cuts in import tariffs and quantitative restrictions on imports. The World Bank's Country Assistance Strategy 2005–08 for India listed reducing average import tariffs and anti-dumping duties as 'priorities' (World Bank 2004).

These reforms directly affected India's food sovereignty as its self-sufficiency in key food products was eroded. The IMF/World Bank loan had the attached conditionality that agriculture be diversified. This resulted in a shift in production from staple food crops to export-oriented cash crops. In ten years, 8 million hectares of food-growing land were converted to exportable crops. With the liberalization of agricultural trade, the switch to cash crops has exposed farmers to price volatility. In addition, the prices of these commodities tend to depreciate over time.[4] Consequently, farmers were plunged into spiralling farm debt and insolvency as they had to borrow to shift cultivation to input-intensive cash crops while their investment did not bring in commensurate returns (Patnaik 2005).

*Increase in input costs* Simultaneously, several policies have reduced farmers' incomes by increasing the cost of farming. For example, the cost of cultivation of wheat has registered a spectacular increase since the 1990s and the expenses

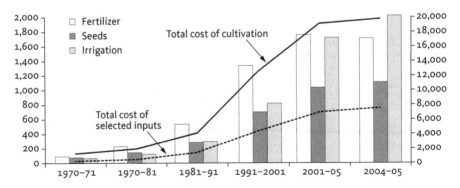

**C3.1** Cost of wheat cultivation in India (Rs/hectare) (source: Raghavan 2008)

on inputs (irrigation, fertilizers, cost of credit and seeds) have ratcheted up the average costs of cultivation (Raghavan 2008) (see Figure C3.1).

In response to the increased cost of cultivation, the demand for agricultural workers has declined, as have their wages. Thus the effects of the increased cost of cultivation affect not only the cultivating households but also the entire agriculture-dependent population, including agricultural workers (ibid.).

*Electricity privatization* Sixty per cent of India's irrigated land depends on private wells (NSSO 2005), and water for irrigation is pumped using electricity.[5] Therefore, the cost of electricity has a strong influence on agricultural income.

Restructuring of the power sector was initiated in the 1990s. The World Bank provided loans for restructuring and imposed the conditionality that market-oriented reforms be introduced (Sreekumar and Dixit 2011). Cross-subsidies to vulnerable sectors were removed and electricity costs soared, affecting the rural and urban poor and small and marginal farmers disproportionately. The price of electricity to farmers (agricultural rates) rose by 97.5 per cent between 2007 and 2012, far more than the average 23.8 per cent increase for the general population (Singh 2012).

*Fertilizers and seeds* India's fertilizer requirement rose by 70 per cent between 1998/99 and 2008/09, but production went up by only 11 per cent, while imports rose by 236 per cent. Government-owned companies were the major producers of fertilizers up to the 1990s. However, their role has since been drastically curtailed. As a result, the fertilizer subsidy bill (i.e. support to farmers to purchase fertilizers) increased from Rs113.87 billion in 1998/99 to Rs966.03 billion in 2008/09, while the costs that farmers have to pay also increased threefold (Raghavan 2008).

Market-oriented reforms have also led to the privatization of the seed sector. There has been a steep rise in the proportion of marketed seeds as opposed to exchanged seeds, enhancing the role of private seed companies (Jafri 2010).

*Rural institutional credit* With increasing dependence on inputs purchased from the market, the credit requirements of farmers have increased. However, access to credit for small and marginal farmers, who comprise the majority of farming households (84 per cent), has worsened since the start of the fiscal reforms in 1991.

Earlier, public sector banks were covered by 'directed credit programmes' that mandated that 40 per cent of their lending should be in 'priority sectors', including agriculture. As a result of the reforms, the rate of growth of credit to agriculture declined drastically, and an increasing number of small and marginal farmers now meet their credit requirements through moneylenders and informal sources (75 per cent of their credit in 2006/07) (Alternative Survey Group 2008).

**Food support schemes**

The Public Distribution System (PDS), the Integrated Child Development Scheme (ICDS) and the Midday Meal Scheme (MDM) have been the cornerstones of the food security policies of the Indian government. In recent decades, they have all suffered from budgetary constraints.

The ICDS provides six essential services to children under six years of age: supplementary nutrition, health check-ups, immunization, non-formal pre-school education, referral services, and nutrition and health education. However, in 2011/12 the national budget allocated only 0.12 per cent of GDP to this scheme. The MDM scheme, which requires the government to provide cooked meals to children in government or government-assisted schools, also received a similar meagre allocation

*Public Distribution System* The PDS distributes subsidized staple foods and commodities, such as wheat, rice, sugar and kerosene, through a network of public distribution shops. It is India's most important food security instrument in terms of both coverage and public expenditure. The Public Distribution Scheme has, progressively, shifted from *universal coverage* (whereby all citizens are eligible) to *targeted* coverage (whereby only specific categories of citizens who are designated as poor are eligible). This has been accompanied by downward shifts in entitlements and an increase in prices of food supplied through the PDS. It is estimated that 50 per cent of the poor are omitted from the priority entitlement list of people designated as 'Below Poverty Line' (BPL) (Right to Food Campaign 2011). Targeting within the PDS is responsible for the decline in foodgrain outflows through the PDS (Swaminathan 2002),

TABLE C3.3 Government procurement, distribution and stocks of foodgrain (in million tonnes)

| Year | Procurement (PT) | Public distribution (PD) | Net addition to stocks (PT–PD) | Stocks as of July |
|------|------------------|--------------------------|-------------------------------|-------------------|
| 1991 | 19.6 | 20.8 | −1.2 | 22.3 |
| 1992 | 17.9 | 18.8 | −0.9 | 15.1 |
| 1993 | 28.0 | 16.4 | 11.6 | 24.2 |
| 1994 | 26.0 | 14.0 | 12.0 | 30.8 |
| 1995 | 22.6 | 15.3 | 7.3 | 35.6 |
| 1996 | 19.8 | 18.3 | 1.5 | 27.0 |
| 1997 | 23.6 | 17.8 | 6.1 | 22.4 |
| 1998 | 26.3 | 18.4 | 7.9 | 28.5 |
| 1999 | 30.8 | 17.0 | 13.8 | 33.1 |
| 2000 | 35.5 | 12.1 | 23.4 | 42.3 |
| 2001 | 31.8 | 8.7 | 23.1 | 61.7 |
| Absolute change 1991–2001 | +14.6 | −10.2 | — | +39.4 |

*Source*: Swaminathan (2002)

while, as discussed earlier, foodgrain stocks held by the government have increased significantly (see Table C3.3).

More recently, there has been a proposal to replace the distribution of food by transfers of cash. Evidence shows that cash transfer schemes work in situations where they supplement rather than replace programmes that offer food to poor families at subsidized rates.[6] Cash transfers that then require people to procure food from private retail outlets place them at the mercy of market forces (Ghosh 2011). However, the Indian government appears keen to introduce cash transfer schemes as substitutes for direct provision of free or subsidized food, to reduce government expenditure on subsidies (Ghosh 2013).

### Challenges to food sovereignty and the risks to human health in the Pacific Islands

The Pacific Islands now have the dubious distinction of leading the world in the already high and growing prevalence of obesity and attendant non-communicable diseases. Globalization has affected local food sovereignty in the twenty-two Pacific Island Countries and Territories (PICTs), particularly as regards participation in decision-making; prioritizing local agriculture to feed local people; and access to land, seeds and water (Plahe et al. 2012).

The economic integration that occurred across the Pacific as a result of colonization in the 1900s, and the accession to the WTO by six PICTs members (Fiji, Papua New Guinea, Samoa, Solomon Islands, Tonga and Vanuatu), has been accompanied by a steady deterioration in traditional food systems, decline in the production of traditional crops and import of less healthy staples and highly processed foods (McGregor et al. 2009). This initiated an ongoing shift in dietary patterns that is associated with a high chronic disease risk, namely reduced consumption of starchy roots and fruits (such as breadfruit and taro) as staple foods, increased consumption of refined cereals (such as white rice and flour), increased consumption of meat and oils, and increased consumption of processed and packaged foods (Hughes 2003).

### Effect on farmers of changing patterns of production

Traditional agricultural practices in PICTs are strongly community- and village-based, and focused on root crop production (Denoon 1997). However, the opening of markets has undermined domestic agriculture and contributed to import dependency. The percentage of imports compared to food expenditure ranges from 36 per cent in Kiribati to 84 per cent in Palau (Parks and Abbott 2009). This in turn has led to policies to increase exports to maintain the balance of payments (Simatupang and Fleming 2005). The focus on export-oriented agriculture has both reduced production of traditional crops and increased intensive production of cash crops and other unsustainable agricultural practices (Thaman and Clarke 1983).

Policies of import liberalization and export promotion have a direct effect on food availability (Thow et al. 2011). For example, the historical experience of Fiji and Samoa demonstrates that economic liberalization is associated with decreased availability of starchy staple foods and increased availability of non-traditional cereals during periods of liberalization (Gittelsohn et al. 2003).

Food imports are also a concern in terms of food affordability and accessibility. The Chamber of Commerce in Vanuatu expressed strong concerns about increasing dependency on imported food staples, both because of the recent surge in the prices of these products, and because of the negative impacts they have had and continue to have on the health of local people. The Chamber stressed the need for investment in training local farmers, in food storage facilities as well as food processing plants, and also emphasized the need to improve the bargaining power of local farmers through developing strong cooperatives.[7]

In the face of soaring global food prices, agriculture experts in Fiji also highlighted the need to invest in processing traditional foods for local consumption. For example, flour from locally grown breadfruit and root crops could easily be used to make food such as chapattis. This, they argued, would reduce Fiji's dependency on imported wheat. Such dependence has had a very negative effect on the landless squatter communities in the urban areas such as Suva, which have suffered from food insecurity as a result of the increase in food prices.[8]

Processes of globalization in the Pacific Island nations have also affected the access of farmers and fisherfolk to inputs, including land, seeds and water. Many countries sell their fishing rights to international corporations and other countries, owing to limited investment capacity. In Micronesia and Fiji, this has contributed to fewer opportunities for local access to fish stocks and other marine resources – and has also contributed to unhealthy diets due to reduced consumption of fresh fish (Cassels 2006).

The shift away from the traditional agriculture to export-oriented agriculture, described above, has also led to some erosion of traditional land tenure, although in most countries a significant proportion of land is still held customarily, which has helped limit extreme poverty and hunger in the region (AusAid 2006). The need to protect land rights is widely understood and recognized in the Pacific Islands.

### Food prices, food accessibility and food culture

Significant changes in food culture have been externally imposed through processes of globalization in PICTs, affecting the control and power of consumers in shaping their food environment. Surveys reveal that consumers prefer traditional foods, but choose to consume imported products for reasons of perceived status, convenience (particularly with changes in working patterns) and variety (Evans et al. 2003).

Globalization has also contributed to constraining the ability of consumers to choose healthier and, in this context, more traditional foods (Thow and Snowdon 2010). The impact of the recent food price crisis in the Pacific Island nations has revealed the vulnerability of the domestic food supply system and the limited options for consumers in achieving food security and healthy diets, owing to this sustained dependence on imports and low investment in agricultural production (ADB 2008). Many countries experience the dumping of low-quality agricultural products from Western countries, which limits the access of consumers to healthy foods (Thow et al. 2011). The Pacific trade in lamb and mutton flaps (breast of lamb interleaved with thick layers of fat) is one example of a dumped commodity. These are generally unacceptable for consumption in their countries of origin, but are integrated into the food systems in lower-income countries owing to their extremely low price (Gewertz and Errington 2009).

Trade and the cash economy have also supported urbanization, which offers a variety of non-traditional employment opportunities, and this has consequently reduced participation in agriculture (particularly subsistence agriculture) (Thaman 1990). Some of the negative aspects of transitioning to an urban environment are the reduced land area available for planting, limited space available for traditional food storage and cooking methods (such as earth ovens), and also difficulties in transporting perishable root crops to urban communities (Parkinson 1982).

**Image C3.4** The WTO agreement has a deep impact on food sovereignty in the South (Benny Kuruvilla)

**Erosion of policy space**

Integration into the global economy and dependence on aid for development have also affected food sovereignty in the Pacific Island nations by reducing the policy space for intervention to improve the food supply and to pursue nutrition and diet-related health goals. While a return to full subsistence farming is unrealistic, policy-makers have identified a need to support local production as the core of the food system and to improve the capacity of farmers and fishermen, including by developing sustainable farming methods (Food Secure Pacific Working Group 2010). In practice, governments have found achieving these goals challenging owing to international pressure to develop extractive industries and to export crops (Plahe et al. 2012). The focus of international aid and development programmes remains firmly on export-oriented agriculture to raise national incomes, despite a demonstrated lack of effectiveness of attempts aimed at reducing income inequities within countries and growing concerns about the harmful impacts on domestic social and health outcomes (Cirikiyasawa 2007).

As part of its accession to the WTO in 2011, Vanuatu agreed to reduce agricultural tariffs and subsidies by a much bigger percentage when compared to other WTO members. Discussion with civil society groups revealed that Vanuatu's negotiating power during the WTO accession process was very weak, resulting in Vanuatu acceding to the WTO under far more onerous terms when compared to much larger countries (Plahe et al. 2012).

A further constraint on food sovereignty is the erosion of domestic policy space as a consequence of international trade and investment agreements. For example, Samoa's accession to the WTO in 2011 resulted in the removal of a four-year ban on turkey tail imports (WTO 2012). The ban had been imposed

---

**Box C3.2 Ban on mutton flap sales in Fiji**

Fiji's ban on sales of mutton and lamb flaps (a fatty meat that was imported in large quantities) was implemented through a joint initiative by the ministers of health and commerce. It was imposed in response to both rising rates of diet-related chronic disease rates (strongly associated with saturated fat intake) and concern about the dumping of these cheap meat cuts on local agricultural production. The ban was accompanied by a health promotion campaign aimed at increasing consumer awareness of the health consequences of consuming high-fat meats. This ban had a significant effect on the food supply. It was strongly supported by consumers, who perceived these cheap meat imports as very unhealthy and 'unfit for human consumption' (Gewertz and Errington 2009).

in order to remove from the market a highly fatty meat product, which was significantly cheaper than other meats. Turkey tails were being 'dumped' on their market, creating an incentive for consumers to consume the cheap and unhealthy product, while reducing the competitiveness of local meat producers (Thow et al. 2010).

In contrast, Fiji has been able to intervene effectively by banning mutton and lamb flap sales (see Box C3.2).

## Conclusion

While they cannot claim to be representative of the whole spectrum of global nutrition and food security, these two case studies individually and together illustrate the complex and dynamic global food and nutrition crisis. They are stark reminders of the urgency of eliminating the 'double burden of nutrition', and of the clear and distressing explications of its national and global social, economic and political contexts. They underline the fact that this human crisis cannot be addressed without confronting and changing its social determinants.

The India case study demonstrates, *inter alia*, the paradox of national food sufficiency and simultaneous widespread hunger and under-nutrition. While food is available within the country, it is clear that access to this food is dangerously limited for a very significant proportion of the population as a result of trade policies often influenced by a global environment inimical to national food sovereignty, and international advice that promotes current economic orthodoxy. Both of these policy thrusts have resulted in large stockpiles of food, but at the same time high food prices and unaffordable agricultural input costs.

The Pacific region case study demonstrates clearly how national food sovereignty and nutrition security have been undermined by the promotion of 'free' trade in the region, resulting in the Pacific Islands (along with an ever-increasing number of other countries) becoming a net food importer. This has resulted in a decline in national food production and in a rapid change from a more traditional and healthier diet to one that is obesogenic, consisting largely of fatty meat and ultra-processed, packaged foods.

## Acknowledgements

The case studies benefited greatly from interviews and personal communications with S. Kannaiyan, Sachin Kumar, Deepa Sinha, Anuradha Talwar, Vijoo Krishnan, Suneet Chopra, Utsa Patnaik, Afsar Jafri, Abhijit Sen, Jayati Ghosh and Veena Shatrugna.

## Notes

1 This chapter draws on a background paper prepared for *The Lancet – University of Oslo Commission on Global Governance for Health Report*, www.med.uio.no/helsam/english/research/global-governance-health/background-papers/food-sovereignty.pdf.

2 For more on the debates about India's calorie intake norms and data, see Patnaik (2007b).

3 Large-scale economic reforms in India were initiated in July 1991 as a response to the external debt and foreign exchange crisis. This

represented an acceleration of a process that had started in the 1980s and which constituted a departure from the post-independence model of planned development. While not formally termed a structural adjustment programme dictated by IFIs, the neoliberal economic reforms, which continue to this day, had most or all of the characteristics of SAPs that were implemented in large parts of Latin America and Africa.

    4  For more details on trends in price variations, see Patnaik (2005).

    5  Rain-fed agriculture accounts for around 56 per cent of India's total cropped area, 77 per cent in the case of pulses, 66 per cent for oilseeds and 45 per cent for cereals

    6  Jayati Ghosh, economist, personal interview, 29 December 2012.

    7  Personal communication, August 2012.

    8  Personal communication, February 2012.

## References

ADB (Asian Development Bank) (2008) *Living with High Prices: A Policy Brief*, Philippines: Pacific Studies Series.

Alternative Survey Group (2008) *Alternative Economic Survey, India 2007–08: Decline of the Developmental State*, New Delhi: Daanish Books.

AusAID (Australian Agency for International Development) (2006) *Pacific 2020: Challenges and opportunities for growth*, Canberra: Commonwealth of Australia.

Cassels, S. (2006) 'Overweight in the Pacific: links between foreign dependence, global food trade, and obesity in the Federated States of Micronesia', *Globalization and Health*, 2(10).

Chandrasekhar, C. P. (2010) 'Financial liberalisation and the agrarian crisis', in M. Kelley and D. D'Souza (eds), *The World Bank in India: Undermining sovereignty, distorting development*, New Delhi: Black Swan.

Cirikiyasawa, P. N. B. (2007) 'Bringing down the barriers – charting a dynamic export development agenda: Fiji Islands, background country report', World Export Development Forum, Montreux, Switzerland: UNCTAD/WTO.

Denoon, D. (1997) 'Pacific Edens? Myths and realities of primitive affluence', in D. Denoon, M. Meleisea, S. Firth, J. Linnekin and K. Nero (eds), *The Cambridge History of the Pacific Islanders*, Cambridge: Cambridge University Press.

Down to Earth (2005) 'Woe the people', 28 February, www.downtoearth.org.in/node/9185, accessed 21 December 2013.

Evans, M., R. C. Sinclair, C. Fusimalohi, L. A. Viliami, V. Laiva'a and M. Freeman (2003) 'Consumption of traditional versus imported foods in Tonga: implications for programs designed to reduce diet-related non-communicable diseases in developing countries', *Ecology of Food and Nutrition*, 42(2): 153–76.

Food and Agriculture Organization (FAO), World Food Programme (WFP) and International Fund for Agricultural Development (IFAD) (2012) *The State of Food Insecurity in the World 2012. Economic growth is necessary but not sufficient to accelerate reduction of hunger and malnutrition*, Rome: FAO.

Food Secure Pacific Working Group (2010) *Towards a Food Secure Pacific: Framework for Action on Food Security in the Pacific, 2011–2015*, Port Vila, Vanuatu: Food Secure Pacific Working Group, www.spc.int/lrd/pafnet-publications/doc_download/1055-towards-a-food-secure-pacific-2011-2015-, accessed 23 December 2013.

Friel, S., R. Labonte and D. Sanders (2013) 'Measuring progress on diet-related NCDs: the need to address the causes of the causes', *The Lancet*, 381(9870): 903–4.

Gewertz, D. B. and F. K. Errington (2009) *Cheap Meat: Flap Food Nations in the Pacific Islands*, Berkeley: University of California Press.

Ghosh, J. (2010) 'The unnatural coupling: food and global finance', *Journal of Agrarian Change*, 10(1): 72–86.

— (2011) 'The cash option', *Frontline*, New Delhi, 26 February–11 March.

— (2013) 'Mad about cash transfers', *Frontline*, New Delhi, 29 December 2012–11 January.

Gittelsohn, J., H. Haberle, A. E. Vastine, W. Dyckman and N. A. Palafox (2003) 'Macro- and microlevel processes affect food choice and nutritional status in the Republic of the Marshall Islands', *Journal of Nutrition, American Society for Nutritional Sciences*, 133(1): 310S–313S.

Hughes, R. G. (2003) *Diet, food supply, and obesity in the Pacific*, Manila: Regional Office for the Western Pacific, WHO.

Jafri, A. (2010) 'The privatisation of seeds', in M. Kelley and D. D'Souza (eds), *The World Bank in India: Undermining sovereignty, distorting development*, New Delhi: Black Swan.

McGregor, A., R. M. Bourke, M. Manley, S. Tubuna and R. Deo (2009) 'Pacific Island food security: situation, challenges and opportunities', *Pacific Economic Bulletin*, 24(2): 24–42.

MoHFW, GOI (Ministry of Health and Family Welfare, Government of India) (2007) *National Family Health Survey – 3*, New Delhi: MoHFW, dhsprogram.com/pubs/pdf/FRIND3/FRIND3-Vol1[Oct-17-2008].pdf, accessed 23 December 2013.

NSSO (National Sample Survey Organisation) (2005) 'Consumer expenditure, employment–unemployment, situation assessment survey of farmers', NSS 58th Round, Report no. 496, New Delhi: Ministry of Statistics and Programme Implementation, Government of India.

Parkinson, S. (1982) 'Nutrition in the South Pacific: past and present', *Journal of Food and Nutrition*, 39(3): 121–5.

Parks, W. and D. Abbott (2009) *Protecting Pacific Island Children and Women during Economic and Food Crises*, Suva, Fiji: UNICEF Pacific and UNDP Pacific Centre.

Patnaik, U. (2003) 'Agrarian crisis and distress in rural India', *Macroscan*, 10 June, www.macroscan.org/fet/jun03/fet100603Agrarian%20Crisis_1.htm, accessed 23 December 2013.

— (2005) 'Theorizing food security and poverty in the era of economic reforms', *Social Scientist*, 33(7/8): 50–81.

— (2007a) 'Neoliberalism and rural poverty in India', *Economic and Political Weekly*, 42(30): 3132–50.

— (2007b) 'Foodstocks and hunger: causes of agrarian distress', in *The Republic of Hunger and Other Essays*, Gurgaon, India: Three Essays Collective.

PIB (Press Information Bureau), Government of India (2012) 'Indian agriculture shows resilience', 24 December, www.pib.nic.in/newsite/erelease.aspx?relid=91149, accessed 23 December 2013.

Plahe, J., S. Hawkes and S. Ponnamperuma (2012) 'The implications of free trade agreements for food sovereignty in the Pacific Island nations', Discussion paper, Suva, Fiji: Pacific Network on Globalisation, pang.org.fj/wp-content/uploads/2013/02/PANG-Ag-Discussion-Paper.pdf, accessed 23 December 2013.

Raghavan, M. (2008) 'Changing pattern of input use and cost of cultivation', *Economic and Political Weekly*, 43(26/27): 123–9.

Right to Food Campaign (2011) *Attack on PDS*, July, www.righttofoodindia.org/data/pds/July_2011_attack_on_pds_english.pdf, accessed 23 December 2013.

Sainath P. (2012) 'Farm suicides rise in Maharashtra, State still leads the list', *The Hindu*, 3 July, www.thehindu.com/todays-paper/tp-opinion/farm-suicides-rise-in-maharashtra-state-still-leads-the-list/article3596457.ece, accessed 23 December 2013.

Shatrugna, V. (2012) 'The wider effects of nutrition research: history of nutrition science and policy', *Infochange News & Features*, July, infochangeindia.org/agenda/malnutrition/the-wider-effects-of-nutrition-research.html, accessed 21 December 2013.

Simatupang, P. and E. M. Fleming (2005) 'Integrated report: food security strategies for selected South Pacific Island countries', Regional Co-ordination Centre for Research and Development of Coarse Grains, Pulses, Roots and Tuber Crops in the Humid Tropics of Asia and the Pacific.

Singh, S. P. (2012) 'Power rate highest in agriculture sector', *Business Standard*, 11 December, www.business-standard.com/article/economy-policy/power-rate-highest-in-agriculture-sector-112121102003_1.html, accessed 23 December 2013.

Sreekumar, N. and S. Dixit (2011) 'Challenges in rural electrification', *Economic and Political Weekly*, 46(43): 27–33.

Swaminathan, M. (2002) 'Excluding the needy: the public provisioning of food in India', *Social Scientist*, 30(3/4): 34–58.

Thaman, R. R. (1990) 'The evolution of the Fiji food system', in A. A. J. Jansen, S. Parkinson and A. F. S. Robertson (eds), *Food and Nutrition in Fiji: A historical review*, vol. 1, Suva, Fiji: Department of Nutrition and Dietetics, Fiji School of Medicine, Institute of Pacific Studies, University of the South Pacific.

Thaman, R. R. and W. C. Clarke (1983) *Food and National Development in the South Pacific*, Suva, Fiji: University of the South Pacific.

Thow, A. M. and W. Snowdon (2010) 'The effect of trade and trade policy on diet and health in the Pacific Islands', in C. Hawkes, C. Blouin, S. Henson, N. Drager and L. Dubé (eds), *Trade, Food, Diet and Health: Perspectives and Policy Options*, Oxford: Wiley-Blackwell, pp. 147–68.

Thow, A. M., B. Swinburn, S. Colagiuri et al. (2010) 'Trade and food policy: case studies from three Pacific Island countries', *Food Policy*, 35: 556–64.

Thow, A. M., P. Heywood, J. Schultz, C. Quested, S. Jan and S. Colagiuri (2011) 'Trade and the nutrition transition: strengthening policy for health in the Pacific', *Ecology of Food and Nutrition*, 50(1): 18–42.

UNDP (United Nations Development Programme) (2007) *Human Development Report, 2007–2008*, New York: UNDP.

UNICEF (United Nations Children's Fund) (2010) *Food and nutrition security in Pacific Island nations and territories*, Suva, Fiji, www.unicef.org/pacificislands/Position_Paper_for_web.pdf, accessed 25 December 2013.

Via Campesina (2007) *Declaration of Nyéléni, 27 February*, Forum for Food Sovereignty, Mali, viacampesina.org/en/index.php/main-issues-mainmenu-27/food-sovereignty-and-trade-mainmenu-38/262-declaration-of-nyi, accessed 24 December 2013.

World Bank (2004) *India – country assistance strategy for India*, Report no. 29374-IN, 15 September, Washington, DC: World Bank, www-wds.worldbank.org/servlet/WDSContentServer/WDSP/IB/2004/09/20/000160016_20040920102445/Rendered/PDF/293740REV.pdf, accessed 23 December 2013.

WTO (World Trade Organization) (2012) 'Briefing note: Samoa's accession to the WTO', Geneva: WTO, 6 September, www.wto.org/english/thewto_e/minist_e/min11_e/brief_samoa_e.htm, accessed 23 December 2013.

# C4 | BREAKING FREE FROM GENDER-BASED VIOLENCE

Gender-based violence (GBV) is understood as violence that is directed against a person on the basis of gender, and is an outcome of gender inequalities and discrimination. It is universal and transcends race, caste, class, culture, ethnicity, identity, disability, religion and regions. However, the forms of violence and their prevalence vary across locations.

The intersections of gender and race, caste, class, religion, sexuality, disability, age, work, etc., create further vulnerabilities to violence (Sama 2013). While women and girls are the primary targets of gender-based violence, boys and men, transgender and queer persons experience violence based on their gender and sexual identities. Gender-based violence is used to assert control and power, to 'punish' supposed transgression of gender, sexuality, religion and caste norms (Sama n.d). For example, in war, racial, ethnic, caste-based and communal violence, sexual violence is used as a tool to punish and dishonour the 'other'.

A range of factors conspire to maintain and perpetuate gender-based violence, considered one of the most severe forms of human rights violations. These include social, economic and political structures, discriminatory legal systems, and cultural systems that legitimize violence. Gender-based violence manifests in various forms – verbal, non-verbal, physical, mental, emotional, social and economic. The forms of gender-based violence include intimate partner violence, non-partner sexual violence (the most prevalent globally), child sexual abuse, trafficking of women and girls, female genital mutilation, sexual harassment at the workplace, forced marriage, forced sterilization, sex selection at birth, etc. (Sama 2013).

## Recognition of gender-based violence as a human rights and public health issue

The Convention on the Elimination of All Forms of Discrimination against Women (CEDAW) was adopted by the United Nations General Assembly in 1979. However, international bodies such as the United Nations did not explicitly articulate a strong position on the issue until 1992, when an expert committee monitoring the CEDAW adopted General Recommendation 19,[1] correcting a major flaw in the Convention. In 1993, at the Vienna Conference, Violence against Women was officially recognized as a human rights violation and the General Assembly adopted the Declaration on the Elimination of Violence against Women (DEVAW) in the same year. A Special Rapporteur on Violence against Women (SRVAW) was established in 1994 as a special mechanism to monitor violence against women, including its causes and consequences worldwide.

In 1995, the Platform for Action of the Fourth World Conference on Women, Beijing, clearly articulated the need to strengthen health systems and to involve healthcare providers in addressing gender-based violence. The core document directed countries to '... develop supportive programmes and train primary health workers to recognize and care for girls and women of all ages who have experienced any form of violence, especially domestic violence, sexual abuse, or other abuse resulting from armed and non-armed conflict' (Section 106(q)).

The World Health Organization (WHO) in its 2009 report on *Women and Health* emphasizes that 'violence is an additional significant risk to women's sexual and reproductive health and can also result in mental ill-health and other chronic health problems' (WHO 2009). In 2013, a declaration of commitment to end sexual violence in conflict was signed by 113 member states at the 68th United Nations General Assembly. In the same year, the fifty-seventh session of the Commission on the Status of Women (CSW) resolved to eliminate all forms of violence against women and girls. Further, it recognized the adverse consequences on health, the need to provide support to victims and survivors, along with affordable and accessible healthcare services, and take necessary steps to sensitize and strengthen the capacity of public officials and professionals and hold them accountable, including in the healthcare sector (CSW 2013).

Women's rights groups, organizations, networks and alliances have been actively involved in country, regional as well as international processes aimed

---

**Box C4.1 UNiTE to End Violence against Women**

The United Nations observes International Day for the Elimination of Violence against Women on 25 November every year. The date marks the brutal assassination, in 1960, of the three Mirabal sisters, political activists in the Dominican Republic.

In 2008, the United Nations secretary-general's UNiTE to End Violence against Women campaign was initiated to raise public awareness and increase political will and resources for preventing and ending all forms of violence against women and girls in all parts of the world. In July 2012 the UN secretary-general proclaimed the 25th of every month as Orange Day to highlight issues relevant to preventing and ending violence against women and girls.

*Source*: UNiTE (n.d.)

at informing and strongly advocating for recognition of gender-based violence as a human rights and health issue.

## Gender-based violence: how prevalent is it?

Global data indicates that 35.6 per cent of women have reported experiencing physical and/or sexual partner violence, or sexual violence by a non-partner (WHO 2013a). The prevalence in different WHO regions is as follows:

TABLE C4.1 Prevalence of gender-based violence

| Region (WHO) | Prevalence % |
| --- | --- |
| South-East Asian | 37.7 |
| East Mediterranean | 37.0 |
| African | 36.6 |
| Region of the Americas | 29.8 |
| European | 25.4 |
| Western Pacific | 24.6 |

Intimate partner violence is the most common type of violence against women, affecting 30 per cent of women worldwide; 7.2 per cent of women have experienced sexual violence by a non-partner (ibid.). The gendered nature of violence is evident from the fact that more than 75 per cent of violence against women globally is committed by male intimate partners (Fleming et al. 2013). Existing figures depict a small part of the entire picture, given the

**Image C4.1** Protest against rising sexual violence in New Delhi, India (Sama Resource Group for Women and Health)

silence and stigma surrounding reporting of gender-based violence and the perceived as well as real risks entailed in its disclosure.

## Consequences for human rights and health

Gender-based violence violates a range of human rights of women and girls, including their rights to Life, Health, Equality and Non-discrimination, Liberty and Mobility, Free Speech and Expression, Social Security, Education, Work and Livelihood, Shelter and Adequate Standard of Living, Participation in Social and Political Activities (Sama 2013). The Right to Health implies freedom from violence and non-discrimination, and gender equality and access to various other socio-economic determinants.

GBV has extremely serious implications for health, both physical and psychological, and has immediate as well as long-term consequences. Women who have been physically or sexually abused by their partners are 16 per cent more likely to have a low-birth-weight baby; they are more than twice as likely to have an abortion, almost twice as likely to experience depression, and, in some regions, are 1.5 times more likely to acquire HIV, as compared to women who have not experienced partner violence. Women who have experienced non-partner sexual violence are 2.3 times more likely to have alcohol use disorders and 2.6 times more likely to experience depression or anxiety (WHO 2013a). Victims of GBV suffer from a range of conditions that affect their reproductive health. Disability, anxiety and post-traumatic stress disorder (PTSD) are also important consequences of GBV. There is also increasing evidence linking intimate partner violence with the health of children (ibid.).

However, despite such evidence, actions to prevent GBV and to address public health consequences remain limited. A public health approach implies multi-sectoral, coordinated efforts to prevent gender-based violence as well as to address the consequences of violence.

## Health system response to gender-based violence

The healthcare system and healthcare providers are often the first point of contact for survivors of violence. Studies have shown that women who have experienced violence are more likely to seek healthcare than those women who have not, even if they do not disclose the violence (ibid.).

However, barriers to accessing healthcare exist in most countries and particularly for survivors of gender-based violence (see Box C4.2). Currently, only a limited number of countries provide comprehensive services to survivors of violence in general and of intimate partner and sexual violence in particular (ibid.). Even when services for dealing with the immediate physical health consequences of GBV are available, mental health services for survivors of violence are widely absent (ibid.). Consequently, not all those experiencing violence directly seek healthcare and yet, when they do, their health problems may not be attributed to violence.

## Box C4.2 Access to care for immigrant and racialized women survivors of sexual assault

The Peel Committee on Sexual Assault (PCSA) was formed in 1989 by a group of service providers concerned about the lack of services in the region of Peel, Ontario, Canada, for survivors of sexual abuse. PCSA conducted a study that examined 'racial inequities of the Canadian Health Care System and its impact on access to primary health care for immigrant and racialized women survivors of sexual assault' in the region of Peel.
Some of the significant findings were:

- Only 6 per cent of sexual assault survivors ever approach police. Most never approach or tell anybody. Most survivors have at least two chronic illnesses.
- One service provider, working with survivors of sexual assault, reported that 75–85 per cent of the women accessing services are racialized or immigrant women.
- Factors that place immigrant and racialized women at risk include: systemic racism, language barriers, isolation, lack of status (legal authorization to remain in Canada), fear, lack of knowledge of resources that can help, and different understandings of what constitutes sexual assault. Respondents reported that women do not ask for help because they fear deportation. One respondent reported: 'For blind women like me, we need to know where to go. When I finally opened my door [to leave my husband], I didn't know where to turn because there was so much fear.'
- Barriers to accessing primary healthcare that were identified included: lack of access to health practitioners; fragmented health services for survivors of sexual assault; lack of practitioner awareness of the complex experiences of racialized and immigrant survivors; and barriers to disclosure. A respondent said: '… you don't have the opportunity to talk with them [doctors] … they say they don't have time for you … how do we open their minds and our hearts that we need more time?'

Clearly, there needs to be a reorganization of primary healthcare services for immigrant and racialized women. The impact of violence and sexual assault on the health of women should be central to their care, particularly for survivors living with chronic illness. Ultimately, the assessment of how gender and race impact women's health could result in possible interventions that will improve individual overall health and health equity in the system.

Further, since the healthcare system may often be the first and the only point of contact that survivors of gender-based violence access, it is an important location for provision of a comprehensive response, including provision and facilitation of referrals. Healthcare providers can play a key role in screening for violence as well as in referring victims to appropriate agencies for help. Health facilities can also play an important role in documenting GBV, which is vital for victims who seek justice.

To effectively reach out to victims of GBV, healthcare systems need to inculcate a 'gendered' approach and build the capacity of healthcare providers to deal with gender, sexuality and violence. Care providers who have undergone training are more likely to enquire about GBV and to feel competent to address the needs of survivors. Survivors are also likely to be more inclined and encouraged to discuss the violence or abuse if they perceive the provider to be sensitive and skilled, and if follow-up is offered (PAHO 2003). Studies have clearly shown that negative attitudes of healthcare providers are identified by women as the primary obstacle to accessing necessary care.

## The way ahead

Policy, law and guidelines on gender-based violence must incorporate a comprehensive health system response. It is necessary to develop clear guidelines, protocols and curricula that are gender- and rights-based. The healthcare sector's response to gender-based violence in humanitarian emergency situations (disasters, conflicts, etc.) needs to be strengthened.

Elimination of gender-based violence requires action at various levels, including steps to address societal issues related to power and dominance, access to resources and entitlements, etc. This is an appropriate moment to review progress and the challenges that remain, as well as to inform future development frameworks and strategies towards preventing and ending gender-based violence.

A new development framework (post-2015) that is transformative must address the structural causes of inequality and marginalization. It must address the convergence of the pernicious effects of globalization, militarism, conflict and fundamentalisms that particularly target women's bodies and livelihoods. Eliminating violence against women must be a target of the post-2015 agenda, along with ensuring decision-making of women in the home, in the community, in development planning and implementation (UN Women 2014).

## Note

1 The General Recommendation no. 19 focused on Violence against Women. It specifically includes GBV within the definition of discrimination and defines GBV as 'violence that is directed against a woman because she is a woman or that affects women disproportionately. It includes acts that inflict physical, mental or sexual harm or suffering, threats of such acts, coercion and other deprivations of liberty.' The GR 19 also appended detailed comments on violence to the different articles of the Convention.

## References

CEDAW (Convention on the Elimination of All Forms of Discrimination against Women) (1979) United Nations General Assembly, www.un.org/womenwatch/daw/cedaw/cedaw.htm, accessed 22 February 2014.

CSW (Commission on Status of Women) (2013) *CSW57 Agreed Conclusions on the elimination and prevention of all forms of violence against women and girls*, www.un.org/womenwatch/daw/csw/csw57/CSW57_Agreed_Conclusions_(CSW_report_excerpt).pdf, accessed 22 February 2014.

Fleming, P. J., G. Barker, J. McCleary-Sills et al. (2013) *Engaging men and boys in advancing women's agency: where we stand and new directions*, World Bank.

PAHO (Pan American Health Organization) (2003) *Gender Based Violence: The Health Sector Responds*, www1.paho.org/English/DD/PUB/ViolenceAgainstWomen-ENG.pdf, accessed 30 January 2014.

Sama (2013) *Gender Based Violence and Health: Strengthening Linkages and Responses*, Information booklet.

— (n.d.) Unpublished draft.

SR-VAW (The United Nations Special Rapporteur on Violence against Women) (2009) *15 Years of The United Nations Special Rapporteur on Violence against Women (1994–2009), Its Causes and Consequences*, www2.ohchr.org/english/issues/women/rapporteur/docs/15YearReviewofVAWMandate.pdf, accessed 22 February 2014.

UN Women (United Nations Entity for Gender Equality and the Empowerment of Women) (2014) 'Member States and civil society organizations in Asia-Pacific endorse a stand-alone gender equality goal for post-2015', Bangkok, 18 February, www.unwomen.org/lo/news/stories/2014/2/ge-post-2015-stand-alone-goal-endorsed, accessed 22 February 2014.

UNiTE (n.d.) 'About UNiTE', www.un.org/en/women/endviolence/about.shtml, accessed 22 February 2014.

WHO (World Health Organization) (2009) *Women and Health: Today's Evidence, Tomorrow's Agenda*, whqlibdoc.who.int/hq/2009/WHO_IER_MHI_STM.09.1_eng.pdf, accessed 22 February.

— (2013a) *Global and Regional Estimates of Violence against Women: Prevalence and effects of intimate partner violence and non partner sexual violence*, apps.who.int/iris/bitstream/10665/85239/1/9789241564625_eng.pdf, accessed 22 February 2014.

— (2013b) *Responding to intimate partner violence and sexual violence against women: WHO clinical and policy guidelines*.

Statistics reflecting the dire state of sanitation in developing countries remain shocking. Inadequate sanitation underlies 2,213,000 deaths per year due to unsafe water and hygiene (Bartram et al. 2012). The Millennium Development Goal to halve the proportion of people without access to sanitation between 1990 and 2015 will not be attained, leaving an estimated 2.5 billion people without even a simple improved latrine and 1 billion still practising open defecation (WHO/UNICEF 2013).

In response, a new approach called Community Led Total Sanitation (CLTS) has taken the sanitation world by storm. From a modest start in Bangladesh, CLTS is now being adopted in the rural areas of many Asian and African countries. The approach has been adopted by the World Bank's Water and Sanitation Programme, the Water Supply and Sanitation Collaborative Council, UNICEF, WaterAid, PLAN International and other international NGOs. Powered by the influence of these organizations, CLTS has been adopted in over forty-four LMICs (Bartram et al. 2012) and at least twenty countries have designated CLTS as their national sanitation approach in rural areas (HEART 2013).

The starting point for CLTS is the argument that communities should control their own development and that 'outsiders' should play the role of 'triggering' community responses. The 'community' ensures that households build their own toilets using their own resources. CLTS facilitators 'trigger' communities to recognize the link between open defecation and disease. The community then formulates its own plan for each household to build a latrine, so eradication of open defecation is 'total'. No subsidy or external technical expertise is provided. A distinctive feature about CLTS is that it forces participants to confront their 'shit' by using this word, visiting places where people openly defecate, and tracing the faecal-to-oral transmission route to a glass of water on the table (Bongartz et al. 2010: 29).

According to practitioners and their academic supporters, CLTS has achieved remarkable success with thousands of rural areas declaring themselves 'open defecation free' (ODF). Few analyses, however, have critically examined CLTS within a broader socio-political and economic context or posed any fundamental challenges to its premises.

CLTS passes responsibility to communities while absolving governments from taking any fiscal or managerial responsibilities towards provision of

**Image C5.1** Community hand pump in India; open defecation pollutes water sources such as this (Nilayan/ActionAid)

sanitation services to poor people in rural areas. It claims to 'trigger' change but does not monitor or intervene if it sparks damaging local actions. CLTS arguably exemplifies several features of a neoliberal approach to development – one which individualizes problems and their solutions and frees governments from promoting the welfare of their citizens.

After outlining CLTS's main tenets, this chapter reviews the main issues around CLTS's effectiveness, particularly sustainability and moving up the sanitation ladder. Its main aim is to explore the value-choices and power dynamics informing CLTS, especially in terms of individual human rights versus the health of the 'community', as well as the balance between a person's right to dignity and their right to access to sanitation. Finally, the chapter places CLTS in a wider global-political perspective.

A lack of local monitoring and data on CLTS's health and social impacts prohibits a more extensive critique. The lack of monitoring systems is surprising, particularly given its energetic promotion by large international organizations.

### Distinctive features of CLTS

Triggering is the primary contribution of the 'facilitator' in CLTS, and aims to harness community energy and thus lead to rapid toilet construction and an open defecation free (ODF) status (Mehta 2014: 8). The core elements of triggering are standard. After some preliminary discussion of the health status of the community, the facilitator insists that participants use the word 'shit' over any protestations of taboo or reference to societal norms. S/he then uses participatory tools to raise awareness of the community's faecal status. A typical 'triggering' session involves the following:

- Participants take the facilitators on the 'walk of shame', to the areas where people defecate in the open. The facilitator pauses to have a discussion there, which forces people to see and smell their 'shit'. Participants draw a map that locates where people openly defecate.
- Having gathered a bit of shit surreptitiously during the walk, the facilitator illustrates faecal–oral contamination visually by silently placing an object with a small amount of shit in water and near food, allowing flies to dart between the two. The implications of open defecation for everyone's health are discussed.
- Facilitated with humour, participants calculate the amount of shit that the community produces annually.

The facilitator then leaves the group to formulate its own plans to construct latrines according to the resources available. Aside from safety information on basic latrine location, no external resources are provided, e.g. training on toilet construction, building materials or subsidies.

Reports suggest that what is frequently referred to as CLTS is actually a 'hybrid' approach that development organizations have fashioned in response to their direct experience. In a 'hybrid' approach the CLTS component is limited to 'triggering', which may then be combined with some training on building toilets, the provision of slabs or some subsidies. Since these hybrids exist in most countries where CLTS is being implemented, the impetus towards and impact of emerging hybrid approaches requires further research. This chapter analyses CLTS in its 'pure' form, as originally conceptualized, as far as possible.

### How sustainable is CLTS?

Efforts to develop new approaches to sanitation were stimulated by the recognition that just building a latrine does not ensure its use. CLTS's precursor – education and awareness-raising through an approach called Participatory Hygiene and Sanitation Transformation (PHAST) – was found to be too didactic. CLTS, which replaces this approach, is premised on the idea that a community-led process will lead to behaviour change that is sustainable in terms of the maintenance and use of latrines.

While previous programmes had outsiders build toilets or advise on their construction, CLTS places the responsibility entirely in the hands of the community. It is assumed that households draw on others' knowledge and that they creatively find local resources. This usually means that poor people end up building very basic latrines – a shallow pit protected by a structure built of local materials, which sometimes collapses in heavy rains or wind.

Thus, most households start at the very bottom of the sanitation ladder. The first rung on the ladder is 'unimproved sanitation', which does not ensure people have no contact with human waste. Latrines built (as described above) are unimproved facilities. The next rung is 'shared systems' that are not considered improved owing to their shared nature, and finally systems per household, considered 'improved sanitation'. Improved sanitation facilities include flush or pour flush (to piped sewer system, septic tank, or pit latrine), Ventilated Improved Pit (VIP) latrine, pit latrine with slab or a composting toilet (WHO/UNICEF 2013: 12).

Without some form of subsidy, poor rural households will generally not be able to afford improvements that would allow them to move up the ladder. In the case of 'pure' CLTS, households within communities that have been triggered and reached ODF status will be considered out of the 'danger zone' and are unlikely to receive the support necessary to move up the ladder.

The second question that needs to be asked is: even at this basic level of sanitation, does CLTS result in lasting behavioural change? While fear and disgust are considered 'particularly effective in public health campaigns in terms of drawing attention to the health threat' (Morales et al. 2012), evidence is 'less clear about the capacity of shocking imagery and texts to influence sustained behaviour change' (Lupton 2014: 4). Not only can poverty prevent the poor from building new toilets, but it may also prevent their being rebuilt after collapsing (Mehta 2014: 12). It has also been argued that, in fact, 'the use of shaming and taunting both disqualifies it [CLTS] as an empowerment approach and is likely to undermine its effectiveness in promoting long-term behaviour change' (Engel and Susilo 2014: 174).

In the CLTS approach it is expected that 'natural leaders' will emerge who will monitor progress and promote maintenance. Natural leaders emerge with enthusiasm about eradicating OD in their area, although their original commitment may be eroded over time, particularly when new priorities arise. Typically such leaders develop a relationship with outsiders who count on them for reports and include them in training, so there is a direct benefit to them in terms of qualifications, experience and networks that can assist them in improving their livelihood and/or improving their standing in the community.

Most surprisingly, given the support and involvement of international organizations, including the World Bank and UNICEF, it does not appear that systems have been put in place to monitor and collect data on the impact and sustainability of CLTS. To date, most analyses are based on anecdotal evidence from selected cases, in support of the authors' perspectives, though there have been a number of calls for a systematic analysis of CLTS (Galvin 2013; Bartram et al. 2012).

At a recent World Sanitation Summit, one presenter recounted a story to illustrate the power of CLTS. In one area where he had worked, the community was triggered but one woman refused to build a toilet. Some community members followed her around the village until she defecated in the bush. They forced her to pick up her faeces and carry it around until she agreed to build a toilet. The conference room erupted in applause (Galvin 2012b). The following section explores how such stories may be understood in terms of a rights-based analysis.

### A rights-based analysis of CLTS

Rights-based issues that arise in relation to the implementation of CLTS relate to the acceptability of CLTS using, or manipulating, negative emotions such as shame and disgust, and the impact that this has on individuals' identities and on community relations, stratification or stigmatization. Critics of the approach question the relationship between individual human rights and the common good, referring to actual accounts of CLTS implementation and its impact on individual human rights (Bartram et al. 2012: 501). They refer to accounts (Chatterjee 2011) that 'squads' threw stones at people openly defecating. Other accounts describe how households' survival was threatened to force them to build a latrine: by cutting off their water supplies or locking them out of their homes (ibid.). An even more horrifying story is one where arbitration was denied to young women and girls who were raped while openly defecating (Mahbub 2009).

> To what extent is it acceptable, in pursuing the *common good* of widespread sanitation, to compromise *individual human rights*: to restrict access [to justice] in the case of rape [if it occurs when openly defecating]; to confiscate property, especially when this represents the source of family income [as a means to force a household to build a toilet]; to threaten physical integrity in the case of stoning; and to withhold water in the case of deprivation of water supply? And to what extent is it tolerable and reasonable to sanction system-atic humiliation of community members who will often represent the least educated and those with the least means to act in the manner demanded? (Bartram et al. 2012: 501)

The second question of rights is not one of level but of substance, of balancing the right to dignity against the socio-economic right to access to sanitation. It has been argued that CLTS is based on a logic that undermines human dignity and is unacceptable. The immediate experience of CLTS infringes people's dignity, with possible long-term implications, and that right to dignity precedes all others. For example, people begin to be considered 'clean' or 'dirty' depending on whether they build and use a toilet (Mehta 2011: 9). It is necessary that we consider 'the morality of punishing the poor for their circumstances' (Engel and Susilo 2014: 174). Within the public health literature, the ethical, moral and political implications of using disgust in campaigns have come under scrutiny. Disgust can 'reinforce stigmatisation and discrimination against individuals and groups who are positioned as disgusting', reinforcing 'negative attitudes towards already disadvantaged and marginalised individuals and societal groups' (Lupton 2014: 1).

## Who takes responsibility?

CLTS proponents hold that any human rights infringements are due to the way some communities or practitioners implement CLTS. Following this logic, it is important to identify who is responsible for such infringements and who can be held accountable. We need to ask whether the coercive actions described in the earlier section are condoned actively or implicitly by those who developed CLTS, promote its adoption, and support its implementation.

'Handing over the stick' to the community, a common reference in participatory rural appraisal to shifting power between the facilitator and participants, can allow those handing over the stick to relinquish all responsibility for what they have sparked. CLTS proponents, with the end of eradicating open defecation in mind, potentially leave the 'community' to its own devices and turn a blind eye to the means of implementation. If infringements of human rights are occurring, even defined in a narrow physical sense, those supporting CLTS are responsible for intervening to stop such behaviour. If CLTS does unleash actions described earlier and cannot be controlled, then CLTS as an approach can result in clear human rights infringements and is unacceptable.

Instead of engaging with the complexity of the entire concept of 'community', its heterogeneity, elitism and conflicts, CLTS tends towards romanticizing the 'community', treating it as a homogeneous blank slate. Yet the impact of CLTS interventions is highly dependent on the nature of individual communities. The CLTS approach feeds on and reinforces deeper pre-existing socio-political dynamics at the community level. Even with the best outside intentions, such interventions can unintentionally lead to negative consequences, such as reinforcing class and other divisions, or result in stigmatization (Galvin 2010).

This takes us back to the original premise of CLTS, that it is 'community-led'. Yet the catalyst of CLTS, the idea and the spark in a community, comes from the outside. It is outsider-driven but community-led. While outside facilitators and a few community leaders may be convinced that CLTS can improve the community's well-being, its actual impact and sustainability may be apparent only in the future.

## Power dynamics of CLTS

A principal premise of CLTS is that one of the main reasons for the failure of sanitation approaches to lead to sustained behavioural change is that they are driven by outsiders. However, the entire approach of CLTS is formulated and introduced by outsiders. Outsiders include international organizations that often are the drivers – the Water and Sanitation Programme of the World

**Image C5.2** Poor community living near a riverbank in Haiti: communities are often forced to use a single water source for a range of activities (Mathieu Poirier)

Bank, UNICEF and DfID and large NGOs, including PLAN and WaterAid. In reality there is an underlying element of control: communities may be implementing, but the path has been defined by these organizations.

CLTS hides behind wider power dynamics of donors and the influential water and sanitation fraternity who promote an approach that embodies the dominant neoliberal paradigm under the guise of good community development. In the 1990s, the World Bank's new approach to sanitation was reinforced by the re-placement of 'supply-side thinking' with a focus on local communities accessing 'water and sanitation services according to their own demands' (WSP 2011). In other words, the neoliberal project and the associated structural adjustment approaches that the Bank applied to public utilities in the 1980s furthered the hostility to state provision of sanitation and water services (Amenga-Etego and Grusky 2005). At the grassroots level, this was presented as a shift to demand-responsive approaches which encouraged the poor to 'take responsibility for their own development' – and, of course, to pay for it!

International organizations have not adopted CLTS owing to evidence of its success, but have done so on 'pragmatic' grounds. By promoting an extremely low-cost approach to sanitation, donors are promoting a solution that LMICs can afford. They need not pressure governments to change their priorities in terms of spending or stepped-up implementation. International agencies simply need to support governments in redirecting their bureaucracies towards a new approach. So CLTS is presently considered by most international donors as the most effective approach to scaling up sanitation.

Countries have an obligation to provide services, and especially services where benefit accrues to the most needy, and to assist people to move up the sanitation ladder. Moreover, investment in sanitation is analogous to investment in vaccination: an individually directed intervention (or household-directed in the case of sanitation) has an additional positive population health effect. If countries do have sufficient funds to provide access to sanitation, introducing CLTS with no support for hardware can be retrogressive. Whether it is in a country like Nigeria, afloat in oil revenues, or in wealthy South Africa, where the government has committed to providing sanitation, '[w]e must question international agencies working with governments to shame poor people into digging their own pits to shit in, while stopping subsidies that assist them to build a proper toilet' (Galvin 2012a). Instead of encouraging governments to adopt CLTS and allowing them to appear to be taking responsibility for sanitation while abrogating responsibility to communities, governments need to be encouraged to develop communities' capacity and to redirect resources towards the poorest.

## Conclusion

CLTS is not a revolutionary magic bullet. There is a need for systematic monitoring and analysis to move past anecdotes about the sustainability and impact of CLTS. What is missing is a basis on which to assess local change in the context of broader impacts of the approach, which may be negative.

The flush toilet was last century's solution to the sanitation crisis in the industrializing world. Today the sanitation crisis is rapidly escalating, with a growing and urbanizing poor population in LMICs and a scarcity of fresh water and infrastructure. The embrace of CLTS by powerful international agencies and NGOs should not deflect attention away from developing and financing novel technologies that could assist the poorest in accessing a more advanced and safer form of sanitation. And those donors, policy-makers and practitioners who are influenced to view CLTS as 'empowering' and the long-sought-for answer to the sanitation crisis should recognize that for some, perhaps many, of the poor, the process may be demeaning and represent a 'victim-blaming' approach to a basic health issue and human right, where an equitable response should be state-supported.

## References

Amenga-Etego, R. N. and S. Grusky (2005) 'The new face of conditionalities: the World Bank and water privatization in Ghana', in D. A. McDonald and G. Ruiters (eds), *The Age of* *Commodity: Water Privatization in Southern Africa*, London: Earthscan, pp. 275–92.

Bartram, J., K. Charles, B. Evans, L. O'Hanlon and S. Pedley (2012) 'Commentary on community-led total sanitation and human rights: should the right to community-wide health be won at the cost of individual rights?', *Journal of Water and Health*, 10(4): 499–503.

Bongartz, P., S. M. Musyoki, A. Milligan and H. Ashley (2010) 'Overview: Tales of shit: Community-Led Total Sanitation in Africa', *Participatory Learning and Action*, 61(1): 27–50.

Chatterjee, L. (2011) 'Time to acknowledge the dirty truth behind community-led total sanitation', *Guardian*, www.guardian.co.uk/global-development/poverty matters/2011/jun/09/dirty-truth-behind-community-sanitation, accessed 23 April 2014.

Engel, S. and A. Susilo (2014) 'Shaming and sanitation in Indonesia: a return to colonial public health practices?', *Development and Change*, 45(1): 157–78, doi: 10.1111/dech.12075.

Galvin, M. (2010) Unintended consequences: development interventions and socio-political change in rural South Africa', in B. Freund and H. Witt (eds), *Development Dilemmas in Post-Apartheid South Africa*, Pietermaritzburg: University of KwaZulu-Natal Press.

— (2012a) *Community Led Total Sanitation: A stunning sanitation solution for Africa?*, www.canadians.org/node/3523, accessed 23 April 2014.

— (2012b) Personal observation communicated by Mary Galvin, Associate Professor, Department of Anthropology and Development Studies, University of Johannesburg.

— (2013) *Addressing Southern Africa's Development Challenges through Community Led Total Sanitation*, Oxfam.

HEART (Health and Education Advice & Resource Team) (2013) 'Community-Led Total Sanitation in Africa', Helpdesk report produced for DfID.

Lupton, D. (2014) 'The pedagogy of disgust: the ethical, moral and political implications of using disgust in public health campaigns', *Critical Public Health*, doi: 10.1080/09581596.2014.885115.

Mahbub, A. (2009) 'Social dynamics of CLTS: inclusion of children, women and vulnerable', CLTS Conference, 16–18 December, Brighton.

Mehta, L. (2011) *Shit Matters: Community Led-Total Sanitation and the Sanitation Challenge for the 21st Century*, Warwickshire: Practical Action Publishing.

— (2014) 'Community Led Total Sanitation and the politics of scaling up', in E. S. Norman, C. Cook and A. Cohen (eds), *Negotiating Water Governance: Why the Politics of Scale Matter*, London: Ashgate Press.

Morales, A. C., E. C. Wu and G. J. Fitzsimons (2012) 'How disgust enhances the effectiveness of fear appeals', *Journal of Marketing Research*, 49(3): 383–93, doi: 10.1509/jmr.07.0364.

WHO/UNICEF (2013) 'Progress on sanitation and drinking-water, 2013', Joint Monitoring Programme for Water, www.wssinfo.org, accessed 23 April 2014.

WSP (2011) 'About WSP', www.wsp.org/wsp/about, accessed 23 April 2014.

# C6 | EXTRACTIVE INDUSTRIES AND HEALTH

Mining is one of the world's most lucrative industries. In 2011, the forty largest companies in the mining industry (representing 80 per cent of the market) made US$700 billion in revenues (PricewaterhouseCoopers 2012) (See Table C6.1). Impacts of this industry on people's health have generated growing concern and raised important questions about the social and political forces and governance structures underpinning these activities. Mining and drilling are seen as necessary to support 'development'. However, the need to better regulate, contain or even eliminate these activities, in certain cases, is pressing.

The health impact of extractive industries encompasses myriad impacts on social determinants of health, ranging from environmental degradation to income inequality to structural violence and beyond. The frustration of communities in which mining and drilling take place has been so extreme and long lasting that many are taking a radical, anti-mining stance, and slogans such as *leave the oil in the soil* are gaining voices.

This chapter summarizes existing findings related to various aspects of mining and health and delineates major challenges to the health and well-being of the 3.4 billion people who live in countries with significant mining operations.

**Image C6.1** Coal mining in the nineteenth century in the USA (Boston Public Library)

TABLE C6.1 Overview of the global extractive industry (major centres)

|  | South Africa | Russia | Australia | Ukraine | Guinea |
|---|---|---|---|---|---|
| Mining as a % of GPD | 18 | 33 | 10 | 6 | 26 |
| Top mining companies | BHP Billiton Anglo American Impala Platinum | Norilsk Nickel Mining Amur Minerals Corp. Anglo American Platinum Ltd | BHP Billiton City Giold | Anika LLC Black Iron Inc. | Newmont Mining Corp. Affinor Resources Inc. Alcoa Inc. Anglo Aluminum Corp. |
| Mineral reserves | $2.5 trillion | $794 billion (iron ore) | $737 billion | $510 billion (iron ore) | $222 billion (bauxite) |
| Mined minerals | Coal Cromium Diamond Gold Platinum | Aluminium Bauxite Coal Copper Diamond Gold Iron ore Nickel Steel | Bauxite Diamond Gold Iron ore Uranium Zinc | Aluminium Coal Diamond Gold Iron ore Uranium | Bauxite Diamond Gold Iron ore Uranium |

*Source*: Hydralok n.d.

## Impact of extractive industries on health

Health impacts of mining occur during every phase of its life cycle. They start with exploration for exploitable deposits, often preceded by the removal of those who own and/or use the land, followed by the construction of mining infrastructure. Then the 'productive phase' involves the mining of the ore and the extraction and beneficiation of the metal. The final closure of an exhausted mine theoretically includes the rehabilitation of the land, but this rarely occurs.

*Direct occupational health effects* Historically mining was among the deadliest of occupations owing to 'brown lung disease', fatal explosions and mine collapses. A large-scale study found that underground gold miners in Australia, North America, South America and Africa suffered from 'decreased life expectancy; increased frequency of cancer of the trachea, bronchus, lung, stomach, and liver; increased frequency of pulmonary tuberculosis (PTB), silicosis, and pleural diseases [see Box C6.1]; increased frequency of insect-borne diseases, such as malaria and dengue fever; noise-induced hearing loss; increased prevalence of certain bacterial and viral diseases; and diseases of the blood, skin, and musculoskeletal system' (Eisler 2003).

Underground explosions of methane and other gases trap and kill thousands of miners every year. Owing to poor ventilation in underground shafts, miners are exposed to harmful gases, dust, toxins and heat, leading to silicosis and

---

**Box C6.1 Silicosis, TB and HIV – the 'perfect storm'**

Approximately 69,000 miners died in accidents in South Africa in the first ninety-three years of the twentieth century and more than a million were seriously injured. In 1993, out of every 100,000 gold miners, 113 died in accidents, 2,000 suffered a reportable injury, 1,100 developed active tuberculosis and of these 25 died; in 1990 about 500 were identified as having silicosis (TRC 1998).

Biological and social factors combine to create a 'perfect storm' for the interaction among silicosis, TB and HIV. Silicosis substantially increases the risk of TB to a magnitude similar to that of HIV infection. The TB risks of silicosis and HIV infection combine multiplicatively. Consequently, the highest recorded rates of TB worldwide have been reported in South African gold miners. The prevalence of TB in gold miners increased from 806 per 100,000 in 1991 to 3821 in 2004. HIV prevalence rose from less than 1 per cent in 1987 to 27 per cent in 2000 (Nelson et al. 2010).

---

other lung diseases, heat stroke and cancer. Large numbers of miners sharing limited underground air create conditions for tuberculosis and other respiratory diseases (Ogola et al. 2002). Coal mining causes extremely high occupational mortality. Uranium miners face elevated levels of lung cancer, silicosis and, together with the surrounding population, are exposed to radiation, causing birth defects, immune impairment and cancer. Poorly maintained mines in the former Soviet bloc are among the most dangerous in the world, with hundreds killed in recent years owing to explosions and collapses (Birn et al. 2009). Despite increasing mechanization, these problems continue.

Loud noise, a ubiquitous hazard across all sectors of the mining industry, can result in significant hearing loss and hypertension (Driscoll 2007; Donoghue 2004). Exposure to vibration due to vehicles and power tools is a risk factor for musculoskeletal conditions, especially lower back and neck injuries (Driscoll 2007). Heat exhaustion can be caused by thermal stress related to surface mines with hot ambient temperatures as well as underground mines with high humidity, geothermal gradients in deep mines and liberation of heat by mining machinery and equipment (Driscoll 2007; Donoghue et al. 2000).

Toxic metals such as mercury are commonly used by miners to amalgamate gold and other precious metals, often with bare hands, leading to occupational exposures as well as environmental exposures once the metals are discarded as waste. A number of studies have found very high levels of mercury in edible fish stocks near mines, which pose particular risks to children (Eisler 2003). Radioactive ores increase the risk of certain cancers (Driscoll 2007).

*Effect on the environment* Of the thirty most polluted places in the world, as documented by the Blacksmith Institute, six are mining sites. In mining sites, the ecosystem suffers through soil, water and air pollution; soil erosion and deforestation; dumping of hazardous mine waste that contain potentially toxic elements into the environment (Sánchez de la Campa et al. 2011). Common contaminants include mercury and arsenic (used as amalgamates) as well as lead and cadmium, which cause health problems such as malacosteon (causing bones to soften), kidney damage and cancers (Ogola et al. 2002; Zhang et al. 2012). Mining is also increasing desertification and coastal erosion, turning millions into 'environmental refugees' (Hens and Boon 1999). A study found an association between risk of dying due to digestive, respiratory, haematologic and thyroid cancers and proximity to Spanish mining industries (Fernández-Navarro et al. 2012).

Mining operations typically leave behind large open pits; seepage of heavy metals, acids and other toxic by-products into the land and rivers destroy forests and kill nearby wildlife. Restoring vegetation to mining areas is dif-

---

**Box C6.2 Gold mining in South Africa: a legacy of impacts**

Gold has been mined in South Africa for more than 120 years, and for several decades the country was the largest gold producer in the world, with production peaking at about 1,000 tons/year in 1975, later declining to less than 200 tons/year. At the current price of gold (about US$1,700/oz), South Africa's cumulative gold production may be valued at US$2.8 trillion, about seven times South Africa's current annual GDP. What is the legacy of this enormous wealth, extracted by the toil of hundreds of thousands of workers?

Employment in gold mines peaked at 531,000 in 1985 (Short and Radebe 2008) but declined to about 157,000 in 2010. The South African mineworkers are drawn from the rural areas of South Africa as well as surrounding countries, such as Mozambique, Malawi, Lesotho, Zambia, Zimbabwe and Angola. An ex-mineworker is typically unemployed, poor, suffering from one or a combination of mine-related diseases (TB, silicosis, HIV/AIDS and/or physical injuries), and with a shortened lifespan.

The legacy of environmental impacts of mining in the world's largest gold and uranium mining basin includes about 400 km² of mostly unlined mine tailings dams and 6 billion tons of tailings (materials left over after separating the valuable fraction) containing 430,000 tons of low-grade uranium. The government has been singularly ineffectual in holding mines to account for the environmental damage caused (Van Eeden et al. 2009).

Investigate Australian mining companies in the Philippines for destructive practices, deception and harassment of residents in mining sites!

Philippine patrimony is not for sale and exploitation!
No to plunder and abuse of people's rights!

pasacь

**Image C6.2** Protests against Australian mining companies in the Philippines (David Legge)

ficult because the mining process causes organic matter, nutrients and water to become either too acidic or too alkaline for plant growth (see Box C6.2).

### Social environment and health

Mining Induced Displacement and Resettlement (MIDR) experienced by environmental refugees is accompanied by the 'resettlement effect', defined as the loss of physical and non-physical assets, including homes, communities, productive land, income-earning assets and sources, subsistence, resources, cultural sites, social structures, networks and ties, cultural identity and mutual help mechanisms (Downing 2002).

A burgeoning sex trade is often a result of mining, as men relocate to work at mines, leaving behind families. In some contexts, the impact is devastating. HIV transmission in southern African countries has been linked to mining work, through the sex trade that often arises around mining communities and the loss of family coherence (Corno and de Walque 2012).

Many miners suffer the stress and economic insecurity of poor employment conditions. Many mining companies in South Africa hire migrant workers from other communities rather than locals, even recruiting from other countries including Swaziland and Lesotho. This strategy reduces worker organization and demands, since 'outsiders' generally know few people in the community and often have a lot to lose if they are fired. Often, these workers are particularly vulnerable, as tensions arise with local residents over employment opportunities or social clashes take place. Large mining companies, increasingly, prefer to subcontract the employment process to local businesses, thus legally distancing these companies from responsibilities for health harms or abrogation of rights.

Mining has also been widely linked to violence and conflict, perpetrated by companies and governments. The recent massacre in South Africa of thirty-four protesting platinum miners is a case in point (see Box C6.3).

Health activists in Ecuador are working to free mining protesters and journalists who have become political prisoners (Sagar 2012). Canadian-owned

---

**Box C6.3 Structural violence and mining**

We must remember the history of mining in South Africa, of cheap black labour, racism and exploitation. This is the model for the rest of Africa too. If we look at Marikana as a microcosm of South Africa and really of mining in Africa, we witness growing discontent, growing inequalities, a widening gap between rich and poor, and all the resultant problems of poverty. The LONMIN workers are victims of structural violence in our society. This is informed by low wages, very bad living conditions, bad nutrition, health and safety problems, HIV and AIDS and no hope for a better life.

Reverend Dr Jo Seoka, 30 October 2012, after the massacre of thirty-four mineworkers in Marikana (South Africa)

---

Barrick Gold, the world's largest gold-mining company, was linked to the repression of dozens of alluvial miners (small-scale diggers) and anti-mining critics in Papua New Guinea, Tanzania and Peru, as well as to thousands of forced evictions of small-scale miners and residents. Since 1997 the world's deadliest conflict has been raging in eastern and southern Congo (killing over 3.9 million people) linked to local and international companies fighting over control of lucrative gold, diamonds and coltan deposits. The Mindanao islands in the Philippines have seen militarization increase with the entry of multinational companies (see Box C6.4).

**Economic benefits: questioning claims**

Mining is often defended on the ground of the economic benefits that accrue to local communities. These claims are not borne out by actual experience. Poverty (people living on less than $1/day) rose from 61 per cent in 1981 to 82 per cent in 1999 in mineral-exporting countries (Langman 2003), and these countries were among the poorest economic performers between 1960 and 1993 (Auty 1998).

The gap between promise and delivery is seen in high-income countries too. Around 80 per cent of the profits from Australian mining leave the country. The mining companies pay an average of 13.9 per cent in corporate taxes, compared to the national 30 per cent personal tax burden, and received substantial taxpayer-funded subsidies (Richardson and Denniss 2011). This illustrates that the burden of coal mining falls disproportionately on society, while the bulk of the benefits accrue to industry owners, executives and investors (Morrice and Colagiuri 2012), often located far away from the site of mining. Most industry-sponsored reports on coal mining overemphasize perceived economic benefits and ignore negative social consequences, with

### Box C6.4  Mining and militarization in Mindanao, Philippines

Since 2005, the Swiss mining company Xstrada Plc and its local counterpart Sagittarius Mines Incorporated (SMI) has been operating in the DS Soccsksargen region on the island of Mindanao in the Philippines. Below is a local resident's testimony:

Since the establishment of SMI–Xstrada in our region, living conditions in our village, Barangay Malawanit, have deteriorated. The mining activity generates environmental damage with impact on our health. Butour community has now come to know a worse enemy: fear. The entire territory has been militarized to prevent our people from revolting. The Tampakan massacre happened in October 2012 in Sitio Alyong, Barangay Kimlawis, Kiblawan, a community close to ours. Juvy Capion, 27 years and a few months pregnant, was killed by the military along with her two sons, while her daughter was injured. We knew her because she was a relative of Daguil Capion, a prominent anti-mining activist. A few months later, Kitari Capion, Juvy's brother-in-law, was also murdered.

Military sometimes occupy our homes for more than a week, loot and destroy our villages claiming they are searching for rebels. They sometimes pose as rebels and if we cooperate with them, they throw us in jail. Others were forced to join the army. We are also facing a food blockade. Out of fear that we might feed the rebels, we need a special permit to go get rice at the farms and we receive only 3–4 kilos at a time. This ration is too low to feed a family for several days. If you venture into the fields at night, you might get killed by the army. By protecting the economic interests of the mine rather than those of the community, the military violates the rights of our people.

By enacting the 1995 Mining Act, the government gave a green light to all companies and foreign multinationals to come plunder our natural resources. The amount of taxes collected by the Philippine government from mining represents only 0.61% of the total in 2011. Despite this low amount, the state continues to encourage foreign investment because it enriches a small local elite. In the name of economic development the State promotes and protects mining multinationals instead of protecting the Filipino people.

*Source*: M3M (2013)

some placing the responsibility for the lack of benefits on the communities themselves (ibid.). For instance, while recognizing 'acute social impacts' of a coal mine in Australia, a study attributes this situation to the 'failure' of the community to capture positive benefits (Lockie et al. 2009).

### Canada: a 'safe haven' for mining companies

Canada stands out as a 'safe haven' for a majority of the world's mining companies, which benefit from a loose fiscal, legislative and cultural regime that favours mining interests both domestically and globally (Deneault and Sacher 2012). The historical and contemporary relationship to mining of this country, where two-thirds of the world's mining companies are based, is instructive in demonstrating a seemingly acceptable practice of governance that is content with private profits, if not profiteering, over wide-scale human rights abuses and the human suffering that follows.

The booming period of exploration coincided with the period when the major treaties governing relations between indigenous nations and the Canadian state were signed (Cranstone 2001). This process was accompanied by dispossession of indigenous lands and severe political and cultural repression, a process still taking place today (see Box C6.5). The wealth generated by mining was, from the early twentieth century, used to finance military adventures and support the nuclear arms race, sealing the alliance between successive Canadian governments and the industry (ibid.). On the other hand, Canadian universities support extractive industries through research and education, as

---

#### Box C6.5 Rights abuses in Canada

The 'Ring of Fire' refers to a cluster of some 30,000 mining claims in northern Ontario, in an area of approximately 10,000 square kilometres. Copper, nickel, diamonds and other minerals have been found, together with one of the world's largest deposits of chromite (an essential ingredient in stainless steel). The situation of indigenous peoples here is one of extreme poverty, high suicide rates, lower life expectancy and continuing systemic racism (MiningWatch Canada 2011).

At a De Beers mine in Attawapiskat, conditions are appalling. Indigenous people living near the mine declared a state of emergency in the winter of 2012 as they were living in harsh sub-zero conditions in substandard housing, including tents, trailers and rotting houses. The Red Cross stepped in when the Canadian government refused to act. Many felt that, in the interest of De Beers' profits, the government was not only reneging on its responsibility to its citizens, but allowing inhuman exploitation within its own borders, and even genocide of the indigenous population (ibid.).

A year later, the chief of Attawapiskat, Teresa Spence, went on a hunger strike, in protest at the conditions in which indigenous peoples live on their own land. It led to the creation of the 'Idle No More' movement. The struggle of 'Idle No More' continues.

well as receiving philanthropic donations which threaten academic freedom (McQuaig and Brooks 2010).

The mining industry has received special attention in Canada, in recent years, after the decline of the manufacturing base since the 1980s. Measures to facilitate the work of mining companies include curbs on the bargaining power of workers (Ontario Ministry of Labour 2012) and changes in environmental law without public consultations (Scoffield 2012). The Canadian government is also utilizing international development aid to mitigate negative consequences of mining on communities affected by the activities of Canadian mining companies (The Current 2012) (see Box C6.6). While Canadian diplomacy is used to support mining companies, Canadian state officials have stepped up attacks on environmentalists. The latter are accused of being influenced by foreign agendas and of working against national interests (Ljunggren 2012).

---

### Box C6.6  Canadian aid follows its mining companies

The restructuring of the Canadian International Development Agency (CIDA) and its integration into the Department of Foreign Affairs, Trade, and Development (DFATD) in April 2013 raises significant concerns. The merger of CIDA with DFATD represents a noticeable shift in Canada's approach to foreign aid.

Canadian development cooperation has long focused on the African continent, with a long list of countries in sub-Saharan Africa being selected based on levels of poverty and resource needs, and with Canada acting as a key donor for health programmes. However, since early on in the Harper administration, Latin America and the Caribbean have been 'rediscovered' as an area of foreign policy focus, linked to the growing importance of the region for Canadian trade and foreign direct investments (FDI), especially for extractive industries and the mining sector. The new country focus list includes only seven African countries, down from fourteen, and excludes some of the continent's poorest countries, five Asian countries and six countries in the Americas (adding Peru and Colombia and including the entire Caribbean region). In particular, the inclusion of Peru and Colombia, both middle-income countries with which Canada has signed FTAs, signals a shift away from an emphasis on the needs of the poorest towards a focus on building relationships with countries that will benefit Canada's commercial interests (Berthiaume 2009).

*Aid to support CSR of mining companies* This geographical shift co-incided with a topical repositioning of Canadian aid in the direction of the promotion of the private sector and corporate social responsibility

(CSR). In 2009, CIDA formally adopted a CSR strategy for the Canadian international extractive sector, with the objective of increasing the competitive advantage of Canadian international extractive sector companies by enhancing their ability to manage social and environmental risks in developing countries (DFATD 2009). The CSR strategy is based on four pillars: to support initiatives to enhance the capacities of developing countries to manage the development of minerals, oil, and gas, and to use the benefits from these resources to reduce poverty; to promote the widely recognized international CSR performance guidelines; to set up the Office of the Extractive Sector CSR Counsellor; and to support the establishment of a CSR Centre of Excellence in Canada (ibid.). According to the government, the overall goal of private sector engagement through CSR is fostering the sustainable development of the extractive/natural resource sector to benefit all segments of the population and increasing government capacity to reduce social conflicts (CIDA 2011).

*The case of Peru* Peru's case is instructive in this context. Canada has strong mining interests in Peru, with Goldcorp, Barrick Gold, Candente Copper Corp and various smaller companies operating in the Latin American country. In 2009, as part of CIDA's aid effectiveness agenda, Peru was selected as one of twenty focus countries for Canadian aid efforts despite its status as an upper-middle-income country. This was followed by a rapid expansion of ODA flows to Peru, from less than Can$15 million in 2009 to close to Can$30 million by 2012. The programming focus of Canada's engagement with Peru historically lay in the areas of education and sustainable economic growth, but has recently shifted towards private sector development and CSR promotion. Indeed, a quick scan of DFATD's project browser reveals that six out of eight projects approved in 2012 and 2013 are focused on private sector development and CSR promotion in the mining sector (DFATD 2013).

As part of a broader CSR pilot project in Peru to promote partnerships between civil society organizations (CSOs) and Canadian mining companies, DFATD is currently investing in building a partnership between World Vision and Barrick Gold. The programme focuses on increasing the income and raising the standard of living of 1,000 families affected by mining operations in the mining community of Quirulvilca, Peru. According to World Vision, the programme will help residents of Quirulvilca, especially women, youths and people with disabilities, become more involved and influential in their own community planning.

In addition to providing loans for people to start small businesses, there will be capacity-building for local leaders to ensure that Quirulvilca follows a path of sustainable development in the long term (World Vision, cited in DFATD 2011).

*Putting a positive spin on the mining industry* However, the real question is whether CSR projects are actually about ensuring better development outcomes for vulnerable populations, as claimed by their proponents; or whether such activities help the Canadian mining industry to put a positive spin on its negative environment and human rights records in Latin America (Carin 2012).

It is also noteworthy that the Canadian mining industry has intensely lobbied the Canadian government to fund CSR projects at mine sites, and is now praising DFATD for doing so (MiningWatch Canada 2012). MiningWatch Canada notes, 'There is reason to believe that CIDA's funding of CSR projects at mine sites is a poorly articulated attempt by the Government of Canada to help mining companies appear to offset the development deficits they are creating at local and national levels' (ibid.: 8). Others see CSR initiatives as evidence of an ongoing trend that has deepened under the Harper administration, towards aggressively advancing the interests of Canadian multinationals in the global South and as a recipe for more violence and social conflict (Gordon 2012).

**Image C6.3** Indigenous people's rally in Guatemala, 2008 (Surizar)

Global structures favour transnational corporations over human rights and the environment and existing legal instruments have generally proved to be toothless. For instance, the Vancouver-based Pacific Rim successfully challenged the El Salvador government at a World Bank tribunal in its decision to prevent further operations at its El Dorado site (Gray 2012). In 2012, the UN Special Rapporteur on the Rights of Indigenous People and other international bodies recommended suspension of operations and land acquisition by the Canadian mining company Goldcorp at Marlin Mine, in Guatemala, until local communities were adequately consulted (see Box C6.7). However, there is no system to enforce this recommendation and there is no sign that it is seriously taken into consideration.

---

### Box C6.7 The Marlin Mine, Guatemala

In 2006, the Canadian mining company Goldcorp bought the Marlin open-pit gold mine, in Guatemala. The mine has been a source of public concern and concrete issues include: (a) water demand from the mine will deny access to communities; (b) the mine will use unsafe processing methods that will contaminate the environment and the water supplies used by downstream people; (c) the rights of indigenous people have been violated as a result of failure by the project to consult with them about its environmental and social impacts; and (d) the presence of the mine is resulting in social conflict, violence and insecurity. Consequently, a protest movement has emerged, encompassing local communities and activists in Canada and Latin American countries.

After several years of struggle, the UN Special Rapporteur on the Rights of Indigenous People, as well as the Inter-American Commission on Human Rights and the International Labour Organization's Committee of Experts, recommended suspension of mining operations and land acquisition until local communities were adequately consulted. However, the Guatemalan president ignored these recommendations and refused to issue any new directives. The Canadian government did not take any steps either.

Within six months of taking office in January 2012, President Molina approved 68 new exploration licences, adding to 387 mining concessions and another 734 pending, many on indigenous lands. Over seventy municipalities have held referendums in which nearly a million people voted against mining in their territories, but these results have not been respected. Meanwhile, targeted attacks against those opposed to mining have intensified (CPO et al. 2012).

**Image C6.4** Keep the oil in the soil (Louis Reynolds)

Moreover, fiscal measures in Canada are used to support mining companies. Canada now has one of the lower corporate tax rates in the developed world (Canadian Press 2012). In addition, it is one of the few jurisdictions that taxes profits (rather than what is actually produced) while also allowing mining companies to legally carry over annual losses to bring their net profit in any given year to zero, and thus pay no tax.[1] Most of the world's mining companies are traded on the Toronto Stock Exchange, and this provides additional benefits to shareholders of mining companies in the form of tax concessions. Further, public pension funds are heavily invested in mining companies (Deneault and Sacher 2012).

## Conclusions: mining justice and better health are possible

The mining sector externalizes the health and environmental costs of its industries to the public sector, workers and communities. The evidence demonstrating the causal relationship between exposure to mining hazards and adverse health outcomes is denied and suppressed by industry advocates. The same is true of the huge contribution of the mining industry to a high burden of disease.

The Occupational Health and Safety Programmes of both the World Health Organization and the International Labour Organization have been systematically starved of adequate resources. Strengthening these programmes will contribute to the achievement of international standards on occupational health and environmental safety.

Human Rights legislation, monitored and effectively enforced, is urgently needed to curb systematic violations of rights by mining companies and country governments that facilitate them. An international criminal court that actively persecutes crimes perpetrated by mining companies (and governments that collude with them) would act as a deterrent for such crimes. At the same time, it is essential that 'mining havens', such as Canada, are eliminated.

Current global governance structures are grossly inadequate in the face of the tremendous power imbalances that exist between communities and mining companies. Mining justice movements exist in many parts of the world to address the tremendous socio-economic and environmental harms that are imposed by mining companies. These movements must be included in the formal and informal governance structures.

Health status is compromised in most communities in which mining activities occur owing partly to pre-existing hierarchies and inequalities and partly to the impact of mining. A comprehensive political, social, economic and environmental approach to solving these problems is urgently required.

## Note

1 See Natural Resources Canada, 'Mining taxation in Canada', 2011, www.nrcan.gc.ca/minerals-metals/business-market/2946.

## References

Auty, R. M. (1998) 'Resource abundance and economic development: improving the performance of resource-rich countries', *Research for Action*, 44, Helsinki: UNU/WIDNER.

Berthiaume, L. (2009) 'CIDA confirms shift to Americas, fewer countries', *Embassy*, 25 February, www.embassynews.ca/news/2009/02/25/cida-confirms-shift-to-americas-fewer-countries/37287?absolute=1, accessed 6 May 2014.

Birn, A., Y. Pillay and T. H. Holtz (2009) *Textbook of International Health: Global Health in a Dynamic World*, Oxford University Press.

Canadian Press (2012) 'Canada's political power shifts westward with population', *CBC News*, www.cbc.ca/news/politics/story/2012/02/08/pol-census-politics-west.html, accessed 6 May 2014.

Carin, B. (2012) 'CIDA, NGOs and mining companies: the good, the bad and the ugly', *iPolitics*, 8 May, www.ipolitics.ca/2012/05/08/barry-carin-cida-ngos-and-mining-companies-the-good-the-bad-and-the-ugly/, accessed 6 May 2014.

CIDA (Canadian International Development Agency) (2011) *Peru: CIDA Report*, www.acdi-cida.gc.ca/INET/IMAGES.NSF/vLUImages/Countries-of-Focus/$file/10-054-Perou-E.pdf, accessed 6 May 2014.

Corno, L. and D. de Walque (2012) 'Mines, migration and HIV/AIDS in southern Africa', *Journal of African Economies*, 21(3): 465–98.

CPO (Western Peoples Council), CIEL (Center for International Environmental Law) and MiningWatch Canada (2012) 'Guatemala's highest court to hear landmark indigenous challenge against mining law', Washington, DC and Guatemala City, 20 July.

Cranstone, D. A. (2001) 'A history of mining and mineral exploration in Canada and outlook for the future', Ottawa: Minister of Public Works and Government Services.

Deneault, A. and W. Sacher (2012) *Imperial Canada Inc.: Legal Haven of Choice for the World's Mining Industries*, Canada: Talonbooks.

DFATD (Department of Foreign Affairs, Trade and Development) (2009) *Building the Canadian Advantage: A Corporate Social Responsibility (CSR) Strategy for the Canadian International Extractive Sector*, Ottawa, www.international.gc.ca/trade-agreements-accords-commerciaux/topics-domaines/other-autre/csr-strat-rse.aspx, accessed 6 May 2014.

— (2011) 'Minister Oda announces initiatives to increase the benefits of natural resource management for peoples in Africa and South America', Ottawa, www.acdi-cida. gc.ca/acdi-cida/acdi-cida.nsf/eng/CAR-929105317-KGD, accessed 6 May 2014.

— (2013) 'Peru – international development projects', International Development Project Browser, www.acdi-cida.gc.ca/cidaweb/cpo.nsf/fWebCSAZEn?ReadForm&idx=01&CC=PE, accessed 6 May 2014.

Donoghue, A. M. (2004) 'Occupational health hazards in mining: an overview', *Occupational Medicine*, 54(5): 283–9.

Donoghue, A. M., M. J. Sinclair and G. P. Bates (2000) 'Heat exhaustion in a deep underground metalliferous mine', *Occupational and Environmental Medicine*, 57(3): 165–74.

Downing, T. E. (2002) *Avoiding New Poverty: Mining-induced Displacement and Resettlement*, London: International Institute for Environment and Development and World Business Council for Sustainable Development.

Driscoll, T. (2007) *Summary Literature Review of Health Issues Related to NSW Mining: Report for the Mines Safety Performance Branch NSW Department of Primary Industries*, ELMATOM Pty Ltd, September.

Eisler, R. (2003) 'Health risks of gold miners: a synoptic review', *Environmental Geochemistry and Health*, 25(3): 325–45.

Fernández-Navarro, P., J. García-Pérez, R. Ramis et al. (2012) 'Proximity to mining industry and cancer mortality', *Science of the Total Environment*, 1(435/436): 66–73.

Gordon, T. (2012) 'Canadian development aid takes on corporate coloring', *Toronto Star*, 29 November.

Gray, J. (2012) 'Pacific Rim Mining locked in closely watched fight with El Salvador', *Globe and Mail*.

Hens, L. and E. N. Boon (1999) 'Institutional, legal, and economic instruments in Ghana's environmental policy', *Environmental Management*, 24(3): 337–51.

Hydralok (n.d.) 'Top five mining companies in the world and their GDP', www.hydralok. net/top-five-mining-countries-in-the-world-and-their-gdp/, accessed 23 June 2014.

Langman, J. (2003) 'Investing in destruction: the impacts of a WTO investment agreement on extractive industries in developing countries', Oxfam America Briefing Paper 1, June, www.jimmylangman.com/uploads/7/1/2/1/7121467/oa-investing_destruction.pdf, accessed 6 May 2014.

Ljunggren, D. (2012) 'Canada blasts foreign "radicals" opposing pipeline', Reuters, www.reuters.com/article/2012/01/09/us-pipeline-idUSTRE8082DN20120109, accessed 6 May 2014.

Lockie, S., M. Franettovich, V. Petkova-Timmer et al. (2009) 'Coal mining and the resource community cycle: a longitudinal assessment of the social impacts of the Coppabella coal mine', *Environmental Impact Assessment Review*, 29(5): 330–9.

M3M (Médecine pour le Tiers Monde) (2013) 'Philippines: à Mindanao la solidarité internationale avec les communautés', 17 July, m3m.be/blog/philippines-%C3%Ao-mindanao-la-solidarit %C3% A9-internationale-avec-les-communaut %C3%A9s, accessed 6 May 2014.

McQuaig, L. and N. Brooks (2010) 'Excerpt: the trouble with billionaires by Linda McQuaig and Neil Brooks', *The Star*, 10 September.

MiningWatch Canada (2011) 'Diamonds and development: Attawapiskat and the victor diamond mine', 15 December, www.miningwatch.ca/article/diamonds-and-development-attawapiskat-and-victor-diamond-mine, accessed 6 May 2014.

— (2012) 'CIDA's partnership with mining companies fails to acknowledge and address the role of mining in the creation of development deficits', Ottawa: Mines Alert, www.miningwatch.ca/sites/www.miningwatch.ca/files/Mining_and_Development_FAAE_2012.pdf, accessed 6May 2014.

Morrice, E. and R. Colagiuri (2012) 'Coal mining, social injustice and health: a universal conflict of power and priorities', *Health Place*, 19: 74–9.

Nelson, G., B. Girdler-Brown, N. Ndlovu et al. (2010) 'Three decades of silicosis: disease trends at autopsy in South African gold miners', *Environmental Health Perspectives*, 118(3): 421–6.

Ogola, J. S., W. V. Mitullah and M. A. Omulo (2002) 'Impact of gold mining on the environment and human health: a case study in the Migori gold belt, Kenya', *Environmental Geochemistry and Health*, 24(2): 141–57.

Ontario Ministry of Labour (2012) 'Minister Jeffrey expresses concern regarding bill c-377 to members of the senate of Canada', Toronto, 19 December, www.labour.gov. on.ca/english/news/2012/ms_20121219.php, accessed 6 May 2014.

PricewaterhouseCoopers (2012) *Mine: The Growing Disconnect*, www.pwc.ch/ user_content/editor/files/publ_energy/ pwc_mine_the_growing_disconnect_e.pdf, accessed 6 May 2014.

Richardson, D. and R. Denniss (2011) *Mining the Truth: The Rhetoric and Reality of the Commodities Boom*, Canberra: Australia Institute.

Sagar, S. (2012) 'The political prisoners of Rafael Correa', *Countercurrents*, 13 December, www.countercurrents.org/sagar131212. htm, accessed 6 May 2014.

Sánchez de la Campa, A. M., J. D. de la Rosa, J. C. Fernández-Caliani et al. (2011) 'Impact of abandoned mine waste on atmospheric respirable particulate matter in the historic mining district of Rio Tinto (Iberian Pyrite Belt)', *Environmental Research*, 111(8): 1018–23.

Scoffield, H. (2012) 'Omnibus bill only the latest move in profound changes for environment, natives', *Maclean's*, 21 October, www2. macleans.ca/2012/10/21/omnibus-bill-only-the-latest-move-in-profound-changes-for-environment-natives/, accessed 6 May 2014.

Short, R. and B. Radebe (2008) *Gold in South Africa 2007*, AngloGold Ashanti, Goldfields, www.goldinsouthafrica.com/images/ Gold_in_SA_2007.pdf, accessed 6 May 2014.

The Current (2012) 'CIDA partnerships', CBC Radio, 26 January, www.cbc.ca/thecurrent/ episode/2012/01/26/cida-partnerships/, accessed 6 May 2014.

TRC (Truth and Reconciliation Commission of South Africa) (1998) *Volume 4: Truth and Reconciliation Commission of South Africa Report*, 29 October, submission by Laurie Flynn, p. 35.

Van Eeden, E. S., M. Liefferink and J. F. Durand (2009) 'Legal issues concerning mine closure and social responsibility on the West Rand', *Journal for Trans-disciplinary Research in Southern Africa*, 5(1): 51–71.

Zhang, X., L. Yang, Y. Li et al. (2012) 'Impacts of lead/zinc mining and smelting on the environment and human health in China', *Environmental Monitoring and Assessment*, 184(4): 2261–73.

# SECTION D

## WATCHING

# D1 | WHO REFORM: FOR WHAT PURPOSE?

In this chapter, we refer to the roots of the global health crisis in the contemporary regime of economic globalization and then argue for a theory of global (health) governance that goes beyond simply listing those international institutions that deal with health issues. An expanded theory of global governance would also recognize imperialism and big-power bullying; acknowledge the historic competition between the nation-state and the transnational corporation as the principal agent of governance; and contextualize governance within the emerging class relations between the transnational capitalist class, the diverse national middle classes and the more dispersed excluded and marginalized classes of both the periphery and the metropolis.

Understanding the global health crisis in relation to the crisis of neoliberal globalization, and locating political control within this expanded theory of governance, the chapter points towards the kinds of capabilities that WHO would need if it were to seriously pursue Health for All (HFA) in this context.

The current reform programme does not rate highly against these criteria. On the contrary, as we noted in GHW1 (GHW 2005), WHO is under continuing pressure to retreat to a purely technical role and to withdraw from any effective engagement with the political and economic dynamics that characterize the global health crisis. We conclude with some notes on civil society advocacy for the WHO that we need.

**Image D1.1** Placard in Rio, Brazil – 'Health shines in Geneva, vulnerability continues here' (Janine Ewen)

## Background to reforms in WHO

WHO has been subject to criticism (as well as appreciation) since its founding (WHO 1958; Farley 2008). In GHW1 (GHW 2005) we reviewed WHO's strengths and weaknesses and explored how it might better fulfil its historic mandate as envisioned in its Constitution (International Health Conference 1946).

Our own criticisms in that chapter focused on lack of resources, poor management and lack of leadership within the Secretariat,[1] and the unequal power play between the rich countries and the low- and middle-income countries (LMICs) in the governance of WHO. We concluded with recommendations concerning: WHO's core purpose, democratization and governance, funding and programming, and leadership and management.

WHO's financial crisis came to a head in 2009 when member states were confronted with the problem of the increasing 'carry-over'; WHO was borrowing against future revenues to maintain its operations. There was self-righteous finger-wagging from many of the rich member states, whose insistence on maintaining the freeze on assessed contributions (ACs) was the fundamental cause of the crisis (see Box D1.1). The debate provided an opportunity to the rich member states to elaborate a range of criticisms of WHO management, almost to the point of suggesting that the freeze on ACs was an act of fiscal responsibility, given the many weaknesses of the organization.

As a consequence, the director general (DG) of WHO was effectively forced into adopting a major reform programme addressing a wide range of management, financing and governance issues (see Box D1.2).

---

### Box D1.1 Member state contributions to WHO

WHO is funded through mandatory contributions from all member states, assessed on the basis of population and GDP (hence 'assessed contributions' or ACs), and voluntary contributions (VCs), most of which are earmarked for particular projects. Since the 1980s there has been a freeze on increases in ACs. Initially, it was a relative freeze in the 1980s (allowing for inflation-adjusted increases), but from 1993 onwards an absolute freeze has been imposed (at the insistence of the United States) (Lee 2009). Meanwhile, VCs have increased to a point where they account for 70 per cent of total WHO expenditure.

The prevailing discourse from those who support the freeze on ACs has been that WHO suffers from administrative inefficiencies and that a tight chokehold is necessary to discipline the organization. In fact, the inefficiencies of the organization are in large degree a consequence of the freeze; certainly, imposing the freeze is not the solution.

Assessed contributions (ACs), the spending of which is untied (i.e. not tied to a particular programme according to donor preference), totalled $475 million in 2012. The amount paid is based on a country's population and GDP using a formula fixed in 1982.

Voluntary contributions (VCs) comprised around $1,539 million in 2012, of which $1,409 million was earmarked (tied) for projects chosen by the donors. Tied funding came from member states ($564 million) and from charities, philanthropies and international financial institutions ($748 million). The five member states making the biggest VCs in 2012 were the USA ($208m, 100 per cent tied), the UK ($104m, 87 per cent tied), Canada ($71m, 100 per cent tied), Australia ($56m, 66 per cent tied) and Norway ($46m, 57 per cent tied).

The proportion of WHO's revenue from ACs fell from 80 per cent in 1978/79 to less than 30 per cent in 2012, owing to the combined effect of the freeze on ACs and the real increases in VCs.

In 2012, 104 member states made VCs, almost all earmarked. Eighty-five of these bilateral donors made no contribution to the core (untied) account. Among the OECD member states only five gave >50 per cent of their VCs to the core account (Greece, Belgium, Luxembourg, Denmark and Ireland). Of the 21 countries globally with GDP >$500 billion, 19 contributed VCs; the donations were completely tied in 13 out of those 19 countries. Of the 149 countries with GDP <$500 billion, 75 contributed VCs; the donations were completely tied in the case of 64 countries.

Among the 33 OECD countries, funds contributed to WHO (assessed/received plus voluntary), expressed as a proportion of GDP ($ contribution per million dollars of GDP, pm GDP), vary very widely:

- 6 countries gave >$50 pm GDP (Luxembourg, Norway, Finland, Canada, UK, Sweden);
- 15 countries gave >$10 pm GDP but <$50 pm GDP (Australia, Netherlands, Denmark, Belgium, Ireland, New Zealand, Switzerland, USA, Germany, Korea, France, Slovenia, Italy, Japan, Austria);
- 6 countries gave >$5 pm GDP but <$10 pm GDP (Mexico, Estonia, Czech Republic, Poland, Slovakia, Turkey); and
- 5 gave <$5 pm GDP (Hungary, Chile, Greece, Spain, Portugal).

*Source:* WHO revenue data from A66/29, A66/29 Add.1 and A66/30. GDP data (in current US$) taken from World Bank data

## Evaluation of the reforms

Let us, first, analyse the different elements of reforms in WHO carried out since 2009. It is possible to identify some elements that are sensibly conceived, rationally framed and likely to be successful. These include:

- improved evaluation practice, building a learning culture;
- harmonization of the work of the six regional offices;
- insistence on donors paying the full overhead costs associated with their earmarked VCs;
- improved accounting; and
- 'organization-wide resource mobilization' (controlling the competition between clusters and regions for donor money).

On the other hand, some of the reforms are likely to have a negative effect on WHO's role in protecting public health. These include:

- Development of new protocols to govern 'the engagement with non-state actors' to protect the governing bodies and the Secretariat from improper influence. The WHO has been very slow in dealing effectively with this issue (see Box D1.5 and D1.6 later).
- The new 'financing dialogue' is about asking the donors to fund the budget rather than WHO agreeing to do whatever the donors are interested in funding. This begs the main issue: the freeze on ACs denies WHO access to adequate, flexible funding to ensure that the work programme adopted by the member states is appropriately funded.

Addressing these weaknesses of the reform programme is important, but there are also more fundamental questions that need to be addressed. These include questions regarding the concrete shape that WHO should acquire, if it is to be effective in dealing with the contemporary global health crisis, having regard to the prevailing structures of global health governance (GHG). (See Chapter A1 of for a detailed account of contemporary neoliberal globalization and how, through different pathways, it has a profound impact on health and healthcare.) Before we envision the role that WHO should be playing and the kinds of reforms that would be needed, we take a closer look at the contemporary landscape of GHG in the context of the global health crisis.

### Global health governance: a sub-domain of global economic governance

While WHO operates in the field of GHG, it is important to understand that this field is a sub-domain of the wider field of economic and political governance. In contrast, much of the discourse around WHO reform and its role in GHG tends to treat GHG as an autonomous domain of governance constituted in largely institutional terms, including: WHO, other UN intergovernmental bodies, the international financial institutions, philanthropic foundations, the myriad public–private partnerships (PPPs) involved in 'development assistance for health (these are discussed in detail in GHW 2008), the pharmaceutical industry and other healthcare supply industries, the large bilateral donors (including in particular USAID, PEPFAR, the UK and the

**Box D1.2  Key elements of WHO reform, 2009–14**

*Management reforms*
- increased focus on outcomes in planning, management, and evaluation;
- improved evaluation practice;
- harmonization of the work of the six regional offices;
- closer alignment of the work of the different levels, from headquarters to regional office to country representative;
- improved risk management;
- improved financial controls;
- improved people management (mobility, performance management, staff development and learning, recruitment and selection).

*Financing reforms*
- adoption of the new 'financing dialogue' (asking the donors to fund the budget rather than agreeing to do whatever they choose to fund);
- insistence on donors paying the overhead costs incurred through their earmarked funding;
- improved accounting;
- improved budgeting and resource allocation;
- 'organization-wide resource mobilization' (controlling the competition between clusters and regions for donor money).

*Governance reforms*
- improved communication between the Secretariat and member states;
- a greater role for the Programme Budget and Administration Committee of the Executive Board;
- streamlined decision-making in governing bodies;
- protection of governing bodies and the Secretariat from improper influence.

EU), non-government organizations (such as Médecins Sans Frontières, Oxfam, World Vision and various specialist professional groupings) and various think tanks and academic centres.

This institutionally defined picture of the global health landscape is useful in thinking through many of WHO's involvements, such as: food standards, vaccine development, distribution of bed nets, and the provision of advice regarding healthcare financing. However, this is a very inadequate picture when it comes to trying to make sense of (for example):

- The USA threatening India with trade sanctions under Special 301[2] over its (TRIPS[3] compliant) patent law, in order to prevent Indians having access to cheap generics;
- the role of investor state dispute settlement in plurilateral trade agreements in preventing countries from regulating for public health;
- the geopolitics of refugee flows and the breaching of human rights standards towards asylum seekers;
- unemployment, poverty and ill-health in rural areas of developing countries in the face of dumped agricultural products;
- the race to the bottom in terms of taxation, public services, labour rights and environmental regulation associated with the auction for foreign investment to create jobs.

The purely institutional view of global health governance does not help if we are hoping to see WHO confront the global health crisis and its roots in the global economic system.

To properly specify the role that WHO should be playing in relation to the global health crisis (recognizing the degree to which that crisis is rooted in neoliberal globalization) requires that we contextualize WHO and its role in relation to the political control of the global economy, not just the institutions that have explicit functions in relation to health. In order to do so, first we need to examine the dialectics in power relations that are part of the political economy of the globe.

Firstly we need to utilize dialectical analysis, in particular locating the institutional picture sketched above in relation to the contentions and solidarities defined by:

- big powers versus small powers; rich countries versus low- and middle-income countries;
- the nation-state, as a unit of governance, versus the transnational corporation; and
- the transnational capitalist class (TCC) (Robinson 2004) versus diverse national middle classes and dispersed excluded and marginalized classes.

The WHO is clearly dominated by the big powers, particularly in their role as donors. Thus it makes limited sense to speak about undifferentiated 'member states' (as if all member states are equal). Big-power 'bullying' is evident in relation to the implementation of resolutions by WHO that the big powers do not like. Big-power threats are normally veiled and delivered behind closed doors, but in the case of WHO's resolution WHA59.26 on 'Trade and health' they have been quite overt (see Box D1.3).

Another useful analytic tool for thinking about GHG is the contention between the nation-state and the transnational corporation as alternative and competing units of global governance. This underlies a central ambiguity in much

---

**Box D1.3 Threat of funding reprisals stymies action around trade and health**

The need to encourage closer policy coherence between trade agreements and public health goals was recognized in a sequence of WHA resolutions from 1996 onwards. The principle was explicitly articulated in Resolution A59.26 on 'Trade and health' in May 2005.

The USA was critical from the first, accusing the Secretariat of being 'against industry, free trade, and intellectual property' when the resolution was being considered in the EB in January 2005. Two very high-profile interventions by US diplomats during 2006 made it clear that effective action on this resolution would not be looked upon favourably (Legge 2013).

Soon after the passage of A59.26 the Secretariat indicated that it was working on a 'tool' to assist countries to assess trade agreements from a public health point of view (WHO n.d.). The tool has never been published although it was submitted to the Secretariat in 2009 (Hawkes et al. 2010).

The Secretariat has done very little at the global level to implement the requests of A59.26 although some regional offices have been able to make some progress under the radar. Nevertheless it is clear that the lack of donor funding and the threats of more drastic funding reprisals have contributed to WHO's failure to effectively implement the resolution on trade and health.

---

of WHO's work, including for example its relationship with the pharmaceutical or the food and beverage industries. The use of terms like 'multi-stakeholder partnerships' to describe WHO's relationships with 'big pharma' and 'big food' obscures the deep conflicts of interest between the corporations and the goals of public health and bestows on the corporations a certain legitimacy to work alongside WHO and the member states who constitute it.

The tension between the nation-state and the TNC is nowhere sharper than in relation to taxation, and indeed whether TNCs should pay tax. Notoriously the prevailing global regime encourages TNCs to arrange their ownership structures and global production chains in such a way as to pay little or no tax. This is of critical importance in terms of health systems development, which is hugely constrained by the refusal of TNCs to pay tax and the pressures of 'tax competitiveness' (the race to the bottom in terms of levels of tax and public expenditure). The emergence of 'investor state dispute settlement' in plurilateral trade agreements also illustrates very clearly the pressure to whittle away the sovereign rights of the nation-state in favour of the stateless TNC.

The absence of class analysis from most (if not all) of the available commentary on GHG is also a limitation. Such an analysis, in the context of neoliberal globalization, needs to take cognizance of the 'transnational capitalist class' (TCC). The TCC has been described as a class group embedded in new global circuits of accumulation rather than in national circuits. The TCC draws its membership from most countries around the world, North and South, and constitutes a nascent global ruling class. The TCC differs sharply from national middle classes and various marginalized groupings in its collective self-consciousness, common assumptions and shared purposes (Robinson 2004).

One of the tools of global governance, which is very much in the hands of the TCC, is 'the discipline of global markets'. The propensity of speculators to buy and sell currencies, commodities, shares, bonds or derivatives in response to the policy choices of sovereign governments is a powerful limitation on such choices. A government which declares that it is planning to protect domestic industry will experience capital outflows, depreciation of its currency and reduced credit ratings. While such decisions by the speculators are generally conceived solely in terms of material outcomes they express in a more pervasive way the interests of the TCC.

Class-based analysis can also provide useful new insights in relation to discussions of 'development' and health, as in 'development assistance', the Millennium Development Goals or the post-2015 'development agenda'. The TCC has been very effective in constructing 'development' as something that refers only to 'underdeveloped' countries (the rich capitalist countries are presumed to have achieved the pinnacle of development); in presenting 'development' as a process mediated by charitable giving (as in 'development assistance'); and in conflating 'development' with the treatment of particular diseases (particularly diseases that jeopardize the legitimacy of the prevailing world order) (see also Chapter C1).

Framing global health governance purely in terms of a pluralism of institutions has the further effect of excluding consideration of the domain of ideas, information, knowledges and ideologies (Althusser 1971; Herman and Chomsky 1988). In the field of GHG ideological assumptions are embedded in highly technical and information-rich discourses, including those produced by some of the leading academic centres, such as Harvard University and the London School of Hygiene and Tropical Medicine or the OECD. The ideology of neoliberalism (Harvey 2005) plays a critical role in maintaining the global economy on its unstable, inequitable and unsustainable trajectory. In doing so it contributes to reproducing the global health crisis.

To construct the global health landscape solely in terms of institutions engaged in health programmes renders invisible some of the key dynamics with which WHO needs to deal. In the lead-up to the post-2015 'development agenda' the WHO Secretariat has campaigned strongly around the slogan of 'universal health coverage' or UHC. The Secretariat negotiated a broad alliance with the World Bank, bilateral donors and various philanthropies in the pursuit of UHC. The price that the Secretariat paid for this alliance is an acceptance of the World Bank's preferred health system model of mixed public/private service delivery and stratified multi-payer health insurance markets with a minimal safety net for the poor. (See Chapter B1 for a more detailed discussion of the dominant model of UHC being promoted today.) The World Bank's policy preferences reflect the power of the neoliberal world view in an institution owned and controlled by the leading capitalist powers.

These analytic frameworks, taken together, provide us with the tools to understand the political environment in which WHO functions. For example, the purchase of political influence by corporations through campaign donations in order to drive trade policy (with consequences for small farmers, manufacturing employment and public policy space) may be understood in terms of both big-power bullying, the agency of particular TNCs and the theoretical tension between the sovereignty of the nation-state and that of the TNC.

### The features and capabilities of the 'WHO we need'

We have sketched a number of different ways of understanding the global health 'landscape' within which WHO works. Much of WHO's present work programme is valuable and essential. Such programmes should be supported and continued. However, in the face of the global health crisis and the prevailing landscape of global health governance, WHO needs new capabilities. We discuss in the following sections some of the most important areas where WHO needs to reorient its approach and acquire new capabilities.

*Abolish dependence on donors* WHO needs to be free of the yoke of the donors if it is to engage with the structures of global governance which reproduce the global health crisis. WHO's dependence on donors (especially those who contribute 'tied' funds) will continue as long as the freeze on assessed contributions remains in place and the Secretariat will remain unable to progress resolutions which challenge the interests of the rich countries. The 'funding dialogue', initiated by the WHO to address the problem of being dependent on donors who provide 'tied' funding, is an expensive charade.

The freeze on ACs has been mainly driven by the USA as part of its opposition to (in sequence): the Code on the Marketing of Breast-milk Substitutes; the Essential Medicines List; the Primary Health Care model; the Framework Convention on Tobacco Control; and most recently (2006) the resolution on Trade and Health.

The prevailing discourse from those who support the freeze on AC has been that WHO suffers from administrative inefficiencies and that a tight chokehold is necessary to discipline the organization. In fact, the inefficiencies of the organization are largely a consequence of having to manage two sources of

**Image D1.2** The World Health Assembly in session in Geneva (Camila Guigliani)

funds, assessed and untied versus tied voluntary contributions. The former, the smaller tranche, is available to support what the WHA commits to, through its resolutions. The latter, vastly overshadowing flexible funds, is available to support what the donors want WHO to do (and by non-funding to prevent WHO from doing what they, the donors, do not support).

The 'financing dialogue' (as part of the current reform programme) was conceived as a way of encouraging donors to support the WHA-adopted programme budget rather than commissioning WHO to deliver the programmes that they favour. However:

- the transaction costs associated with the financing dialogue and the mix of revenue sources are huge, in terms of senior-person time and cash expenditure on dialogue;
- the large donors (bilaterals, private philanthropies, corporations and IFIs) continue to exercise control over WHO's programme;
- important initiatives commissioned through the WHA are being held up for want of funding support; these include: medicines regulation, trade and health, action on junk food.

The urgent needs now are to increase assessed contributions and to increase the flow of voluntary contributions to the core account: first, by increasing the proportion of voluntary contributions going to the core (untied), which is presently very low, and secondly, by increasing the level of voluntary contributions from the emerging economies (presently very low). The Stage II External Evaluator (PricewaterhouseCoopers 2013) has called upon member states to fulfil their 'duty of care' to the organization. This is an important and timely warning.

---

### Box D1.4  The story of IMPACT

An item appeared on the agenda of WHA61 (May 2008) which surprised a number of member states. The item, named 'Counterfeit medical products', had not been mandated by any resolution of the Assembly, but had been included on the agenda at the request of the UAE and Tunisia (at the EB122 in January 2008) without substantive discussion.

The accompanying Secretariat document (A61/16) described with some pride the establishment of the International Medical Products Anti-Counterfeiting Taskforce (IMPACT) and the work which had been progressed through IMPACT since its launch in 2006. The document listed the IMPACT 'stakeholders', including strong representation of the research-based pharmaceutical manufacturers.

The Taskforce had been established in 2006 and was funded (nearly US$2.6 million) by contributions through the European Commission and the governments of Australia, Germany, Italy and the Netherlands (altogether 68 per cent) and by WHO (28 per cent). It also benefited from significant in-kind support from the pharmaceutical industry.

The purpose of IMPACT from an industry point of view was to drive stronger IP protection. The strategy involved highlighting the dangers of substandard or falsified medicines while promoting policy initiatives which were directed to protecting branded pharmaceuticals from generic competition. Critical to this strategy was the ambiguous use of the term 'counterfeit'. In the TRIPS agreement 'counterfeit' is defined as a trademark violation, but under pressure from the pharmaceutical industry WHO had adopted a definition which conflated IPRs and quality, safety and efficacy (QSE).

The shortfalls with respect to medicines regulation which had allowed the flow of substandard medicines was a consequence of the funding crisis of WHO and lack of donor support for comprehensive medicines regulation. However, this had led to a situation where, because falsified or adulterated drugs were circulating widely, the scare campaigns implemented by IMPACT were effective in persuading some governments to adopt higher levels of IP protection. A key element in this hoax was the conflation of IP protection with QSE standards.

For more details regarding the IMPACT saga, see GHW3 (2011). For follow-up reporting, see also WHO Watch (2013).

---

*Preserve WHO's status as an intergovernmental organization (IGO)* WHO's status as an IGO must be preserved; the governance of WHO should not be shared with PPPs, philanthropies, bilaterals or IFIs. TNCs are obliged to focus on profit and shareholder value. Their purposes are not congruent with the mission of the WHO. The PPPs, philanthropies, bilaterals and IFIs are all, in various ways, accountable to different sets of TNCs and see the world in ways which privilege the interests of the TNCs.

The member states have previously rejected the Committee C proposal (which would have created a forum within the World Health Assembly in which private sector players would have an institutionalized place in the governance of WHO). Member states also rejected the proposal for a Global Health Forum which would have provided a similar entré but outside the formalities of the WHA. Nevertheless calls for the governance structures to be opened to the donor institutions continue to surface, most recently in a report prepared by PricewaterhouseCoopers (ibid.) evaluating the progress of the reforms.

The principles of democracy are poorly realized in the modern nation-state but at least there is a rhetorical commitment to popular sovereignty. As the TNC displaces the nation-state as the principal agent of governance, so the role of citizen is reduced to that of consumer. In the neoliberal view market forces have the magical capacity to translate the aspirations of the erstwhile citizen into reality more effectively and more efficiently than the forum and the ballot box. This is a dangerous idea; it would be hard to reverse.

*WHO's engagement with non-state actors* One of the most controversial items on the WHO reform agenda has been 'engagement with non-state actors'. This reflects the continuing advocacy of NGOs such as IBFAN and the watchfulness of a small number of LMIC delegations in the governing bodies. The Secretariat has shown itself to be susceptible to the benevolence of the pharmaceutical industry (most notably in the IMPACT saga – see Box D1.4).

To maintain its integrity and preserve its reputation WHO needs robust risk management protocols to identify and manage the risk of improper influence, whether that influence be mediated by corporations, philanthropists, PPPs or bilateral donors. The fact that such protocols are not yet in place is reflected in the story of World Psoriasis Day (Box D1.5).

---

**Box D1.5  World Psoriasis Day (WHO Watch 2014)**

Psoriasis appeared on the agenda for the 133rd meeting of the Executive Board of the WHO (EB 133, May 2013) without any note as to how it got there. The Secretariat report (B133_5-en.pdf) provided an overview of psoriasis, still with no account of how it came to be on the agenda. In the course of EB133, a draft resolution, entitled 'World Psoriasis Day', appeared and was discussed under this item. This draft resolution, which had not been posted in the papers for the EB, Resolution (EB133.R2), was adopted after some discussion.

World Psoriasis Day is sponsored by the International Federation of Psoriasis Associations, which is supported by, among others, Pfizer, Novartis, Lilly, Leo, Celgene and Abbvie. Furthermore, twenty-two of the forty-two member associations with active websites (13 June 2013) acknowledge drug company support on their websites (including AbbVie, Leo, Janssen, Pfizer, Abbott, Ducray, La Roche-Posay, Pierre FabrieDermatologie, Janssen-Cilag). At least one national association receives drug company support of several million US dollars per year.

The Psoriasis Association (UK) (whose representative spoke under the banner of the International Association of Patients Organisations, IAPO) is supported by grants from AbbVie, Dermal Laboratories Ltd, Forest Laboratories Ltd, Galderma (UK) Ltd, LEO Pharma, MSD and T&R Derma. IAPO also receives extensive support from pharmaceutical companies, individually and through the IFPMA.

Drugs for treating psoriasis are among the top revenue-earning drugs in the world. Three of these – adalimumab (marketed by AbbVie as Humira), etanercept (marketed by Pfizer as Enbrel) and infliximab (marketed by Janssen as Remicade) – have been identified by Forbes in 2012 as being among the top ten revenue-earning drugs ever. The combined sales of just these three products were US$25 billion. These high revenues have, in large measure, been sustained by IP protection and monopoly pricing. All these drugs are extremely expensive and are therefore inaccessible in LMICs; on average, a year's treatment with any of these drugs cost about $20,000. They are also key to the healthy profit margins of the companies involved; Humira sales accounted for 51.7 per cent of the revenues of AbbVie in the first quarter of 2013.

It appears probable that the involvement of drug companies in supporting the IFPA (and its member associations), and their support for World Psoriasis Day, is part of a marketing strategy directed at expanding the global market for their products.

WHO's de facto endorsement of an event planned and organized by an organization such as the IFPA, which is funded and promoted by the pharmaceutical industry, contravenes WHO's stated position regarding engagement with non-state actors. At the very least the Executive Board should have been advised of these relationships, but they were not.

The WHO has a legitimate role in raising awareness regarding psoriasis, in promoting access to treatment and in harnessing research capacity towards finding better remedies. However, WHO's endorsement of World Psoriasis Day cannot be seen as an appropriate way to pursue these objectives.

## Box D1.6 Regulation of transnational corporations

There is a powerful public health case for regulation of the TNCs (including those involved in tobacco, junk food, alcohol and medicines). There is also powerful opposition to any regulation of TNCs, including through the increasing prevalence of investor protection provisions in plurilateral trade agreements. This contradiction illustrates starkly the tension between the nation-state and the TNC as the dominating units of global governance.

The rich countries, the USA in particular, have repeatedly opposed the regulation of TNCs for public health objectives, preferring to speak in terms of 'multi-stakeholder collaboration', and obscuring the conflicts of interest between the corporations and public health.

The classic case is the Code on the Marketing of Breast-milk Substitutes, which started life as a proposal for a binding treaty but emerged in the form of a voluntary code because of a promise that the USA would not vote against it (which in the end they did; see Richter 2002). However, while the Code has had a positive influence, its voluntary status is a clear limitation. Recent data (WHO 2014) indicate that just over half of 199 member states reporting had implemented any principles from the Code through national legislation and just thirty-seven member states (22 per cent) had fully implemented the Code.

In contrast the Framework Convention on Tobacco Control (FCTC) is a binding treaty and requires states parties to implement the basic set of regulatory measures. The struggle to conclude the FCTC was fiercely contested by big tobacco and their allies (Roemer et al. 2005) and the struggle to control tobacco continues. The attempt by Australia to implement plain packaging (in accordance with the FCTC) has been challenged in the WTO (by Ukraine, Honduras, the Dominican Republic, Cuba and Indonesia, all of whom as member states of WHO are bound by the FCTC) and under investor state dispute settlement provisions of the Hong Kong Australia Investment Treaty by Phillip Morris Asia.

The alcohol and food and beverages industries, and their nation-state sponsors, have learned much from the fights over tobacco control and are determined to prevent the international regulation of the marketing of alcohol and junk foods.

The attempts by the Pacific Island countries to regulate the importation of fatty meats and the marketing of unhealthy lifestyles are revealing (see Chapter C3). The Pacific Island countries have high rates of obesity, diabetes and other non-communicable diseases and have explored a range of strategies to 'make healthy choices easier choices'. However, they have faced powerful opposition, particularly from the USA, in this project. In 2008, the US delegate to the Western Pacific Regional Committee of WHO, in opposing WHO engagement with issues of trade, stated that, 'Diet, physical activity and health behaviour involve complex personal choices and individual priorities. The Regional Action Plan should address those complexities and the responsibility of individuals in changing their behaviour' (Legge 2013).

*Collaboration with other UN agencies* Inter-sectoral collaboration has been part of public health rhetoric since Alma-Ata in 1978, but WHO's collaboration with other intergovernmental organizations (IGOs) within the UN system has been weak. In contrast WHO works closely with the World Bank on health systems and with WTO on trade issues. The World Bank is structured to represent the interests and perspectives of the rich world, notwithstanding its rhetoric about poverty alleviation. The WTO is structurally committed to the neoliberal faith in globalized free trade. WHO should treat Bretton Woods institutions with caution. Their accountabilities, and therefore their world views and their policies, are all shaped by the interests and perspectives of the rich world.

On the other hand UNDP and the UNHRC have valuable expertise in relation to health systems and UNCTAD and the UN Department of Economic and Social Affairs (UN DESA) have high levels of expertise in trade and global economics. The UN system retains a one country, one vote constituency and in this degree remains committed to a pre-eminent role for the nation-state. In view of the ascendant role of the TNC this is an important advantage over the Bretton Woods organizations, which have no such commitment.

WHO's collaborations with UNDP, UNCTAD, UN DESA, UNEP, UNHRC and other IGOs of the UN system need to be strengthened if it is to take effective action on the right to healthcare, trade and investment, the availability and quality of work, the regulation of TNCs (see Box D1.6), the environment, taxation (tax avoidance and tax 'competitiveness') and technology transfer (focusing on 'technologies which are critical for health'), refugees, war and climate change. This is not to suggest that WHO should seek to exercise pre-eminent authority in these matters but to ensure that the decisions and programmes developed in these different UN-system IGOs reflect an understanding of the health dimensions.

*Engagement in monitoring, coordinating and accountability of development assistance* While WHO's country representatives (WRs) are frequently involved in assisting countries to access 'development assistance for health', WHO's lack of involvement at the global level is striking. In the current debates about 'health in the post-2015 development agenda' WHO has been preoccupied

**Image D1.3** 'Watchers' at the World Health Assembly (John Mahama)

with the funding of its own programmes, in particular 'universal health coverage', and has failed to exercise effective leadership in relation to the flow of funds under the broad rubric of 'development assistance for health'. Two recent initiatives in this area were the 'Maximising positive synergies' project (MPS) and the International Health Partnership + (IHP+). In both cases an extremely diplomatic approach was taken so as not to cause offence, but the consequence was not to cause change either.

The 'developing countries' necessarily approach the idea of 'development' very differently from the donors whose 'development assistance' is directed at demonstrating their concern for the poor while doing nothing about tax evasion and capital flight and continuing to drive free trade and economic integration policies which are very problematic for any meaningful programme of development. It is in the interests of the LMICs to authorize the WHO to play a more active role in relation to 'development assistance for health'.

*Support engagement of LMICs in WHO's decision-making bodies* There is an urgent need for increased support for the LMICs to play a more active role in the governing-body discussions, including capacity-building and more strategic caucusing. The rich countries come to the GB meetings having carefully researched the issues at stake and evaluated possible policy strategies. The European Union countries come to the GB meetings with a single policy position reflecting careful consideration of issues and options.

Certainly the regional committees provide an opportunity for some preparation by LMICs, especially in relatively homogeneous regions such as Africa and South-East Asia. However, caucusing in regional committees is constrained in various ways by the presence of regional directors and Secretariat staff. While Secretariat staff can contribute in providing background and options in relation to particular items they have their own interests and accountabilities. UNASUR and the South Centre and other regional coordination bodies do provide space for this kind of caucusing but there is considerable scope for strengthening this kind of support.

*Stronger accountability at all levels* There is a need for stronger accountability on the part of the member states for their involvement in WHO at all levels. Governments and their delegations need to be more accountable for their preparation for governing-body debates, for the policy positions they adopt and in some cases for their implementation of WHO resolutions. In particular they need to be accountable to the people who have most to gain from a more equitable and more sustainable global regime. Civil society organizations have an important part to play in holding both the member states and the Secretariat to account.

### Scorecard for the current reform programme

The current reform programme does not address the real requirements as regards changes in WHO's capabilities and approach. It is not based on any coherent conception of WHO's role in confronting the global health crisis, nor a realistic account of the structures and dynamics of global (health) governance. Rather the reform identifies and seeks to address specific management weaknesses, many of which can be traced in part to the policy of zero nominal growth and the absurd funding situation WHO is in.

The proposals for a focus on harmonization (across the regions), alignment (across the levels) and 'organization-wide resource mobilization' all arise from an earlier approach to the funding crisis in which clusters and regions were encouraged to be more entrepreneurial and seek donor funding directly. The consequence of that strategy was to vastly increase tied voluntary donations, which in many cases did not cover organizational overheads (which therefore increased the drain on ACs) and which contributed to a dispersal of focus and functional incoherence at the organization-wide level.

There have been references to WHO's role in GHG in the discourse around the current reform programme but only in very general and rhetorical terms. Certainly there is nothing in the current reform programme which might strengthen WHO's ability to address the roots of the global health crisis in the instabilities, imbalances and inequities of the global economy.

The tensions among the member states and within the Secretariat over improper corporate influence and the necessary risk management protocols do not seem likely to be resolved soon. The USA, the EU and Japan see

**Box D1.7  WHO Watch: democratizing global health governance**

WHO Watch is a programme of engagement with the World Health Organization and global health governance (GHG) more generally, undertaken by the People's Health Movement (PHM) in association with a number of CSO partners. The broad goal of the initiative is to improve the global environment for health development by changing the information flows, power relations and alliances which frame global health decision-making and implementation. This will require developing countries finding a stronger voice in global decision-making, supported by a broadly based popular mobilization which rejects the prevailing neoliberal paradigm.

WHO is a central agent in global health governance and worth engaging with for this reason alone, but building a 'watching' capacity in relation to WHO will provide a firm basis for extending the project to the wider field of GHG. The main activities which comprise WHO Watch include:

- recruiting and training 'watchers';
- maintaining a high-quality website (www.ghwatch.org/who-watch) dealing in an integrated way with WHO governing-body meetings, agenda items and policy issues and providing a portal to other resources;
- monitoring, participating in and lobbying around meetings of WHO's governing bodies (World Health Assembly, Executive Board, regional committees);
- collaborating with developing-country governments and delegations in policy analysis around global health issues under consideration by WHO;
- strengthening the links between the local and thematic campaigns being undertaken by PHM country circles and PHM thematic networks and activism around the structures and dynamics of global health governance;
- engaging in national-level consultation with government officials regarding global health issues through delegations, deputations, national workshops and stoking a national policy dialogue around GHG issues.

the health of their TNCs as more important than the health of the global South and see a strong corporate influence on WHO's work as desirable and appropriate. The pressure to expand and formalize the input of the PPPs, philanthropies and IFIs into WHO decision-making is likewise set to continue.

**An advocacy programme for civil society: 'Save WHO!'**

'The WHO we need' will not emerge from the current reform programme. However, the capabilities described earlier provide the basis for a realistic alternative reform programme for which civil society organizations and LMICs should be arguing. Box D1.7 describes 'WHO Watch', which is a project of the People's Health Movement (PHM) and partner organizations seeking to strengthen the accountability of WHO at all levels.

It would be a serious mistake to write off WHO as an institutional failure. It has played a key role in global health and has the potential to continue to play a powerful and positive role. It is vital for civil society to engage with WHO (at all levels); as an arena of struggle, as an agent of change and as an authoritative voice.

## Notes

1 WHO comprises 'the Secretariat', which includes the staff of the organization in Geneva and in regional and country offices, and the 'governing bodies', the World Health Assembly, the Executive Board and the regional committees.

2 Section 301 of the US Trade Act authorizes the listing of countries which do not provide 'adequate and effective' protection of intellectual property rights or 'fair and equitable market access to United States persons that rely upon intellectual property rights'.

3 Trade Related Intellectual Property Rights Agreement.

## References

Althusser, L. (1971) 'Ideology and ideological state apparatuses', in L. Althusser (ed.), *Lenin and Philosophy and Other Essays*, New York and London: Monthly Review Press, www.marx2mao.com/Other/LPOE7oii. html#s5, accessed 8 March 2014.

Farley, J. (2008) *Brock Chisholm, the World Health Organisation and the Cold War*, Vancouver: UBC Press.

GHW (2005) 'World Health Organization', in Editorial Team (eds), *Global Health Watch 2005–2006: An alternative world health report*, London and New York: Zed Books, www.ghwatch.org/sites/www.ghwatch.org/files/E1.pdf, accessed 6 March 2014.

— (2008) 'The global health landscape', in Editorial Team (eds), *Global Health Watch 2: An alternative world health report*, London and New York: Zed Books, www.ghwatch. org/sites/www.ghwatch.org/files/d1.1.pdf, accessed 6 March 2014.

— (2011) 'World Health Organisation: captive to conflicting interests', in Editorial Group (eds), *Global Health Watch 3: An alternative world health report*, London and New York: Zed Books, www.ghwatch.org/sites/www.ghwatch.org/files/D1_0.pdf, accessed 6 March 2014.

— (2014) 'The health crises of neoliberal globalization', in Editorial Group (eds), *Global Health Watch 4: An alternative world health report*, London and New York: Zed Books.

Harvey, D. (2005) *A Brief History of Neoliberalism*, Oxford: Oxford University Press.

Hawkes, C., C. Blouin, S. Henson, N. Drager and L. Dubé (2010) 'Trade, health and dietary change', in C. Hawkes, C. Blouin, S. Henson, N. Drager and L. Dubé (eds), *Trade, Food, Diet and Health: Perspectives and policy options*, Chichester: Blackwell.

Herman, E. S. and N. Chomsky (1988) *Manufacturing Consent: The political economy of the mass media*, New York: Pantheon Books.

International Health Conference (1946) *The constitution of the World Health Organisation*, online, apps.who.int/gb/bd/PDF/bd47/EN/constitution-en.pdf, accessed 28 August 2012.

Lee, K. (2009) *The World Health Organization (WHO)*, London and New York: Routledge.

Legge, D. G. (2013) *Trade and Health: An Enquiry into the Role of the World Health Organisation in promoting Policy Coherence across the fields of Trade and Health and in particular, the Origins, Implementation and Effectiveness of World Health Assembly Resolution 59.26 on International Trade and Health*, Oslo, www.med.uio.no/helsam/english/research/global-governance-health/background-papers/who-trade.pdf, accessed 6 March 2014.

PricewaterhouseCoopers (2013) *WHO Reform Stage 2 Evaluation Final Report*, Geneva, apps.who.int/gb/ebwha/pdf_files/EB134/B134_39-en.pdf, accessed 10 March 2014.

Richter, J. (2002) *Codes in Context: TNC regulation in an era of dialogues and partnerships*, online, Newton, Dorset: The Corner House, www.thecornerhouse.org.uk/sites/thecornerhouse.org.uk/files/26codes.pdf, accessed 7 January 2014.

Robinson, W. I. (2004) *A Theory of Global Capitalism: Production, Class, and State in a Transnational World*, Baltimore, MD: Johns Hopkins University Press.

Robinson, W. I. and J. Harris (2000) 'Towards a global ruling class? Globalization and the transnational capitalist class', *Science & Society*, 64(1): 11–54.

Roemer, R., A. Taylor and J. Lariviere (2005) 'Origins of WHO Framework Convention on Tobacco Control', *American Journal of Public Health*, 95: 936–8.

United Nations (2013) *The Millennium Development Goals Report, 2013*, New York, www.un.org/millenniumgoals/pdf/report-2013/mdg-report-2013-english.pdf, accessed 1 July 2012.

WHO (World Health Organization) (1958) *The first ten years of the World Health Organization*, Geneva: WHO.

— (2014) *Maternal, infant and young child nutrition*, Geneva, apps.who.int/gb/ebwha/pdf_files/EB134/B134_15-en.pdf, accessed 12 March 2014.

— (n.d.) *A forthcoming guide for policy makers: diagnostic tool on trade and health*, www.who.int/trade/trade_and_health/Diagnostic_Tool_on_Trade_Summary.pdf, accessed 9 January 2013.

WHO Watch (2012) *WHO reform 2010–2012*, People's Health Movement, online, www.ghwatch.org/who-watch/topics/whoreform, accessed 6 March 2014.

— (2013) *SFC & QSE @ WHO (2003–2013)*, WHO Watch, online, www.ghwatch.org/who-watch/topics/sfcchronology, accessed 6 March 2014.

— (2014) *Psoriasis*, WHO Watch, online, www.ghwatch.org/who-watch/topics/psoriasis, accessed 6 March 2014.

World Bank (2014) *Data: Indicators*, online, Washington, DC: World Bank, data.worldbank.org/indicator/NY.GDP.MKTP.CD, accessed 12 March 2014.

## D2 | A NEW 'BUSINESS MODEL' FOR NGOS?

### Introduction

In the last two decades, there has been an upsurge in the number of organizations in the 'third sector'[1] and a tremendous growth in their mandates. Financed by government, voluntary and private sources, civil society organizations are now involved in a range of sectors, such as health, education, development programmes (including relief and rehabilitation), peace, human rights and environmental issues (Bagci 2007), and serve multiple functions to influence policy processes; from agenda-setting to implementation and evaluation (Pollard and Court 2005).

The term 'civil society' is not new. It has been in use and intensely contested for centuries. Nineteenth-century scholars (such as Alexis de Tocqueville) viewed civil society as a pluralist space in which ideas and beliefs were shaped by virtue of associations. Such 'associational life' was seen as inculcating a sense of civic and political participation as well as providing a counterweight to the state in guaranteeing individual liberties.

Among the different concepts that try to theoretically capture civil society, that of Antonio Gramsci seems to be the most promising (Gramsci 1982). Gramsci did not conceptualize civil society as completely separate from the political sphere of the state. On the contrary: the political sphere (the administration, the regulatory and legal apparatus of states) is closely linked with civil society (the political parties, the media, trade unions, grassroots organizations, the corporate sector, the NGOs). According to Gramsci's concept of civil society the 'World Social Forum' is as much part of civil society as is the industry-driven 'International Forum on Economy'.

In fact, civil society is not about particular actors, but more about a space. It is the space of societies where opinion-making happens, where political decisions are prepared, where – as Gramsci put it – the struggle for cultural hegemony occurs.

Thus, descriptions of civil society as a 'sphere separate from both the state and market' (as the WHO defines civil society), indicating the non-state and non-profit characteristics, or occupying a space between the public and the private, are at best misleading. In the complex contemporary global architecture, traditional boundaries between what constitutes 'public' and what is 'private' are being eroded. The dichotomy is blurred in particular by the contemporary growth of private foundations registered by corporations (corporate-owned NGOs). Scholars have also noted a growing trend of *agencification* that implies the 'carving out of independent agencies from the state, either through corporatisation or the formation of societies at the state levels' (Prakash and Singh 2007: 4). These agencies operate as legally and financially independent structures with greater operational flexibility in terms of recruitment, funding, payment systems and outsourcing services. This trend has resulted in 'diffusion of power and authority' (Baru and Nundy 2008: 66), by effecting relationships between the state and non-state actors, thereby posing a challenge to accountability (Kapilashrami 2010).

It has also been argued that the term 'civil society' enables a dishonest creation of an idealized space where a large collection of individuals and organizations are assumed to pool their interests to secure optimal outcomes (Amoore and Langley 2004). This notion of civil society underplays differences and power relations between CSOs, conferring unfounded legitimacy on policy decisions and the actions of international agencies, thereby widening the 'democratic deficit' within international systems (Kapilashrami and O'Brien 2012).

CSOs include a very wide range of institutions, networks and social and political (and identity-based) movements. These include social and political movements, faith-based institutions, community groups/community-based initiatives, professional associations, consumer groups, trade unions, media organizations, scientific and research institutes, policy think tanks and non-governmental organizations (NGOs).

NGOs, the most recognizable component of civil society, are emerging as a strong force in the global political economy of the world: 3,900 organizations have consultative status in UN ECOSOC, and representation in the governing body of UNAIDS and the Security Council, among others. NGOs have come to be recognized as important actors in the landscape of international development, from leading international campaigns against trade liberalization, aid reforms and tackling poverty (such as 'Make Poverty History') to humanitarian and reconstruction efforts in post-conflict and disaster-hit nations. Their growth in numbers, scope and influence reinforces the observation that the 'global associational revolution' brought about by the rise of NGOs may prove to be as significant to the early twenty-first century as the rise of the nation-state was to the nineteenth century (Salamon 1994: 1). Traditional actors such as the World Bank and other bilateral agencies (such as USAID) are now joined by a myriad of institutions such as those referred to as Global Health Initiatives (GHIs) to channel aid to LMICs through NGOs to achieve development goals. An estimate suggests that in 2004 NGOs were recipients of one third of total overseas development assistance, approximately US$23 billion (Riddell 2007: 53). Their increasing share within the aid market is accompanied by a growing legitimacy that has enabled their movement beyond support services into the realm of provision and financing (Kapilashrami 2010).

## Conceptual and definitional ambiguity

The growth of NGOs over the past two decades has given them an increasingly important role and the recognition of a distinctive sector within civil society. However, the term is often used interchangeably (and almost consciously) with the term 'civil society'. One of the problems in defining this term is its local meaning. Every government has its own indigenous organizational structures, thus defining structures outside those poses new challenges for this concept. Many sociologists define NGOs as organizations with four defining characteristics which enable them to be distinguished from other organizations in civil society. They are: voluntary, formal, not-for-profit, self-governing (Edwards and Hulme 1992; Lewis and Kanji 2009). Combining these operational-structural elements, a useful definition regards NGOs as 'self-governing, private, not-for-profit organisations that are geared to improving the quality of life for disadvantaged people' (Vakil 1997: 2060). While all NGOs are non-profit-oriented, and institutionalized, they may differ considerably in their objectives, affiliation, methods of action and internal structure (Frantz 1987), each aspect having a bearing on the others. For instance, some NGOs direct their action towards clearly defined problems in society, while others act with much broader mandates, addressing wider upstream determinants. Some act with a charitable intent, while others shape their efforts in a more political fashion, working with other groups in pursuit of a common goal. Frantz (ibid.) also suggests a distinction between NGOs which act to minimize the perverse effects of economic liberalization and those which redirect these same processes.

## Numbers and scope

Definitional ambiguity in the term and varied data sources make precision on numbers difficult. According to one estimate, the number of NGOs operating internationally (INGOs) has grown from 1,083 in 1914 (Anheier et al. 2001) to over 50,000 in the early twenty-first century (Union of International Associations n.d.). In 1992 about seven hundred NGOs were granted consultative status with the UN Economic and Social Council; today the number has increased to 3,900 organizations.[2] In 2009 the number of NGOs in India was estimated at around 3.3 million, many times the number of primary schools and primary health centres.[3]

The policy and political influence enjoyed by these INGOs merits a better understanding of their organization and factors underpinning their growth. The rapid increase in their numbers and reach is attributed to several factors, foremost being the change in the aid architecture, which has witnessed the ascendancy of private foundations and philanthropies like the Bill and Melinda Gates Foundation (BMGF). Other reasons include the rise of democracy, cheaper information technology, economic and political globalization, decreasing public confidence in governments and corporations, and growing normative

### Box D2.1 Save the Children – perils of 'corporatization'

Save the Children UK is one of the largest INGOs operating today in the humanitarian and development world.

Save the Children UK has come under criticism, however, for its relationship with large corporations (its income from large corporations has increased more than fivefold, from £3.9 million in 2009 to £22.5 million in 2013[4]), such as British Gas, GSK and Unilever, and also for its lack of independence in criticizing the UK government.

In a *Panorama* report aired in the UK in 2013, a former staff member of Save the Children UK (SCUK) argued that the INGO operated self-censorship on various occasions, including on a campaign against fuel poverty in the UK. This self-censorship, later denied by SCUK's CEO, was aimed at not jeopardizing funding from EDF (a UK-based energy corporation). Yet emails obtained by the *Independent* show that:

> [A] manager in charge of winning new partnerships wrote: 'I am really conscious that this will need to be handled carefully so as not to jeopardise what could end up being a long-term partnership.' A few days later a second email stated that the charity's head of advocacy was 'of the feeling we should not risk the EDF partnership'.[5]

The INGO's association with GSK[6] (worth £15 million over five years[7]) also causes concerns as GSK's reputation is far from untainted: a bribery scandal in China in 2013, a criminal fraud in the USA in 2012, the 2008 Paroxetine scandal, the resistance to allowing other companies to produce its drugs at a cheaper price, the lack of transparency of the pharmaceutical giant in terms of its pricing policies or its attempts to foster monopoly, for example, all contribute to giving GSK a bad reputation. Considering these repeated allegations against the pharmaceutical giant and the general lack of transparency surrounding pharmaceutical companies' activities, any financial association with them should indeed cause concern.

A further example of this corporatization of SCUK is its association with Unilever. Unilever states that, through this association,[8] it will increase consumer outreach and cause-related marketing[9] and plans to double the size of its business.[10] Yet the SCUK 'consumers' are supposedly children who should be accessing SCUK's services freely rather than through any form of market exchange.

Various SCUK staff members, who prefer to remain anonymous (which in itself is a sign of an issue within the NGO), were told to stop criticizing the international development arm of the UK government as SCUK was now a partner rather than a critic of DfID. This desire for collaboration may serve a higher goal, but it certainly jeopardizes the independence and neutrality of SCUK. This feeling of unease with the direction taken by SCUK in terms of policy messaging is also reflected in the very low staff morale unearthed by the 2013 staff survey. This survey shows that the policy department of SCUK is extremely unhappy about the values of the organization. Yet no one dares talk about it.

support for INGOs as legitimate actors. The rise of private foundations as global actors has enabled some NGOs to function as large multinational enterprises (McCoy et al. 2009) (see also Box D2.1). For example, the Seattle-based, BMGF-funded Programme for Appropriate Technology in Health (PATH) had assets in excess of $130 million in 2006. An even wider range exists in numbers and operations of national NGOs, which have proliferated in low- and middle-income countries (LMICs) in the last two decades.

NGOs are increasingly viewed as the solution for achieving universal coverage in countries with deficient public systems. Recent examples of NGO involvement in service delivery and management contracts include running urban or rural primary health centres in Cambodia, Bolivia, Bangladesh and India, or offering treatment, counselling and care services in disease-specific programmes. This shift to greater engagement of the third sector and the undermining of the role of the state is underpinned by multiple and often contrasting discursive shifts in ideas and policy.

The ascendancy of the discourse on new public management (NPM) and the neoliberal emphasis on free markets, privatization and a reduced state emerged in response to the claim of ineffective and inefficient public bureaucracies (Anheier 2009). Pushed by World Bank and other aggressive proponents of the structural adjustment programmes, such reform policies emphasized greater involvement of the private sector, both for- and not-for-profit, on several grounds, not least the economic imperative for government reforms. More recently, the principles of NPM are reinforced by the rise of the public–private partnership paradigm and demands and prescriptions of global health actors for participatory governance, thereby opening decision-making spaces for NGOs and transforming their role as partners or even as competitors. This is a significant departure from (and extension of) their role of complementing state provision by addressing particular demands of equity.

Within this new managerialism, NGO involvement is often seen as a panacea for democratic deficiencies that characterize governance and development programmes. This argument rests on the participatory and civic engagement (or community-building) function of civil society considered as a prerequisite for the success of development programmes (and the economic objectives these serve) and necessary for enforcing contracts and development of both markets and democratic institutions (ibid.).

Further, non-profit entities are viewed as instruments for improving citizenship and social accountability. With rights, empowerment and equality core to the vision of most NGOs, they are often viewed as ensuring wider and more democratic representation of people's voices (Anderson and Rieff 2004; Scholte 2001). The rationale for this discursive shift in ideas of governance rests on the widely held but largely unexamined notion of the comparative advantage that NGOs have in reaching the poorest more effectively, compassionately and efficiently than public services (Pfeiffer 2003).

Regardless of whether NGOs remain centre-stage (or peripheral) to aid reforms, the contemporary aid delivery mechanisms (which continue to be neo-liberal in their approach) have deepened the *contracting* culture and enhanced the role of NGOs in service delivery along with private sector actors. This has happened against a growing consensus on and policy salience of universal access and improvements in services (through stronger and responsive health systems). Further, the ongoing economic crisis has strengthened the rationale for finding more efficient ways of meeting the health crisis. Arguably, non-state agencies, in particular the NGO sector, are viewed as a viable option. Consequently, strengthening primary care and improving health financing is being delegated to a growing number of non-profit and for-profit entities coming together through contracting measures and partnerships in delivery and health financing (through social health insurance schemes).

## Implications for governance and health systems

NGOs have been subjected to fierce criticism on several grounds. Among these, a major critique concerns the institutionalization and 'taming' of critical voices and radical grassroots action. NGOs are seen as drawing social movements and activism into the safe professionalized and often depoliticized world of development practice (Lewis and Kanji 2009).

This affects spaces for debate and generation of ideas and theory that backs action, and warrants specialization (from demands of efficiency), which sometimes facilitates their transformation into service providers or single-issue lobbyists of international institutions (Kaldor 2003). Such apolitical conceptions of NGOs are reinforced in their interface with global health institutions, raising questions around internal democracy (or lack of participation and transparency in decision-making) within their organization.

A recent analysis of governing boards of top 100 INGOs reveals the disjunction between the world NGOs seek to create and the world their governance structures reproduce (Tom 2013). Seventy-two per cent had their headquarters in the North (predominantly in North America and Europe), and boards were predominantly of European origin with degrees from Northern universities. Another staggering finding of the survey was that over 55 per cent of NGO

DEVELOPMENT
PARTNER

RICH
DONOR

F & B
INDUSTRY

CORPORATE
NGO

"We are together in the business of CHARITY"

**Image D2.1** Many NGOs are part of the establishment today (Indranil Mukhopadhyay)

boards had some professional affiliation with either the banking sector or the arms and tobacco industries. Such leadership is clearly inconsistent with the promotion of justice and social development goals that the NGOs endorse.

### Two vignettes of NGO-led 'interventions'

At the country level, these relationships of power and inequality are enacted in myriad ways that profoundly shape health systems and policies. This is further explored through two case vignettes examining NGO involvement in primary healthcare and HIV programmes.

*The case of INGOs and foreign agencies and primary healthcare* Describing such a scenario through an ethnography of INGOs in Mozambique, Pfeiffer (2003) demonstrates how foreign aid channelled through NGOs intensifies local social inequality and creates a culture of competition with high social costs to primary healthcare. Project-specific funding emphasized demonstration of short-term results, i.e. improvements in health outputs, such as under-five mortality or nutrition indicators, over short project periods. Further, the professional pace and skill sets of expatriates were in stark contrast with highly demotivated (and low-paid) staff in provincial health facilities.

However, existing health systems (and programmes) are key to the operations of foreign agencies, which seek to either graft their projects on to the health system or create parallel structures and fund local NGOs. In the case of the former, ministries were confronted by the challenge of managing foreign agency competition and their overlapping interests in supporting specific components of the programme. Coordination mechanisms/meetings emerged as sites of turf conflicts (and 'behind-the-scenes deal-making') to seek patronage of ministry officials for respective projects by offering them a range of financial incentives. Such incentives and personal favours for high-level officials became quintessential for favourable evaluations of their projects and continuity of donor funding received by INGOs. Additionally, participation in NGO-sponsored seminars, evaluations, surveys and training programmes resulted in the emptying out of health directorate offices and the departure of qualified personnel for donor consultancies, thereby affecting routine health systems' work. In terms of health outcomes, Pfeiffer highlights several systemic dysfunctions resulting from disjointed aid projects, including reduced mobile vaccination brigades, absenteeism from regular duties, under-the-table payments for free services, and loss of skilled personnel. All these undermined the effectiveness of the national health system (ibid.).

*The case of NGO networks and HIV management in India* In an ethnography of the AIDS industry undertaken in India, Kapilashrami points to a similar proliferation of INGOs and development agencies (such as UNOPS and HIV Alliance among others) whose movement into countries can be traced to the inflow of GHI funding (Kapilashrami and McPake 2013). A prominent part of this industry is national networks of affected communities which emerged, expanded and diversified in the wake of GHI demands for inclusion of voices in AIDS policy and governance. The Global Fund, for instance, opened up possibilities of engaging with 'beneficiaries' as 'activist experts', and in this process gave a boost to the presence of institutions representing them and their activities. This was evidenced in the case of the Indian network of people with HIV, whose outreach expanded from national to sub-national (state and district) level: 102 networks were established in the districts of 'high-prevalence' states within the first two years of the Global Fund's operations in India. This quantum leap in reaching out to people with HIV implied improved access to care and support services, and potential opportunities for reporting grievances with respect to unavailability of drugs, quality of treatment and other rights violations. However, these district networks also emerged as convenient sites for much of the development work around HIV and AIDS, and as organizations running multiple projects (access to care and treatment; prevention of parent-to-child transmission; drop-in centres) with multiple funding sources and significant overlaps in their activities. The following excerpt from Kapilashrami and O'Brien (2012) describes this transition phase, which saw the emergence of professionalized and activity-oriented agencies.

> Formally registered as societies, each district level network (DLN) has a
> separate governance and organisational structure which comprises of a board

and project staff varying with the number of projects implemented. The infrastructure usually comprises of four or five rooms, each run as a dedicated unit, distinguished by the Funder's name mounted on a nameplate at the entrance of each room, for the respective funding agency whose project is being implemented. ... Typically, most DLNs I visited had on an average five to six projects being implemented. These included Global Fund, HIVOS, Elton John Foundation, Gates Foundation, US Centre for Disease Control, Danish International Development Agency (DANIDA), Canadian International Development ment Agency (CIDA), GlaxoSmithKline Positive Action, Family Health International (FHI), Concern Worldwide, UNDP etc. ... A few projects were designed specifically to build capacities and orient staff to donor mechanisms, for example, strengthening the network's involvement with the CCM [Country Coordinating Mechanism] and other national processes. Moreover, a clear overlap could be seen across projects, wherein service oriented activities such as support meetings, pre- and post-test counseling, and referrals, were supported by more than one funding agency. A consequence of managing these multiple demands of different funding agencies was that a single intervention was recorded and reported under different projects.

Both case vignettes highlight programme-wide and system-wide effects as a consequence of competition and resulting opportunist behaviours among staff. These effects in the latter case included poor quality of counselling and care services, competition in achieving and demonstrating targets arising from sustainability concerns of projects and institutions, and friction between GHI-funded project staff and the demotivated public health facility staff. However, both vignettes reveal that fragmentation of primary healthcare systems and services is not simply an outcome of problems of aid coordination and management but also of the structural transformation at national and local levels brought about by NGOs' interface with aid and its tenuous relationship with the state. This transformation is characterized by a shift from critical to increasingly technical, apolitical and professional discourses to fit formalized models and frameworks of mainstream development agencies, and the changing nature of 'expertise' that values technical skills and qualifications over activism and community engagement experience.

### Risk of co-option

Advocates of greater autonomy and an enhanced role for third-sector organizations argue that involvement in national-level decision-making forums (such as programme management units, task forces and CCMs) can alter power dynamics and make governments more accountable to their citizens. Literature points to a contrary effect. At the service level, there is evidence of co-option, and departure from NGOs' traditional watchdog role to that of an implementing agency (and a 'partner') of the state. The risk of such co-optation rises as some NGOs are increasingly drawn 'into service delivery functions and market relations' and 'an increasing number became part of a growing corporate social responsibility industry of service providers' (Utting 2005: 376). In the case of Global Fund in India, this was evident from the corporate sector involvement in civil society consortia that were developed to deliver HIV care as part of the Global Fund grants. With the growing engagement of NGOs in business-type activities 'a whole commercial market develops around shaping, assessing, and consulting on the desired dimensions of social responsibility' (Shamir 2004: 678). Thus NGOs' dependency on aid tends to redirect accountability away from their grassroots constituencies, towards corporations and funders – both state and foreign agencies.

The above system-wide and governance effects run counter to the premise on which NGO/civil society participation is sought, i.e. democratic legitimacy, people-centred and appropriate care, rebuilding and strengthening communities, and reinforcing the public interest role of states. Within an overwhelming focus on targets and deliverables in-built in service delivery projects, their capacity to affect structural change to benefit the poor and disenfranchised they claim to represent through these projects (or advocacy efforts) is severely undermined. Such fragmented efforts not only weaken state capacities but also reduce the viability of downwardly accountable community-led groups, and the creation of an organic civil society free from corporate and donor influence and interests.

### In lieu of a conclusion

As our discussions have shown, NGOs have been remarkably flexible in adapting to changing global power relations. It is, hence, virtually impossible to summarize the potential role that NGOs are likely to play in the future. However, it would be useful to end by indicating some of the 'red lines' that are beginning to be defined quite sharply in relation to the activities of NGOs.

That 'pragmatism' guides many NGOs today should not come as a surprise. It is part of the current hegemonic discourse that abhors utopian thinking by demanding realism. Many NGOs perceive 'business-oriented' management practices as a proof of 'professionalism'. Most donors require that NGOs plan their activities so that they are 'measurable, realistic and time-bound' (Doran 1981). Such standards may be useful for the production of commodities but in the social and political arena they distort the possible role of NGOs in social change.

The impact of managerial economics is visible in the depoliticization of NGOs. 'Business talk' has seamlessly entered the lexicon of NGOs. With increasing frequency NGOs speak of 'stakeholders', 'controlling mechanisms', 'impact analysis' and 'investments'.

As NGOs become increasingly beholden to donor funding, they are being overtaken by the agenda set by donors. Unfortunately, instead of supporting people to mobilize against unjust power relations at different levels, donor-driven cooperation focuses on the provision of techniques, management know-how and motivational support to help cope with adversities.

## Notes

1 The term 'third sector' has been used interchangeably with voluntary sector to refer to the sphere of social activity undertaken by the non-profit and non-governmental sector. This classification refers to civil society as both a group of organizations and a social space in between government (public sector) and market (private sector).

2 See NGO Branch, Department of Economic and Social Affairs, 2013, csonet. org/?menu=100.

3 See 'India: more NGOs, than schools and health centres', OneWorld.net, 7 July 2010.

4 See www.independent.co.uk/news/uk/home-news/the-price-of-charity-save-the-children-exposed-after-seeking-approval-of-energy-firms-8994225.html.

5 See www.independent.co.uk/news/uk/home-news/the-price-of-charity-save-the-children-exposed-after-seeking-approval-of-energy-firms-8994225.html.

6 See www.savethechildren.org/site/c.8rKLIXMGIpI4E/b.8685351/k.C027/GSK.htm.

7 See www.theguardian.com/business/2013/may/09/save-the-children-teams-up-glaxosmithkline.

8 Unilever Foundation is also associated with Oxfam, UNICEF, WFP and PSI.

9 See www.savethechildren.net/about-us/our-corporate-partners/unilever-foundation-and-save-children.

10 See www.unilever.co.uk/aboutus/foundation/aboutunileverfoundation/.

## References

Amoore, L. and P. Langley (2004) 'Ambiguities of global civil society', *Review of International Studies*, 30: 89–110.

Anderson, K. and D. Rieff (2004) '"Global civil society": a sceptical view', in H. Anheier, M. Glasius and M. Kaldor (eds), *Global Civil Society*, London: Sage, pp. 26–39.

Anheier, H. K. (2009) 'What kind of nonprofit sector? What kind of society?', *American Behavioural Scientist*, 52(7): 1082–94.

Anheier, H. K., M. Glasius and M. Kaldor (2001) 'Introducing global civil society', in H.

Anheier, M. Glasius, M. Kaldor, D. Osgood, F. Pinter and Y. Said (eds), *Global Civil Society Yearbook 2001*, London: Oxford University Press.

Bagci, C. (2007) 'Historical evolution of NGOs: NGO proliferation in the post-Cold War era', Turkish Weekly (originally published in Avrupa Gunlugu, 4, 2003, pp. 299–326), www.turkishweekly.net/article/222/historical-evolution-of-ngos-ngo-proliferation-in-the-post-cold-war-era.html, accessed 26 June 2014.

Baru, R. and S. Nundy (2008) 'Blurring of boundaries: public–private partnerships in health services in India', *Economic Political Weekly*, 43(4): 62–71.

Doran, G. T. (1981) 'There's a S.M.A.R.T. way to write management's goals and objectives', *Management Review*, 70(11): 35–6.

Edwards, M. and D. Hulme (eds) (1992) *Making a Difference: NGOs and development in a changing world*, London: Earthscan.

— (1996) *Beyond the Magic Bullet: NGO performance and accountability in the post-cold war world*, West Hartford, CN: Kumarian Press under the auspices of the Save the Children Fund.

Frantz, T. R. (1987) 'The role of NGOs in the strengthening of civil society', *World Development*, 15, Supplement 1(0): 121–7, doi: dx.doi.org/10.1016/0305-750X(87)90150-1.

Gramsci, A. (1982) *Selections from the Prison Books*, London: Lawrence and Wishart.

Kaldor, M. (2003) 'Civil society and accountability', Journal of Human Development, 4(1): 5–26.

Kapilashrami, A. (2010) 'Understanding public–private partnerships: the discourse, the practice, and the system wide effects of the global fund to fight AIDS, tuberculosis, and malaria', PhD thesis, Queen Margaret University, etheses.qmu.ac.uk/369/1/369.pdf, accessed 26 June 2014.

Kapilashrami, A. and B. McPake (2013) 'Transforming governance or reinforcing hierarchies and competition: examining the public and hidden transcripts of the global fund and HIV in India', *Health Policy and Planning*, 28(6): 626–35, doi: 10.1093/heapol/czs102; 10.1093/heapol/czs102.

Kapilashrami, A. and O. O'Brien (2012) 'The global fund and the re-configuration and re-emergence of "civil society": widening or closing the democratic deficit?', *Global Public Health*, 7(5): 437–51, doi: 10.1080/17441692.2011.649043; 10.1080/17441692.2011.649043.

Lewis, D. and N. Kanji (2009) *Non-governmental Organisations and Development*, Oxford: Routledge.

McCoy, D., S. Chand and D. Sridhar (2009) 'Global health funding: how much, where it comes from and where it goes', *Health Policy and Planning*, 24(6): 407–17, doi: 10.1093/heapol/czp026; 10.1093/heapol/czp026.

Pfeiffer, J. (2003) 'International NGOs and primary health care in Mozambique: the need for a new model of collaboration', *Social Science & Medicine*, 56(4): 725–38.

Pollard, A. and J. Court (2005) 'How civil society organisations use evidence to influence policy processes: a literature review', Working Paper 249, London: Overseas Development Institute.

Prakash, G. and A. Singh (2007) 'Outsourcing of health care services in Rajasthan: an exploratory study', Paper presented at IIM, IMR Conference, Bangalore.

Riddell, R. C. (2007) *Does Foreign Aid Really Work?*, Oxford: Oxford University Press.

Salamon, L. M. (1994) 'The rise of the nonprofit sector', *Foreign Affairs*, 1 July.

Scholte, J. A. (2001) 'Civil society and democracy in global governance', CSGR Working Paper no. 65/01, University of Warwick.

Shamir, R. (2004) 'The de-radicalization of corporate social responsibility', *Critical Sociology*, 30(3): 669–89.

Tom, F. E. (2013) 'Diversity and inclusion on NGO boards: what the stats say', *Guardian*, 7 May.

Union of International Associations (n.d.) *Yearbook of International Organisations*, www.uia.org/, accessed 31 January 2014.

Utting, P. (2005) 'Corporate responsibility and the movement of business', *Development in Practice*, 15(3/4): 375–88.

Vakil, A. (1997) 'Confronting the classification problem: toward a taxonomy of NGOs', *World Development*, 25(12): 2057–71.

# D3 | PRIVATE SECTOR INFLUENCE ON PUBLIC HEALTH POLICY

There is extensive evidence that the promotion of markets in healthcare leads to an increase in health inequities and inefficiencies. Despite such evidence, globally, privatization of the health sector is being vigorously promoted. This policy push is a result of the strong influence the private sector wields on health policy-making. Private sector influence has risen exponentially with an increase in large private foundations and public–private partnerships. These operate on the basic assumption that public sector management is inefficient and adoption of private sector management practices[1] is the solution. This increase in private sector influence on health policy formulation is at the cost of transparency and accountability. There are concerns about the role, effect and lack of accountability of private foundations (McCoy et al. 2009; Barkan 2014).

The process of privatization has been accompanied by growing influence of international management consulting services in the public sector. International management consulting services are an integral part of the 'policy community' (Player and Leys 2012) that promotes back-door privatization of the health sector through constant campaigning. They have little or no experience of health policy issues and count large healthcare and pharmaceutical firms as their major clients. These operate inside and outside the ministries of health. The revolving door ensures that the corporate voice is always represented. Ex-ministers, officials and civil servants profit from lucrative positions in private health companies. Management consultancy professionals move from ministerial adviser to policy drafter at the Department of Health to private health company to insurance company to think tank to lobby group and round again (ibid.). The death blow dealt to the British National Health Service is a very recent example of the interplay of these forces (see Chapter B2). These financial consultancy firms further strengthen the case for privatization through the 'hollowing' of state coffers by assisting their clients in tax evasion.

In this chapter we look at some of the major players who wield enormous power on public policy, especially in the health sector.

## The Gates Foundation

The Bill and Melinda Gates Foundation is the world's largest private grant-making foundation, estimated to have disbursed about $36 billion since its inception (Parry et al. 2013). The remit of the Bill and Melinda Gates

Foundation's influence can be assessed from the fact that it has association with a majority of key global health actors through funding arrangements. These include WHO and UNICEF, the Global Fund, GAVI, universities, non-governmental organizations, policy think tanks and the World Bank. It has also awarded two grants to the International Finance Corporation, whose mandate is to support private sector development (see also Chapter D6). It sits on the governing structures of many global health institutions, and has the ear of government and business leaders (McCoy et al. 2009; McCoy 2009).

The private management consulting organization McKinsey and Co. (whose operations we examine later in the chapter) enjoys a close relationship with the Gates Foundation[2] and conducts studies for it.[3]

Despite the strong influence the Gates Foundation exerts on global health policies the effect of the policies it promotes has never been evaluated. This lack of accountability distinguishes it from other global health institutions. It is based on the false premise that private foundations built on private wealth are not publicly accountable. This overlooks the fact that these foundations: intervene in public life through the political power they exert owing to the finances they funnel; are publicly subsidized through tax exemptions; and reinforce the problem of plutocracy – the exercise of power derived from wealth (Barkan 2014).

The Gates Foundation has an advisory board, but no formal governing body.[4] It has an advisory board. While it consults widely, some in the health community feel it listens only to what it wants to hear (McCoy 2009).

The Gates Foundation engages in policy-making to achieve 'catalytic change'.[5] It has representatives that sit on the governing structures of many global health partnerships (McCoy et al. 2008). It is also a part of a self-appointed group of global health leaders known as the H8 (together with WHO, the World Bank, GAVI Alliance, the Global Fund, UNICEF, the United Nations Population Fund (UNFPA) and UNAIDS); and has been involved in setting the health agenda for the G8 (McCoy et al. 2009; Reich and Takemi 2009).[6]

The Bill and Melinda Gates Foundation's endowment mainly comes from Bill Gates' personal fortune and stock in Berkshire Hathaway given to the Foundation as a gift from Hathaway's CEO, Warren Buffett (Stuckler et al. 2011).[7] The Foundation's corporate stock endowment is heavily invested in the food industry, directly and indirectly. The Foundation holds significant shares in McDonald's (10 million shares representing about 4 per cent of the Gates portfolio) and Coca-Cola (34 million shares, 14 per cent of the Foundation's portfolio, not counting Berkshire Hathaway holdings).[8, 9]

Previously it invested in pharmaceutical companies. In 2009 it sold extensive pharmaceutical holdings in Johnson & Johnson (2.5 million shares), Schering-Plough Corporation (14.9 million shares), Eli Lilly and Company (about one million shares), Merck & Co. (8.1 million shares) and Wyeth (3.7 million shares) (ibid.).

The Bill and Melinda Gates Foundation does not disclose the detailed discussions that take place among its board members when funding decisions are made. The Foundation's management committee oversees all the Foundation's efforts. Several members of the management committee, leadership teams, affiliates and major funders are currently or were previously members of the boards or executive branches of several major food and pharmaceutical companies, including Coca-Cola, Merck, Novartis, Pfizer, General Mills, Kraft and Unilever, raising conflict-of-interest issues (ibid.). The Foundation has also secured the services of people who have served in senior positions in the United Nations, the World Bank and state institutions.[10]

The blurring of the boundaries between the Foundation's objectives and its portfolio investment is evident in Foundation grants that encourage communities in developing countries to become business affiliates of Coca-Cola, in which the Foundation has substantial holdings (McCoy et al. 2009; Stuckler et al. 2011). The Foundation held stock in Merck at a time when it developed partnerships with the African Comprehensive AIDS and Malaria Partnership and the Merck Company Foundation to test Merck products (Stuckler et al. 2011).

## The Global Fund

The Global Fund for AIDS, TB and Malaria is a global public–private partnership. Country aid budgets constitute approximately 95 per cent of its funding. On 1 January 2009, the Global Fund became an administratively autonomous international financing institution, separating from the World Health Organization (WHO). The Global Fund, however, retains its status as an international institution with privileges and immunities similar to UN organizations in Switzerland and the United States.[11]

The private sector influence on the Global Fund is disproportionately large compared to its 5 per cent contribution. The Global Fund board consists of eight 'constituencies' comprising twenty voting and eight non-voting members. All voting constituencies participate equally. The private sector is one of the voting constituencies. The Global Fund's definition of private sector is broad. It includes interested corporations including pharmaceuticals, oil and gas, banking, management consulting, food and beverages (among others).[12] Thus, the Global Fund directly provides a voice and a vote on its policies to the private sector. Industries such as pharmaceuticals, food and beverages have interests that often conflict with public health policies. The remit of private sector influence also extends to the Global Fund constituencies of foundations and civil society, which it funds.

The Global Fund hires Local Fund Agents (LFAs) (Table D3.1) to oversee, verify and report on grant performance.[13] LFAs are supposed to serve as the 'eyes and ears' of the Global Fund within recipient countries during the pre-grant phase, the grant implementation period and the grant renewal process (McCoy 2013). All LFA reports to the Global Fund are confidential and released by the Global Fund with LFA permission (Global Fund 2007).

LFAs are mainly international management or auditing firms such as PricewaterhouseCoopers and KPMG, known for their 'financial management' skills.

TABLE D3.1 Local Fund Agents of the Global Fund

| Local Fund Agent | Number of countries |
| --- | --- |
| Crown Agents | 1 |
| Finconsult | 2 |
| Grant Thornton | 2 |
| KPMG | 12 |
| Swiss TPH | 15 |
| UNOPS | 15 |
| PricewaterhouseCoopers (PwC) | 75 |
| Grupo Jacobs | 6 |
| Cardno EM | 5 |
| TL Company Analytics | 1 |

*Source*: www.theglobalfund.org/en/lfa/

The Global Fund entrusts LFAs with important oversight roles for technical health issues in which they hold negligible or limited expertise. LFAs are viewed as expensive and of questionable quality (McCoy 2013).

LFAs are expected to interact closely with grant recipients. They can attend Country Coordinating Mechanism (CCM) meetings (Global Fund 2007). Country Coordinating Mechanisms are country-level multi-stakeholder partnerships. These include representatives from both the public and private sectors, including governments, multilateral or bilateral agencies, non-governmental organizations, academic institutions, private businesses and people living with diseases. CCM meetings provide LFAs with an opportunity to interact with other development partners and legitimize their role in public health interventions in which they hold no expertise. Rotation of personnel between LFAs, the Global Fund and grant recipients is common, giving rise to potential conflicts of interest.

### The GAVI Alliance

The GAVI Alliance is yet another public–private partnership in which private sector influence is disproportionately high compared to its contribution. Just as in the case of the Global Fund, GAVI chose not to continue to be based in a UN agency (in this case UNICEF) and became an independent Swiss foundation.[14] Seventy-five per cent of GAVI's funding is from governments and 25 per cent from foundations, corporations and individuals.[15] The Bill and Melinda Gates Foundation holds one of the four permanent seats on GAVI's board. Other permanent seats are held by UNICEF, WHO and the World

Bank. As a public–private partnership, GAVI professes to represent the sum of its partners' individual strengths: WHO's scientific expertise; UNICEF's procurement system; the financial know-how of the World Bank; and the market knowledge of the vaccine industry.[16]

Serious concerns have been expressed about GAVI's close association with the pharmaceutical industry. GAVI's Advanced Market Commitment (AMC) has been criticized as subsidizing big drug companies with aid money. GSK and Pfizer received such money from GAVI for their pneumococcal vaccines (Arie 2011).

GAVI's country eligibility criteria and co-financing policy have been criticized for their risk aversion.[17] Countries must contribute a sum (proportionate to their gross national income per capita) towards immunization programmes with a pledge to subsequently fund these entirely themselves. The countries must already have at least 70 per cent coverage for the DTP3 vaccine (the third dose of the combined diphtheria, tetanus and pertussis vaccine). This implies that the poorest countries most in need of the programme cannot afford to launch immunization programmes with the support of GAVI (GAVI Alliance 2011a; Arie 2011).

A majority of GAVI's organizational and programmatic evaluations have been undertaken by private management consulting firms.[18] The GAVI Alliance shares a close relationship with the global consulting firm McKinsey & Co. McKinsey was involved in developing the financing mechanisms for GAVI. Further, the Accelerated Development and Introduction Plans (ADIPs) for pneumococcal and rotavirus vaccines for the five-year period 2003–07 were based on a commissioned report by McKinsey.[19] GAVI seeks McKinsey's assistance on issues ranging from development of business plans to conducting self assessments (GAVI Alliance 2011b).

The influence of private management consulting firms and the private sector is reflected in GAVI's policies geared towards aligning private sector interests. The *GAVI Second Evaluation Report* concluded that vaccine prices have been an 'area of weak performance' for the Alliance. It also pointed out that 'the assumption that creating a large market for vaccines would lead to a rapid reduction in vaccine prices has not occurred' and that 'GAVI has not actively addressed strategies for reducing vaccine prices and has relied on natural market force'.[20] However, GAVI continues to support a non-transparent system of pricing by vaccine manufacturers. In a report to the GAVI Alliance board in 2011, the GAVI Alliance noted:

> While increased transparency on individual historical product prices has evident benefits, GAVI must be aware of the risk of inadvertently 'setting a price' as there is a limited number of manufacturers in the market. Similarly, sharing the vaccine specific end-to-end roadmaps which outline the long-term vision for the market and potential supply and procurement strategies may

undermine GAVI's ability to negotiate with manufacturers. To mitigate these risks, procurement tactics will remain confidential as will prices until contracts are awarded. (ibid.)

## The role of McKinsey and Co. in the privatization of the NHS

The privatization of the National Health Service (see Chapter B2) is a stark tale of how sharp-elbowed private healthcare companies have bought influence and advantage through a revolving door between former ministers, civil servants, private companies, McKinsey & Co. and other management consultancy firms.[21] These reciprocal relationships ensured that successive governments in the UK pursued the goal of privatizing the NHS irrespective of party lines. All changes to the NHS have been directed at accommodating the needs of the private healthcare sector and building a strong foundation for it to flourish, and terms have been continuously rigged to serve the interests of private providers.

The full extent of McKinsey & Co.'s involvement, as the key architect of the NHS reforms, emerged in the official documents disclosed, under the Freedom of Information Act, to Tamasin Cave from Spinwatch (Spinwatch monitors the lobbying industry). Such was McKinsey's influence that despite being paid public money, the names of its staff were blacked out. Repeated requests from Tamasin Cave were refused by the Department of Health on the grounds that McKinsey advice was 'provided in confidence', or was subject to 'commercial confidentiality' (Rose 2012).

McKinsey's close association with ruling political parties dates back to the seventies, when Sir Keith Joseph (one of Margaret Thatcher's key advisers) introduced McKinsey and Co. into the NHS in 1973.[22] The first major re-organization of the British National Health Service in 1974 was largely based on work and concepts developed by McKinsey and a team from Brunel University (Scott-Samuel et al. 2014).[23]

A 1973 letter to the *British Medical Journal* about this issue said: '... more and more people are realizing that Sir Keith Joseph's managerial revolution – drafted by McKinsey's, the management consultants – will take health care in all its aspects even further away than it now is from public surveillance and interest'.[24]

These words were to prove prophetic. McKinsey continued to promote pro-market policies in healthcare by working closely across all parties and governments. It slowly formed enduring relationships with ministers and civil servants to promote policy measures that ensured returns for itself and its private sector clients at the expense of the public exchequer and public health. A revolving door between McKinsey and the NHS ensured McKinsey employees were already embedded in critical NHS jobs prior to the full enactment of the proposed radical reforms (Rose 2012; Player and Leys 2012).

Besides penetrating the government, McKinsey also plays a key role in the

King's Fund and the Nuffield Trust, the two dominant healthcare pro-market think tanks that have pushed the privatization agenda in the UK (Rose 2012). Both have senior McKinsey partners on their boards, and while they portray themselves as 'independent' they routinely endorse models of care that replicate the US health system (ibid.).

McKinsey also exploited its privileged access to the NHS reform Bill to 'share information' with its corporate clients – which include the world's biggest private hospital firms – which are now set to bid for the health service (ibid.).

## The tax avoidance industry

Accounting firms are also at the centre of a huge tax avoidance industry (Sikka 2013). Some scholars call it the 'hollowing out of the state' (Momani 2013). Tax avoidance by the richest corporations and individuals ultimately translates into fewer resources for public services, such as for healthcare.

The US Senate Permanent Subcommittee on Investigations, 2003, 2005, found that the Big Four accountancy firms (PricewaterhouseCoopers, Deloitte and Touche, KPMG and Ernst & Young) have created a complex architecture of transactions to enable corporations and rich individuals to obtain tax benefits that were (probably) not directly intended by those responsible for passing the relevant legislation (Sikka 2013).

The UK tax authorities have referred to Ernst & Young as 'probably the most aggressive, creative, abusive provider' of avoidance schemes (Guardian 2009) and courts have ruled that a PricewaterhouseCoopers scheme was a 'circular, self-cancelling scheme designed with no purpose other than to avoid tax' (Sikka 2013).

## Conclusion

Public–private partnerships entail a substantial involvement of management/accounting/financial consultancy firms. Such involvement provides platforms for closer interaction between governments, multilateral and bilateral agencies and the private sector. Over time, management/accounting/financial consultancy firms and the private sector gain legitimacy and the respect and admiration of civil servants through repeated interactions. These platforms provide the private sector with opportunities to influence policies and strategies that affect public health. Conflicts of interest get legitimized by constant interaction between the private sector, governments and multilateral agencies. Moreover, tax-exempt private foundations and for-profit corporations are increasingly engaging in relationships that can influence global health.

Public policy-making is being influenced on a global scale by private actors, accountable only to their board members. There is also a clear nexus between different private actors – private foundations, consulting and accounting firms, private industry and global public–private partnerships. The precise role of this unholy nexus in subverting public policy needs to be examined systematically.

## Notes

1 Promoted under the banner of New Public Management (NPM) (Scott-Samuel et al. 2014).

2 This nexus between the Gates Foundation and McKinsey has also come under close scrutiny and criticism in the United States for promoting privatization of public education. See Parry et al. (2013).

3 Response of the WHO to Knowledge Ecology Initiative's (KEI's) letter regarding McKinsey, vaccine policy and competing interests, keionline.org/node/1084, accessed 10 April 2014.

4 The Gates Foundation and other philanthropic institutions have been characterized as '... the least democratic of institutions' (see Parry et al. 2013).

5 www.gatesfoundation.org/How-We-Work/General-Information/How-We-Develop-Strategy, accessed 11 April 2014.

6 www.moldova.org/h8-meeting-of-global-health-leaders-underway-in-seattle-201622-eng/, accessed 11 April 2014.

7 In 2006, Buffett made a pledge to gradually give away all of his stake in Berkshire Hathaway. At the end of 2008, the Bill and Melinda Gates Foundation Trust had US$29.6 billion assets under its management: $13.5 billion was in corporate stock, $1.8 billion in corporate bonds, $6.1 billion in US and state government obligations, and $8.2 billion in other investments, land and temporary holdings (Stuckler et al. 2011).

8 Berkshire Hathaway, a conglomerate holding company, owns several subsidiary companies, including banks, railroads, candy production, retail and utilities. Berkshire Hathaway's second-largest investment is in Coca-Cola. It also owns stocks in Kraft and Procter & Gamble. Since Buffett is gradually transferring ownership of Berkshire Hathaway stock to the Bill and Melinda Gates Foundation, the Foundation will soon be the largest stakeholder of Coca-Cola and Kraft in the world (Stuckler et al. 2011; www.nasdaq.com/quotes/institutional-portfolio/berkshire-hathaway-inc-54239#ixzz3ofyocfjy, accessed 4 May 2014).

9 www.nasdaq.com/quotes/institutional-portfolio/bill--melinda-gates-foundation-trust-98131.

10 www.gatesfoundation.org/Who-We-Are/General-Information/Leadership/Management-Committee/Geoff-Lamb, accessed 4 May 2014.

11 www.theglobalfund.org/en/mediacenter/ newsreleases/2008-12-19_The_Global_Fund_becomes_an_administratively_autonomous_institution_as_of_2009/, accessed 6 May 2014.

12 www.theglobalfund.org/en/documents/governance/.

13 www.theglobalfund.org/en/lfa/.

14 Gavi Alliance, *Overview – GAVI Alliance Strategy and Business Plan 2011–2015*.

15 www.gavialliance.org/funding/donor-profiles/#sthash.6BM8xZsK.dpuf.

16 www.gavialliance.org/about/governance /gavi-board/composition/.

17 www.iffim.org/funding-gavi/eligible-countries/, accessed 4 May 2014.

18 See more at: www.gavialliance.org/results/evaluations/#sthash.iupB30AM.dpuf.

19 McKinsey Consulting, *Report to the GAVI Board*, April 2004.

20 CEPA LLP, 'Applied strategies', *GAVI Second Evaluation Report*, September 2010, www.gavialliance.org/resources/GAVI_Second_Evaluation_Report_Final_13Sep2010.pdf.

21 www.lobbyingtransparency.org/15-blog/general/62-revolving-door-is-unhealthy, accessed 14 April 2014.

22 bevansrun.blogspot.com/2012/01/market-failure-in-healthcare-part-2.html.

23 Former health minister Lord Owen revealed that reforms in the seventies had been drawn up by McKinsey and were scrapped after it was decided they 'were going to be an unparalleled, expensive disaster' (Rose 2012). McKinsey also advised John Major's government on the disastrous Railtrack privatization (ibid.).

24 bevansrun.blogspot.com/2012/01/market-failure-in-healthcare-part-2.html.

## References

Arie, S. (2011) 'How should GAVI build on its success?', *British Medical Journal*, 8 September, doi: dx.doi.org/10.1136/bmj.d5182.

Barkan, J. (2014) 'How to criticize "Big Philanthropy" effectively', *Dissent, a Quarterly of Politics and Culture*, 9 April, www.dissentmagazine.org/blog/how-to-criticize-big-philanthropy-effectively, accessed 2 July 2014.

Davis, J. and R. Tallis (eds) (2013) *NHS SOS: How the NHS was Betrayed and How We Can Save It*, London: Oneworld.

GAVI Alliance (2011a) *Country Eligibility Policy*,

www.gavialliance.org/about/governance/
programme-policies/country-eligibility/,
accessed 2 July 2014.

— (2011b) *Draft Vaccine Supply and Procurement Strategy 2011–2015*, www.gavi
alliance.org/Library/GAVI-documents/
Supply-procurement/GAVIAlliance %e2%
80%99s-Draft-Vaccine-Supply- and-
Procurement-Strategy-2011-2015--for-public-
comments/, accessed 2 July 2014.

Global Fund (2007) 'The role of the Local
Fund Agent (LFA)', Workshop on grant
negotiation and implementation of TB
grants, December, www.who.int/tb/events/
archive/gf_presentations/14_lfa_role.pdf,
accessed 2 July 2014.

Guardian (2009) 'Gilt-edged profits for profession's "big four"', *Guardian*, 7 February,
www.theguardian.com/business/2009/
feb/07/tax-gap-avoidance-schemes,
accessed 2 July 2014.

Letwin, O. (1988) *Privatising the World: A Study
of International Privatisation in Theory and
Practice*, London: Cassell.

McCoy, D. (2009) 'The giants of philanthropy',
*Guardian*, 5 August, www.theguardian.
com/commentisfree/2009/aug/05/gates-
foundation-health-policy, accessed 2 July
2014.

— (2013) 'The Global Fund and corruption',
*Panorama*, BBC, www.medact.org/
medact-blog/bbc-panorama-global-fund-
corruption/, accessed 2 July 2014.

McCoy, D., G. Kembhavi, J. Patel and A. Luintel
(2009) 'The Bill & Melinda Gates Foundation's Grant-making Programme for Global
Health', *The Lancet*, 373: 1645–53.

McCoy, D., A. Ntuli and D. Sanders (2008)
'Gates Foundation', in D. McCoy, A. Ntuli
and D. Sanders (eds), *Global Health Watch
2*, London: Zed Books.

McKee, M. and D. Stuckler (2011) 'The assault
on universalism: how to destroy the
welfare state', *British Medical Journal*, 343,
20 December, doi: dx.doi.org/10.1136/bmj.
d7973.

McNeil, D. G. (2008) 'Gates Foundation's influence criticized', *New York
Times*, 16 February, www.nytimes.
com/2008/02/16/science/16malaria.
html?_r=0, accessed 2 July 2014.

Momani, B. (2013) 'Management consultants

and the United States' public sector', *Business and Politics*, 15(3): 381–99.

Parry, M., K. Field and B. Supiano (2013) 'The
Gates effect', *Chronicle of Higher Education*,
14 July, chronicle.com/article/The-Gates-
Effect/140323/, accessed 2 July 2014.

Pirie, M. and E. Butler (1988) *The Health
Alternatives*, London: Adam Smith Institute,
www.adamsmith.org/sites/default/files/im-
ages/uploads/publications/The_Health_Al-
ternatives.pdf, accessed 2 July 2014.

Player, S. and C. Leys (2012) 'McKinsey's
unhealthy profits', *Red Pepper*, July, www.
redpepper.org.uk/mckinseys-unhealthy-
profits/, accessed 2 July 2014.

Reich, M. R. and K. Takemi (2009) 'G8 and
strengthening of health systems: follow-up
to the Tokyo Summit', *The Lancet*, 373(9662):
508–15, doi: 10.1016/S0140-6736(08)61899-1.

Rose, D. (2012) 'The firm that hijacked the NHS:
MoS investigation reveals extraordinary
extent of international management consultant's role in Lansley's health reforms',
*Mail Online*, 12 February, www.dailymail.
co.uk/news/article-2099940/NHS-health-
reforms-Extent-McKinsey--Companys-role-
Andrew-Lansleys-proposals.html, accessed
2 July 2014.

Scott-Samuel, A., C. Bambra, C. Collins,
D. J. Hunter, G. McCartney and K. Smith
(2014) 'The impact of Thatcherism on
health and well-being in Britain', *International Journal of Health Services*, 44: 53–71.

Sikka, P. (2013) 'The tax avoidance industry',
*Critical Perspectives on International Busi-
ness*, 9: 415–43.

Sridhar, D. and R. (2008) 'Misfinancing global
health: a case for transparency in disburse-
ments and decision making', *The Lancet*,
372(9644): 1185–91.

Stuckler, D., S. Basu and M. McKee (2011)
'Global health philanthropy and institutional relationships: how should conflicts of
interest be addressed?', *PLoS Medicine*, 8.

Stuckler, D., A. B. Feigl, S. Basu and M. McKee
(2010) 'The political economy of Universal
Health Coverage', Background paper for
the Global Symposium on Health Systems
Research, Montreux, www.pacifichealth
summit.org/downloads/UHC/the%20
political%20economy%20of%20uhc.PDF,
accessed 2 July 2014.

# D4 | THE TRIPS AGREEMENT: TWO DECADES OF FAILED PROMISES

In 1994 the agreement on Trade Related Intellectual Property Rights (TRIPS) was signed as part of the World Trade Organization (WTO) agreement. Low- and middle-income countries (LMICs) were aware of the grave risks posed by the TRIPS agreement to sustainable access to medicines. The TRIPS agreement harmonized laws that protect intellectual property (IP) in all countries and thus forced LMICs to allow patents on medicines, irrespective of the domestic situation. However, at the insistence of many LMICs, the TRIPS agreement incorporated a number of 'flexibilities' (also called 'health safeguards') that were designed to mitigate the adverse impact of a strong patent regime in LMICs. Almost two decades have gone by since the signing of the TRIPS agreement and there is substantial experience regarding the actual use of TRIPS flexibilities. In this chapter we take stock of the experience of using TRIPS flexibilities. We also examine a number of emerging trends in the global trade environment that act as barriers to medicines access in different parts of the world.

## TRIPS flexibilities: do they work?

The global consensus regarding the use of TRIPS flexibilities to ensure access to medicines was articulated in the 'Doha Declaration on Public Health and the TRIPS Agreement' (announced at the ministerial meeting of the WTO in Doha, in 2001), which stated '... we affirm that the Agreement can and should be interpreted and implemented in a manner supportive of WTO members' right to protect public health and, in particular, to promote access to medicines for all. In this connection, we reaffirm the right of WTO members to use, to the full, the provisions in the TRIPS Agreement, which provide flexibility for this purpose' (WTO 2001). This consensus, subsequently, found mention in resolutions and outcome documents of various international conferences and summits – for example, the MDG declaration, declarations on HIV/AIDS and non-communicable diseases (NCDs), and the Rio +20 declaration. However, the experience of the past two decades shows us that LMICs have found it extremely difficult to make effective use of the TRIPS 'flexibilities'. We discuss below the constraints faced by LMICs in this regard.

*Low technological capacity in LMICs* A majority of LMICs, including almost all least developed countries (LDCs), lack manufacturing capacity in the

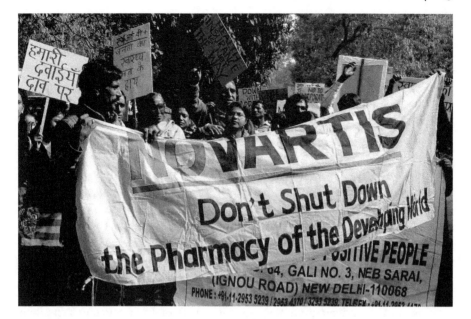

**Image D4.1** Opposition to Novartis in India after it challenged India's patent law (Rajeev Chaudhury)

pharmaceutical sector. Most LMICs import pharmaceutical products, especially Active Pharmaceutical Ingredients (APIs). In the absence of local manufacturing capacity, most LMICs cannot make effective use of TRIPS flexibilities as they are dependent on imports from, and therefore on IP laws that exist in, the exporting countries. The TRIPS agreement was amended to allow imports to countries without manufacturing capacity, unencumbered by obligations imposed by the TRIPS agreement (MSF 2010). However, the mechanism proposed by the amendment required extremely cumbersome procedures. This made it almost impossible for countries to use the new mechanism to procure affordable generic medicines through imports. As a result, there have been only two instances of this mechanism being used.

*Bilateral pressures by HICs* Often high-income countries (HICs), especially the USA and those in the European Union (EU), try to prevent the use of TRIPS 'flexibilities' in LMICs through various means. In 2007, when Thailand issued a compulsory licence (CL), the EU Commissioner wrote a letter stating 'neither the TRIPS Agreement nor the Doha Declaration appear to justify a systematic use of compulsory license wherever medicine exceeds certain prices'.[1] Similarly, in August 2013, the US International Trade Commission asked that an investigation be launched against India. This investigation, entitled 'Trade, Investment and Industrial Policies in India: Effects on the US Economy', interrogates India's domestic policies related to the local content requirements in green technologies and information technology, and IP protection and enforcement in the area of patent and copyrights (Gopakumar 2014). Further, the USA, under its 'Special 301 process', regularly identifies countries that do not provide 'adequate and effective' protection for intellectual property rights. US law also empowers the United States Trade Representative (USTR) to impose unilateral retaliatory measures (Flynn 2010).

*Pharmaceutical companies block entry of generic medicines* Pharmaceutical companies use multiple strategies to block or delay the entry of affordable generic medicines. These include the filing of numerous patent applications for the same medicine (termed 'patent clusters' or 'patent thickets') to delay or block the market entry of generic medicines (ibid.). Another common ploy used is to extend the life of a patent by a method known as 'evergreening', where small changes are made to the original patented molecule, in order to perpetuate the patent monopoly of the originator company. Under the TRIPS agreement, countries have the flexibility to determine what is patentable under national law. This means that country laws can have provisions that prevent 'evergreening' – a clear example is Section 3(d) of India's Patent Act. In a landmark judgment in 2013, the Supreme Court of India upheld the validity of this section of the Indian law (which had been challenged by the Swiss MNC, Novartis). Now, Argentina and the Philippines also incorporate such provisions in their national laws and attempts are under way in Brazil and South Africa to do likewise.

*Weak laws and regulatory systems in LMICs* In order to use the TRIPS 'flexibilities', these have to be incorporated in country laws on IP. Many LMICs have not done so, or have done so very inadequately (MDG Gap Taskforce 2012). Further, optimum use of the flexibilities requires, as a first step, a national system to examine patents that are filed (so that national priorities are reflected in decisions regarding which patents should be allowed). Many LMICs do not have such a system in place (South Africa, for example). Moreover, under the guise of providing 'technical assistance', international organizations such as the WTO and the World Intellectual Property Organization (WIPO) misguide LMICs and encourage patent examination systems that mimic those in HICs. When LMICs incorporate such 'advice' in their national systems, they give up the advantages that are allowed in the TRIPS 'flexibilities' (Birkbeck and Roca 2010). A similar role (of providing biased assistance) is also regularly played by the European Patent Office (EPO), the US Patent and Trademark Office (USPTO) and the Japanese Patent Office (JPO) (Drahos 2007).

HICs are also engaged in undermining TRIPs flexibilities by working for a harmonization of the process of examining patent applications (thus imposing their standards of patent examination on the entire world). They have made a

**Image D4.2** Communities oppose free trade agreements in Colombia (Third World Health Aid)

proposal to reform the Patent Cooperation Treaty (PCT), which would treat a patent application as granted in PCT member states if the patent is granted in three member states of PCT (Syam and Li 2009).

*Lobbying and biased 'technical assistance'* LMICs that have country laws which incorporate TRIPS 'flexibilities' face further challenges in ensuring that the flexibilities are actually used. Many do not have the financial and human resources that are necessary for effective implementation of national laws. In situations where regulatory capacity is weak, HICs intervene to derail the working of patent offices in LMICs. The EPO, USPTO and JPO regularly train personnel in patent offices of LMICs, thereby introducing a bias in how the latter work.

HICs also attempt to influence judges, so that they interpret IP laws in a manner that is beneficial to the interests of HICs. For instance, since 2003, the George Washington University (GWU) Law School coordinates an IP lobby programme known as the 'India Project'. GWU coordinates an annual visit to India by a delegation consisting of pro-IP academics, corporate executives and judges of Federal Circuit Courts.[2] This delegation meets Indian judges of High Courts and the Supreme Court to advocate the need for strong IP protection.

*Barriers to the issue of compulsory licences (CLs)* The compulsory licensing system lies at the heart of TRIPS 'flexibilities'. Countries have the right to grant licences to domestic generic companies, so that they can manufacture and market patented drugs. When used, CLs curb the monopoly of MNCs and have been effective in reducing medicine prices by 95 per cent or more. However, too few CLs are actually being issued – just twenty-four have been issued in seventeen countries since the signing of the TRIPS agreement. Most CLs issued to date are for HIV/AIDS treatment, and a few for the treatment of NCDs (including a CL issued in India in 2013 for an anti-cancer drug, sorafenib).

There are several reasons why more CLs have not been issued. As we have noted earlier, the lack of local manufacturing capability acts as a major barrier against the optimal use of CLs. HICs regularly pressurize LMICs, asking them not to issue CLs (as we noted earlier, in the case of Thailand). LMICs are also reluctant to issue CLs, fearing reprisals from MNCs that control their pharmaceutical market. Further, most LMICs have inadequate or ineffective institutional mechanisms to monitor the impact of patented drugs on access to medicines. As a result they are unable to use the CL provisions, even when they are incorporated in their domestic laws (to issue a CL, evidence needs to be generated to show that a patent monopoly is a threat to public health).

### Free trade agreements: going beyond TRIPS

Free trade agreements (FTAs) are now the preferred route adopted by HICs to impose even higher standards of IP protection than what the TRIPS agreement demands (hence IP provisions in FTAs are called 'TRIPS plus' measures). An examination of 165 FTAs (in force or under negotiation) found that one quarter of them had provisions that undermine the ability of LMICs to incorporate flexibilities regarding the criteria for patentability. Further, a majority of FTAs involving the USA incorporate pharma-related provisions (Valdés and Tavengwa 2012).

Many FTAs involving the USA contain provisions that can result in patent terms that go beyond the twenty years mandated by the TRIPS agreement. The ongoing negotiations on the Trans Pacific Partnership Agreement (TPP) may lead to a treaty with very serious consequences for medicines access, and public health in general (see Box D4.1).

---

**Box D4.1  The Trans Pacific Partnership (TPP)**

The proposed Trans Pacific Partnership Agreement started out (in 2005) as a trade agreement between Brunei, Chile, New Zealand and Singapore. It was then known as the Trans-Pacific Strategic Economic Partnership Agreement.

In 2008 the USA proposed expanding the agreement to include a diverse range of countries bordering the Pacific, hence the Trans Pacific Partnership Agreement. The negotiating countries comprise Peru, Chile, the USA, Mexico, Canada, Japan, Vietnam, Malaysia, Singapore, Brunei, Australia and New Zealand. Reports from the negotiations all describe the USA as the main proponent, preparing draft materials for meetings of negotiators, and promoting the most extreme provisions.

The proposed TPP agreement includes twenty-nine chapters, most of which go far beyond traditional trade issues such as tariffs and quotas. The bulk of the chapters deal with the regulatory environment within which corporations operate. It appears that the USA is pursuing two objectives: first, regulatory harmonization so as to reduce the complexities of working across different jurisdictions; and secondly, creating a more accommodating environment within which US corporations might operate. These 'economic integration' chapters deal variously with trade in services, intellectual property (easier patents, greater privileges, tighter enforcement), investment protection, pharmaceutical pricing, capital controls, operations of state-owned enterprises, non-tariff barriers, government procurement, e-commerce, labour standards, environmental standards, and dispute settlement.

The negotiations are conducted in secret with national negotiating teams committed to tight security regarding the proposals and debates. The exception is the trade policy committees which advise the US Trade Representative (USTR). It appears that around six hundred corporate lobbyists and industry association officials have full access to the negotiating texts. Notwithstanding the tight security there have been some important leaks of chapters (Behsudi 2014) and memoranda (Washington Trade Daily 2014).

The debates around the agreement involve broadly three sets of stakeholders: US corporations, exporters from other negotiating partners seeking access to the US market, and a mixed constituency of opponents, based in the USA and beyond. Driving the USTR is the aggregate clamour from various corporations and industries in the USA seeking new markets (lower tariffs, tighter disciplines on state-owned enterprises, etc.); extended privileges for information-rich industries in the form of extended intellectual property rights and stronger enforcement; new privileges for investors in the form of investor state dispute settlement arrangements and new constraints on national economic autonomy (e.g. forgoing capital controls, new disciplines on monetary policy) (English 2012).

While most of the USA's negotiating partners are apprehensive regarding the implications of such extreme demands, what holds them at the table is the possibility of access for their exports to the US market. New Zealand wants access for dairy; Vietnam wants access for clothing and footware; Australia wants access for sugar, and so it goes. Japan may be an exception in that the Japanese corporates share many of the aspirations of their US counterparts but are apprehensive about the costs to specific Japanese industries of reducing protection and about the terms of the agreement privileging the USA vis-à-vis Japanese corporations.

The third group of stakeholders comprises a wide range of civil society interests concerned about the impact of some or all of the US programme on public interest policy space (e.g. regulation for public health), on access to information-rich technologies (e.g. pharmaceutical pricing), on domestic economic autonomy, on labour standards and environmental protection and other public interest areas. This group stands outside the negotiating rooms and with the exception of occasional leaks is not privy to negotiating texts. However, over the course of the negotiations this loose coalition of opposition networks has exercised increasing influence over policy-makers as mainstream commentators have picked up on their warnings.

From a health perspective the main concerns are: the impact of the extreme IP agenda on the prices of and access to medicines (UNITAID 2014); the proposed prohibition on the use of cost-effectiveness criteria in price-setting for reimbursement and procurement programmes; the reduced policy space for public health regulation associated with investor state dispute settlement (Gleeson and Friel 2013; Mitchell et al. 2014; Aldis et al. 2013).

The TPP is not a trade agreement. It is designed to promote economic integration of the participating countries on terms which are designed to serve the interests of US corporations. According to the TPP strategists, once the agreement is signed pressure will be brought to bear on other countries to join on a take-it-or-leave-it basis. In parallel with the TPP are the more recently launched negotiations for a Trans Atlantic Trade and Investment Partnership (TTIP), which would broadly reproduce the provisions and purposes of the TPP (European Commission 2013).

The TPP represents the corporate world's response to the stalemate in the WTO, where the demands by LMICs for the dismantling of agricultural protection in the rich world, and the demands of the rich countries for market access for industrial and information-rich products, have arrested the project of economic integration.

The principal economic significance of the TPP lies in the project of global economic integration, which promises short- and medium-term profit for the large transnationals but which accelerates the imbalances which threaten further economic crises, the inequalities which lock millions into marginalization and exclusion and the processes of ecological destruction. In geopolitical terms the purpose of the TPP is to 'contain' China. It is not clear how seriously China takes this threat.

Within the USA there is rising opposition to the TPP, in particular around the theme of 'exporting American jobs'. The concerns of the labour, environment and internet freedom movements are expressed in the refusal of the Democrats in the US Congress to give the US Trade Representative (USTR) 'fast track trade negotiating authority'. Fast-track authority would enable the USTR to finalize the negotiations without congressional deliberation and then present the Congress with a final text for acceptance or rejection (Congressional Research Service 2012).

## Using the bogey of 'counterfeit' to criminalize generic drugs

Over the past several years, multinational pharmaceutical companies and some developed countries have been pursuing what has come to be known as the 'Intellectual Property (IP) Enforcement Agenda'. This involves lobbying with governments to introduce strict IP enforcement norms in their laws and to involve public authorities funded by taxpayers' money to enforce their IP rights. Recently, attempts have been focused on redefining the term *counterfeit*, which generally refers to trademark disputes. This has been done by blurring the lines between issues of real public health concern (i.e. spurious, substandard and adulterated drugs) with counterfeits.

The issue blew up into a major international incident in 2009 when generic drugs from India, being exported to Latin America, were confiscated in transit in several European ports (Khor 2009) on the suspicion that they were 'counterfeit'. These drugs were manufactured legally in India and were being exported to countries where these drugs were also legal. The incident served to focus attention on the possible ways in which the IP enforcement agenda could be turned into a ploy to criminalize generic drugs.

Since then, the issue of 'counterfeits' has been a subject of considerable discussion in the WHO. Also controversial has been the role of a body called IMPACT (International Medical Products Anti-Counterfeiting Taskforce), which is engaged in criminalizing generic medicines by using the bogey of 'counterfeit'.[3] IMPACT works closely with several organizations such as Interpol, the Organisation for Economic Co-operation and Development (OECD), the World Customs Organization (WCO), the World Intellectual Property Organization (WIPO), the European Commission and the International Federation of Pharmaceutical Manufacturers Associations (IFPMA). Led by India and Brazil, several countries of the South were able to force

WHO to stop hosting IMPACT. Since then a new term (SSFFC – Substandard/spurious/falsely labelled/falsified/counterfeit medical products) has been developed by the WHO to identify the different ways in which medicines can be of compromised quality. A 'member state mechanism' (MSM) has also been developed within the WHO to discuss ways in which medicines of compromised quality can be eliminated. However, IMPACT continues to promote its agenda and ambiguities continue to be present in the WHO's definition of 'counterfeit' medicines.

### Voluntary licences and differential pricing

Voluntary licences (VLs) are licences negotiated by originator companies and domestic generic companies on mutually agreed terms. They differ from CLs, as in the case of CLs the government issues a licence to a generic company irrespective of whether the originator company is willing to part with its monopoly (hence CLs are also called 'non-voluntary' licences). MNCs use VLs to co-opt generic companies (with whom they enter into an agreement) and thus effectively stop the possibility of a CL being issued. VLs usually impose restrictive conditions on the licensee. These can include restrictions that prevent local production, geographical restrictions that prevent marketing in some territories, etc. Such restrictive conditions have limited the effectivity of the 'Medicines Patent Pool' initiative (MSF 2013).

MNCs also try to pre-empt the issuing of CLs by entering into differential pricing arrangements (also called 'tiered' pricing) in LMICs (Saez 2014). Typically differential pricing leads to a lowering of the price of medicines in a country, but never to a level that could be reached if a CL was issued to encourage competition in the market. The mechanism is used to deflect criticisms regarding the very high prices of patented drugs. At the same time MNCs retain control over the price at which their product will be sold and also the countries that will be covered by a differential pricing mechanism. Typically originator companies keep many medium-income countries (in addition to all HICs) outside the ambit of differential pricing.

### International investment agreements

Investments agreements – either as discrete Bilateral Investment Treaties (BITs) or as part of FTAs – are increasingly being used by MNCs to retain their monopoly over pharmaceutical markets. These agreements contain provisions to protect the investment of foreign investors. They allow foreign investors to seek compensation from the state for actions that undermine their investment, through an international arbitration. Since the definition of investment includes intellectual property, the use of TRIPS flexibilities such as CLs, the rejection of patent claims, etc., can be interpreted as grounds for initiating legal action against country governments (Biadgleng 2013). For example, Eli Lilly has recently filed an arbitration notice against Canada, seeking compensation

---

**Box D4.2 A 'broken' system of innovation**

Problems in the IP-based system of innovation have been frequently articulated. These include the problem that such a system incentivizes only those innovations where profits based on a patent monopoly are secured. There are efforts under way to work towards an innovation system that looks beyond the framework of IP. It is widely recognized that current R&D incentives fail to address the majority of global health priorities in LMICs. Therefore, any comprehensive and sustainable solution should include innovative approaches to govern publicly funded R&D that ensures both needs-driven innovation and affordable access. A way to achieve this is to encourage the use of incentive mechanisms that facilitate knowledge sharing and incorporate the principle of delinkage (i.e. delinking the cost of innovation from the cost of a drug by supporting innovation through public investment and other forms of support).

---

of CAN$500 million for the rejection of patents on Strattera and Zyprexa under the investment protection provisions of the North American Free Trade Agreement (NAFTA) (Public Citizen 2013).

**The way forward**

Our discussions have focused on the legal, institutional and political bottlenecks which prevent the effective use of TRIPS flexibilities. This situation has prompted the 'Global Commission on HIV and Law' to observe that 'TRIPS has failed to encourage and reward the kind of innovation that makes more effective pharmaceutical products available to the poor, including for neglected diseases. Countries must therefore develop, agree and invest in new systems that genuinely serve this purpose, prioritising the most promising approaches including a new pharmaceutical R&D treaty [see Box D4.2] and the promotion of open source discovery' (Global Commission on HIV and Law 2012).

Clearly, there is an urgent need to think beyond a framework that is bound by the TRIPS agreement. The negotiated outcomes of various international conferences and summits, including the post-2015 development agenda, should go beyond the use of TRIPS flexibilities and clearly state that public health, human rights and inclusive development take priority over IP protection. Finally, LMICs should insist on the initiation of the mandated reviews of the TRIPS agreement, including a review of the implementation of TRIPS under Article 71.1 of the agreement.

## Notes

1 The letter can be accessed at www.wcl. american.edu/pijip/documents/mandelson 07102007.pdf.

2 For a brief description of the India Project, see www.law.gwu.edu/Academics/ research_centers/india/Pages/Overview.aspx, accessed 31 October 2009. See also see the interview with the dean of GWU Law School, available at: www.law.gwu.edu/Academics/ research_centers/india/Documents/India_ article.pdf.

3 For a detailed discussion on the IMPACT story see: 'World Health Organization: captive to conflicting interests', *Global Health Watch 3*, Zed Books, London, 2011, pp. 237–43.

## References

Aldis, W., C. Oh, K. Bhardwaj and K. Timmermans (2013) 'The Trans-Pacific Partnership Agreement: a test for health diplomacy', *Journal of Health Diplomacy*, 1.

Behsudi, A. (2014) 'Trade leak feeds Democratic insurgency', *Politico*, 16 January.

Biadgleng, E. T. (2013) 'IP rights under investment agreements: the TRIPS-Plus implications for enforcement and protection of public interest', Research Paper 8, South Centre, www.southcentre.int/wp-content/ uploads/2013/05/RP8_TRIPs-Plus-Implications_EN.pdf, accessed 3 May 2014.

Birkbeck, C. D. and S. Roca (2010) *WIPO, An External Review of WIPO Technical Assistance in the Area of Cooperation for Development*, www.wipo.int/edocs/mdocs/mdocs/en/ cdip_8/cdip_8_inf_1-annex1.pdf, accessed 4 May 2014.

Congressional Research Service (2012) *The Trans-Pacific Partnership Negotiations and Issues for Congress*, Washington, DC, www. fas.org/sgp/crs/row/R42694.pdf.

Drahos, P. (2007) '"Trust me": patent offices in developing countries', Working paper, Centre for Governance of Knowledge and Development, www.anu.edu.au/fellows/ pdrahos/pdfs/2007Drahostrustmessrn.pdf, accessed 4 May 2014.

English, P. (2012) 'The Trans-Pacific Partnership: an opportunity for American leadership in the Asia-Pacific economy', *Ripon Forum*, 46: 13–14.

European Commission (2013) *European Commission's initial position on TTIP*, www.

bilaterals.org/IMG/pdf/tpc-ttip-non-papers -for-1st-round-negotiatons-june20-2013.pdf.

Flynn, M. S. (2010) *Special 301 of the Trade Act of 1974 and Global Access to Medicine*, papers.ssrn.com/sol3/papers.cfm?abstract_ id=1654011, accessed 4 May 2014.

Gleeson, D. and S. Friel (2013) 'Emerging threats to public health from regional trade agreements', *The Lancet*, 381: 1507–9.

Global Commission on HIV and Law (2012) *UNDP 2012*, www.undp.org/content/dam/ undp/library/HIV-AIDS/Governance%20 of%20HIV%20Responses/Commissions% 20report%20final-EN.pdf, accessed 6 May 2014.

Gopakumar, K. M. (2014) 'Intellectual Property Issues dominate the USITC', Third World Network, www.twnside.org.sg/title2/health. info/2014/hi140201.htm, accessed 3 May 2014.

Khor, M. (2009) 'Row over European seizures of low-cost drugs', *Third World Resurgence*, 228/229: 4–5, www.twnside.org.sg/title2/ resurgence/2009/228-229/health1.htm, accessed 24 April 2014.

MDG Gap Taskforce (2012) *The Global Partnership for Development, Making Rhetoric a Reality*, www.un.org/millenniumgoals/2012_ Gap_Report/MDG_2012Gap_Task_Force_ report.pdf, accessed 5 May 2014.

Mitchell, A. D., T. S. Voon and D. Whittle (2014) 'Public health and the Trans-Pacific Partnership Agreement', *Asian Journal of International Law*.

MSF (2010) 'Seven years on, "August 30 Decision" has failed to improve access to medicines and remains virtually unused. WTO must reform the rules', www.msfaccess. org/about-us/media-room/press-releases/ seven-years-'august-30-decision'-has-failed- improve-access, accessed 3 May 2014.

— (2013) *Untangling the Web of Antiretroviral Price Reductions*, 16th edn, www.msfaccess. org/sites/default/files/AIDS_Report_UT16_ ENG_2013.pdf, accessed 3 April 2014.

Public Citizen (2013) 'U.S. pharmaceutical corporation uses NAFTA Foreign Investor Privileges Regime to attack Canada's patent policy, demand $100 million for invalidation of a patent', www.citizen.org/documents/ eli-lilly-investor-state-factsheet.pdf, accessed 3 April 2014.

Saez, C. (2014) 'Global Fund and tiered medicines pricing under debate', *IP Watch*, 7 April, www.ip-watch.org/2014/04/07/global-fund-and-tiered-medicines-pricing-under-debate/, accessed 3 May 2014.

Syam, N. and X. Li (2009) 'Suggested PCT reforms could lead to a system of "world patents"', *South Bulletin*, 22 September.

UNITAID (2014) *The Trans-Pacific Partnership Agreement: Implications for Access to Medicines and Public Health*, www.unitaid.eu/images/marketdynamics/publications/TPPA-Report_Final.pdf.

Valdés, R. and R. Tavengwa (2012) *Intellectual Property Provisions in Regional Trade Agreements*, WTO Economic Research and Statistics Division, www.wto.org/english/res_e/reser_e/ersd201221_e.pdf, accessed 6 May 2014.

Washington Trade Daily (2014) 'Environmental options', *Washington Trade Daily*, 23.

WTO (2001) *Declaration on the TRIPS Agreement and Public Health*, www.wto.org/english/thewto_e/minist_e/min01_e/mindecl_trips_e.htm, accessed 5 May 2014.

## D5 | CHOLERA EPIDEMIC IN HAITI

Popular consciousness of the Haitian cholera epidemic in donor countries has been based on a fabricated narrative which has centred on the plight of the refugees affected by the January 2010 earthquake. According to this narrative, these internally displaced persons (IDPs), having lost everything in the earthquake, were reduced to living in such miserable conditions that the spread of disease became inevitable. With news coverage conflating these issues and NGO appeals for donations often using phrases like 'Since the outbreak in October 2010 in the aftermath of the devastating earthquake that shook the country' or prominently featuring pictures of IDP tent cities in appeals for donations (UN 2013), it is understandable that this narrative should continue to dominate the conceptual landscape. This narrative has also been the base of the international health interventions rolled out after the outbreak. This narrative is not only misleading, it misses out on the political context in which the epidemic took place. This chapter will examine the roots of the epidemic and examine the international response in this light.

### Haiti: a history of occupation

In 1804 the Haitian slaves of the French colony of Saint-Domingue did the impossible: they decimated Napoleon's army and created the first state founded by ex-slaves. However, the price to be paid would be an initial political isolation and a debt to France, to compensate former slave owners for their loss of property, including loss of their slaves, that was fully paid off only in 1947 (Gebauer 2010).

After a century and a half of troubled history, in the 1970s Jean-Claude Duvalier (Baby Doc), son of brutal dictator François Duvalier, moved in to reorient the Haitian economy. What came to be popularly known as *the American plan*, owing to the role the USA played in its design, was a World Bank and International Monetary Fund (IMF) programme that involved moving Haitian agriculture away from subsistence farming and towards the production of export crops, along with developing an assembly industry in Port-au-Prince that would absorb the 'excess' rural population (Schwartz 2008). It was presented in optimistic tones – Haiti would become the 'Taiwan of the Caribbean' (Farnsworth 1984).

In the early 1980s, using the excuse of recent droughts and famines in the Northwest province, the USA sent massive amounts of food aid (most of which arrived months after the disaster). This dumping of unneeded food

**Image D5.1** Children at a relief camp in Haiti after the earthquake (Pijuano)

proved catastrophic for local subsistence farmers. It is argued that malnutrition increased after the arrival of foreign food. As part of the American plan, protective tariffs on imported rice were reduced in 1985 and again in 1995, and soon Haiti was importing large amounts of (subsidized) 'Miami rice' from the USA (Bell and Field 2010). Within a few years, Haiti went from being a net rice producer to becoming a net rice importer (Schwartz 2008).

In the face of their livelihood being lost, Haitian peasants had few options: move to increasingly crowded Port-au-Prince, cross the border to cut cane in the Dominican Republic under conditions that amounted to slavery (Lemoine 1985), or risk their lives as boat people in an attempt to reach the promised land of Miami. This social context sets the background for the disaster that followed the 2010 earthquake.

### Structural adjustment programmes and UN presence

Jean-Claude Duvalier was overthrown by a popular uprising in February 1986. Over the next four years various military-led governments were formed and failed as Haitians demanded real democracy. In December 1990, Father Jean-Bertrand Aristide, a Haitian priest schooled in the Liberation Theology tradition, was elected with nearly 70 per cent of the vote. It was a time of great hope and people spoke of Haiti's 'second independence'.

In January 1991, a first coup attempt against Aristide, before he was even sworn in, was foiled by a massive outpouring of people in Port-au-Prince. In September, the coup staged by the army was successful and Aristide was sent into exile after less than seven months in office. While the Bush administration publicly denounced the coup, it is believed that they provided support for the plotters (Chossudovsky 2004). The USA was also involved in forming and supplying FRAPH (Front révolutionnaire pour l'avancement et le progrès en

---

**Box D5.1  Haiti's adjustment policy**

The Paris plan, in many ways a new American plan, was then described by journalist Allan Nairn as follows.

Haiti commits to eliminate the jobs of half of its civil servants, massively privatize public services, 'drastic[ally]' slash tariffs and import restrictions, eschew price and foreign exchange controls, grant 'emergency' aid to the export sector, enforce an 'open foreign investment policy,' create special corporate business courts 'where the judges are more aware of the implications of their decisions for economic efficiency,' rewrite its corporate laws, 'limit the scope of state activity' and regulation, and diminish the power of President Aristide's executive branch in favor of the more conservative Parliament. In return, Haiti is to receive $770 million in financing, $80 million of which goes immediately to clear up debt owed to international financial institutions. Compliance with the plan is to be closely monitored by missions from the World Bank, the IMF and the Inter-American Development Bank. (Nairn 1994)

---

Haiti), an organization that functioned as a death squad targeting Aristide supporters (Hallward 2007).

In the face of ongoing and widespread resistance to the military government and ongoing human rights violations, the Clinton administration decided that returning a defanged Aristide to power was their best option (Chossudovsky 2004). In 1994, the 'Paris plan' was worked out to return Aristide to power in what would become a second US occupation, this time accompanied by draconian structural adjustment policies (see Box D5.1) and expensive political concessions. These included that Aristide would leave office approximately two years after his coming back.

While the return of Aristide to Haiti in September 1994 was accomplished primarily by the US military, security functions were handed over to a UN force in March 1995. That force remained in Haiti until June 1996 and UN-supported police training continued until 2000. The rationale for the deployment of the UN forces was legally dubious. The UN charter authorizes the Security Council to intervene in the internal affairs of countries only when there are 'threats to the peace, breaches of the peace and acts of aggression' (UN 1945). But none of these conditions applied to Haiti, which is not at war and does not pose a threat to its neighbours. Nor is there an internal armed conflict going on in Haiti. The only purpose of the UN forces was to control the civilian population, especially in the face of the draconian economic policies to be implemented.

In 2000, Aristide ran for president again and won 92 per cent of the votes in an election boycotted by the opposition. In a sign of opposition, the

**Image D5.2** Camp in Jacmel, Haiti, for earthquake victims (Charles Eckert/ActionAid)

USA banned any aid to Haiti from going through the Haitian government. A 'destabilization plan' was complemented by military incursions from the Dominican Republic by ex-army members (Chossudovsky 2004). In February 2004 Aristide left Haiti as a US-supported military force entered the capital, perpetrating a second coup against the elected president (Hallward 2007). Once again the Marines were in Port-au-Prince. As had been the case in 1991, a violent campaign was unleashed against Aristide supporters (ibid.).

The Marines were just the prelude for another UN-sanctioned force now called MINUSTAH (United Nations Stabilization Mission in Haiti), which currently comprises 5,794 troops and 2,413 police (MINUSTAH 2014). The force was authorized for six months but has been in Haiti now nearly ten years. Since its arrival, MINUSTAH has been, in essence, a tool for US political control.

### The earthquake and its aftermath

On 12 January 2012 an earthquake hit Port-au-Prince, causing extensive damage to the city and many thousands of deaths. As mentioned earlier, this natural disaster took place in a particular social context. The population of Port-au-Prince had swelled from around 700,000 in the mid-1980s to over two million, mostly living in precarious housing. It can be argued that the level of damage caused by the earthquake was a 'the result of human action, social structure, and policy, together with the individual families making their way through the labyrinth of neo-liberal restructuring. As a product of human action, it could have been avoided' (Schuller and Morales 2012: 5).

The international response (see Box D5.2) was best characterized by Canadian author Peter Hallward:

---

**Box D5.2 The international community's response to the earthquake**

The USA already had a policy that no aid should go through the Haitian government. This policy was confirmed by the 'international community' after the earthquake. On 31 March 2010 the Interim Haiti Recovery Commission was set up in New York City at the UN to handle international donations to Haiti. It was chaired initially by the Haitian prime minister, Jean-Max Bellerive, and UN Special Envoy former US president Clinton (Lessons from Haiti n.d.). This commission would approve all projects; the World Bank would then supervise their implementation. The commission was supposed to be 'Haitian-led' but was first made up of a majority of non-Haitian members. The representation was later brought to half Haitian and half non-Haitian. However, Haitians complained that they had no real power and their only role was to endorse the decisions made by the director and Executive Committee (Bernadel et al. 2010).

An estimate made in 2012 found that the Haitian government had received only 1 per cent of the humanitarian aid given for the earthquake and 15–21 per cent of longer-term assistance (Ramachandran and Walz 2011). The reconstruction funds that bypassed the Haitian state went to various corporations and NGOs specializing in what has been called 'disaster capitalism'. This process was described in a Wiki-leaked cable from US Ambassador Merton entitled 'The gold rush is on' (Herz and Ives 2011).

One of the Clinton Foundation's first projects is emblematic of what happened. A community was promised 'hurricane-proof' schools that turned out to be poorly constructed mobile homes without ventilation, water or latrines. They had been purchased from Clayton Homes, the same company that had provided the notorious formaldehyde-contaminated trailers after Hurricane Katrina hit New Orleans. Clayton Homes is owned by one of Warren Buffett's holding companies. Buffett is a large donor to the Clinton Foundation (Macdonald and Doucet 2011).

---

Nine days after the devastating earthquake that struck Haiti on January 12, 2010, it's now clear that the initial phase of the U.S.-led relief operation has conformed to the three fundamental tendencies that have shaped the more general course of the island's recent history. It has adopted military priorities and strategies. It has sidelined Haiti's own leaders and government, and ignored the needs of the majority of its people. And it has proceeded in ways that reinforce the already harrowing gap between rich and poor. (Hallward 2010)

It is in this context that the cholera epidemic surged.

**Two tales and an epidemic**

The source of the cholera epidemic can be traced to the small city of Meille, host city of a MINUSTAH base staffed with soldiers from several countries, including Nepal (Piarroux et al. 2011). Negligence on the part of a contractor and the UN troops led to untreated sewage contaminating the Artibonite river, causing the first epidemic in the cities downstream of the country's largest river (Cravioto et al. 2011). None of these cities experienced significant damage from the earthquake and this first epidemic phase was not affected by hurricanes or seasonal rains (Gaudart, Rebaudet et al. 2013). A second, explosive epidemic phase fuelled by Hurricane Thomas soon followed in the Artibonite and Centre departments, still outside the earthquake disaster zone (ibid.). Finally a succession of epidemic waves carried the disease to every corner of the country. Despite these facts, even some esteemed cholera epidemiologists have been influenced by the popular narrative, claiming that the outbreak could be due to earthquake damage to water and sanitation infrastructure and unhygienic living conditions in IDP camps. This conjecture was strongly rejected by the consortium which first investigated the outbreak (Gaudart, Moore and Piarroux 2013).

As of December 2013, there had been an estimated 694,842 cases and 8,494 deaths attributable to cholera, although these are probably underestimates due to underreporting and sub-clinical infection (Jackson et al. 2013). The attack rates experienced in some areas are of orders of magnitude larger than those experienced in the 1991 Latin American epidemic as well as more recent African epidemics. However, IDP camp residents have consistently been found to have lower rates of cholera than surrounding communities (IASC 2013). What became clear from the manner in which this epidemic spread is that its cause was the long-standing lack of access to safe water and sanitation.

Remittances from migration are estimated to account for 25 per cent of GDP (Maldonado et al. 2012); however, migration also means a continual loss to the country of the majority of the skilled and educated population. Data shows that whereas only 5.7 per cent of the low-skill labour has emigrated, 83.4 per cent of highly skilled labour has left the country (Docquier and Rapoport 2009). The number of migrating physicians ranged from 34.9 to 66.6 per cent annually from 1991 to 2004 (Bhargava et al. 2011). It is in this context that a complex health intervention against the cholera epidemic had to be launched.

**The response from the international community**

The first two years of interventions against the disease were characterized by extreme fragmentation of organizations and activities and a dependency on the charity of donors. This in turn partially explains the paradoxical linking of IDPs with the cholera epidemic in popular media, despite there being no connection between the introduction or even the propagation of the disease with IDPs. The charity model of humanitarian aid had led most groups to focus on the most visible suffering to maximize donations, which would keep them operating in the country. Furthermore, a significant proportion of their resources was expended on IDP camps because humanitarian groups were already operating in these areas and rightly feared that, without action, cholera would run rampant in the crowded living conditions (UN 2013). While the sparing of these IDPs from the brunt of the epidemic can be pointed to as a success, the weakness of the response would soon become apparent.

Two years later, donations to NGOs slowed dramatically, resulting in a drop from 120 humanitarian organizations in 2011 to 43 in 2013 and a concurrent drop in cholera treatment centres from 250 in 2011 to 150 in 2013 (UN 2014). The international funds had not been invested in building the Haitian health system. Further, the underlying mode of transmission of disease remained largely unchanged with only 64 per cent of the population having access to safe drinking water and 26 per cent having access to improved sanitation (ibid.). Even the hitherto protected IDP camps, although now fewer in number, may be transitioning to higher risk with fewer NGOs and resources engaged every year (ibid.; UN 2013). In view of this deceleration of progress, a Haitian government-led unified approach to cholera elimination has been proposed.

The National Plan for the Elimination of Cholera in Haiti (MSPP 2013) marks a shift from the earlier strategy. The ten-year plan lays out a series of goals for the control and eventual elimination of the disease. The plan refers to the challenges of 'institutional fragmentation' and loss of national staff to NGOs and funding providers. While developed in conjunction with major bilateral and multilateral partners, the plan proposes a lead role for the Haitian government. The National Directorate for Water Supply and Sanitation (DINEPA) aims to increase potable water access to 85 per cent and sanitation coverage to 90 per cent of the population by 2022. It is planned to deploy one community health worker for 500 to 1,000 persons. The total budget for the plan is approximately US$2.2 billion for ten years.

With a total government expenditure of approximately US$3 billion per annum, of which over half comes from foreign grants and loans, it is clear that financing will depend on external donor funding (MEF 2012). A shortfall in funding is already apparent, and less than 50 per cent of funds for the first two years of the plan have been committed (UN 2014). Further, large NGOs and major funders such as USAID are reluctant to channel resources through the national fund as they fear loss of control over disbursement of their resources (CEPR 2013). A truly unified national plan to eliminate cholera may never come to fruition owing to the reliance on a charity funding model, which perversely depends on conditions worsening to spur sufficient funding pledges.

**Conclusion**

Several models which would allow for reliable and sufficient levels of aid to flow to programmes such as the cholera elimination plan have been proposed. One such proposal is a tax on highly skilled migrants lost to higher-income countries (see also Chapter B9) imposed on the host country as compensation for lost education and opportunity costs. Indeed, it has been calculated that there are more Haitian doctors in New York City than in all of Haiti, and Haitian medical schools continue to train doctors who will practise overseas.

But the first, necessary step for any progress is an end to foreign government intervention in Haitian internal affairs. The very presence of MINUSTAH is a reminder that Haitians continue to organize themselves politically to fight the occupation. MINUSTAH, which has admitted responsibility for the introduction of cholera into Haiti in their own report (Cravioto et al. 2011), has received US$5.98 billion over the last ten years from the United Nations (CERFAS 2013), i.e. two and a half times the funds required for the cholera elimination plan!

Each year there is an international day of solidarity with Haiti on 1 June calling for the withdrawal of foreign troops. Uruguayan movements, organized under the Coordinadora Uruguaya por el Retiro de las Tropas de Haití, have persuaded the Uruguayan government to pull its troops out of Haiti. Citizens of other countries that support MINUSTAH have a clear example to follow, in demanding an end to the occupation of Haiti.

## References

Bell, B. and T. Field (2010) '"Miami rice": the business of disaster in Haiti', *Other Worlds*, 9 December, www.otherworldsarepossible. org/miami-rice-business-disaster-haiti, accessed 23 April 2014.

Bernadel, J., L. Bernard, J.-M. Bourjolly et al. (2010) 'Letter from the Haitian members of the Interim Haiti Reconstruc-tion Commission to Co-Chairmen of the Commission' [unofficial translation], *Le Matin*, 14 December.

Bhargava, A., F. Docquier and Y. Moullan (2011) 'Modeling the effects of physician emigra-tion on human development', *Economics and Human Biology*, 9(2): 172–83.

CEPR (Center for Economic and Policy Research) (2013) 'New details emerge on elimination plan as cholera continues to spread', *Haiti: Relief and Reconstruction Watch*, 12 June, www.cepr.net/index.php/ blogs/relief-and-reconstruction-watch/ new-details-emerge-on-elimination-plan-as-cholera-continues-to-spread, accessed 24 April 2014.

CERFAS (Centre de Recherche de Reflexion de Formation et d'Action Sociale) (2013) 'A general overview of development assistance for Haiti', Bulletin no. 3, Port-au-Prince: Observatory on Public Policies and on International Cooperation.

Chossudovsky, M. (2004) 'US sponsored coup d'etat: the destabilization of Haiti', Center for Research on Globalisation, 29 February, globalresearch.ca/articles/CHO402D.html, accessed 24 April 2014.

Cravioto, A., C. F. Lanata, D. S. Lantagne et al. (2011) *Final Report of the Independent Panel of Experts on the Cholera Outbreak in Haiti*, www.un.org/News/dh/infocus/haiti/UN-cholera-report-final.pdf, accessed 24 April 2014.

Docquier, F. and H. Rapoport (2009) 'Quantify-ing the impact of highly-skilled emigration on developing countries', Policy Report no. 1, Politics, Economics and Global Governance: The European Dimensions (PEGGED), May.

Farnsworth, C. (1984) 'Haiti, Taiwan of the Caribbean', *The Age*, 23 July.

Gaudart, J., S. Moore and M. Piarroux (2013) 'Environmental factors influencing epi-demic cholera', *American Journal of Tropical Medicine and Hygiene*, 89(6): 1228–30,

www.ncbi.nlm.nih.gov/pmc/articles/
PMC3854908/, accessed 24 April 2014.

Gaudart, J., S. Rebaudet, R. Barrais et al. (2013) 'Spatio-temporal dynamics of cholera during the first year of the epidemic in Haiti', *PLOS Neglected Tropical Diseases*, 7(4), www.plosntds.org/article/info%3 Adoi%2F10.1371%2Fjournal.pntd.0002145, accessed 24 April 2014.

Gebauer, T. (2010) 'Odious debts and global responsibilities: Haiti's example shows how foreign debt can lead a defenseless population into a catastrophe', *Social Medicine*, 5(3): 139–40.

Gladstone, R. (2013) 'Rights advocates suing U.N. over the spread of cholera in Haiti', *New York Times*, 8 October.

Hallward, P. (2007) *Damming the Flood: Haiti, Aristide, and the Politics of Containment*, London: Verso.

— (2010) 'Securing disaster in Haiti', Center for International Policy, 22 January.

Herz, A. and K. Ives (2011) 'WikiLeaks Haiti: the post-quake "gold rush" for reconstruction contracts', *The Nation*, 15 June, www.thenation.com/article/161469/wikileaks-haiti-post-quake-gold-rush-reconstruction-contracts#, accessed 24 April 2014.

IASC (Inter-Agency Standing Committee) (2013) 'Haiti: situation snapshot in the IDPs camps', Office for the Coordination of Humanitarian Affairs (OCHA).

Jackson, B. R., D. F. Talkington, J. M. Pruckler et al. (2013) 'Seroepidemiologic survey of epidemic cholera in Haiti to assess spectrum of illness and risk factors for severe disease', *American Journal of Tropical Medicine and Hygiene*, 89(4): 654–64.

Lemoine, M. (1985) *Bitter Sugar: Slaves Today in the Caribbean*, Chicago, IL: Banner Press.

Lessons from Haiti (Office of the Secretary General's Special Adviser on Community-based Medicine & Lessons from Haiti) (n.d.) 'Interim Haiti Recovery Commission', www.lessonsfromhaiti.org/relief-and-recovery/interim-haiti-recovery-commission/, acccessed 24 April 2014.

Macdonald, I. and I. Doucet (2011) 'The shelters that Clinton built', *The Nation*, 11 July, www.thenation.com/article/161908/shelters-clinton-built, accessed 24 April 2014.

Maldonado, R., N. Bajuk and M. L. Hayem (2012) *Remittances to Latin America and the Caribbean in 2011: Regaining Growth*, Washington, DC: Multilateral Investment Fund, idbdocs.iadb.org/wsdocs/getDocument.aspx?DOCNUM=36723460, accessed 24 April 2014.

MEF (Ministère de l'Economie et des Finances de la République d'Haïti) (2012) *Loi de Finances de l'Exercice 2012–2013*, Port-au-Prince.

MINUSTAH (United Nations Stabilization Mission in Haiti) (2014) 'MINUSTAH facts and figures', United Nations, www.un.org/en/peacekeeping/missions/minustah/facts.shtml, accessed 24 April 2014.

MSPP (Ministère de la Santé Publique et de la Population) (2013) *National Plan for the Elimination of Cholera in Haiti 2013–2022*, Port-au-Prince.

Nairn, A. (1994) 'Aristide banks on austerity', *Multinational Monitor*, 16(7/8), July/August.

Piarroux, R., R. Barrais, B. Faucher et al. (2011) 'Understanding the cholera epidemic, Haiti', *Emerging Infectious Diseases*, 17(7): 1161–8.

Ramachandran, V. and J. Walz (2011) 'Haiti: where has all the money gone?', Policy paper, Center for Global Development, 14 May.

Schuller, M. and P. Morales (ed.) (2012) *Tectonic Shifts: Haiti since the Earthquake*, West Hartford, CN: Kumarian Press.

Schwartz, T. T. (2008) *Travesty in Haiti: A True Account of Christian Missions, Orphanages, Food Aid, Fraud and Drug Trafficking*, BookSurge Publishing.

UN (United Nations) (1945) *Charter of the United Nations*, New York City.

— (2013) *UN Fact Sheet: Combating Cholera in Haiti*, Office for the Coordination of Humanitarian Affairs (OCHA), Haiti, July, www.un.org/News/dh/infocus/haiti/Haiti%20Cholera%20Factsheet%20July2013.pdf, accessed 24 April 2014.

— (2014) *Haiti: Humanitarian Action Plan 2014*, OCHA, docs.unocha.org/sites/dms/CAP/HAP_2014_Haiti.docx, accessed 24 April 2014.

# D6 | THE INTERNATIONAL FINANCE CORPORATION'S 'HEALTH IN AFRICA' INITIATIVE

In 2007 the International Finance Corporation[1] (IFC) launched a report sponsored by the Bill and Melinda Gates Foundation and researched by McKinsey & Co. (IFC 2011a; IEGWB 2009: 86). The report, *The Business of Health in Africa: Partnering with the Private Sector to Improve People's Lives*, outlined the IFC's laudable aim of developing and enforcing quality standards for private healthcare, but also made significant claims about the role of the private sector in healthcare in the continent. IFC states that the private sector already delivers half of all healthcare across sub-Saharan Africa and even more for the poorest people (IFC 2011a: vii), and that private healthcare is often more affordable for poor people than government provision (IFC 2010: 2; IFC 2011a: 26). The report asserts that private sector enterprises can 'stimulate higher efficiency and quality standards' through competition, and set national benchmarks for higher-quality healthcare. The report also says that up to two-thirds of needed investments to scale up and improve health services in sub-Saharan Africa may need to come from non-state actors.

IFC claims about the performance and potential of the for-profit private sector in health remain largely unsubstantiated, and have since been challenged (Oxfam International 2009; Basu et al. 2012). Yet in 2008, the IFC launched

**Image D6.1** IFC is a part of the World Bank Group

the Health in Africa initiative – a $1 billion investment project which aimed to 'catalyse sustained improvements in access to quality health-related goods and services in Africa [and] financial protection against the impoverishing effects of illness', with 'an emphasis on the underserved' (Investment Climate Advisory Services 2013: 1). Health in Africa would achieve these objectives by harnessing the potential of the private health sector, specifically by improving access to capital for private health companies, enabling them to grow and expand, and through assisting governments to incorporate the private sector into their overall healthcare system. Health in Africa would aim to ensure the private health sector became 'an additional and powerful instrument to progress towards the Millennium Development Goals' with 'extra efforts to improve the availability of health care to Africa's poor and rural population' (Brad Herbert Associates 2012: 11).

Health in Africa enjoys the backing of many international actors, including the governments of France, Japan and the Netherlands, and the Bill and Melinda Gates Foundation (IFC and World Bank 2012: 1). Other partners include the African Development Bank and the German development finance institution DEG (IFC n.d. a). Within the Bank the initiative was characterized as 'a new direction for the World Bank Group in health', and formed part of the Bank's larger health strategy (World Bank Group 2012: 1).

### IFC's track record in health

Until the early 1990s, IFC had only a few, sporadic health projects and no health department or specialized health staff (ibid.: 77). However, IFC's operations have grown exponentially and its current investment commitments total $50 billion, involving nearly 2,000 companies in 126 countries. (IFC (n.d. c). An assessment in 2009 found a number of IFC health projects implemented between 1997 and 2002, where operations resulted in abandonment of project construction, or complete failure of the business and bankruptcy of the sponsor company. Development outcomes were also low, with a number of hospital projects reporting significant underutilisation of facilities (World Bank Group 2012: 83). The IFC's health operations showed some improvement in the following decade, but saw continuing low development outcomes in a number of its hospital projects. Only a third of its advisory services met or exceeded expected outcomes and the cost-effectiveness of projects was considered low. The IFC's experience in health projects was assessed as limited, sporadic and predominantly based outside of Africa in low-risk middle-income countries. Far from benefiting the underserved, IFC health projects were found to have 'benefited primarily upper- and middle-income people', the so-called 'top of the pyramid' (ibid.: 90).

The pattern of low performance has continued with the Health in Africa initiative. The independent mid-term review of the initiative published in 2012 identified some limited areas of success, but overall found its performance had been uneven with a failure to deliver across a number of key objectives (Brad Herbert Associates 2012: 11). The review commends the IFC for establishing a new equity fund that aims to incentivize health sector investments that will benefit people at the so-called 'base of the pyramid'. However, as discussed later, a closer look at this incentive mechanism reveals serious flaws that render it largely meaningless as an effective approach to ensure poor people benefit from the equity fund investments.

## Poor progress on Health in Africa investments

It is clear that Health in Africa's activities have failed to deliver anywhere near the scale of healthcare investments and reforms they set out to achieve. The poor progress has led many stakeholders to label Health in Africa as merely 'talk and paper', and to suggest that the initiative should 'stop wasting everybody's time' (ibid.: 47, 50).

Health in Africa aimed to generate $1 billion via three main investment mechanisms: a $300 million equity vehicle; a $500 million debt facility mobilizing loans from local banks to private healthcare actors; and $200 million in technical assistance (IFC 2010; IFC and World Bank 2012: 4). The equity and debt schemes aimed to provide capital for nascent small and medium enterprises (SMEs) by channelling smaller, more manageable investments than the average large endowments made directly to companies by the IFC (World Bank Group 2012: 1).

Health in Africa's equity vehicle comprises investments in two private equity funds: the Africa Health Fund managed by the Abraaj Group (IFC n.d. a), and the Investment Fund for Health in Africa (IFHA) established by the Dutch PharmAccess Foundation in February 2007 (IFC n.d. b). The two funds had collectively raised $172 million at Health in Africa's mid-point in June 2011 (Brad Herbert Associates 2012: 6), with IFC contributing over $26 million.[2] However, only $24 million had actually been disbursed (ibid.: 32). The remainder sat unused in the equity funds but was still culled for hefty management fees.[3] Moreover, this $24 million constituted Health in Africa's total investment as of June 2011– just 2.8 per cent of the $850 million target.[4]

In recent years, owing perhaps directly to the significant failure to make any real progress towards Health in Africa's $1 billion target, the IFC has now begun marketing its own direct health investments in sub-Saharan Africa. The largest of these totalled more than $93 million, almost four times Health in Africa's own investments (ibid.: 4).

*Reaching the poorest: Health in Africa's commitment to 'the underserved'* The IFC's literature has repeatedly emphasized the intention of Health in Africa to focus on benefiting 'underserved' populations in sub-Saharan Africa. Its plan presented to the World Bank board in 2007 emphasized improving the 'availability of health care to Africa's poor and rural population' (ibid.: 4). Despite this, there is clear evidence of systematic failings across all work streams to impact on poor people. This includes failure to analyse how to reach poor people effectively via the private sector; failure to direct investments for the benefit of poor people; and failure to even measure whether poor people are being reached (ibid.: 4, 18, 41).

The independent mid-term review found Health in Africa's analytic work completely failed 'either by omission or design' to 'engage with the most single important global controversy with regard to the role of the private sector in health in Africa: the role – if any – that the private health sector can and should play in achieving development impacts'. Despite the stated focus on the 'underserved', the IFC had made no attempt to answer the question: 'does strengthening the private health sector improve health outcomes for the poor' (ibid.: 4, 18, 20). A further concern is the apparent lack of consideration of gender equity, both in terms of whether the initiative seeks to promote gender equity and, if so, how this will be measured. Given that women are disproportionately represented among poor and rural populations, this is a worrying oversight and is at odds with the World Bank Group's commitment to promote gender equity.

Publicly available information suggests Health in Africa's investments to date have in practice almost uniformly been in expensive, high-end, urban hospitals offering tertiary care to African countries' wealthiest citizens and expatriates. The intention to target the elite, including those rich enough to seek care overseas as health tourists, is made explicit in several investment decisions. Clinique La Providence in Chad was to receive an IFC loan of $1.5 million to make available 'locally, health care services for which Chadians are currently travelling abroad' (IFC Projects Database 2014a). Togo's already well-established Clinique Biasa received a $1.7 million investment and describes itself as 'one of Lomé's top three private hospitals' (Private Equity Africa 2012). And in Nigeria (a country bearing 14 per cent of the entire global maternal mortality burden) the Africa Health Fund has invested $5 million in West Africa's first IVF centre with an objective, to quote Jacob Kholi, managing partner of the Africa Health fund, to 'provide world-class infertility treatments' (Abraaj Group 2012).

IFC's biggest Health in Africa investment to date has been in Life Healthcare – South Africa's second-largest multimillion-pound company with services spanning a network of sixty-three hospitals plus other facilities across the country (IFC Projects Database 2014b). Life Healthcare's services remain unaffordable even for many comparatively wealthy South Africans.[5] Moreover, Life Healthcare is rapidly expanding, but predominantly outside African markets; its main growth since the $93 million Health in Africa investment has been the 2011 acquisition of a 26 per cent stake in one of the largest hospital groups in India (Hasenfuss 2011).

Some Health in Africa investments have targeted smaller companies but their hospitals still deliver the same kind of expensive, inaccessible services. At the Health in Africa-supported Nairobi Women's Hospital, even the most basic maternity package would cost an average Kenyan woman three to six months' worth of wages at $463. This goes up by almost $280 if an obstetrician is involved and by more again if a caesarean section is required. The hospital claims to cater for low- and middle-income Kenyan women and their families, yet their average reported inpatient cost was $845 in 2011. Two thirds of Kenyans would have to forgo at least their entire income for well over a year to pay such a fee.[6]

Any genuine availability of services for poor people in Health in Africa's investment portfolio seems to be limited to tokenistic corporate social responsibility schemes on a tiny scale, such as the donation of 250 blankets; sponsorship of eight water pumps in schools; and two days of free eye screening for 200 people (Nakasero Hospital n.d.: 1, 4).

### High-cost, low-impact investments

Health in Africa has failed across its investment portfolio to prove claims of superior efficiency and cost-effectiveness in the private healthcare sector. Instead there are numerous examples of high-cost, low-impact investments which make a negligible contribution to the overall scale of health coverage. Health in Africa's investment in Chad's Clinique La Providence translates to a cost of $50,000 per additional bed. The lack of transparent and accurate information makes it impossible to investigate why the costs are so high. Similarly, Health in Africa invested in Tanzania's so-called leading health insurance provider, Strategis Insurance (IFHA n.d.), which had just 30,000 people enrolled. The East Africa-wide health maintenance organization, AAR Health Care Holdings, has benefited twice from IFC investments[7] yet currently provides outpatient services for only 500,000 people per year across the region (IFC 2013). AAR's growth target of serving an additional 600,000 outpatients per year by 2018 (ibid.) would see it reaching a mere 1.9 per cent of the total population of the three countries in which it operates by this date.

### Turning a blind eye to measuring impact

The IFC's approach to Health in Africa is at odds with World Bank Group president Jim Kim's emphasis on evidence-based approaches and the 'science of delivery' (Kim 2012). The independent mid-term review states that 'the topic of the private health sector is controversial, and this should have led Health in Africa to be more engaged with defining its anticipated results and then assessing them. This has not happened, and as a result it is now difficult to assess the extent to which HiA has had any real impact' (Brad Herbert Associates 2012: 4).

The particular failure of the IFC to measure the extent to which Health in Africa impacts on people living in poverty is nothing less than surprising.

---

**Box D6.1 IT workers' health insurance scheme**

A series of schemes partnering the IFC-supported company Hygeia (IFC and World Bank 2012) in Nigeria have been celebrated for extending health coverage to low-income Nigerian communities. One Health in Africa scheme, receiving $6.1 million from IFC, set out to subsidize health insurance for 22,500 low-income IT workers in Lagos over five years starting in 2008 (GBOPA n.d.). The pilot scheme automatically excludes the poorest and most vulnerable Nigerians as enrollees are required to be in formal employment and earning 300,000 naira a year or less (the equivalent of approximately $5 per day, while 68 per cent of Nigerians live on $1.25 or less per day).

Such exclusion is even clearer when looking at the costs of the scheme. In the first year enrollees pay $10 to join. By year five, as the IFC subsidy is reduced, the cost rises to $53. Beyond the project's five-year term it can only be assumed that the full cost of the $93 insurance premium will fall to individual members unless the government can be persuaded to take it on. To achieve the latter on a country-wide scale would require tripling the current government per capita health expenditure.[8]

Even at this unaffordable cost the insurance scheme excludes a number of key healthcare services, including cancer treatment, intensive care, family planning, any major surgery, as well as several other essential health services.[9]

According to the project information available, the scheme has failed to reach its target number of enrollees. Today, a year after the project was supposed to close, fewer than 40 per cent of the planned beneficiaries have been reached and only 54 per cent of the IFC funding has been disbursed.[10]

---

The performance indicators outlined in the business plan for Health in Africa are inadequate to measure any impact on the underserved (ibid.: 32). Health in Africa equity funds are tasked with 'serving underserved and low-income people' through their investments but neither do so, nor measure their attempts to do so. The investment fund for Health in Africa simply requests its portfolio companies to complete a questionnaire on environmental, social and development impact and makes a series of assumptions, including that extension of insurance, tele-medicine and other products and services will increase equitable access to healthcare impact (IFHA 2012). The tele-medicine provider supported by the fund (a South African company called 'Hello Doctor') has since been branded unethical by the Health Professions Council of South Africa, forcing the organization to withhold its services (Umar and Rondganger 2011).

The mid-term review notes that a results framework has 'finally been developed' for Health in Africa but despite the authors' requests to date, the IFC has not yet made this available for us to review (ibid.: 4).

## Unaccountable and opaque: use of financial intermediaries

The absence of any genuine attempts to measure development impact through Health in Africa is compounded by the initiative's use of financial intermediaries (FIs) to invest on its behalf. In 2011, over half of IFC's total portfolio was made up of lending through this route and research by Oxfam has identified several worrying associated problems (Oxfam 2012: 1). These include opacity, complexity, focus on financial returns over development impact, focus on financial risk over environmental and social risk, lack of oversight or ability to influence the business practices of investee companies, and remoteness from the projects ultimately financed and the impacts they have on poor people (ibid.: 3–6; Nash 2013).

A 2012 report from the Compliance Advisor Omdbudsman (IFC's watchdog) found that IFC is unable to track whether or not its investments via FIs are causing harm to poor people and the environment, let alone measure whether they bring development benefits (CAO 2012: 24–5). This dearth of information can make it impossible for communities to find out whether the IFC is even involved in a project, much less know that they could access grievance and redress mechanisms through the CAO (Nash 2013).

## The World Bank's response to Health in Africa's mid-term evaluation

The official World Bank Group response (World Bank Group 2012) to the critical findings of Health in Africa's mid-term evaluation was largely to emphasize the pilot nature of the initiative and that the IFC team were committed to an approach of 'learning by doing'. This defence is later undermined by their admission that monitoring and evaluation, a prerequisite for learning by doing, did not receive sufficient attention in the first year. In fact, Health in Africa did not have an overarching results framework until 2011. Further emphasizing the IFC's poor understanding of the purpose of monitoring and evaluation, the response commits to defining a verifiable criterion for judging the success of Health in Africa 'by the time it concludes' (ibid.: 6).

In response to the lack of focus on the underserved the World Bank management response appears at odds with the Health in Africa literature in claiming that the initiative 'did not intend to have a direct focus on the underserved in everything that it did, especially its policy work'. It goes on to assert that its work has indirect benefit by, among other things, improving the operating environment for the private sector. The response throughout reasserts IFC's ongoing and unsubstantiated assumption and expectation that the improvement and growth of the private sector in the lowest-income countries will automatically benefit poor people (ibid.: 4–6).

## Conclusion

The evidence available suggests that IFC's Health in Africa initiative works at odds with the commitment from the World Bank Group leadership to universal and equitable health coverage. While the failure of the initiative to mobilize its target level of investment is of interest, of significant concern is the lack of focus on poor people, and particularly women. The absence of any robust and comprehensive framework to measure impact, particularly on poor people, undermines IFC claims that it has taken a 'learning by doing' approach and has done nothing to challenge the weight of evidence demonstrating the risks and inequity of healthcare commercialization. There is little, if anything, in the official World Bank response to the mid-term evaluation to reassure critics that the IFC is committed to a pro-poor, evidence-based approach. The World Bank leadership should fully review the IFC's operations in health and question how they fit with, and are accountable to, the overarching goals to end extreme poverty and promote shared prosperity.

## Notes

1 IFC is a member of the World Bank Group. On its website (www.ifc.org), IFC claims that it is 'the largest global development institution focused exclusively on the private sector in developing countries'.

2 IFC invested $6.79 million in IFHA (IFC n.d. b).

3 For example, Aureos Capital takes 2.25 per cent from the Africa Health Fund as 'management fees'. See Lister (2013).

4 The $850 million target comprised $500 million for equity, $300 million for debt and $50 million for associated technical assistance (Brad Herbert Associates 2012: 32).

5 See Life Healthcare's website for examples of the additional costs of private doctors (outside of medical aid schemes) at Life Hospitals: Life Westville Hospital, www.lifehealthcare.co.za/Hospitals/DisplayHospital.aspx?nHospitalId=61; Life East London Private Hospital, www.lifehealthcare.co.za/Hospitals/DisplayHospital.aspx?nHospitalId=14; Life Faerie Glen Hospital, www.lifehealthcare.co.za/Hospitals/DisplayHospital.aspx?nHospitalId=20, accessed 11 May 2014.

6 Nairobi Women's Hospital's 'shortmat' maternity package costs KSh40,000 (confirmed in correspondence with Nairobi Women's Hos-

pital, February 2014, and converted at xe.com March 2014).

7 A $4 million equity investment due to be disbursed (IFC Projects Database 2014c) and an additional purchase of a 20 per cent stake by the Investment Fund for Health in Africa (Private Equity Africa 2010).

8 According to WHO figures the Nigerian government spent $29.6 per capita in 2011 (WHO Global Health Expenditure Database n.d.).

9 Including high-technology services (CT scans, MRI, etc.); epidemics affecting more than 10 per cent of the population; injuries resulting from natural disaster, war or riots; dialysis; congenital abnormalities; provision of spectacles, hearing aids or dental care; and drug abuse.

10 The scheme had 8,862 enrollees out of a target of 22,500 as of May 2013.

## References

Abraaj Group (2012) 'Aureos managed Africa Health Fund invests US$5 million in Nigerian assisted reproductive centre', www.abraaj.com/news-and-insight/news/aureos-managed-africa-health-fund-invests-us5-million-in-nigerian-assisted/, accessed 11 May.

Basu, S., J. Andrews, S. Kishore et al. (2012) 'Comparative performance of private and public healthcare systems in low- and middle-income countries: a systematic review', *PLOS Medicine*, 9(6): e1001244.

Brad Herbert Associates (2012) *Health in Africa Mid-Term Evaluation – Final Report*, March.

CAO (Office of the Compliance Advisor Ombudsman for the International Finance Corporation) (2012) *CAO Audit of a Sample of IFC Investments in Third-Party Financial Intermediaries*, 10 October.

GBOPA (World Bank Global Partnership of Output-Based Aid) (n.d.) 'Pre-paid health scheme pilot in Nigeria', www.gpoba.org/project/P104405, accessed 11 May 2014.

Hasenfuss, M. (2011) 'South Africa's life health-care picks 26% in max', *Business Standard*, 13 October, www.business-standard.com/article/finance/south-africa-s-life-healthcare-picks-26-in-max-111101300095_1.html, accessed 11 May 2014.

IEGWB (Independent Evaluation Group World Bank) (2009) *Improving Effectiveness and Outcomes for the Poor in Health, Nutrition and Population – an Evaluation of World Bank Group Support since 1997.*

IFC (International Finance Corporation) (2010) *The Business of Health – Policy Notes*, 1, January, www.hha-online.org/hso/system/files/Policy%20Note%20Private%20Roles%20Web.pdf, accessed 11 May 2014.

— (2011a) *The Business of Health in Africa: Partnering with the Private Sector to Improve People's Lives*, Washington, DC.

— (2011b) 'Nakasero Hospital to expand affordable quality health care in Uganda', ifcext.ifc.org/IFCExt/pressroom/IFCPressRoom.nsf/0/2429484A4DA055DC8525774C005885F9, accessed 11 May 2014.

— (2013) 'IFC invests in AAR to improve health services in East Africa', 2 July, ifcext.ifc.org/IFCExt/pressroom/IFCPressRoom.nsf/0/2F42686363308FFE85257B9C004550F1, accessed 11 May 2014.

— (n.d. a) 'IFC backs Africa health care fund', www.ifc.org/wps/wcm/connect/region_ext_content/regions/sub-saharan+africa/news/health_equity_fund, accessed 10 May 2014.

— (n.d. b) 'Investment fund for health in Africa: summary of proposed investment', ifcext.ifc.org/ifcext/spiwebsite1.nsf/ProjectDisplay/SPI_DP26516, accessed 10 May 2014.

— (n.d. c) 'What do we do', ifc.org/wps/wcm/connect/CORP_EXT_Content/IFC_External_Corporate_Site/What+We+Do/Investment+Services, accessed June 2014.

IFC (International Finance Corporation) and World Bank (2012) *2012 Factsheet*, Washington, DC.

IFC Projects Database (2014a) 'Chad Clinic: summary of investment information', ifcndd.ifc.org/ifcext/spiwebsite1.nsf/78e3b305216fcdba85257a8b0075079d/fb9298fb97103a0885257b5d005f5948?opendocument, accessed 11 May 2014.

— (2014b) 'Life healthcare – summary of proposed investment', ifcext.ifc.org/ifcext/spiwebsite1.nsf/ProjectDisplay/SPI_DP29199, accessed 11 May 2014.

— (2014c) 'AAR healthcare: summary of investment information', ifcndd.ifc.org/ifcext/spiwebsite1.nsf/78e3b305216fcdba85257a8b0075079d/571e1e97915da5ca85257b6b006a2541?opendocument, accessed 11 May 2014.

IFHA (Investment Fund for Health in Africa) (2012) *Environmental, Social and Development Performance Report*, www.ifhafund.com/uploads/ESDPR%202012%20FINAL.pdf, accessed 11 May 2014.

— (n.d.) 'Private equity – Strategis Insurance (Tanzania) Limited', www.ifhafund.com/index.php?page=strategis-insurance-tanzania-limited, accessed 11 May 2014.

Investment Climate Advisory Services (2013) *The Health in Africa Initiative: Improving the Role of Private Sector in Healthcare*, www.wbginvestmentclimate.org/advisory-services/health/health-in-africa/upload/HiA-Factsheet_October-2013.pdf, accessed 10 May 2014.

Kim, J. Y. (2012) 'Remarks as prepared for delivery: World Bank Group president Jim Yong Kim at the annual meeting plenary session', World Bank, 11 October.

Lister, J. (2013) *Health Policy Reform: Global Health versus Private Profit*, Libri Publishing.

Nakasero Hospital (n.d.) 'Nakasero hospital (NHL) – Deseret International eye camp', www.nakaserohospital.com/images/documents/eyeclinic.pdf, accessed 11 May 2014.

Nash, R. (2013) 'Does the World Bank speak with forked tongue on land grabs', 15 April, oxfamblogs.org/fp2p/does-the-world-bank-speak-with-forked-tongue-on-land-grabs/, accessed 11 May 2014.

Oxfam (2012) *Risky Business: Intermediary Lending and Development Finance*, Issue Briefing, 18 April.

Oxfam International (2009) 'Blind optimism: challenging the myths about private health care in poor countries', Oxfam International.

Private Equity Africa (2010) 'IFHA injects funds into East African healthcare', 15 December, www.privateequityafrica.com/countries/ifha-injects-funds-into-east-african-healthcare/, accessed 11 May 2014.

— (2012) 'Aureos in $1.7m Clinique Biasa deal', 4 July, www.privateequityafrica.com/uncategorized/aureos-in-1-7m-clinique-biasa-deal/, accessed 11 May 2014.

Umar, R. S. and L. Rondganger (2011) 'Hello Doctor under fire', *IOL News*, 10 May, www.iol.co.za/news/south-africa/kwazulu-natal/hello-doctor-under-fire-1.1066992#.UkrU1K416eZ, accessed 11 May 2014.

WHO Global Health Expenditure Database (n.d.) 'Health Systems Financing country profile: Nigeria, 2011', viewed 11 May 2014, apps.who.int/nha/database/Standard Report.aspx?ID=REPORT_COUNTRY_PROFILE, accessed 11 May 2014.

World Bank Group (2012) *World Bank Group Management Response: Health in Africa Independent Mid-Term Evaluation*, Washington, DC, August.

Clinical trials represent a crucial stage in the R&D process in new drug development. Between 60 and 70 per cent of the R&D budget is allocated to them, or $80–90 billion out of the $130 billion spent annually by the pharmaceutical industry worldwide (Clark 2009). Efficacy and safety of newly discovered compounds are tested on humans. Companies do this in three phases of trials, which serve as the basis for the marketing authorization of a drug (i.e. licensing). A fourth phase is sometimes undertaken for the purposes of complementary research following licensing.

Although the majority of clinical trials are conducted in the United States and Europe, there is a movement towards offshoring to low- and middle-income countries (LMICs) and countries in eastern Europe. The proportion of trials conducted in LMICs increased from 10 per cent in 1991 to 40 per cent in 2005. Between 2006 and 2010 it continued to increase, while the proportion of clinical trials conducted in western Europe and the United States fell from 55 to 38 per cent (Mroczkowski 2012). These figures are broad estimates as there are no international norms for reporting clinical trials. However, all current estimates indicate that offshoring is increasing, particularly for the most expensive Phase III trials (Thiers et al. 2008). Major new destinations for clinical trials include China, India, Brazil, Russia, Argentina, Ukraine and South Africa (Mroczkowski 2012).

Offshoring leads to a significant reduction in the costs of clinical trials (ibid.) – the overall cost in China is a third of that in the United States (Homedes and Ugalde 2012). Recruiting in LMICs can also reduce the length of a trial by up to six months on average (ibid.). Licence to market a drug early leads to enormous benefits for pharmaceutical companies – each additional day of marketing a drug in a monopoly situation (i.e. protected by a patent) can be worth in excess of a million dollars (IMS Health 2012).

However, this 'globalization of clinical trials' does not result in better access to treatment in LMICs and, further, entails major ethical violations. This chapter examines the major issues related to the ethics of offshoring clinical trials.

## Offshoring: at what price?

A number of international ethical standards have been drawn up over the years. These include: the Declaration of Helsinki (DoH), adopted by the World

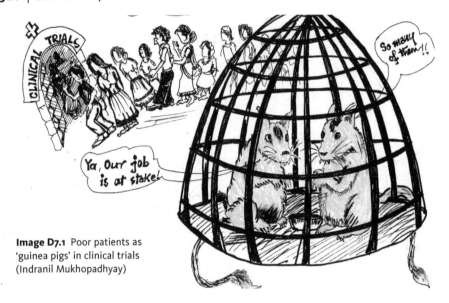

**Image D7.1** Poor patients as 'guinea pigs' in clinical trials (Indranil Mukhopadhyay)

Medical Association in 1964 and subsequently amended several times (WMA n.d.); and the Guidelines on Good Clinical Practice (GCP) published in 1996 by the International Conference on Harmonization of Technical Requirements for Registration of Pharmaceuticals for Human Use (ICH 1996). The Council of Europe and the Council for International Organizations of Medical Sciences (CIOMS) have also developed ethical rules governing biomedical research on human subjects (Council of Europe 1997; CIOMS 2002). All these texts place the rights of trial subjects above those of science and society.

A major section of the people in LMICs and eastern Europe do not have access to social security and universal healthcare. Thus, often, taking part in a clinical trial represents for many the only hope of receiving some form of care (especially in the case of conditions which have few treatment options, and/or where medicines required are very expensive). The recruitment of vulnerable subjects is a clear ethical violation as trial subjects are presumed to be 'volunteers', and is tantamount to the exploitation of the vulnerability of local populations (Aultman 2013).

On the other hand, risks of ethical violations are higher as regulations are generally lax in LMICs and capacity to monitor compliance is less developed (Glickman et al. 2009). A number of recent investigations by the media and civil society organizations (CSOs) have reported serious deficiencies in the process of obtaining the informed consent of trial participants, the problematic use of placebos as proof of efficacy, failure to pay compensation in cases of serious adverse events, and access to treatment at the end of trials[1] (see Box D7.1). While pharmaceutical companies deny the existence of double standards with regard to protection, ethical violations have been confirmed by recent investigations conducted by the Berne Declaration in Argentina, Russia, India and the Ukraine (Berne Declaration 2013d; Berne Declaration n.d.), and by the Wemos Foundation in South Africa and in Kenya (WEMOS n.d.). As trials often take place simultaneously in several different locations internationally, if one branch of a trial is tainted by ethical violations or lack of scientific reliability, the entire clinical trial is compromised (Lang and Siribaddana 2012).

---

### Box D7.1 The most frequent ethical violations in LMICs

*Exploitation of people's vulnerability* Trial participants often agree to be part of trials because this could be the only option available to receive treatment, and/or there is a small monetary incentive. We need to question whether it is ethical to exploit the vulnerability of people in LMICs (because they are poor and because they may not have easy access to healthcare) in order to test drugs at the lowest possible cost. Research carried out within vulnerable populations is justified only if the trial sponsor (usually a pharmaceutical company) ensures that the treatment will be available and accessible to those volunteering (Declaration of Helsinki (2013), Arts 20 and 34). This is seldom the case as a new product, marketed after successful clinical trials, is usually covered by a patent and is prohibitively expensive for patients in LMICs.

*Absence of free and informed consent* Any person taking part in a trial must give his/her free and informed consent.[2] This requirement is often not met in LMICs, where trial subjects could be illiterate or semi-literate, and unaware of the risks involved. Sponsors of trials and contract research organizations (CROs) recruit doctors to in turn recruit trial subjects. Such doctors often exert inappropriate influence on patients to become part of clinical trials (Berne Declaration 2013d; Hirschler 2011). Trial subjects are frequently unaware that they are part of an experiment (Glickman et al. 2009; Homedes and Ugalde 2012).

*Improper use of placebos* The use of a placebo makes it easier to obtain clear results and allows the efficacy of a drug to be evaluated in a patient receiving no treatment. However, if drugs exist that have already been used and are known to be effective for the type of pathology being studied, and if the absence or interruption of treatment represents a risk, using a placebo constitutes an ethical violation (Declaration of Helsinki (2013), Art. 33).[3]

*Absence of compensation norms in cases of serious adverse events* When injury or death occurs in the context of clinical trials and is linked to the drug being tested, financial compensation must be provided.[4] Frequently, any link between the injury caused and the drug being tested is not evaluated independently but by those responsible for the trial. Compensation is almost never offered when the cause of death or injury is uncertain, even when there are indications that it is trial related (Berne Declaration 2013d).

*No access to treatment at the end of the trial* A person who agrees to participate in a study should be guaranteed access to the treatment when the trial ends if the drug was found to be beneficial during the trial, or to any other treatment or appropriate benefit (Declaration of Helsinki (2013), Art. 34). In reality, treatment is often stopped at the end of the trial, a problem which is all the more acute in countries where access to medicines is limited (Berne Declaration 2013d; Berne Declaration n.d.; WEMOS n.d.).

### Lack of transparency and accountability

Data from clinical trials is routinely used to obtain marketing authorization of drugs (Barlett and Steele 2011). However, it is impossible to know, solely on the basis of information in the public domain, upon which clinical trials the marketing authorization of an individual drug is based, nor the details of such decisions (Berne Declaration 2013c). Worse still, half of all clinical trials conducted in the world are never published, particularly those presenting unfavourable results (Goldacre 2012). In the case of those that are made public, unfavourable data is concealed or minimized in order to present the drug being tested in a better light (ibid.). This leads to drugs of dubious efficacy and/or safety being marketed (Gøtzsche 2011). Given that 80 per cent of all clinical trials are industry-sponsored (Clark 2009), there are virtually no avenues available for public scrutiny of decisions by regulatory agencies (Doshi et al. 2012). In 2010 the European Medicines Agency adopted a more open policy on access to clinical trial data. However, its full implementation has been regularly challenged by the pharmaceutical industry (Hai Europe 2013).

When drugs are tested on volunteers, the results should logically be made available to society and considered a public good (Gøtzsche 2011). In making their bodies available in the interests of science, participants in clinical trials are in fact taking a risk. However, pharmaceutical companies consider trial-related data as proprietary and attempt to keep it confidential (Hai Europe 2013).

Most trial sponsors, i.e. pharmaceutical companies, are located in western Europe and the United States. Regulatory agencies in these regions have a duty to demand that the same ethical standards that are mandated in their home countries are followed when trials are offshored. The European Medicines Agency has recently recognized the need to strengthen ethical controls on clinical trials conducted abroad and require that relevant information in this regard be submitted along with marketing authorization applications in the EU. This is designed to ensure that trials in non-EU locations have been conducted in accordance with the same ethical standards as applied in the EU (European Medicines Agency 2012). However, drug regulatory agencies in other high-income countries (prominently in the United States) do not follow this practice (Berne Declaration 2013c).

## Case studies: deficient regulatory environments

*Russia and Ukraine*[5] Russia and Ukraine are host to an increasing number of clinical trials – recruitment of subjects is reported to be up to twenty times faster than in western Europe. Both countries are attempting to align their regulatory framework with that in western Europe, but effective changes are yet to be implemented. Both countries are characterized by a public health system in decline and plagued by corruption.

Ukraine has seen a rapid rise in offshored clinical trials for several reasons. It is situated at the gateway to the European Union, and its population is genetically close to that of western Europe. Patients are easy to recruit, given the decay in Ukraine's public health system and a deeply entrenched economic crisis. There has been a sharp rise in the number of facilities authorized to conduct drug trials, from 175 in 2001 to more than 1,300 in 2009 (although many of the municipal hospitals involved do not have the necessary infrastructure). Conducting a drug trial costs half of what it costs in western Europe.

The sudden rise in trials in Ukraine has been accompanied by an increased risk of ethical violations. Regulations are weak and regulatory mechanisms are not fully operational. Ethics committees (which are supposed to ensure that ethical violations do not occur during the conduct of a trial) are plagued with issues of conflict of interest – doctors in charge of trials are members of such committees. The agency in the ministry of health, responsible for overseeing clinical trials, ceased functioning in mid-2012.

Patients are at the mercy of a medical profession which stands to benefit financially, by conducting trials. Doctors are known to deliberately mislead patients by recruiting them in what they term a 'humanitarian programme that provides treatment free of charge'. Informed consent norms are frequently violated, with reports that hospital employees sign consent forms on behalf of the recruited patients. Such systemic deficits in the regulatory system have led to instances of gross violation of ethics (see Box D7.2).

In 2010, Russia legislated for the establishment of decentralized ethics committees. The central agency in the ministry of health, overseeing clinical trials, is poorly staffed and overworked. The inspectors at Russia's medicines

---

**Box D7.2 Orphans as guinea pigs**

In March 2013, members of the Ukrainian parliament claimed that three clinical trials – conducted by international companies between 2011 and 2012 on orphan children – clearly violated national laws. One of these trials was conducted by the Swiss firm Actelion, on a drug called Tracleer (a treatment for pulmonary arterial hypertension). Informed consent procedures were waived in the case of many children, though the national law mandates that in the case of orphans, a representative of the state must provide consent. In addition, the trials were said to have taken place at facilities not in possession of the necessary accreditations. The Ukrainian authorities denied the accusations, while the companies concerned remained silent. An official inquiry was launched, but its results were not published.

---

agency are powerless, owing partly to a lack of resources but mostly because the law does not permit serious sanctions to be imposed on doctors involved in research or on clinical trial facilities. Local ethics committees (just as in Ukraine) are plagued with the problem of conflict of interest, with doctors in charge of trials also sitting on ethics committees.

Patients are also recruited through misleading advertisements on the internet, where they are enticed by being asked to join an 'observation programme'. Doctors, who use unethical means to recruit trial participants, benefit financially from the clinical trials (up to several times their basic salary). The trials are often poorly supervised and the trial results are, thus, unreliable.

A number of ethical violations were reported during the conduct of a trial by Novartis of Gilenya (used to treat multiple sclerosis). Consent was not sought from several patients before the start of the trial and no compensation was provided to those who experienced trial-related side effects. In fact, between 2007 and 2009 not one of the more than 70,000 patients insured against treatment-related side effects received compensation.

*Argentina: deceptive appearances*[6] Argentina is listed third among countries hosting the largest number of drug trials in South America, behind Brazil and Mexico. Although it is often cited as a reference for best practice, investigations report serious problems in the conduct of clinical trials. Argentina has no national law on regulation of drugs trials, its national ethics committees are only nominally independent, and its medicines agency (Anmat) appears to lack rigour when permitting clinical trials.

In the absence of a public regulatory system governing ethics, 'independent ethics committees' are responsible for ensuring that ethical norms are followed.

These committees are not accountable to the public and appear to 'rubber-stamp' applications, without carrying out any serious evaluation of proposals that they receive. Two 'independent ethics committees' approve 80 per cent of the trials carried out in Argentina. One of them, the FEFyM, audits the protocols of 85 per cent of the clinical trials conducted by Roche and Novartis.

The quality of the FEFyM's work was called into question by an analysis of thirty-six clinical trial protocols (thirty of which were approved) received in 2005 and 2006. The analysis identified nearly a hundred points in 85 per cent of the protocols examined that did not comply with the standards in force. (See Box D7.3 and Box D7.4, which describe two cases of ethics violation.)

Moreover, there is a total lack of transparency surrounding the decisions of the ethics committees. There is no national public registry of clinical trials. 'Ethics committee shopping' is rampant – a practice where trial sponsors (whose protocol is rejected by a particular ethics committee) serially submit their application to several committees, till one of them accepts it.

The only major case where a trial sponsor has been found guilty (and fined) for ethics violations involves GlaxoSmithKline's (GSK) trial of Synflorix (a vaccine against pneumonia, otitis and meningitis). The trial was conducted between 2007 and 2011 on 14,000 infants. Fourteen babies died during the trial period, causing outrage and triggering an inquiry. The inquiry found that parental consent was often obtained by alarming parents about the health of their baby and ignoring their refusal to have their baby vaccinated. GSK paid $350 to researchers for each baby recruited, an enormous sum for doctors whose monthly salary was about $1,200–1,400. Even though it was not possible to prove a clear link between the vaccine and the deaths, the Argentinian authorities imposed a fine on GSK, for ethical violations. The decision was upheld by the Argentinian justice system.

---

### Box D7.3 Schizophrenia patients denied treatment

Placebo trials, where an effective treatment is withheld to test a new drug against patients who receive no treatment, are a violation of ethics. Merck, in a clinical trial begun in 2010 in a number of countries in the southern and eastern hemispheres, tested the use of an anti-psychotic drug, Saphris (Asenapine), on adolescents suffering from schizophrenia. In Argentina, the trial placed many trial participants in grave danger by withdrawing all their medication (antipsychotic, antidepressant, etc.), and replacing them with a placebo. Anmat finally suspended the trial after this was reported by an anonymous whistle-blower. However, no legal proceedings were initiated and a veil of secrecy surrounds the case.

---

---

**Box D7.4  Off-label use of a drug during a clinical trial**

In 2008, Roche tested the use of an immunosuppressant, ocrelizumab, in the treatment of lupus nephritis (an autoimmune disorder causing kidney disease). Conducted in several countries, the trial was finally suspended owing to serious side effects. In Argentina, in addition to ocrelizumab or the placebo, patients also received CellCept (mycophenolate mofetil), an immunosuppressant used to prevent rejection of transplants. CellCept is not authorized for the treatment of lupus in Argentina, although doctors prescribe it unofficially ('off-label'). The 'off-label' use of a drug is a clear violation of Argentinian law.

---

*India: taking advantage of a dysfunctional regulatory regime*[7] Before 2005, foreign companies were not allowed to conduct clinical trials in India unless they repeated the trial from a previous phase in the country (called 'phase lag'). This dissuaded foreign sponsors from conducting trials in the country. However, the regulatory system was changed in 2005, and the 'phase lag' provision was amended. This led to a steep rise in the number of clinical

---

**Box D7.5  Victims of industrial genocide as guinea pigs**

Perhaps the worst industrial 'genocide' in the world took place in the central Indian city of Bhopal in 1984. Over three thousand people were killed because of a poisonous gas leak (methyl isocyanide) from a chemicals plant run by Union Carbide (since acquired by the chemical giant Dow Chemicals). Over ten thousand more people have died since because of long-term effects. Victims were left scarred for life, and 300,000 people who live in the vicinity of the Union Carbide plant now live with varying degrees of disability.

In 2004, around ten firms, including Pfizer, GlaxoSmithKline and Astra Zeneca, conducted clinical trials in the hospital in Bhopal reserved for victims of the industrial genocide. The clinical trials were not of medicines that could treat the health problems that the gas victims are facing. The trials were called off in 2008 on the orders of the hospital's management. While the trials were under way, numerous irregularities had been recorded in procedures related to recruitment and consent. The conduct of trials on victims of a disaster, in a hospital where patients come to be treated free of charge, for drugs that are not even useful, is truly diabolical.

---

## Box D7.6  India – pittance paid for deaths and serious adverse events

Adverse events during drug trials are seldom acknowledged, and weak regulatory systems rarely pick them up. Official data shows that, between 2005 and 2012, approximately 2,600 deaths were reported in 40,000 participants of clinical trials in India. More than half of those (1,317) were documented between 2010 and mid-2012.

Because of lax oversight it has not been possible to establish the cause of death in an overwhelming majority of cases. Evidence is available to link only twenty-two of these deaths to the drugs tested in 2010, and only sixteen in 2011. Families received compensation of around US$3,000–4,000 – a pittance in comparison to the millions earned from drug sales by companies. The situation is no better for those who suffered serious side effects, and patients have to go through a tedious process to prove a link between the adverse event and the drug tested.

The Indian lawmakers are now engaged in drafting fair compensation norms and procedures.

---

trials – from fewer than a hundred before 2005 to over a thousand within four years. While the floodgates were opened, regulatory structures did not keep pace with the virtual explosion of clinical trials in India. Trials in India are typically two to three times less expensive than in Europe, and there is a huge pool of potential trial subjects (driven, as in the case of Ukraine and Russia, by a poor public health system and widespread poverty).

In the wake of various scandals involving unethical clinical trials, the Supreme Court had to intervene in 2013 to virtually stop clinical trials (attempts are under way to persuade the court to modify its ban).

Many ethical violations have taken place since 2005, involving procedures related to recruitment, consent and compensation (see Boxes D7.5 and D7.6).

Trial participants in India are largely of rural origin (80 per cent) and tend to be poor. Most are recruited by their treating doctor, in whom they have blind confidence. In addition, there is the prospect of receiving treatment free of charge, treatment that would otherwise be unaffordable.

As in the other countries studied, there is an obvious conflict of interest when the doctor is at the same time the principal investigator of the trial and when he or she receives payment for every patient recruited. Ethics committees do little to combat such conflicts of interest.

Further, a large number of 'institutional' ethics committees in India are linked to health facilities that benefit financially from clinical trials. It is rare for these committees to verify consent procedures: they barely check whether the correct form exists. Such violations occur even though Indian law now says that any deficiency in procedure is equivalent to a refusal of consent (including when the person responsible does not read the form, when it is not understood by the participant, or when any undue influence is exerted on the patient to sign).

## Conclusion

The case studies reflect a common trend in some of the preferred destinations of offshored clinical trials. All the countries studied have weak regulatory systems and a vulnerable population constitutes a pliant pool of clinical trial subjects. Violation of ethics is rampant and increasing. The case studies collected by the Berne Declaration[8] are the proverbial tip of the iceberg. The gross rights and ethical violations are taking place owing to a nexus between multinational pharmaceutical companies, domestic regulatory agencies, pliant doctors leading clinical trials and regulatory agencies in the North. The continuance of the trend described in the chapter has several implications. Poor and vulnerable patients are dying because of unethical and poorly designed clinical trials. The data generated by these clinical trials is often unreliable, but is being used to get marketing approval in countries across the world, thereby jeopardizing the health of patients in both the North and the South. It is imperative that the health community takes cognizance of the very serious challenges to public health that are posed by the offshoring of clinical trials.

## Notes

1 Among the NGOs, in particular, are Dutch-based Wemos Foundation, www.wemos.nl, and SOMO, www.somo.nl, as well as Swiss-based Berne Declaration, www.evb.ch/en.

2 This requirement is made explicit in all ethical and good clinical practice guidelines mentioned previously.

3 For some concrete cases, see the recent investigations carried out by Wemos and Berne Declaration (Berne Declaration 2013d; Berne Declaration n.d.; WEMOS n.d.).

4 This requirement is made explicit in all ethical and good clinical practice guidelines mentioned previously.

5 Based on Berne Declaration (2013e, 2013b).

6 Based on Berne Declaration (2013a).

7 Based on Berne Declaration and Sama (2013).

8 The case studies presented in this chapter were collected by Berne Declaration as part of a research project.

## References

Aultman, J. M. (2013) 'Abuses and apologies: irresponsible conduct of human subjects research in Latin America', *Journal of Law, Medicine and Ethics*, 41(1): 353–68.

Barlett, D. L. and J. B. Steele (2011) 'Deadly medicine', *Vanity Fair*, January.

Berne Declaration (2013a) *Clinical Drug Trials in Argentina: Pharmaceutical Companies Exploit Flaws in the Regulatory System*, Research on clinical trials, Lausanne, September.

— (2013b) *Clinical Drug Trials in Ukraine: Myths and Realities*, Research on clinical trials, Lausanne, September.

— (2013c) *Clinical Trials in Developing Countries and Swissmedic's Role in Protecting Vulnerable Participants*, Research on clinical trials, Lausanne, September, www.evb.ch/cm_data/1309_SWISSMEDIC_Final_Report_ENG.pdf, accessed 7 May 2014.

— (2013d) 'Human guinea-pigs on the cheap: clinical trials', *BD Magazine*, special edn, Lausanne, September, www.evb.ch/cm_

data/DB-Solidaire-229-ang_-_septembre_
2013.pdf, accessed 7 May 2014.

— (2013e) *Russia: The Mirage of Swiss Clinical
Trials*, Research on clinical trials, Lausanne,
September.

— (n.d.) *Investigations*, www.evb.ch/en/p21761.
html, accessed 7 May 2014.

Berne Declaration and Sama (Sama-Resource
Group for Women and Health) (2013) *Exploratory Study on Clinical Trials Conducted
by Swiss Pharmaceutical Companies in India:
Issues, Concerns and Challenges*, September.

CIOMS (Council for International Organizations of Medical Sciences) (2002) *International Ethical Guidelines for Biomedical
Research Involving Human Subjects*, Geneva.

Clark, T. D. (2009) *The Case for Globalization:
Ethical and Business Considerations in Clini-
cal Research*, Value of Insight Consulting
Inc., July.

Council of Europe (1997) *Convention for the
Protection of Human Rights and Dignity of
the Human Being with regard to the Application of Biology and Medicine: Convention
on Human Rights and Biomedicine*, Oviedo,
4 April, conventions.coe.int/Treaty/en/
Treaties/Html/164.htm, accessed 7 May
2014.

— (2005) *Additional Protocol to the Convention on Human Rights and Biomedicine
concerning Biomedical Research*, Strasbourg,
25 January, conventions.coe.int/Treaty/en/
Treaties/Html/195.htm, accessed 7 May
2014.

Doshi, P., T. Jefferson and C. Del Mar (2012)
'The imperative to share clinical study
reports: recommendations from the tamiflu
experience', *PLoS Med*, 9(4): e1001201.

European Medicines Agency (2012) 'Reflection
paper on ethical and GCP aspects of clinical
trials of medicinal products for human
use conducted outside of the EU/EEA and
submitted in marketing authorisation applications to the EU Regulatory Authorities',
London, 16 April.

Glickman, S. W., J. G. McHutchison, E. D.
Peterson et al. (2009) 'Ethical and scientific

implications of the globalization of clinical
research', *New England Journal of Medicine*,
360: 816–23.

Goldacre, B. (2012) *Bad Pharma: How Drug
Companies Mislead Doctors and Harm
Patients*, London: Fourth Estate.

Gøtzsche, P. (2011) 'Why we need easy access
to all data from all clinical trials and how to
accomplish it', *Trials*, 12: 249–62.

Hai Europe (2013) 'Protecting citizens' health:
transparency of clinical trial data on medicines in the EU', Policy paper, Amsterdam,
October.

Hirschler, B. (2011) 'Special report: big pharma's
global guinea pigs', Reuters, 6 May.

Homedes, N. and A. Ugalde (eds) (2012) *Ética y
Ensayos Clínicos en América Latina*, Buenos
Aires: Lugar Editorial.

ICH (1996) *Guideline for Good Clinical Practice*,
ICH Harmonized Tripartite Guideline
E6(R1), May, www.ich.org/products/
guidelines/efficacy/article/efficacy-
guidelines.html, accessed 7 May 2014.

IMS Health (2012) *Restoring Innovation as
Global Pharma's Center of Growth: How to
Optimize Clinical Trial Performance and Save
$1 Billion Annually*, White Paper Clinical
Trials.

Lang, T. and S. Siribaddana (2012) 'Clinical trials
have gone global: is this a good thing?',
*PLoS Medicine*, 9(6): e1001228.

Mroczkowski, T. (2012) *The New Players in Life
Science Innovation: Best Practices in R&D
from Around the World*, New Jersey: FT
Press.

Thiers, F. A., A. J. Sinskey, E. R. Berndt et al.
(2008) 'Trends in the globalization of clinical trials', *Nature Reviews Drug Discovery*,
7: 13–14.

WEMOS (n.d.) www.wemos.nl, accessed 7 May
2014.

WMA (World Medical Association)
(n.d.) *WMA Declaration of Helsinki –
Ethical Principles for Medical Research
Involving Human Subjects*, www.wma.net/
en/30publications/10policies/b3/index.
html, accessed 7 May 2014.

SECTION E

# RESISTANCE, ACTIONS AND CHANGE

## E1 | REFRAMING HEALTH IN BOLIVIA AROUND THE CONCEPT OF 'LIVING WELL'[1]

### Background

Bolivia's population has one of the highest percentages of native indigenous people in Latin America.[2] Its wide-ranging cultural diversity was recognized for the first time with the creation of the Plurinational State of Bolivia and the adoption of a new constitution through a referendum in January 2009.[3]

Bolivia is currently transitioning from a 'nation-state' to a plurinational state. 'Living well' constitutes the fundamental theoretical foundation of this new state, oriented to building development alternatives based on recovering national cultural identity and state sovereignty, building a participatory democracy, and restoring natural resources. This change drew on the Andean and Amazonian people's world view.

During the 300 years of Spanish colonialism and 200 years of Creole colonialism – when the native indigenous peoples of Bolivia were reduced to slavery and feudal serfdom, and faced ruthless discrimination and exploitation – indigenous rebellions and uprisings were hoisting the banner of 'living well' as a development alternative (García Linera 2012).

Two social movements are driving this process of change in Bolivia, each with its own proposals for transforming the state: the native indigenous

**Image E1.1** Julia Ramos, executive secretary of the Bolivian Peasant Women's Confederation Bartolina Sisa; indigenous people now lead the social transformation of Bolivia (Rafael Gonzalez Guzman)

peoples' movement and that of wage earners and the self-employed. Together they launched the struggle against colonialism, the oligarchy and neoliberal capitalism, setting the course for political change and mapping out plans for development of the new plurinational state. They proclaimed the emancipation of native peoples, communitarianism and equal rights and opportunities for all cultural, ethnic and language groups, and called for reclaiming a society free of capitalist exploitation. In the early twenty-first century, these social forces were active in the water and gas wars. These grassroots rebellions surged and became a cohesive force in the struggles of the Bolivian social and native movements and brought about the collapse of the capitalist system (García Linera 2011).

Bolivia today is undergoing a complex process of transition that has been described as post-capitalist, which involves searching for types of development that are alternatives to capitalism. This search has resulted in the formation of the current development paradigm in Bolivia, based on two currents:

1  The first, based on agrarian peasant and indigenous realities, rooted in the land and in family labour, reaffirms the value of the community–nature relationship and practices that defend the balance among people, biodiversity and environment in all its complexity – 'living well'. This reality underpins 'the imagination of the future by relying on the memory of the past' (Matthew Gildner 2012) in breaking with the current state of capitalism.
2  The second is based on the realities of urban wage earners and the self-employed that reaffirm the ideals of people's sovereignty, democratic freedoms, republican brotherhood, the idea of equality, and the principle of solidarity inherent in the social state. These ideals make it possible to expand citizens' political, civil and social rights, and equally, in this context, take advantage of advances in science and technology, from this perspective, to address the complex problems of the present.

The process of change in Bolivia is heavily influenced by the modern and traditional world views and knowledge of native peoples and peasant and indigenous organizations, and by ancestral socio-economic and cultural structures (García Linera 2010). This influence is producing a shift away from ethnocentric and anthropocentric views, since it calls for a cosmocentric perspective, which includes life in all its forms, nature and Mother Earth, who is now threatened. This perspective is being positioned as the ethical foundation of a pattern of development in opposition to individualism, the market and hegemonic privatizing capitalism. As a concept of development, 'living well' is based on a harmonious and respectful relationship among human beings and between humans and other living beings that cohabit in nature, rather than on the production of commodities or on generation of profit.

This process of change, using the concept of 'living well', has caused bewilderment in all political organizations, particularly those of the liberal and neoliberal right, and in the churches, which have become its biggest opponents (García Linera 2011).

This historical and political shift triggered a broad, plural process of ideological, political, philosophical and cultural discussions (Heredia Miranda 2008), to advance an alternative aimed at the following: promoting the exercise of the right to health; considering health as a public good; applying new categories of analysis of reality; understanding the social determinants of health; and in the Ministry of Health, developing the policy for the Single, Universal, and Free Health System in the framework of the Family, Community and Intercultural Health (FCIH) policy (MSD 2006).

## Living well

To explain the meaning of living well first requires addressing certain central semantic aspects. From an understanding of the term, we can then identify its influence on the design of health policies in Bolivia, in particular the FCIH policy. This is the alternative to the single macroculture of global commercial modernity and the tenets of 'health reform' promoted by international cooperation organizations and agencies.

The concepts inherent in living well respond to several cultural terms of the primarily agrarian Andean and Amazonian peoples, such as the Aymara, Quechua, Guarani and others, living in Bolivia and other countries. The terms are, in Aymara, '*sumaqamaña*'; in Quechua, '*sumak kawsay*'; and in Guarani, '*ñandereko*' and '*takevoporã*'. These words mean living in relationships of harmonious coexistence, pleasant to everyone, and in balance with everything: 'living in peace', 'living comfortably', 'living well together', leading a 'sweet life', or 'nurturing the life of the world'. The closest translation in English would be 'abundant life'.

The Aymara believe that in order to *live well* or to *have an abundant life*, one first has to be well and in harmony with oneself, and then know how to relate to and coexist with all forms of life and non-life. To practise living well, we must be in harmony with the cycles of family and community life, with Mother Earth, and with the universe (Huanacuni Mamani n.d.).

To live well and to live well together, we must work (*thaki*) and the fruits of our labour must be shared in solidarity (*ayni*), for both work and social solidarity are values that give meaning to 'how to live well'. With regard to work, this means relationships that are not exploitative, nor harmful to nature. These products have a use value, to be redistributed among individuals, couples, families, communities and the world above (*Alaj Pacha*) and the one below (*Pacha Mama*). Working in mutual solidarity leads to a life of social harmony with family, community and nature, with no imbalances of wealth or power. The enjoyment of living well is tied to work as a creative, productive, liturgical and recreational activity that flows among everyone in the community. Thus, it is contrary to exploitation, direct and indirect abuse and the subjugation of others.

Living well, therefore, produces concern and responsibility for others; it requires caring for all members of the community, caring for the children and the elderly. It gives recognition and social prestige. In contrast, exploiting or abusing others and nature directly or indirectly, subjugating your neighbour, lying, stealing or not working with your hands constitute living poorly. Further, it involves living as an integral part of a community that offers protection, without harming it or nature. One cannot live well if others live poorly. Loosely it can be related to the concept of 'integrated sustainable development' (Huanacuni Mamani 2010).

The differences between living well and the neoliberal concept of 'living better' are summarized in Table E1.1.

TABLE E1.1 'Living better' versus 'living well'

| Living better | Living well |
|---|---|
| Accumulation is the main concern: winning is everything, the only thing. | Accumulation is not the main concern; rather, being in constant harmony with everything is. This suggests not consuming more than the ecosystem can tolerate, preventing production of waste that we cannot safely absorb; it encourages us to reuse and recycle everything we use. |
| A logic of privilege and merit and not of real community need. | |
| The existence of a winner implies that there are many losers. This means that for one person to be happy, many must be unhappy. | |
| The urge to live better has produced an unequal, imbalanced, predatory, consumerist, individualistic, insensitive, anthropocentric and unnatural society. | Living well cannot be envisaged without the community. It is emerging to contradict capitalist thinking – its inherent individualism, the monetization of life in all its spheres, the denaturalization of humans and a view of nature as a 'resource that can be exploited, a lifeless thing, an object to be used'. |
| For North Americans and Europeans to live better, millions in the Third World have had to live badly, in the past and today. | |
| This is the contradiction of capitalism. | |

This view is located in the dialectical relationship between social forces, decision-making levels and the exercise of integrated and harmonious power. It assumes a multi-causal approach to the health–disease process, requiring a holistic understanding oriented to taking care of individuals, families and communities on the physical and spiritual planes. Living well includes many facets:

• integrated health practices in relation to the natural environment and land, including collective ownership, the protection, preservation and recovery of ancestral territories and food sovereignty systems;

**Image E1.2** Traditional practitioner from Bolivia in People's Health Assembly, 2012; protection of traditional medicine is one of the pillars of Bolivia's health policy (People's Health Movement)

- opportunities and conditions for the protection of traditional medicines, including current spiritual practices for harmony and balance;
- preservation of indigenous peoples' languages, education systems, legal frameworks, food cultures, etc., as political-organizational elements aimed at strengthening the organizational structures of each marka (region) and ayllu (community), which in turn strengthen the different types of healthcare systems of the indigenous peoples.

Criticism of the concept of living well stems from the premise that it could mask a conservative approach to the social inequalities generated by the capitalist system, since it negates the power of social contradictions and of class, gender and native peoples' struggles. This could ultimately favour the reproduction of capitalism. The dialectic of living well views reality from the principle of the complementarity of opposites in the natural and social environment, in which society is a whole in balance and in harmony, and where social conflict is an exception. The negation of the determination of capitalist relations in Bolivian society would negate the nature of Bolivian social formation (Matthew Gildner 2012). The determination of capitalist relations of production is key to understanding the social reproduction of health.

Through health policies, the government is attempting to harmonize the understanding of living well with social determinants of health, proposing that both are paradigms that are different and not interchangeable, although they are complementary.

**Structural changes in the health sector: 'mobilized for the right to health and life' for living well**

The current government believes that the plurinational state has a social health debt to the Bolivian people that has been accumulating since the colonial period. The debt has grown over the past twenty years because of neoliberal health policies that have involved privatization of the sector, commoditization of services and the creation of an individualistic culture of health (MSD 2006, 2010).

As part of the process of change, the government accepts that to repay this debt there first needs to be a radical transformation of society, including its means of production and distribution of wealth. Moreover, this is to be accomplished by addressing social determinants of health; substantially improving the conditions under which people are born, live, work and grow old; and fighting unequal distribution of power, wealth and services. It recognizes that this cannot be done in a capitalist society that favours individual and corporate profits above collective well-being and in which health becomes a commodity.

In 2006, Bolivia overhauled its health policy, based on the economic and social development guidelines in the National Development Plans for 2006–10 and 2009–13 from the Ministry of Development Planning. These plans establish that health and social security policies and institutions shall assume three substantive commitments:

1 Function as specific instruments for the development of social welfare, so that all people can live well.
2 Protect the entire population against social and biological risks, to improve quality of life and health status.
3 Ensure equal access to services, benefits and funding through public policies and regulations that prevent social exclusion for economic, cultural, ethnic, gender and other reasons.

These commitments are aligned to provisions in the Constitution on social rights, for the protection of health and for social security, meaning that they represent shared social values and priorities. To achieve these substantive goals, the Health Sector Development Plan sets out policies, strategies, programmes and projects that aim to build a new model of social protection in health; a single, integrated, decentralized, participatory public system, with autonomous management in the provinces, municipalities and indigenous regions; and a unified social security system, with health priorities in nutrition, education, environment and safe water, with social monitoring of public policies and services and the ethical exercise of public service.

The current priorities are implementation of the Single Health System and the Family, Community and Intercultural Health (FCIH) policy, recovery of health sovereignty, and inter-sectoral action to address social determinants of health.

The FCIH policy provides regulations, methods and operational backing for the following:

- a model that promotes participation by communities and social organizations in decision-making for the shared management of health, reflection and analysis on health issues (Health Information Analysis Committees);
- community and municipal assemblies for health, as well as strengthening organizational systems in each community and ayllu for governance of health systems;
- redefining the family as the structure for guidance and for fostering personal principles and values and for the collective development of health plans for each community;
- the reorientation of services and benefits of traditional medicine and natural medicine, and fostering interculturalism in health.

The guiding principles of FCIH are community participation, intersectoral work, interculturalism and comprehensiveness (Government of Bolivia 2008).

All this is geared towards universal access to a unified family, community, and intercultural healthcare-based health system, respectful of indigenous and native cultures, and enriched by traditional medicine. It is not easy to advance to this since the inherited system has major gaps which need to be addressed, while improving services provided by the Ministry of Health. It is also geared towards an inclusive, equitable, supportive, good-quality and friendly system, for which the first generations of doctors are being trained in family, community and intercultural healthcare.

## Conclusion

The current Bolivian context is affected by the crisis in the neoliberal model, which has lost some of its hegemony but still remains dominant. In contrast, social movements based on the principle of living well have initiated irreversible historical processes in the quest for an alternative to capitalist development. 'Living well' is contributing, at a structural level, to the dismantling of colonialism and neoliberalism. It is doing so by promoting communitarianism and interculturalism, which are restoring social solidarity, reciprocity, complementarity and equity as the guiding principle for action in the health sector.

## Notes

1 The Bolivian chapter of the Latin American Association of Social Medicine (ALAMES) held a series of presentations and discussions, in October and November 2013, to address, interpret and understand the meaning of 'living well' (*vivir bien* in Spanish) as part of the process of developing the unified family, community and intercultural health system and attaining the right to health. This chapter includes some of the main points from those discussions.

2 According to the 2001 census, 62.2 per cent of Bolivians declared themselves to be of native indigenous origin (INE 2001). The results of the 2012 census have not yet been formally released.

3 Since 2009, Bolivia has been a Unitary Social State of Plurinational, Community-based Law. Plurinational refers to its thirty-six First Nations, and community-based refers to living, understanding and sharing life together (Bolivia 2009).

## References

Bolivia (Plurinational State of Bolivia) (2009) *Political Constitution of the State*, La Paz, February.

García Linera, A. (2010) 'El socialismo comunitario: un aporte de Bolivia al mundo', *Revista de Análisis: Reflexiones Sobre la Coyuntura*, 3(5), Vicepresidencia del Estado Plurinacional, Presidencia de la Asamblea Legislativa Plurinacional, www. vicepresidencia. gob.bo/IMG/pdf/revista_analisis_5.pdf, accessed 26 April 2014.

— (2011) *Las Tensiones Creativas de la Revolución: La Quinta Fase del Proceso de Cambio*, Vicepresidencia del Estado Plurinacional, Presidencia de la Asamblea Legislativa Plurinacional, La Paz, www.alames.org/ documentos/tensiones.pdf, accessed 26 April 2014.

— (2012) 'Bolivia: la constitución política del Vivir Bien', *Agenda Latinoamericana Año 2012*, servicioskoinonia.org/agenda/ archivo/obra.php?ncodigo=749, accessed 26 April 2014.

Government of Bolivia (2008) *Nuevo Modelo Sanitario, Decreto Supremo No. 29601*, 11 June.

Heredia Miranda, N. (2008) 'El derecho a vivir bien, más allá de un enunciado', *Revista Posibles*, 1: 10–20.

Huanacuni Mamani, F. (2010) *Vivir Bien/Buen Vivir: Filosofía, Políticas, Estrategias y Experiencias Regionales*, Coordinadora Andina de Organizaciones Indígenas (CAOI), Lima, February, www.dhl.hegoa.ehu.es/ficheros/ 0000/0535/Vivir_Bien_1_.pdf, accessed 26 April 2014.

— (n.d.) 'Pachamama: sagrada madre tierra', Culturande, www.culturande.org/ Upload/20126413473Pachamama.pdf, viewed 26 April 2014.

INE (Instituto Nacional de Estadísticas) (2001) *Censo de Población y Vivienda 2001: Población por Organizaciones Comunitarias*, La Paz.

Matthew Gildner, R. (2012) 'La historia como liberación nacional: creando un pasado útil para la Bolivia posrevolucionaria', *Revista Ciencia y Cultura*, 29, La Paz.

MSD (Ministerio de Salud y Deportes) (2006) *Bases del Plan Estratégico 2006–2010*, La Paz, www.paho.org/hq/index.php? option=com_content&view=article&id=4290 &Itemid=3 513&lang=en#bolivia, accessed 26 April 2014.

— (2010) *Plan Sectorial de Desarrollo 2010–2020: 'Hacia la Salud Universal'*, La Paz.

## E2 | SOCIAL CHANGE IN EL SALVADOR AND THE HEALTH SECTOR

### Historical backdrop

June 2009 marked the beginning of a new era in the history of El Salvador, when, through democratic elections, the first ever left government came to power in the country. This had been preceded, starting in 1932, by fifty years of military dictatorship, which, in the 1970s, erupted into a civil war (1979–92) that only ended with the negotiated Peace Accords. This was followed by four neoliberal administrations.[1]

At the end of the nineteenth century and in the early period of the twentieth century, a model of production based on an agro-exporting economy led to a polarized society: on one side was an oligarchy that amassed wealth produced by mono-crop plantations, and on the other the masses of poor peasants and daily labourers, who earned cash from harvesting these crops and then tended their own subsistence crops the rest of the year.[2] In the 1950s and 1960s, the United States, anxious about the explosive situation in Salvadorean society, pressured the local oligarchy to invest its huge profits in industrialization of the nation (Lindo-Fuentes et al. 2007). The objective was to promote export-oriented industrialization that would make it possible to reduce social polarization and develop a middle class. It was hoped that this would alleviate the high levels of poverty and exclusion that were fuelling social discontent, roused, in turn, by the example of the recent victory of the Cuban revolution.[3]

Attempts by the USA to implement this new model quickly fizzled out, and in 1969 led to the war between El Salvador and Honduras (known as the Soccer War).[4] This was the immediate trigger for the emergence of political-military organizations in El Salvador in the early 1970s (ibid.).

### The struggle against military dictatorship

The revolutionary movement in El Salvador grew fast, spawning a broad organization of the mass of people and a guerrilla army. In 1980, the movement took a qualitative leap, from its initial sporadic urban attacks, as it initiated combat against the army of the dictatorship, which was militarily and economically aided by the US government.

The war transformed the nature of outmigration, which until then had been for economic reasons. It swelled to increasingly include people fleeing political persecution at the hands of the military dictatorship. The vast majority of migrants went to the United States, and in a few years their numbers ballooned to almost one third of the Salvadorean population (approximately two million).[5] They became the greatest source of foreign exchange for the country by sending remittances to relatives they had left behind.

The people's struggle against the military dictatorship expanded to the entire country. The guerrillas took control of large areas and the fighting spread to the countryside, which seriously affected agricultural production. The landed oligarchy abandoned the agro-export model and adopted a service-based economic model aimed at capturing burgeoning family remittances. This was accompanied by a boom in consumption, development of the banking system, and increasing commerce, culminating in the 'dollarization' of the economy.

### The health system in El Salvador

Development of the Salvadorean health system has been determined by the succession, development and dominance of these economic models.

While the agro-export model was dominant and society was split between a landowning bourgeois oligarchy and broad masses of labourers and peasants, the health system was primarily a charitable network of health services for the poor, which had unreliable government funding.

When the door was opened to export-oriented industrialization, in order to guarantee the productivity of the industrial labour force and respond to the demands of the emerging middle class, the Salvadorean Social Security Institute was established, modelled on the classic Bismarckian tripartite financing system (government, workers and employers). It led to the development of a model which provided 'high end' curative care. On the other hand the public system, designed for the poorest segments of society lacking formal employment, provided extremely limited services. However, the social security system never covered more than 20 per cent of the population, leaving large groups of people grossly neglected and excluded (CDHES 2005).

During the worst years of the war and the transition to a service economy, the aggressive commercial and financial bourgeoisie identified, in the Salvadorean Social Security Institute, an opportunity to make more money through privatization. Starting with hospital services and speciality care, they later attempted to privatize the entire model, replacing it with a variety of private insurance providers, which provided services according to people's ability to pay.

By the beginning of the twenty-first century the war had ended and social movements started regaining strength.[6] In the early 2000s, attempts to privatize the social security system and the primary level of care provided by the Ministry of Health's service network unleashed a wave of public protests. Several new organizations were created and fought privatization of health (Orellana 2013). They were successful in overturning legislative decrees and other manoeuvres aimed at privatizing the Social Security Institute.

During this period, and in juxtaposition to the neoliberal governments' attempts to privatize services, the social movements developed numerous

**Image E2.1** Defence of the health reforms proposed by President Funes in El Salvador (Boris Flores)

proposals to reform the national health system. These proposals aimed to create a health system that would be more equitable, less segmented, less fragmented and more identified with the defence of the right to health.

## The new government and health reform

People's awareness of the need for a health system with the above characteristics and an organized movement born out of the anti-privatization protests found a channel for their aspirations with the electoral victory of the current government, in 2009.

A broad-based process of consultations with public participation was organized to develop a National Health Policy that would guide the new government. Inputs came from several sources: discussions among the social movements and FMLN[7] grassroots party members (through Open Social Dialogue Roundtables); the FMLN's election platform 'Hope is Born, Change is Coming'; the Citizens' Alliance against Privatization of Health; and the FMLN's Health Task Force.

After being elected, the new president, Mauricio Funes, called on the country and the international community to form 'a grand nationwide alliance around the issue of health, an alliance capable of achieving real change that benefits everyone, especially the most vulnerable' (Rodríguez et al. 2009: 5).

President Funes pledged his political will and committed to raising the necessary resources to build a national health system. Based on the recognition of health as a public good and a fundamental human right that must be guaranteed by the state, the new system would assume the task of the collective, democratic and participatory development of health. The system's programmatic underpinnings would include a human rights approach; intersectoral work to address the social determinants of health; development of an equitable, efficient, fair and universal national health system funded by general revenues; and the integration, complementarity and development of sub-regional and regional health policies (ibid.).

Building a system with these characteristics posed a historic challenge for the health sector. Alongside the new system, a broad, militant, organized community would need to be strengthened to enable the people to fully exercise their right to health and to carry out their role of monitoring government policies.

Thus, the policy goal is to: 'Guarantee the right to health of all Salvadoreans through a National Health System that steadily strengthens its public segments (including social security) and effectively regulates its private segments, and provides access to health promotion, prevention, care, and rehabilitation, and a healthy, safe environment, including (but not limited to) the creation and maintenance of an efficient health care system, with high problem-solving capacity and equitable access to quality services for all' (ibid.).

To operationalize this goal, eight fundamental core areas of action were designed, to be implemented during the five-year term of office of the 'Government of Change':

- A comprehensive, integrated health services network, based on universal coverage and comprehensive provision of promotion, prevention, treatment and rehabilitation services throughout the life course, and definition of a set of uniform services for each level of care.
- A National Medical Emergency System, to provide timely, effective, round-the-clock care, along with the creation of a Control Centre coordinating with the national civilian police and the armed forces, and including specialized agencies and the community, to overcome the current fragmentation and poor quality of emergency medical services.
- Drugs and vaccines: guarantee the accessibility of essential drugs and vaccines with the necessary quality, safety and efficacy, promoting their rational use, removing conflicts of interest, and strengthening a single pharmaceutical regulatory authority.
- Inter- and intra-sectoral work, including work with institutions from non-health sectors, to discuss and address determinants of health problems and inequities among population groups.
- National Health Forums: a permanent venue for organizing local communities and different sectors to participate in and give their support to democratic decisions regarding health.
- National Institute of Health: a technical scientific organization under the Ministry of Health, responsible for developing and promoting institutional research policies.
- Unified Health Information System: an information system to systematize and analyse data to facilitate informed decision-making at all levels of the national health system.

- Human Resources for Health (HRH): creation of an HRH Development Unit to promote actions and strategies aimed at effective and productive work, with conviction, capacity, motivation and commitment to the reform process.

## The reform process

The importance accorded by the government to health reform is reflected in increases in budgetary allocations – more than 70 per cent for primary care and more than 50 per cent for the hospital network between 2008 and 2013 (MINSAL 2013a).

The first measure taken by the current administration was to abolish every type of fee in the public system, to do away with the appalling cost recovery programme that used so-called 'voluntary fees', which in reality were mandatory. These fees were charged to people seeking services in the public system and constituted a barrier to access to health services. Abolition of the fees spurred a 25 per cent increase in demand for services across the country in one year, from 2009 to 2010 (Menjival 2012).

This was followed, in 2010, by the roll-out of Community Health Teams (*Equipos Comunitarios de Salud* or Ecos) in the country's poorest 125 municipalities, charged with bringing primary-care services to these traditionally excluded areas (MINSAL 2011b).

At the same time, the country undertook the largest infrastructure and equipment project for the health services network in its history, with a total investment of over US$228 million. The number of primary-care facilities was

**Image E2.2** Popular support for the Medicines Act (Boris Flores)

doubled with US$38 million of this money, and another US$190 million was spent on the hospital network (MINSAL 2013b).

Created in May 2010, the National Health Forum steadily grew and gained expertise.[8] Inter-sectoral work made headway in identifying and addressing social determinants of health (MINSAL 2013a). An especially difficult task that was accomplished was the setting up of a legal framework to regulate the pharmaceutical sector, the private sector and human resources.[9] Over forty information systems were merged into one unified system in a Linux-based platform, the SUIS (*Sistema Único de Información en Salud*).[10] It has become the backbone of an extensive information and monitoring system (ibid.).

In the face of open hostility from the pharmaceutical industry, the Medicines Act was passed. The Act ensures a unified regulatory system and has removed pharmaceutical manufacturers from the regulatory board. It has also instituted a price regulation system and quality control mechanisms.[11]

### Evidence of success

The breadth and depth of these changes have impacted institutional indicators, reflecting the recovery of the public system and its reorientation towards a rights-based approach and towards comprehensive primary healthcare (not as a level of care, but rather in the original spirit of Alma Ata). In brief, indicators of success include:

- El Salvador has met the target for MDG 5 on maternal mortality (Orellana 2012).
- The private-to-public spending ratio moved from 50 per cent private and 50 per cent public in 2004, to 37 per cent private and 63 per cent public in 2012 (MINSAL 2013a).
- Price reductions of up to 60 per cent for drugs are expected to further bring down household out-of-pocket spending on healthcare.
- Prenatal care coverage is up to 90 per cent and institutional delivery coverage is up to 95 per cent (PAHO and MINSAL 2013).
- Hospital beds increased from 0.7/1,000 population in 2009 to 1.14/1,000 in 2013 (ibid.).
- Institutional child and infant mortality dropped by 20 per cent between 2007 and 2012, owing to improvements to the hospital network and to teamwork across all levels of care (MINSAL 2013a).
- Drug shortages in the public network were reduced from 60 to 20 per cent between 2008 and 2013 (Secretaria de Comunicaciones 2013).
- For the most part, the inequitable distribution of human resources in service facilities was resolved, and municipalities in poorer locations were allocated additional human resources (PAHO and MINSAL 2013).

Moreover, El Salvador was in the forefront in the Americas in the control of dengue fever outbreaks (with the lowest case fatality rate in the Americas), influenza A (H1N1), socio-natural disasters related to climate change, etc. (MINSAL 2013a; MINSAL 2011a; MSPAS 2010c). This was accomplished by developing and implementing innovative methods, including school-based screening, tiered alerts, intensive mass training of human resources on important topics, and much more.

### Obstacles and constraints

Every attempt to regulate an area of the private sector was met with resistance. The Medicines Act led to a tussle with the pharmaceutical industry; the Breastfeeding Policy was opposed by marketers of breast-milk substitutes; regulation of toxic agrochemicals was opposed by agribusiness; the Sexual and Reproductive Health policy met resistance from ultra-conservative religious groups; modernization of the public hospital network was resisted by the powerful medical-industrial complex; regulation of groundwater contamination from heavy metals was opposed by the mining industry; and the list goes on.

Despite this, the main challenge for the next government will be the sustainability and expansion of the reform process. This will involve a sweeping reorganization of the fragmented legal framework and far-reaching fiscal reforms to broaden the tax base and substantially reduce tax avoidance, tax evasion and corruption. The goal is to obtain the resources necessary for the sustainability of the health reforms and other social programmes implemented by the 'Government of Change', including educational reforms and other programmes linked to implementation of a universal social safety net.

El Salvador has embarked on a challenging process to ensure the irreversibility of the achievements made thus far and to intensify the health reform process. The alternative would be a return to the exclusionary past of only five years back. The left once again won the presidency in March 2014, but this time by a razor-thin margin. Health was a major issue in the elections. El Salvador continues to be a battleground for emerging economic and political clashes reminiscent of the Cold War.

### Notes

1 Alfredo Cristiani, 1989–94, Armando Calderon Sol, 1994–99, Francisco Flores Perez, 1999–2004, and Antonio Saca, 2004–09.

2 For more information, see Velásquez Carrillo (2011).

3 On the impact of the Cuban revolution on politics in the Americas, see Wright (2001).

4 For more on the Soccer War, see Anderson (1981).

5 For more information on migration from El Salvador, see Migration Policy Institute at www.migrationpolicy.org/. See also Gammage (2007).

6 See Blandino (2000).

7 Frente Farabundo Martí para la Liberación Nacional, the recently elected left-wing political party.

8 See 'Building social participation in health', www.phmovement.org/es/node/2914.

9 See 'La eficacia de la ayuda: progreso y statu quo de la apropiación democrática y la participación significativa de la sociedad civil en el sector de la salud', www.actionforglobal-health.eu/, and Posada (2013).

10 See suis.salud.gob.sv/.

11 For more information on the controversies, see BBC Mundo (2013), MINSAL (n.d.), Diario de Hoy (2010) and MINSAL (2011b).

## References

Action for Global Health (2011) *La eficacia de la ayuda: progreso y statu quo de la apropiación democrática y la participación significativa de la sociedad civil en el sector de la salud*, www.actionforglobalhealth.eu/.

Anderson, T. (1981) *The War of the Dispossessed: Honduras and El Salvador, 1969*, Lincoln: University of Nebraska Press.

BBC Mundo (2013) 'El Salvador: polémica por la reducción del precio de medicinas', *BBC Mundo*, 2 April, www.bbc.co.uk/mundo/.

Blandino, R. (2000) 'Las luchas populares en El Salvador', Presentation at 'Encuentro sobre experiencias de poder popular en América Latina', América Libre, São Paulo, 26–30 October, www.nodo50.org/americalibre/.

CDHES (Comisión de Derechos Humanos de El Salvador) (2005) 'Informe sobre las condiciones de salud en El Salvador', *Derecho a la salud: Situación en países de América Latina*, Plataforma Interamericana de Derechos Humanos, Democracia y Desarrollo, Asociación Latinoamericana de Medicina Social, pp. 119–36.

Diario de Hoy (2010) 'El anteproyecto de la Ley de Medicamentos es anticonstitucional', 29 March, www.saludyfarmacos.org/.

Gammage, S. (2007) 'El Salvador: despite end to civil war, emigration continues', Migration Policy Institute, 26 July.

Lindo-Fuentes, H., E. Ching and R. Lara-Martinez (2007) *Remembering a Massacre in El Salvador: The insurrection of 1932, Roque Dalton, and the politics of historical memory*, University of New Mexico Press.

Menjívar, V. (2012) 'Redes integrales e integradas de servicios de salud: avances y desafíos', Presentation at the international forum 'Logros de la reforma de salud en El Salvador y desafíos para su consolidación', San Salvador, 30 August.

MINSAL (Ministerio de Salud de El Salvador) (2011a) *Informe de Labores 2010–2011*, San Salvador, June, www.salud.gob.sv.

— (2011b) *Lineamientos operativos para el desarrollo de actividades en los Ecos familiares y Ecos especializados*, San Salvador, March, www.salud.gob.sv.

— (2013a) *Informe de labores 2012–2013*, San Salvador.

— (2013b) *Rendición de Cuentas 2012–2013*, San Salvador, 14 August, www.salud.gob.sv.

— (n.d.) '50 preguntas más frecuentes sobre la Ley de Medicamentos', www.salud.gob.sv.

MSPAS (Ministerio de Salud Pública y Asistencia Social) (2010a) *Acuerdo No. 126 Política Nacional de Salud 2009–2014*, Diario Oficial, San Salvador, February.

— (2010b) 'En respuesta a las declaraciones del Dr Rodolfo Canizález', Press release, Unidades de Comunicaciones, San Salvador, 29 December.

— (2010c) *Informe de Labores 2009–2010*, San Salvador.

Orellana, G. S. (2012) 'MINSAL cumplió el objetivo 5 del Desarrollo del Milenio', *Diario Co Latino*, 14 June, nuevaweb.diariocolatino.com/.

— (2013) 'ACCPS: diez años de lucha contra la privatización de la salud', *Diario Co Latino*, 8 October, nuevaweb.diariocolatino.com/.

PAHO (Pan American Health Organization) and MINSAL (Ministerio de Salud de El Salvador) (2013) *El Salvador: Aportes de la reforma de salud en El Salvador al desarrollo del sistema de salud y los objetivos de cobertura universal y dialogo político para la sostenibilidad de los logros*, September.

Posada, M. (2013) 'Rol de la sociedad civil y el desempeño de los recursos humanos en la RIISS', Foro Nacional de Salud (FNS), San Salvador, December, rrhh.salud.gob.sv/files/webfiles/foro2013/lic_Posada_presentacion9.pdf.

Rodríguez, M. I., E. Spinoza and V. Menjívar (2009) *Building Hope, Strategies and Recommendations for Health*, Ministry of Health, El Salvador, May, www.salud.gob.sv/archivos/pdf/salud_para_todos/HEALTH_POLICY_EL_SALVADOR_(Building_Hope).pdf, accessed 26 June 2014.

Secretaria de Comunicaciones (2013) 'Presidente Funes desmiente publicación sobre desabastecimiento de medicinas en hospitales', *Transparencia Activa*, 13 August, www.transparenciaactiva.gob.sv/.

Velásquez Carrillo, C. (2011) 'La consolidación oligárquica neoliberal en El Salvador y los retos para el gobierno del FMLN', *Revista América Latina*, 10, Universidad ARCIS, pp. 161–202.

Wright, T. (2001) *Latin America in the Era of the Cuban Revolution*, New York: Praeger.

# E3 | VENEZUELA: THE IMPACT ON HEALTH OF SOCIAL CHANGE

## New vision of health in the 1999 Constitution

The election of a government led by Hugo Chávez in 1998 ushered in a new period in Venezuela's history. The new government resolved to bring about social change by advancing a model grounded in social inclusion and new ways of organizing Venezuelan society through popular participation.

From its outset, this innovative attempt at social change had a major impact on the health sector. The new vision for health was enshrined in the Constitution of the Bolivarian Republic of Venezuela (CRBV 2000), as follows:

> Health is a fundamental social right and the responsibility of the State, which shall guarantee it as part of the right to life. (Article 83)

> Financing of the public health system is the responsibility of the State ... The State guarantees a health budget such as to make possible the attainment of health policy objectives. ... The State shall regulate both public and private health care institutions. (Article 85)

> In order to guarantee the right to health, the State creates, exercises guidance over, and administers a national public health system that crosses sector boundaries, and is decentralised and participatory in nature, integrated with the social security system and governed by the principles of gratuity, universality, completeness, fairness, social integration, and solidarity. ... Public health assets and services are the property of the State and shall not be privatised. The organised community has the right and duty to participate in the making of decisions concerning policy planning, implementation, and control at public health institutions. (Article 84)

Thus, the new Constitution recognizes health as a fundamental human right and as a social right. Consequently, the state is responsible for guaranteeing it, counter to the liberal and neoliberal concept in place until that time, which had viewed health as an individual good, a commodity, according to which everyone enjoys the level of health that they can afford (Feo 2003).

## Transforming health: Mission Barrio Adentro

The Venezuelan government has clearly articulated that it aims to build a single National Public Health System with the active participation of the people. In order to makes this possible there was, at the outset, the necessity

TABLE E3.1 Phases of Barrio Adentro

| Phases | Began | Components | Achievements |
|---|---|---|---|
| Barrio Adentro I | 2003 | Primary care level. Implementation of primary healthcare strategy in the entire country, including: popular medical dispensaries, consultation points (in family homes), dental clinics and optical centres, applying the principles of universality, equity and free cost. Health as a right and a public good. | In 1998: 5,360 popular medical dispensaries; no optical or dental services. In 2012: 13,731 popular medical dispensaries. 500 million no-cost medical consultations. 492 optical centres. 3,500 dental units. |
| Barrio Adentro II | 2005 | Secondary level of care. Provides comprehensive, no-cost service to all citizens through comprehensive diagnostic centres, high-technology centres and comprehensive rehabilitation services. | In 2012: 1,939 comprehensive diagnostic centres operating around the country, treating 59 million emergencies, 500,000 admissions for intensive care, and 927,751 surgeries. |
| Barrio Adentro III | 2006 | Modernization of the country's hospital network, using the traditional hospital network and increasing the number of facilities and number of hospital beds. | In 2012: Hospitals: from 278 in 1998 to 304. Hospital beds: from 17,822 to 27,620. |
| Barrio Adentro IV | 2006 | The main objective is to build healthcare centres for specialized areas of care in very low supply; e.g. opening the Gilberto Rodríguez Ochoa Children's Cardiology Hospital. | Child heart surgery: from 140 surgeries per year in 1998 to 1,500 per year at present. |

to bring about a paradigmatic transformation of the neoliberal health policy that had driven the health system earlier. The new system, it was clear, would no longer be founded on hospital-based, individual, curative medical care, understood as a commodity. It was also understood that policies on health need to include not just healthcare, but also action to promote decent housing, secure employment, a healthy environment and access to recreational facilities.

In light of this premise, Mission Barrio Adentro (Inside the Neighbourhood) was created in 2003. Barrio Adentro incorporates a strategy that includes development of a new health system and a new public institutional framework in which social inclusion and public participation are key ingredients (see Table E3.1). Mission Barrio Adentro has been described as 'the culmination of over 25 years of experience in Latin America and the rest of the world in transforming health systems through the primary health care strategy'. Further, it is seen as an 'experiment in bilateral co-operation between two sister countries [Venezuela and Cuba] on an unprecedented scale … to create a comprehensive

**Image E3.1** Barrio Adentro health centre in a low-income area (Jose Leon Uscategui)

care model that emphasises both health promotion and disease prevention; to implement broad-scale primary health care in urban areas; to form integrated service networks, and to develop an innovative infrastructure of establishments, and new mass human resources education programmes ...' (PAHO 2006).

Barrio Adentro has gone beyond the treatment of sick people in the country's poorest areas, to become the linchpin of the government's social policy. The latter prioritizes local-level efforts, and links the major components of a new social policy. Included are:

- a *social economy* (productive development), through cooperatives, micro-enterprises, a People's Bank, a Women's Bank, and urban family gardens;
- in *education*, implementation of several educational missions and community information centres;
- in *urban improvement*, granting land titles to people who built homes on government land; and
- in *nutrition*, through communal cafeterias, community kitchens, MERCAL grocery stores and the establishment of child care centres (Muntaner et al. 2008).

Barrio Adentro relies on a new type of political and organizing strategy: the creation of urban land committees, health committees, Bolivarian Circles (political and social organizations of workers' councils), technical water boards, community councils, communes, and local public planning councils, among others. Barrio Adentro is contributing to the development of a network of social networks, the embryo of the new social fabric of Venezuela.

## Developing a health workforce and social participation

A National Education and Training Plan has been developed to train human resources, as part of building the Single National Public Health System. For example, people employed in traditional health services are part of a re-education programme to inculcate the new ethics for public servants. Locally, the government is training community health leaders and comprehensive community health workers.

The goal is to train 70,000 Venezuelan physicians, through the various training programmes, to be comprehensive community physicians, who will work for and with the community. They will join the new single health system, through Mission Barrio Adentro, throughout the country. In 2013, the first 14,000 graduated and 10,000 are currently in school. Additionally, 3,200 physicians received graduate training in comprehensive general medicine (family medicine). Further, in collaboration with the Cuban medical mission, 1,823 students received graduate-level training in comprehensive general dentistry, and 1,413 received advanced-level technical training in primary healthcare nursing.

Extraordinary strides have been made in *social participation*. Over eight thousand health committees have been formed. The Ministry of Health is working to strengthen public participation and mobilization through mechanisms such as social auditing of the public administration, formation of community councils, and more recently the creation of communes. Progress is also being made in giving power to the people, guaranteeing their participation in policy-making, planning, monitoring, oversight and evaluation in the health sector (Contraloría Comunitaria en Salud 2004).

The Ministry of Health has been clearly designated as the steward of the health system by the Constitution. The government is addressing issues of corruption that arose from neoliberal decentralization, which consisted of minimizing the role of the state, reducing social spending and targeting the poorest sectors of society. Also being promoted are interconnections and complementarity among the different social missions, which are developing an inclusive and universal social policy.

## The results are evident

The results are evident, as shown by the following data (though partial and limited in scope) (MPPEF n.d.). Owing to growth in employment, 2,124,208 people escaped extreme poverty from 1999 to 2007; during the same period, the percentage of households in poverty dropped from 42.0 to 28.3 per cent. The unemployment rate decreased from 16.6 per cent in 1999 to 7.1 per cent in 2008. Moreover, the employment rate in the formal sector has increased, reducing the size of the informal sector.

Aggregate social spending increased from US$12.5 million in 1999 to US$330.6 million in 2009, and the health budget as a percentage of the national budget went from 6.09 per cent in 2000 to 26.08 per cent in 2006

**Image E3.2** A secondary-level health facility in Venezuela (Jose Leon Uscategui)

(PAHO 2006: 13). In 1998, there were 229,900 pensioners and by 2013 there were more than two million.

Since 1989, the legal minimum wage has kept ahead of the cost of the standard food basket. Household income inequality (Gini coefficient) dropped from 0.4874 in 1997 to 0.3928 in 2009 (a Gini coefficient near 0 indicates equal income distribution and, near 1, unequal distribution).

The net enrolment rate in primary education increased from 86.2 per cent in 1999 to 92.3 per cent in 2009, and in secondary education from 34.7 per cent to 60.6 per cent (MPPEF n.d.).

Health-related indicators have shown marked improvement. Some key indicators are as follows (MPPS n.d., 2009a, 2009b; MPPA 2008):

- The child mortality rate (under five years) in 1998 was 23.4/1,000 live births, dropping to 16.9 by 2009;
- During that same period, infant mortality (under one year) dropped from 21.36 to 14.4, and post-neonatal mortality dropped from 8.0 to 4.01;
- Antiretroviral therapy was being provided free of charge to 7,170 HIV/AIDS patients in 2002 and to 32,302 in 2009, almost the entire infected population.

- The tuberculosis mortality rate fell from 3.35/100,000 population in 1998 to 1.94 in 2009;
- The prevalence of undernutrition decreased from 21 per cent in 1998 to less than 6 per cent in 2009;
- Energy availability in the Venezuelan diet (in calories) increased from 2,127 in 1999 to 3,182 in 2011 (2,720 calories a day are needed for adequate food intake) (AVN 2013);
- The percentage of babies exclusively breastfed up to six months of age increased from 7 to 27 per cent from 1990 to 2008;
- At the primary-care level, there were 5,360 facilities in 1998, increasing to 13,731 in 2012 (MPPCI 2012);
- At the secondary-care level (comprehensive diagnostic centres, high-technology centres, comprehensive rehabilitation services), 1,939 facilities had been built and equipped by 2012, up from 310 facilities in 1998;
- The percentage of the population with access to safe drinking water increased from 68 per cent in 1990 to 95 per cent in 2009;
- During the same period, waste-water collection increased from 52 to 84 per cent.

On balance, the progress cannot be classified as anything other than highly positive. However, it is not free of failures, limitations and contradictions.

**The struggle ahead**

Today, Venezuela is in the midst of a fierce onslaught from the imperial US government, which sees its global hegemony jeopardized, and from its internal allies in the country (the oligarchy, private media, the Catholic Church hierarchy, political parties now led by neo-fascist groups, etc.). At the same time, its people are mourning the death of Hugo Chávez. In the face of these challenges, the people of Venezuela continue to strive to usher in a new stage, a new time, to implement the two main tasks still pending: 1) to finish building the Single National Public Health System, with the active participation of the people, putting into practice their understanding of what 'living well' and 'living fully' mean; and 2) the political task of bringing to life a true democracy, which can be summed up in the Zapatista slogan, 'Here the people rule and the government obeys'.

**References**

AVN (Agencia Venezolana de Noticias) (2013) 'Disponibilidad energética en dieta del venezolano aumentó 49.6% en 13 años', 4 June, www.avn.info.ve.

Contraloría Comunitaria en Salud (2004) *Temas para el debate*, Maracay: IAES.

CRBV (Constitución de la República Boliva-riana de Venezuela) (2000) *Gaceta Oficial No. 5.453*, 24 March.

Feo, O. (2003) *Repensando la salud. Propuestas para salir de la crisis. Análisis de la experiencia venezolana*, Maracay: Universidad de Carabobo.

MPPA (Ministerio del Poder Popular para la

Alimentación) (2008) 'Lactancia materna exclusiva se ha incrementado 200% en Revolución', www.minpal.gob.ve/.

— (n.d.) 'Venezuela disminuyó en 50% índice de subnutrición', www.minpal.gob.ve/index.php?option=com_content&task=view&id=25 o&Itemid=6.

MPPCI (Ministerio del Poder Popular para la Comunicación y la Información) (2012) 'Venezuela pasó de 5,360 centros de salud a 13,731', 23 July, radiomundial.com.ve/.

MPPEF (Ministerio del Poder Popular de Economía y Finanzas) (n.d.) www.mppef.gob.ve.

MPPS (Ministerio de Poder Popular para la Salud) (2009a) *Anuario Estadístico del Ministerio del Poder Popular para la Salud de la República Bolivariana de Venezuela 2009*, www.mpps.gob.ve.

— (2009b) *Alimentación de niños y niñas en los dos primeros años de Vida: Venezuela 2006–2008*, Caracas: Instituto Nacional de Nutrición.

— (n.d.) www.mpps.gob.ve.

Muntaner, C. et al. (2008) '"Barrio Adentro" en Venezuela: democracia participativa, cooperación sur–sur y salud para todos', *Medicina Social*, 3(4): 306–22.

PAHO (Pan American Health Organization) (2006) *Mission Barrio Adentro: The Right to Health and Social Inclusion in Venezuela*, Caracas: PAHO, July.

In Colombia, neoliberal reforms initiated in the 1990s began dismantling the edifice of the social security system. As part of these, reforms were initiated in the health system in 1993 through enactment of what is known as 'Law 100'. The reforms sought to develop a healthcare model that was primarily based on individual private insurance. The Colombian 'model' was held out as a 'success story', and in fact was showcased as the model for achieving Universal Health Coverage (UHC) (see Chapter B1). However, the story told by the Colombian people is very different.

The reforms in the Colombian health system soon became an arena of struggle, revealing the disparity between those who defended the commercial model of healthcare and those who disputed this model from an understanding of health as a public good and a human right. During the last twenty years, this political contention around health policy has generated significant social mobilization against privatization of health, and has led to the emergence of a social movement for the right to health.

### Law 100 and its impact on the right to health

Colombia was one of the most 'faithful' among Latin American nations in embracing and promoting the guidance provided by multilateral financial organizations. An adherence to this 'guidance' led to adoption of polices in the economic, social and political spheres. These policies (located within the logic of neoliberal globalization) promoted liberalization of markets and other standard measures that are the hallmark of 'structural adjustment' (see Chapter A1). A series of reforms were pushed through, in both the state apparatus (judicial and administrative reforms) and the economic and social sectors (tax, education, labour, social security and health reforms). These reforms were directed at bringing about a reorientation of the state. The state's primary role was now seen as that of a 'regulator' instead of a direct provider of social services such as education, health, housing, etc. In the health sector, Colombia followed the prescriptions outlined by the World Bank in its 1988 document entitled *Financing health services in developing countries: an agenda for reform* (World Bank 1988).

The 1991 Constitution is in line with this new orientation. It does not define health as a human right but as a public service that can be provided by public or private institutions, thus establishing the basis for social security reforms through 'Law 100 of 1993'. This led to the creation of the General

**Image E4.1** National campaign for health and social security in Colombia (People's Health Movement)

System of Health Social Security (*Sistema general de seguridad social en salud*, SGSSS). SGSSS is a model based on individual insurance and regulation by market mechanisms. Health insurance companies (*Entidades promotoras de salud*, EPS) form the linchpin of this model.

Law 100 of 1993 is premised on an understanding of health as a 'private good'. It places responsibility on individuals to access health services from the market. In this system, the state addresses the needs of people who cannot pay through targeted subsidies. Through the operation of this law over the past twenty years, the concept of health as a commodity has been established, as opposed to an understanding of health as a human right and a duty of the State (Torres-Tovar and Paredes 2005).

The functioning of the SGSSS has led to a number of negative effects, and these have been the cause of the emergence of social struggles for the right to health. Some of these effects include:

1 the weakening of public institutions in social security and health leading to structural weaknesses in the development of policies and programmes for public health, health promotion and prevention, health surveillance and disease control;
2 the deterioration of the health status of the people and of conditions of employment of workers in the health sector;

3 increased barriers in accessing health services for almost the entire population, as evidenced by the high rates of legal action seeking protection by the state.

## Collective social action for the right to health

Collective social action for the right to health over the past twenty years in Colombia can be divided into three phases. The first phase involved the articulation of demands. During this phase, in the period just after the implementation of Law 100, different sections of the population articulated sectional demands. Workers demanded protection of labour rights; students demanded increased budgets for education and health and for maintaining vocational training; users of health services demanded a better quality of services; groups of health professionals demanded the recognition of their social and employment status; and the indigenous peoples demanded a specific law that recognized their traditions and practices in health.

Each social group carried out its own analysis of the impact of the new law. They also, individually, sought legal recourse for protection of their rights. These separate strands of action were later to coalesce into a broad social movement.

A second phase, involving the politicization of the struggle, began in 2000. This phase commenced with preparation for and organization of the First National Congress for Health and Social Security. A collective called *Acciones Sociales Colectivas por el Derecho a la Salud* (Social Actions for the Right to Health – ASCDS) used this opportunity to provoke a broad public debate on the right to health.

This phase of activity promoted public debates that shaped the proposal to build a social movement for health and a process of political mobilization. The contours of a new model of health were agreed at the Second National Conference on Health in 2004. Key elements of the proposal for a new health system include that it should:

1 be based on an understanding of health as a human right linked to well-being and quality of life;
2 be universal, equitable, solidarity based and cognizant of differences (cultural, gender, age);
3 be administered with a public ethos, without insurance companies functioning as intermediaries;
4 be financed from the national budget, through a national public fund and regional funds;
5 prioritize health promotion, prevention and education;
6 implement a national system of health information;
7 respond to people's needs and include technological developments (equipment, medicines, etc.);

**Image E4.2** Health professionals march in Bogotá against the reforms (Mauricio Torres)

8  incorporate the cultural and intellectual heritage of indigenous medicine and medicine of other ethnic groups;
9  be subject to social surveillance and control with a high participation of citizens.

Over a period collective actions grew and there was a greater politicization of the movement. This was based on the realization among different partners in the movement that the structural causes of state policy needed to be countered by collective action. Thus, while actions on specific demands continued, different sections opposing the reforms began working together in a coordinated manner.

A significant development in this phase was the election of a non-neoliberal government in the city of Bogotá. The new government of the city sought the help of ASCDS and this enabled district-level public health policy to be designed from the perspective of human rights. It was also possible to incorporate some elements of the proposal described earlier (Vega-Romero et al. 2008). Valuable experience was gained regarding challenges that exist, at the local level, to the reorientation of state policy (away from the premises of Law 100).

Since early 2011, a third phase of the struggle has been taking shape. This phase of the movement has progressed in shaping a collective identity of the struggle and has also accomplished further concretization of the alternative proposals. Through years of working together in the common struggle, different sections that are active have developed common positions on many issues. Consequently, the movement is much less fragmented now.

The progress in shaping a collective identity for the struggle has been very valuable in channelling the collective outrage of the people against measures by the national government to forcibly implement a system that helps the insurance companies. These measures are clearly against the interests of the people, as well as of health workers and professionals (Torres-Tovar 2010). Two processes are now taking place simultaneously: convergence of a movement around health as a right, and a conceptual clarity against an insurance-based model of healthcare that is represented by the model promoted by Law 100.

Protests in Colombia escalated in 2013, brought on by the condition of the health system and outrage in the face of the Bill introduced by the national government. This Bill is designed to further deepen the impact of Law 100 and will exacerbate the health crisis in Colombia. Protests are taking place in various ways: blockades, marches, pot-banging, permanent assemblies, public discussions, information dissemination through social networks, rejection letters through virtual platforms, etc. The streets are filling up with protesters, many of whom are medical students and young graduates.

## Looking forward

The experience gained in the past twenty years has sharpened the understanding that there is a need to confront a political class, a national government and a parliament that do not represent the interests and needs of society. The movement for better healthcare is also now a movement for increased political participation of the people in the shaping of policies.

This implies that all social, academic, legal, technical and political efforts must be continuously directed at increasing people's dissatisfaction with the present system. The movement has the task of channelling people's anger and their growing consciousness to build a political platform for the right to health. Such a platform would not just seek a new healthcare system, but would also demand initiatives around health promotion, prevention and rehabilitation.

### Note

1 This chapter is based on research conducted by the 'Social Collective Action for the Right to Health in Colombia' from 1994 to 2010, published as *Lucha social contra la privatización de la salud*, Ediciones Cinep, Bogotá, 2013.

### References

Torres-Tovar, M. (2010) 'Colombia: declaratoria de emergencia social. Salvavidas para el negocio de la salud', *Le Monde Diplomatique*, 86: 2–3, Bogotá.

Torres-Tovar, M. and N. Paredes (2005) 'Derecho a la salud. Situación en países de América Latina. El caso colombiano, "El mercado no es para todos y todas"', *Gerencia y Política de Salud*, 4(8): 169–85.

Vega-Romero R. et al. (2008) 'Health policy in Bogotá (2004–2008): an analysis of the experience with primary health care', *Social Medicine*, 3(2).

World Bank (1988) *Financing health services in developing countries: an agenda for reform*, Policy study, Washington, DC: World Bank.

# E5 | PERU: SOCIAL MOVEMENT AGAINST NEOLIBERAL REFORMS

## Introduction

At the time when Ollanta Humala was running for president of Peru, he had repeatedly talked about the need to create a universal health system accessible to all, based on a health policy that would prioritize the public health system (Ríos Barrientos 2013). However, once he took office in July 2011, people-centred health system reforms disappeared from his priorities, to be replaced by market-led reforms (ibid.). On 8 January 2013, through a presidential decree, President Humala entrusted the Peruvian National Health Council (NHC) with developing guidelines for the proposed health sector reform (Resolución Suprema N° 001-2013-SA). By that time, the Humala administration that had taken power on a centre-left platform was effectively following the same neoliberal path the country had been on since 1992 (Tejada Guerrero 2013). This call for reform was framed as a deepening of the existing model of income-based access to health, including limited insurance packages for the poor and growing influence of health insurance and pharmaceuticals companies.

The NHC has been criticized for its lack of representatives from civil society (only one civil society representative out of twelve members) and because its decisions are advisory in nature.[1] Charging this body with developing the reform guidelines made clear that the government's intent was to avoid deep reforms to the existing system but rather to envisage more of the same model. From the outset, social movements, represented in the NHC by ForoSalud (a network of health rights organizations and activists), demanded the inclusion of all stakeholders in the discussion, as well as that the scope of reform should be defined before guidelines were developed. Both requests were rejected by the Ministry of Health (MoH) and the majority of NHC's members (essentially health service providers or funders).

## Key numbers and the failure of universal health insurance

To have a better understanding of the reality of the Peruvian health system, a few numbers are useful. For 2013, the country's health expenditure was composed as follows (Torres 2013):

- Out-of-pocket spending: US$4.353 billion.
- General public government spending and insurance for the poor: US$4.257 billion (US$400 million on insurance for the poor).

- Contributions from employees and employers to the social security health system: US$2.927 billion.
- Private insurance premiums: US$650 million.
- Total health spending: US$12,187 billion.

Public spending is only around 35 per cent of total health spending. Although around 25 per cent of resources go to the social security health system, these contributions are not part of the public budget. Peru lags behind most Latin American countries in terms of public investment in health as a share of GDP, with only 1.6 per cent compared to 3.5 per cent for the continent (CMP 2013b). It also lags behind in terms of total investment in health, with only 5.1 per cent of GDP, compared to an average of 7.6 per cent in Latin America in 2012 (CNS 2013). The health financing structure itself is a barrier to achieving the right to health for all.

The main argument in favour of passing the Universal Health Insurance Law of 9 April 2009 (Law 29344) was that increasing the number of people insured would mean that more people would be financially supported in accessing their health needs. It was argued that with more insured people, there would be greater financial protection and therefore less out-of-pocket spending. However, five years into the universal health insurance programme, the reality has proved otherwise. In 2009, household out-of-pocket spending was around US$3.4 billion, and it was estimated that in 2013 families spent around US$4.35 billion (see Table E5.1). Even though the insured population increased from 40 to 70 per cent, this has not provided effective financial protection. Because of this, the government's reform plan was and continues to be the object of substantial criticism.

TABLE E5.1 Household out-of-pocket health spending, 2009–13

|  | 2009 | 2010 | 2011 | 2012 | 2013 |
|---|---|---|---|---|---|
| Household spending (billions of Peruvian sols) | 8,580 ($3,400) | 8,660 | 9,740 | 10,520 | 11,320 ($4,350) |

*Source*: Estimates based on online database of the Ministry of Economy and Finance, cross-checked with other sources

## Resistance against the reforms

In mid-2013, nearing the end of the time period given to the NHC to develop the reform guidelines, the Peruvian Medical Federation (PMF, Federación Médica de Perú, the largest doctors' association) went on a nationwide strike over pay and job security (TeleSur 2013). In recent times, the nationwide doctors' strike has been the only show of strength that has successfully put pressure on the government. This strike opened the road for several actions by different groups of health workers (see Box E5.1).

---

### Box E5.1 Doctors' strike spreads into health workers' strikes

Peruvian doctors are among the worst paid in Latin America, with a monthly remuneration of close to US$1,000 (La República 2014). In 2012, PMF had reached an agreement with the government for a substantial pay increase following a month-long strike. Claiming that the agreement had not been honoured by the government, the federation raised the issue of pay, job security and further health sector reforms, and called for a nationwide strike on 16 July 2013. A month after the strike began, with at least 70 per cent of health services shut down in Lima and the country's twenty-six regions, the government agreed to an average effective raise of around US$550 (La República 2013c). This outcome strengthened the physicians' leadership and set off similar actions by other organizations.

While the doctors' strike was ongoing, the Peruvian Federation of Ministry of Health Nurses, FEDEMINSAP, an organization of 50,000 public sector nurses, began an action on 18 July 2013. In the midst of heightened tensions, the MoH stepped in to resolve the issues raised by the nurses, prioritizing them above the doctors. The government agreed to an increase in pay and appointment of contractual staff. A month after the end of the doctors' strike, FENUTSSA, a national federation of around 100,000 health sector professional, technical and administrative workers, went out on strike on similar lines (Alvarado 2013).

In September 2013, the government had issued Legislative Decree 1153 that 'Regulates the Comprehensive Policy on Compensation and Economic Payments for Health Personnel in Government Service'. This regulation distorts the employment relationship, replacing 'remuneration' with 'compensation', and affects professional laws and the acquired rights of health sector employees. Health workers overwhelmingly opposed this regulation and, in October, the Peruvian Medical Association challenged its constitutional standing (CMP 2013a). The law is under review by the Constitutional Court.[2]

---

While sparked by wage and job security demands, the health workers' strikes also included a criticism of the government's health reform agenda. The government responded to PMF demands by asserting that one of the components of the six-point health sector reform would be a comprehensive health workforce remuneration policy (Le República 2013b). Despite the government's rhetoric focused on 'providing better services to the public', the confrontation between MoH and PMF exposed the anti-people nature of the reform process and the half-truths of the government in general and the MoH in particular. The return to the bargaining table,

**Image E5.1** Community monitoring of health services – ForoSalud meeting (Rafael Gonzalez Guzman)

after a month of the PMF's strike, strengthened a wave of resistance to the proposed reforms.

It is at this point that the relationship between social movements (coordinated through ForoSalud) and health workers' organizations began to develop. The government argues for the continuation and expansion of the existing health insurance system. On the other hand, social organizations and health workers' organizations argue for the need to deal with the structural problems of the country's health system, including sustainable financing, equality of access and services, social participation, regulation of the health market, and decent work policies.

The reforms led to the enactment of twenty-three new health laws in December 2013. These twenty-three regulations deepen the reforms initiated in 2008, through the passing of three pieces of legislation that create a larger space for private players in the Peruvian health sector (Cuba García 2014). The most recent legislation was drafted by government officials and consultants in the Ministry of Economy and Finance (MEF) and MoH, and enacted pursuant to 'special powers' the Peruvian Congress granted the executive branch. The NHC's contribution to this process, in the form of guidelines published in July 2013,[3] can best be understood as a 'formality' required by the government to legitimize its claim that it was a participative process. Faced with the government's plans to expand a health insurance system based on 'structured pluralism',[4] social organizations and health workers' organizations have been moved to organize a coordinated movement to counter these new health laws.

### Forging an inclusive social movement

The resistance to the neoliberal health reforms is being led by an alliance of social organizations and health workers' organizations. The alliance could be effectively built as a result of a number of supportive developments involving the alliance partners. The new leadership of ForoSalud (elected in November

2013) was politically committed to building a broad movement and proposed an alliance with health workers. The former president of the PMF, César Palomino, was elected chairman of the Peruvian Medical Association (PMA). He had previously headed the doctors' strike and his election marked a crucial policy shift in PMA, which had traditionally been conservative. In PMF, a leadership supportive of alliances with social movements was re-elected. The alliance also works in coordination with FENUTSSA and FEDEMINSAP.

The newly forged alliance was soon provided with an opportunity to show its collective strength. In February 2014, an 'International Seminar: Towards Universal Health Coverage'[5] was organized in Lima by the Peruvian government, the World Health Organization, the Pan American Health Organization, the World Bank and the Inter-American Development Bank. Invitees to the seminar included representatives from ministries of health of different countries around the world. The organizations of health workers, professional associations or social organizations were not invited. At the seminar, the MoH and the Peruvian government received the support of the WHO for deepening a market-led health insurance system (Chan 2014). However, WHO director-general Margaret Chan was faced by 5,000 protesters gathered outside the hotel where the seminar was taking place in Lima's financial district (ForoSalud 2014c).

The lines are now clearly drawn: on one side stands a strengthened alliance of social movements coordinated by ForoSalud, PMA and the major health workers' organizations; on the other side are the pro-insurance market operators (serving the interests of insurance and pharmaceutical companies) currently heading the MoH, ESSALUD (the social health security system), SUNASA (the Superintendence of Health) and SISOL (a municipal public–private partnership system). It is worth noting that the people who are formally in charge of the Peruvian health system come from USAID health projects carried out over the past ten years in Peru (Ramos 2013a), or are agents directly related to private insurers, as in the case of SUNASA.

The challenge today is to strengthen the alliance by involving more nation-wide organizations engaged in various struggles, and for the health sector to be able to extend its relationship with the medical profession. The progress in recent months shows that, with all its complexities and underlying differences in perceptions, the resistance is expanding. This alliance has a medium-term target for the presidential elections of April 2016, to ensure that the movement is sufficiently consolidated and strong to be able to push the debate on Peru's health system on the political agenda.

Several coordinated actions by the alliance are already being organized (ForoSalud 2014a). The 6th National Health Conference of ForoSalud, held in late 2013, issued a Political Declaration[6] that rejects the reform process, and supports broad alliances and the development of a universal health system. This position found resonance in the 9th National Medical Congress of the PMA, held in Lima in March 2014.[7]

Debates on health usually focus on the healthcare system, leaving out discussions on the social determinants of health and the need to move beyond a biomedical focus. The new health laws strip the MoH of any responsibility for health promotion. The struggle for health is much more than the fight to reorient the health system. However, today in Peru, owing to the neoliberal legal barrage of twenty-three new laws, the resistance is concentrated on the defence of the public system and the need to recognize the right to health as the basis of universality, comprehensiveness and solidarity. It is no coincidence that in the midst of the reform process the government is issuing tenders to private national and transnational capital for equipment, laboratories, testing, health services and management of the main public hospitals of Lima, through public–private partnerships (Perú 21 2013). It is no coincidence that international insurance companies have partnered with Peruvian companies. It is no coincidence that banks and insurance companies are being offered the opportunity to build hospitals in different regions and run them for fifteen or twenty years through the mechanism of 'works for taxes'. These developments foreshadow the battles that need to be fought in the future.

## Notes

1 See Ley del Sistema Nacional Coordinado y Descentralizado de Salud, Ley N° 27813.

2 As of March 2014, the court decision was still awaited.

3 See CNS (2013).

4 See the structured pluralism model of Frenk and Londoño (Londoño and Frenk 1997).

5 For more information, see the conference page of the MoH website, appminsa.minsa.gob.pe/cus/, accessed 22 April 2014.

6 See ForoSalud (2014b).

7 For more information, see the event webpage, congresomediconacional.org/, accessed 22 April 2014.

## References

Alvarado, G. (2013) 'Trabajadores del Minsa inician huelga indefinida', *La Primera*, 19 September, www.laprimeraperu.pe/online/actualidad/trabajadores-del-minsa-inician-huelga-indefinida_149842.html, accessed 22 April 2014.

Chan, M. (2014) 'Reforma de salud: Perú en el camino correcto', Speech delivered at the international seminar 'Towards Universal Health Coverage', Lima, 20 February, www.paho.org/per/, accessed 22 April 2014.

CMP (Colegio Médico del Perú) (2013a) 'Colegio médico presentó hoy acción de inconstitucionalidad contra DL 1153', 18 October, www.cmp.org.pe/component/content/article/56-ultimas/1833-colegio-medico-presento-hoy-accion-de-inconstitucionalidad-contra-dl-1153.html, accessed 22 April 2014.

— (2013b) 'El presupuesto de salud 2013', 24 July, www.cmp.org.pe/component/content/article/56-ultimas/1629-el-presupuesto-de-salud-2013.html, accessed 22 April 2014.

CNS (Consejo Nacional de Salud) (2013) *Lineamientos y Medidas de Reforma del Sector Salud*, Lima: Government of Peru, July.

Cuba García, H. (2014) 'Artículo de opinión: el proceso de reforma de la salud en el Perú y el traspaso de recursos públicos al sector privado', Presentation at the IX Congreso Médico Nacional, 20–22 March, Lima, congresomediconacional.org/, accessed 22 April 2014.

ForoSalud (Foro de la Sociedad Civil en Salud) (2014a) 'Consultas ciudadanas en hospitales de Lima y Callao', www.forosalud.org.pe/actividades567.html, accessed 22 April 2014.

— (2014b) *Declaración política de la VI conferencia nacional de salud: derecho a la salud para todas y todos ¡por un sistema universal de salud ahora!*, www.forosalud.

org.pe/declaracionpolitica.pdf, accessed 22 April 2014.

— (2014c) 'Gran movilización por el derecho a la salud', www.forosalud.org.pe/actividades 569.html, accessed 22 April 2014.

La República (2013a) 'Huelga médica nacional fue levantada luego de treinta días', *La República*, 14 August, www.larepublica. pe/14-08-2013/huelga-medica-nacional-fue-levantada-tras-acuerdo, accessed 22 April 2014.

— (2013b) 'Juan Jiménez: Aumento de remu-neraciones en sector salud es cuestión de días', *La República*, 1 August, www. larepublica.pe/01-08-2013/juan-jimenez-aumentos-en-sector-salud-es-cuestion-de-dias, accessed 22 April 2014.

— (2013c) 'Huelga médica: acuerdos a los que llegaron médicos y el Gobierno', *La República*, 14 August, www.larepublica. pe/14-08-2013/huelga-medica-acuerdos-a-los-que-llegaron-medicos-y-el-gobierno, accessed 22 April 2014.

— (2014) 'Médicos peruanos tienen uno de los sueldos más bajos de Latinoamérica', 22 February, www.larepublica.pe/22-02-2014/medicos-tienen-uno-de-los-sueldos-mas-bajos-del-area, accessed 22 April 2014.

Londoño, J. L. and J. Frenk (1997) 'Structured pluralism: towards an innovative model for health system reform in Latin America', *Health Policy*, 41(1): 1–36.

Perú 21 (2013) 'Hay 80 empresas interesadas en alianza público–privado con el Minsa', *Perú 21*, 5 January, peru21.pe/actualidad/ hay-80-empresas-interesadas-alianza-publico-privado-minsa-2164331, accessed 22 April 2014.

Ramos, R. (2013a) 'Esta es la USAID, qué les parece: misión, programas, proyectos de USAID en el Perú', Agencia Latinoamericana de Información (alainet), 4 May, alainet. org/active/63773&lang=es, accessed 22 April 2014.

— (2013b) 'Huelga de médicos: la inutilidad de los reclamos y compromisos', Agencia Latinoamericana de Información (alainet), 9 August, alainet.org/active/66323, accessed 22 April 2014.

Ríos Barrientos, M. (2013) 'Luz verde a reforma de la salud mercantilista', Agencia Latinoamericana de Información (alainet), 22 August, alainet.org/active/ 66659&lang=es, accessed 22 April 2014.

Tejada Guerrero, U. (2013) 'Ollanta, un 28 de reformas y protestas', Agencia Latinoameri-cana de Información (alainet), 28 July, alainet.org/active/66009, accessed 22 April 2014.

TeleSur (2013) 'Crisis sanitaria en Perú cumple un mes sin acuerdos con el Gobierno', TeleSur, 12 August, www.telesurtv.net/ articulos/2013/08/12/crisis-sanitaria-en-peru-cumple-un-mes-sin-acuerdos-con-el-gobierno-3781.html, accessed 22 April 2014.

Torres, D. (2013) 'Crisis del sector salud: una visión económica', *Patio de Sociales*, 15 August, www.patiodesociales. com/2013/08/crisis-del-sector-salud-una-vision.html, accessed 22 April 2014.

Your heart is a weapon the size of your fist. Keep fighting, keep loving.

The global economic crisis has had a deep impact on people's lives in large parts of Europe (see Chapter A2). As the crisis and its consequences continue to escalate, waves of protests and resistance movements have started sweeping large parts of the continent, akin to the anti-IMF demonstrations of the 1980s and 1990s (Kondilis et al. 2013). These target the austerity packages being imposed by the 'Troika' (the European Commission, the International Monetary Fund (IMF) and the European Central Bank) and also the EU–US negotiations for a new free trade agreement (the Transatlantic Trade and Investment Partnership, or TTIP), which poses imminent threats to democratic decision-making and social protection systems across Europe. In this chapter we provide brief vignettes of the rising tide of resistance in Europe against austerity measures being imposed by neoliberal governments in many parts of the continent.

### National mobilisations in different countries

In Spain, the moves to privatize healthcare services face resistance from both popular movements of civil society and workers in the public healthcare system. A historic unity, linking the entire range of health professionals (doctors, nurses, health workers), has resulted in the organization in Madrid and other regions of a huge movement, called '*marea blanca*' (white tide). The movement has organized a prolonged strike and massive street protests (Washington Post 2012). Several initiatives, designed to resist the attempts to demolish the edifice of the public health system, have been forged, which unite civil society groups and health workers. These range from advocacy groups, such as the Federation of Associations for the Defence of Public Health (La Federación de Asociaciones para la Defensa de la Sanidad Pública) and the Dempeus per la Salut Pública and Centre d'Anàlisis i Programes Sanitaris in Catalonia, to a platform of neighbourhood groups that self-manage Primary Assistance Centres – 'Platform of people affected by healthcare cuts' (Plataforma de Afectadas por los Recortes Sanitarios).[1]

In the face of these struggles, in January 2014 the conservative government of the region of Madrid cancelled its planned outsourcing of management and services at six local hospitals. If implemented, the plan would have transferred six public hospitals to private healthcare management groups, adversely affecting the healthcare of 1.2 million people and the careers of 5,000 health workers (Marcos 2014). While this has been a small victory, *marea blanca* warns that

**Image E6.1** Demonstration in Athens against denial of healthcare (Alexis Benos)

the protests should not stop, since a large part of the regional healthcare is now managed or owned by private firms. A very large demonstration was organized in Madrid in March 2014, three years after the *indignados* 15-M protests, in which over a million people participated in a '22 M dignity march'. Many others, travelling to the capital on buses and trains, were blocked by the police. The 22 M Manifesto called for the defence of the right to work, housing and social services. It further demanded a halt in cuts in welfare, a moratorium on debt payments, and a rejection of the austerity package imposed by the Troika (Marchas de la Dignidad n.d.).

In Portugal, since the onset of the crisis, four general strikes and a series of national mobilizations involving all sections of the population have been organized to protest against privatization of health services. These include a strike by doctors, in July 2012, which saw the participation of over 80 per cent of health professionals (Soares 2012); and street protest and demonstrations, in September 2012, by hundreds of thousands in all big cities of the country.

Public mobilizations in defence of public healthcare have been less prominent in Italy. A march by health professionals' trade unions in defence of the national healthcare service (NHS) was held in October 2012 (Quotidiano Sanita 2012). A campaign to 'Save our NHS' was launched in May 2013, supported principally by health workers (Salviamo il nostro SSN n.d.). Another campaign that has attracted popular support is led by the main Italian 'anti-Mafia' group. It calls for greater transparency and better governance of the NHS, including mechanisms for increasing citizens' participation (Riparte il Futuro n.d.). A grassroots-driven campaign has been launched by the 'Network for

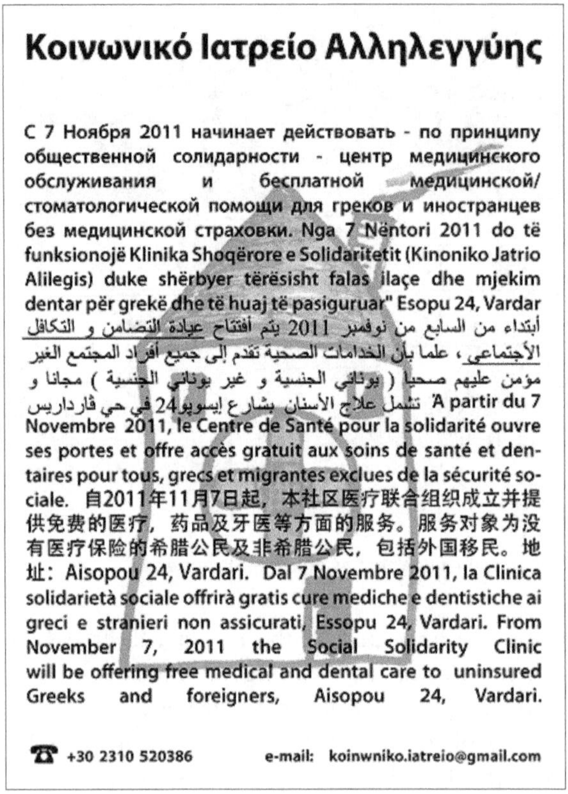

## Κοινωνικό Ιατρείο Αλληλεγγύης

С 7 Ноября 2011 начинает действовать - по принципу общественной солидарности - центр медицинского обслуживания и бесплатной медицинской/стоматологической помощи для греков и иностранцев без медицинской страховки. Nga 7 Nëntori 2011 do të funksionojë Klinika Shoqërore e Solidaritetit (Kinoniko Jatrio Alilegis) duke shërbyer tërësisht falas ilaçe dhe mjekim dentar për grekë dhe të huaj të pasiguruar" Esopu 24, Vardar أبتداء من السابع من نوفمبر 2011 يتم أفتتاح عيادة التضامن و التكافل الأجتماعى، علما بأن الخدمات الصحية تقدم إلى جميع أفراد المجتمع الغير مؤمن عليهم صحيا ( يونانى الجنسية و غير يونانى الجنسية ) مجانا و تشمل علاج الأسنان بشارع إيسوبو24 فى حى فارداريس A partir du 7 Novembre 2011, le Centre de Santé pour la solidarité ouvre ses portes et offre accès gratuit aux soins de santé et dentaires pour tous, grecs et migrantes exclues de la sécurité sociale. 自2011年11月7日起，本社区医疗联合组织成立并提供免费的医疗，药品及牙医等方面的服务。服务对象为没有医疗保险的希腊公民及非希腊公民，包括外国移民。地址: Aisopou 24, Vardari. Dal 7 Novembre 2011, la Clinica solidarietà sociale offrirà gratis cure mediche e dentistiche ai greci e stranieri non assicurati, Essopu 24, Vardari. From November 7, 2011 the Social Solidarity Clinic will be offering free medical and dental care to uninsured Greeks and foreigners, Aisopou 24, Vardari.

☎ +30 2310 520386    e-mail: koinwniko.iatreio@gmail.com

**Image E6.2** Poster announcing the opening of a Social Solidarity Clinic in Thessaloniki (Alexis Benos)

sustainability and health' (MDF 2013). It is promoted by the 'health and degrowth' group of the Italian Association for Happy Degrowth, which advocates against the paradigm of unlimited (and unsustainable) economic growth. The network comprises a wide range of groups and associations, ranging from older social medicine movements of the 1970s (Democratic Medicine, Democratic Psychiatry), to newer groups advocating for the independence of the health sector from private interests. It also includes the Italian Observatory on Global Health (a think tank on global policies/politics and their impact on health), the Association for Person-centred Medicine (which calls for the integration of traditional and non-conventional medicines in the healthcare system), and the Secretariat of the Italian Medical Students (SISM).

Beyond the health sector, grassroots movement are claiming (back) basic rights for the population. In October 2013, a large demonstration in Rome – promoted by radical trade unions – included movements for the right to housing, and movements against 'unnecessary imposed mega projects', such as the high-speed train in northern Italy (No Tav movement). Following the national demonstration, actions have continued to happen in cities – often involving student movements – while the leading groups are increasingly and violently being targeted by police and legal authorities.

In the UK, several public campaigns targeted the top-down reorganization of the National Health Service (NHS) (see Chapter B2). An organization called 'Keep Our NHS Public', which is a network of several local affiliates, has been at the forefront of this campaign (Keep Our NHS Public n.d.). After the comprehensive reform of the NHS was pushed through by the government in 2012, a group of health professionals decided to create a new political party to challenge the health reforms at a political level. The National Health Action party is set to challenge the privatization of the NHS and the fragmentation of care accelerated by the Health and Social Care Act and aims to restore the NHS to a service that provides publicly funded healthcare, free to all at the point of need (Lancet 2012).

In Belgium, efforts are under way to develop a coordinated campaign against the privatization of healthcare. The 'Action platform for health and solidarity' brings together trade unions and grassroots organizations (Santé & Solidarité n.d.). The Platform is also an endeavour to unite the resistance to neoliberal reforms in the health sector at a European level (Brussels being the main seat of the European Commission). In February 2014, the Platform organized a day of protest followed by an international conference of the 'European network against privatisation and commercialisation of health and social protection'. The Platform has released a campaign manifesto against the privatization of healthcare and for the promotion of a comprehensive, non-commodified healthcare system based on equal access (European Network 2014).

**Image E6.3** A popular singer participating in a solidarity concert for the Social Solidarity Clinic (Alexis Benos)

## Box E6.1 'Doctors for the People' in Belgium

'Doctors for the People' (DFTP) is a network of eleven community-based primary healthcare centres in Belgium. Currently it employs approximately a hundred healthcare professionals and sixty administrative assistants. It is being supported by hundreds of volunteers. Thirty-five thousand patients are registered in the different healthcare centres (Doctors for the People n.d). DFTP was founded over four decades ago in the wake of the May 68 movement, when family doctors settled in working-class neighbourhoods. Instead of pursuing a profitable career, they shared the living conditions of their patients and struggled together with them for better living and working conditions. Doctors and other DFTP employees choose to work for modest wages and medical care is free for all registered patients. Over the past forty years DFTP has developed into an organization that is able to influence national debates and struggles on a range of issues. DFTP is also a training centre for general practitioners, and the organization works together with several Belgian universities. Daily medical practice is consciously linked with social campaigning, international solidarity with the popular struggle for the right to health around the globe and scientific research on social topics. Many health workers with DFTP have worked (or continue to work) in international solidarity initiatives in the Philippines, El Salvador, Lebanon, Palestine, the Democratic Republic of Congo, Burkina Faso, Cuba, Iraq and Venezuela.

While the impact of the crisis in Europe and the neoliberal response to this crisis has mounted in Belgium, DFTP has been active in supporting the key demands of trade unions: no austerity cuts in public transport or healthcare, a interdiction on closure of companies still making a profit, no wage freeze, etc. DFTP combines work at the local level with wider actions and mobilization at regional and national levels.

The general physicians of DFTP see it as their duty to put their privileged social position and their access to academic and scientific resources at the service of popular struggles for better working and living conditions and access to healthcare. They actively take part in these struggles by organizing and participating in campaigns that result from their research. These campaigns defy corporate interests and clearly demonstrate how the present regime in Belgium is harmful for public health. Following are some examples of how DFTP combines medical care with research, activism and solidarity actions.

*Research as a tool for empowerment and struggle* As life expectancy has increased steadily over the last decades, many European governments have raised the retirement age to balance the ratio of employed people and dependent ones. In 2010, an observational study by DFTP assessed the health status and the 'employability' of 2,028 patients aged from fifty-five to sixty-five (Ruelens 2013). The study suggested that early retirement, when their physical or mental ability to work is impaired, should be an option for workers after the age of fifty-five. This study supports the labour movement in its struggle for more humane working conditions, as well as for the retention of the right to early retirement with preservation of full pension rights.

DFTP is also associated with an ongoing project between general practitioners (GPs) of DFTP in Antwerp and the trade unions of a public transport company (De Lijn). The project investigates the working conditions of local bus and tram drivers and was initiated after some GPs noticed a high incidence of low back problems and stress-related health problems among urban bus drivers. De Lijn, as a result of austerity measures, has reduced the number of bus lines and cut down on staff, leading to an increased workload for workers and overcrowded buses. Through focus group discussions with drivers, three principal problems were identified – badly designed seats leading to low back ailments, work overload and repressive measures at the workplace addressing absenteeism (Van Bever et al. n.d.). A survey addressing these problems was initiated among drivers, in the face of negative propaganda by the company. The results of the survey demonstrated a clear link between the drivers' ill health and poor working conditions. These results have been shared with the trade unions and workers and the unions are using the results of the project to demand improved working conditions. During the project, a lot of attention was paid to the participatory approach of research as a strategy for social change.

Another example of DFTP's work on employment conditions is the research work of Karel van Bever, a young DFTP general physician, working in Zelzate, a small industrial town in the north of Belgium. In order to understand the psychological, social and physical problems of his patients with temporary jobs, Karel worked as a temporary worker in the port of Antwerp for nine months. He wrote down his experience in a diary and published his testimony under the title 'Doctor in Overalls' (Van Bever 2008). Karel's book has created a deep impression among trade unions in Belgium. He wrote in his book: 'Never in my life have I worked this hard, have I been this tired, or has my social life been so non-existent' (ACW 2008).

*Tackling pollution in Genk* Sledderlo is a deprived area surrounding an Arcelor-Mittal steel factory in Genk. In 2005 the general physicians of

DFTP in Genk detected an abnormally high prevalence of respiratory problems among patients living near the factory. An investigation by DFTP in the region confirmed the high incidence of respiratory problems. The research results were presented to the Genk city council and a comprehensive investigation into the different sources of pollution in the area followed. DFTP supported a petition, by the local community, against the polluting industry. Eventually the municipal authorities decided to move the locality's elementary school from the polluted zone. Popular mobilization and media attention forced the regional government to initiate a health survey and the federal government started an investigation in order to detect other polluting hot spots. Ultimately more stringent pollution control norms were imposed on the factory.

*The struggle for affordable and quality healthcare* Within the national health insurance system of Belgium, since the 1990s, the costs of medicines have contributed the most towards increase in expenditure on healthcare (RIZIV-NIHDI n.d.). Between 1997 and 2004, expenditure on medicines rose twice as fast as the overall expenditure of the national health insurance system (RIZIV-NIHDI 2008). In 2004, DFTP physician Dirk van Duppen published a book, *The Cholesterol War. Why drugs are so expensive.* The book analyses the malpractices indulged in by 'big pharma' and the origin of their enormous profits. It also discusses a specific strategy to ensure lower drug prices, inspired by the drug policy of New Zealand: the so-called 'Kiwi model'. This policy is based on a scientific analysis of national drug needs and the use of a collective drugs purchase system that minimizes prices.

The campaign in the wake of the publication of this book stimulated a broad public debate in the Belgian media, and the commissions on Social Affairs and Public Health organized a joint hearing on the topic. Late in 2005 a coalition of DFTP, civil society groups and the healthcare workers' trade unions gathered 100,000 signatures for the application of the 'Kiwi model' in Belgium. In 2006 pharmaceutical companies started what they called 'their biggest lobby campaign ever' to stop approval of the Bill for the application of the 'Kiwi model' in Belgium. Though they were successful in stalling the Bill, public pressure forced pharmaceutical companies to drastically reduce the prices of 900 drugs. This resulted in an overall reduction of 400 million euros in the costs of the National Health Insurance System in 2006 alone. However, a much larger reduction in costs (an estimated 300 million euros per year in savings for National Health Insurance and a further 110 million euros per year saving for individual patients) would be possible if the 'Kiwi model' were to be implemented in Belgium.

In Germany, 'Blockupy' protests – promoted by radical anti-capitalist political groups and networks – took place mainly in Frankfurt in 2012 and 2013 and are poised to continue in 2014, drawing increasing participation every year (Blockupy n.d.).

A rising tide of protests, demonstrations and mobilizations is confronting the planned dismantling of the public health system in Greece (see Chapter A2). Massive gatherings have laid siege to administrative offices of public hospitals, protesting against the levy of a five-euro registration fee for outpatients. In March 2014, primary healthcare doctors, administrative personnel and patients 'occupied' several primary healthcare centres to protest against the closure of 380 units by the Health Ministry. As a result of the closures more than 8,500 doctors and primary-care personnel will be sent home with 75 per cent of their salary, and will eventually be assigned to new workplaces, many of them several hundred kilometres away. The decision is part of the latest Greek healthcare reform which threatens to make patients' access to primary care even more difficult, especially in the countryside and on islands (Keep Talking Greece 2014). In parallel, solidarity movements are being assembled to protect the growing number of jobless people who are being excluded from public health insurance schemes, and solidarity clinics are being organized all over the country. These clinics combine solidarity and mobilization of both health workers and patients against the current policies, which are denying healthcare access to millions of people.

---

**Box E6.2  Solidarity in response to the 'crisis'**

Responding to the catastrophic health crisis in Greece, a vibrant grass-roots-driven movement for the right to healthcare is taking shape. Massive protests have been organized in several cities against closures of public hospitals and the dismantling of primary-care services. The movement is also forging a unity between workers in public services unions, local organizations and common citizens. Open popular assemblies are being organized to mobilize for the right to health and healthcare services.

The sudden impoverishment of hundreds of thousands of people has created an immediate need for shelter, food and healthcare. A unique solidarity movement is growing, based on the principle 'to let no one alone during the crisis'. Solidarity kitchens, shelters for the homeless and solidarity clinics are being organized around the country.

The Social Solidarity Clinics are designed to protect those who are excluded from any form of health insurance scheme. These have spread to different parts of the country, and provide primary-care services. These clinics are managed and sustained collectively by health workers, activists and patients (Solidarity 4 All 2013; Hellenext 2012).

The very process of setting up solidarity clinics is throwing up new lessons for the principles of solidarity, democratic participation and self-organizing. For example, one of the first solidarity clinics set up in Thessaloniki began as a neighbourhood solidarity action to support immigrant workers (Fotiadis 2013). Subsequently the assembly of the solidarity activists decided to keep working together and formed a Social Solidarity Clinic that would respond to the healthcare needs of both immigrants and the local population. The clinic is supported by a wide network of volunteer health workers, and by a parallel movement that collects medicines to be distributed free of cost, and involves a network of health workers, workers' unions, pharmacists and patients.

The solidarity clinics are not organized around a 'charity model' and do not seek to replace necessary public health services. Instead they combine solidarity and mobilization of both health workers and patients against the austerity measures being imposed in Greece. Patients are sensitized to understand that they are not mere passive users of healthcare services but are partners in the movement for the right to health. The collectives that run the solidarity clinics periodically organize visible actions demanding comprehensive healthcare services and articulate the acute healthcare needs of the people (Nissiotis 2014).

The Social Solidarity Clinics incorporate a new vision regarding the organization of healthcare services. Patients and health workers work together in open assemblies and in a non-hierarchical fashion to collectively decide how best to run and expand the solidarity clinics and the solidarity movement for the right to health. The solidarity clinics are fast becoming the backbone of the movement for health as a social right.

While the clinics provide healthcare to people who are most in need, they have also stimulated ideological discussions about the development of a new paradigm for popular movements and their relationships with progressive political parties and organizations. There are several experiences of the social solidarity clinics that could have implications for the building of progressive movements in Europe. These clinics have grown out of a spontaneous upsurge, have been sustained as a continuing grassroots activity, and are managed exclusively by general assemblies.

The Social Solidarity Clinics and the growing movement around them share common characteristics with other 'anti-austerity' movements in Greece. The massive movement against the privatization of water companies was founded on a similar perspective, and is now organizing a plebiscite against water privatization. Other similar groupings include movements against extractive industries, unfair taxation (the 'no pay' movement) and evictions.

## Transnational solidarity and mobilization

Europe is also seeing the rise of transnational solidarity and political actions. A characteristic that is common to many of these actions is that they are being organized by networks of community groups, with little or no connections with traditional political parties and trade unions. At the same time, more structured initiatives by traditional political formations are also visible.

In December 2013 the Spanish government declared abortion to be illegal except in the case of rape or when there's a risk to the physical and mental health of the mother. While protests mount in Spain, solidarity actions were organized all over Europe in front of Spanish embassies, on 1 February 2014, and again on 8 March on the occasion of International Women's Day. The European network against privatization and commercialization of health and social protection met in Brussels in early February 2014, to demonstrate against the widespread dismantling of public health and welfare systems across Europe. With the aim of influencing candidates before the European elections scheduled for May 2014, a week of action was organized around World Health Day on 7 April.

## The movement against 'Unnecessary Imposed Mega Projects'

An important issue that is linking national struggles in Europe is the movement against 'Unnecessary Imposed Mega Projects' (UIMPs). It was scheduled to organize its fourth international forum in Roşia Montană (Romania) in May 2014. The movement brings together diverse groups such as those in Susa Valley (Italy) fighting against a high-speed train project, in Notre-Dame-des-Landes (France) struggling against the construction of a new airport in Nantes, in Stuttgart struggling against the new underground railway station, the UK-based 'Stop H2S' movement against the proposed ultra-high-speed railway line, and the Romanian anti-mining movement. March 22 2014 was observed as a day of action in many countries in solidarity with the endangered communities of Notre-Dame-des-Landes, the Susa Valley and Halkidiki (Greece) (the latter struggling against a gold-mining project; see Chapter E7). The struggles against UIMPs incorporate a broader critique of the current policies of the EU, and a call for a different Europe which prioritizes well-being, freedom, solidarity, justice and democracy rather than finance, markets and competition.

---

### Box E6.3  Statement against UIMPs

The movement against UIMPs issued the following statement before the 2014 European elections:

UIMPs are Crimes against Humanity, which have caused immeasurable losses to tens of millions of people and destroyed entire ecosystems.

These crimes are committed by our rulers who are slaves of the laissez-faire ideology of the free market and unhindered competition, by financial institutions and bankers obsessed with global hegemony and by entrepreneurs compulsively seeking to gain the most profit at any cost. … Mega Projects represent a new means to plunder and colonise from within. These projects always keep the persons affected outside of the decision-making process. … UIMPs produce ecological, socio-economic and human disasters; they cause the destruction of natural areas and farmlands, of artistic and cultural treasures; they contribute to producing noxious and degenerative effects and environmental pollution with grave consequences for inhabitants. … These initiatives generate enormous debt, they do not create employment, they concentrate wealth in the hands of the ruling elite, they impoverish society, they permit global predators to tighten their control of the world and they cause irreversible damage to ecosystems. (FAUIMP4 n.d.)

### Struggles against extractive industries

The diverse struggles against extractive industries are being supported by international mobilizations, across Europe, and in other parts of the world. The solidarity actions recognize that these ecologically and socially unsustainable mining projects are being promoted, across the world, by very similar strategies (false economic justification, intimidation and criminalization of protest movements) and often by the same companies (including a number of Canadian companies) (see Chapter C6). For example, communities in Roşia Montană (Romania) face loss of livelihoods and environmental degradation, as a consequence of the activities of the biggest gold-mining project in Europe, run by the Canadian company Gabriel Resources. Promoted through corrupt means, intimidation and repression, the project is fraudulently presented by the company and the Romanian government as a tool for growth and employment. The movement against the project, initiated in 2000, has snowballed into the biggest social and environmental struggle against the Romanian government's neoliberal policies (ibid.). Communities in Bulgaria, Greece (Halkidiki) and Turkey (Bergama) are fighting similar battles (Franco and Norras 2013; Coban 2004).

### The struggle against the Transatlantic Trade and Investment Partnership (TTIP)

Another terrain of struggle at a pan-European level is the growing movement against a free trade agreement between the EU and the United States, the Transatlantic Trade and Investment Partnership (TTIP) (see Box E6.4).

**Box E6.4 What is TTIP?**

TTIP is designed to create the world's largest free-trading bloc. The stated aim of the TTIP is to increase trade between the EU and the USA, not just in goods, but also in services and procurement, by harmonizing existing regulations on international commerce, customs tariffs and non-tariff standards (most notably uniform environmental, health and social security standards). While TTIP is ostensibly about promoting growth and job creation, the evidence advanced for this is weak. On the basis of industry-funded research, a 1 per cent increase in GDP growth has been promised together with the creation of 'hundreds of thousands of jobs'. However, the European Commission's own impact assessment concluded that a growth rate of 0.1 per cent would constitute a more realistic expectation. On the other hand, the potential socio-economic and environmental risks could be catastrophic. The increased competition associated with the liberalization of trade could trigger economic restructuring that leads to job losses. Generally, US laws and regulations offer significantly less protection to citizens than in Europe and the proposed harmonization of legislation would greatly undermine the level of social protection still available in Europe. The TTIP seeks to harmonize rules and regulations in almost every economic and social sphere – ranging from agriculture to financial services, investment, social services such as healthcare, intellectual property rights (IPR), labour rights, etc. In other words the TTIP has the potential to radically change the already crumbling edifice of the welfare state in Europe.

As is the case with all free trade agreements, negotiations on the TTIP are being conducted in secret. The negotiated text is not shared with elected representatives of member-state parliaments or with civil society groups (apart from when leaked documents become available); on the other hand, the corporate sector has been invited to make many formal submissions. If the treaty is signed, the European Council, together with the European Parliament (and the Congress for the USA), can only approve or reject the final text, without making any amendments (European Network 2014; Bizzarri 2013).

In late 2013 and early 2014, demonstrations against the agreement were held in a number of cities, including in Brussels and Rome (during the visit of President Obama). Platforms against TTIP are being created, both within existing movements and as new networks. In Italy, a national campaign against TTIP was launched in February 2014. In Belgium, the Alliance D19-20 is trying to bring together trade unions and grassroots organizations in the struggle against the agreement. In December 2013, the European district in Brussels (encompassing the headquarters of the European Commission, the European Parliament and the Council of Ministers) was successfully blocked by several hundreds of protesters (Alliance D19-20 n.d.).

## Note

1 See Federación de Asociaciones para la Defensa de la Sanidad Pública (n.d.), www. fadsp.org; Dempeus per la Salut Pública (n.d.), dempeusperlasalut.wordpress.com; Centre d'Anàlisis i Programes Sanitaris (n.d.), www. caps.cat; A las Barricadas (n.d.), www.alasbar-ricadas.org; Cooperativa Integral Catalana (n.d.), cooperativa.cat/en/; and cooperativa. ecoxarxes.cat, accessed 6 May 2014.

## References

ACW (2008) *Medisch Dossier*, Welzijnszorg.
Alliance D19-20 (n.d.) www.d19-20.be/en, accessed 6 May 2014.
Bizzarri, K. (2013) *A Brave New Transatlantic Partnership: The proposed EU–US Transatlantic Trade and Investment Partnership (TTIP/TAFTA), and its Socio-Economic & Environmental Consequences*, Brussels: Seattle To Brussels Network (S2B), October, www.s2bnetwork.org/fileadmin/dateien/downloads/Brave_New_Atlantic_Partnership.pdf, accessed 6 May 2014.
Blockupy (n.d.) blockupy.org/en/, accessed 6 May 2014.
Coban, A. (2004) 'Community-based ecological resistance: the Bergama movement in Turkey', *Environmental Politics*, 13(2): 438–60, kentcevre.politics.ankara.edu.tr/Coban EnvPolitics04.pdf, accessed 6 May 2014.
Doctors for the People (n.d.) www.gvhv-mplp. be, accessed 6 May 2014.
European Network (European Network against Privatization and Commercialization of Health and Social Protection) (2014) *Health and Social Protection Are Not for Sale!: Manifesto of the European Network against Privatization and Commercialization of Health and Social Protection*, Brussels, 7 February, www.sante-solidarite.be/sites/default/files/manifest_english.pdf, accessed 6 May 2014.
FAUIMP4 (The 4th Forum Against Unnecessary Imposed Mega Projects) (n.d.) rosiamon-tana.org/fauimp4/, accessed 6 May 2014.
Fotiadis A. (2013) 'Greece: what lies ahead?',

Open Society Foundation, 16 December, www.opensocietyfoundations.org/voices/greece-what-lies-ahead, accessed 6 May 2014.
Franco, J. and S. M. Norras (2013) *Land Concentration, Land Grabbing and People's Struggles in Europe*, Transnational Institute (TNI) for European Coordination, Via Campesina and Hands off the Land network, June, www. tni.org/sites/www.tni.org/files/download/land_in_europe-jun2013.pdf, accessed 6 May 2014.
Hellenext (2012) '"We're all in this together": volunteers respond to Greek crisis with a free clinic', Reinventing Greece Media Project, 29 March.
Keep Our NHS Public (n.d.) www.keepournhs public.com/index.php, accessed 6 May 2014.
Keep Talking Greece (2014) 'Doctors protest as Greek Health Minister closes down Primary Health Care units for one month', 17 February, www.keeptalkinggreece. com/2014/02/17/doctors-protest-as-greek-health-minister-closes-down-primary-health-care-units-for-one-month/, accessed 6 May 2014.
Kondilis, E., C. Bodini, P. de Vos et al. (2013) 'Fiscal policies in Europe in the wake of the economic crisis: implications for health and healthcare access', Background paper for *The Lancet*, University of Oslo Commission on Global Governance for Health, www. med.uio.no/helsam/english/research/global-governance-health/background-papers/fiscal-policies-eu.pdf, accessed 6 May 2014.
Lancet (2012) 'A new UK political party to fight for the NHS', *The Lancet*, 380(9856): 1792.
Marchas de la Dignidad (Marchas de la Dignidad 22 de Marzo – Grupo Madrid) (n.d.) marchasdeladignidadmadrid.wordpress. com/, accessed 6 May 2014.
Marcos, J. (2014) 'Madrid abruptly cancels plans to outsource management at public hospitals', *El País*, 27 January,

elpais.com/elpais/2014/01/27/ineng-lish/1390844787_448815.html, accessed 6 May 2014.

MDF (Movimento per la Decrescita Felice) (2013) 'Decrescite, sostenibilita e salute – resoconto e video', Rome, 29 October, decrescitafelice.it/2013/10/decrescita-sostenibilita-e-salute-diretta-streaming/, accessed 6 May 2014.

Nissiotis, G. (2014) 'Protesters hold a banner reading in Greek "resist to death", during protest ...', 30 January, news.yahoo.com/photos/protesters-hold-banner-reading-greek-quot-resist-death-photo-160357602.html, accessed 6 May 2014.

Quotidiano Sanita (2012) '"Diritto alla cura, diritto a curare": la manifestazione nazionale del 27 ottobre', Gli Speciali, www.quotidianosanita.it/eventi.php?evento_id=11461, accessed 6 May 2014.

Riparte il Futuro (n.d.) *Difendiamo il bene più prezioso: la nostra salute*, www.riparteilfuturo.it/sanita/, accessed 6 May 2014.

RIZIV-NIHDI (2008) *Monitoring of Reimbursement Significant Expenses Semi-annual Report 2008*, www.riziv.fgov.be/drug/all/drugs/statistics-scientific-information/report/pdf/morse200802.pdf, accessed 6 May 2014.

— (n.d.) *Farmaceutische kengetallen: 1997– 2007*, www.riziv.fgov.be/drug/nl/statistics-scientific-information/pharmanet/

pharmaceutical-tables/index.htm, accessed 6 May 2014.

Ruelens, E. (2013) 'Van consultatie tot empowerment. Hoe kan de huisarts arbeidsrisico's aanpakken?', ICHO (Interuniversitair Centrum voor Huisartsen Opleiding), Ghent.

Salviamo il nostro SSN (n.d.) www.salviamo-ssn.it/pagine/751/it/salviamo-ssn, accessed 6 May 2014.

Santé & Solidarité (Plate-forme d'action Santé & Solidarité) (n.d.) www.sante-solidarite.be, accessed 6 May 2014.

Soares, M. (2012) 'Medicos dizem ter feito a maior manifestação de sempre', *Publico*, 11 July, www.publico.pt/sociedade/noticia/sindicatos-esperam-quatro-mil-medicos-na-manifestacao-1554444, accessed 6 May 2014.

Solidarity 4 All (2013) *Solidarity is People's Power: Towards an International Campaign of Solidarity to the Greek People*, Athens, March, www.solidarity4all.gr/files/aggliko.pdf, accessed 6 May 2014.

Van Bever, K. (2008) *Dokter in Overall*, Antwerpen-Berchem: EPO.

Van Bever, K., K. Vangronsveld, H. de Witte et al. (n.d.) 'Hoe gezond zijn onze oudere werknemers?'

Washington Post (2012) 'Thousands protest austerity, proposed sell-offs of parts of Spain's national healthcare', 9 December.

### Background

In December 2003, the assets of the Cassandra Mines (in north-east Halkidiki, Greece) and mining concessions covering 317 square kilometres of public forest were transferred to the Greek state for 11 million euros. They were sold the same day to Hellas Gold S.A. for the same price without prior economic assessment of the assets and without an open tender being floated.[1] Eldorado Gold Corporation (based in Vancouver, Canada) owns 95 per cent of the assets of Hellas Gold S.A. The market capitalization value of Eldorado Gold is 2.3 billion euros, and the value of the minerals in Halkidiki is estimated to be 15.5 billion euros (over seven times the current assets of Eldorado Gold). Eldorado Gold has full ownership of the minerals in the concessions granted and there are no arrangements through which the government can claim royalties (Triantafyllidis 2012).

The holdings of Hellas Gold S.A. include an existing mine, a new open-pit and underground mine in Skouries, an underground mine in Olympiada, an 8.5-kilometre underground tunnel for the transport of ore, a copper-gold metallurgy plant, a sulphuric acid plant, four tailing disposal and storage sites, an industrial port, and rights to the exploration of fourteen other potential mining areas (HELLAS GOLD S.A. – ENVECO S.A. 2010). In July 2011 the Greek state approved the plan for mining in the area after an Environmental Impact Assessment (EIA). The assessment is supposed to have included public consultations, but the government made a complete mockery of the process to legitimize its sale of the mining concessions to Hellas Gold S.A. (Technical Chamber of Greece 2011).

### Impacts

Several independent studies have shown that the proposed mining project exceeds the carrying capacity of the area. The impacts and consequences will be significant and irreversible both on the environment and on the local economy, which is based on agriculture and tourism.[2]

The Kakkavos mountain supplies water to the entire region of north-east Halkidiki (Triantafyllidis 2012) and the proposed mining activity will directly and irreversibly affect the region's water resources. Ore dust will pour huge amounts of toxic pollutants into the region's environment. It has been estimated that full-scale mining operations will throw up 4.324 tonnes of ore dust every

**Image E7.1** Protesters facing tear-gas shells from police in Halkidiki (Hellenic Mining Watch)

hour (HELLAS GOLD S.A. – ENVECO S.A. 2010). The dust will have high levels of sulphur compounds of heavy metals, such as antimony, arsenic, barium, cadmium, chromium, copper, iron, manganese, nickel, lead, mercury, zinc, etc. The soil will be contaminated with heavy metals and the mining activity will cause the topsoil to dry up over a radius of several kilometres from the open pit. Severe soil erosion is expected to occur, leading subsequently to catastrophic floods (Panagiotopoulos 2012).

The mining activity poses serious risks for workers, residents and visitors to the region. Workers in gold mines are known to have a lower life expectancy. They often suffer from many kinds of cancer (trachea and bronchi, lung, stomach and liver), pulmonary tuberculosis, silicosis, pleural diseases, hearing loss, increased prevalence of bacterial and viral infections, diseases of the blood, skin and musculoskeletal system. The presence of heavy metals, even at very low concentrations, increases the risks of a number of conditions such as anaemia, hypertension, central nervous system disorders (especially in children), a range of respiratory disorders, renal failure, gastroenteritis, kidney disease, liver damage, cancer, hepatitis and liver cirrhosis (Benos A 2012).

### Genesis of a popular struggle

The sale of the mining concessions to Hellas Gold S.A. is a transfer of public assets for the accumulation of private profits. In the process, extremely serious and wide-ranging environmental impacts have been transferred on to local communities. The government of Greece has imposed a decision that will not lead to any economic benefit to the country or the people in the region. At the same time, the government's decision condemns the region to

**Image E7.2** March in Thessaloniki, Greece, against the mining project in Halkidiki (Alexis Benos)

environmental degradation and destruction. A clear realization of these issues has led to the development of a popular and sustained struggle in the region against the mining contract.

To take forward the struggle against the mining contract, several scientific studies have been commissioned by local community organizations, which rebut the hollow claims made by the government. Lawsuits have been filed at the Council of State (Greece's Supreme Administrative Court) challenging the state's 2011 EIA approval. The struggle has led to mass mobilization of the people in the area and campaigns are being organized to inform people about the impending threats posed by the mining company. Several demonstrations have taken place in the cities of the regions and in the habitations, higher up in the mountains.

The Greek government continues to disregard the voices of communities struggling against the project. After initially ignoring the growing protests, the government has now begun a disinformation campaign, claiming that the struggle is being led by a small minority of people in the region. The government has also dubbed the struggle as 'anti-development' and as being led by 'a terrorist organization'. State repression and police violence have escalated rapidly since March 2012.[3] The popular struggle of Halkidiki has been attacked repeatedly, and the government has tried various methods to discredit and criminalize the struggle. Unfortunately, a significant section of the mainstream Greek media has chosen to side with the government's position.

A 2012 Reuters article entitled 'Greece's triangle of power' draws attention to the 'interplay between politics, big business and powerful media owners' (Grey and Kyriakidou 2012). The attitude of the mainstream media in Greece is in sharp contrast to the response by significant sections of the international media. The struggle against the mining contract in Halkidiki has received wide coverage in the *New York Times*, *Le Monde*, Associated Press, *France2*, *Weiner Zeitung*, *El País*, ARD, the *New Statesman*, Inter Press Service, the *Globe and Mail* and the *Independent*.

In 2012, three big demonstrations in the Kakkavos mountain (in August, September and October[4]) were countered by the police with extreme violence. The police used tear gas and shot rubber bullets at the protesters, beat up and injured several of them, and arrested many others (Amnesty International 2012). After the demonstration in August, the special police forces invaded the village of Ierissos and indiscriminately attacked people (including children, the elderly, pregnant women and even tourists).

Since February 2013, Halkidiki has become the target of what can only be described as a 'police state'. The residents of the area face intimidation and repeated violation of civil, political and human rights. Instances abound of arbitrary arrests of large numbers of people (including young students), disappearances of citizens, and several hours of interrogation of those arrested.

In March 2013, more than two hundred riot policemen invaded the village of Ierissos. The police resorted to unjustified and excessive use of force, made extensive use of chemicals (including in a schoolyard filled with students) and

**Image E7.3** Popular mobilization in Greece against the mining project in Halkidiki (Hellenic Mining Watch)

even injured an eleven-month-old baby. A few days later, at 3 a.m., armoured special police forces invaded the homes of two residents by forcibly breaking into their houses. They were arrested after sustained interrogation. Three months later, two more residents were imprisoned and all four were kept in prison for periods ranging from four to six months.

The movement in Halkidiki includes peaceful people who have diverse ideologies. The only 'weapons' they use are scientific evidence, objective information, social action and solidarity. They are supported by collectives, institutions, organizations, parliamentary and non-parliamentary parties, political institutions, Canadian politicians and European social and political organizations. The strength of the movement is manifest in the participation of thousands of people in demonstrations and other public activities.

Women are playing a central role in this social struggle. They have left behind their 'traditional' roles, and are participating in all facets of this struggle. In their open letter[5] they introduce themselves as follows:

We are the great-grandmothers who experienced the occupation during World War II and decided – never again fascism. We are the grandmothers who experienced civil war and declared – never again war.

We are the mothers who saw our children becoming immigrants and declared – never again racism. We are the daughters who experienced the dictatorship and declared – never again authoritarian regimes.

We are the granddaughters who have never before experienced occupation, civil war, immigration or dictatorship and are now experiencing all of them simultaneously. We are the great granddaughters who dream, who hope, who demand a better future.

They also state:

They attacked us with tear gas and chemicals, they chased after us, they beat us, they arrested us, they interrogated us, they invaded our homes and schools. They accused us of not respecting the laws. They called us uneducated, uninformed and disobedient women, liars and even terrorists! We endured though all this. Besides, we brought our children into this world with untold pain and we are raising them with incredible effort. We will not be intimidated by terrorizing practices.

The society in Halkidiki was traditionally conservative, but the threat of the mining project has radicalized it. People have learned to organize without 'leaders'. They have learned to discuss, to listen, to understand and then to synthesize the opinions of many different people. They now understand the deeply political nature of the present conflict with the company and the government and they now also understand the need to take positions on all social issues. Halkidiki's movement states:

Our movement could only be against all social and political structures that are based on authoritarian and racist attitudes. We are opposed to segregation and discrimination of people based on origin, sex, skin colour, religious beliefs, sexual orientation or political ideology. The authoritarian and racist attitudes – especially in these difficult times experienced by our societies – tend to perpetuate a vicious cycle of violence. A cycle of violence that we strive to crack.

The experiences of their struggle have led people to start believing that perhaps the natural state of humans is not selfishness, but cooperation and solidarity. They now question the economy that is based on over-consumption and over-exploitation of nature. The people of Halkidiki strive for the right to live with dignity. They are fighting against the rape of nature, justice and human rights. They are struggling for the right to participate in the decision-making processes. They strive to keep alive a creative dialogue of many different voices.

## Notes

1 Law N 3220/2004, *Official Government Gazette*, 15A/28.01.2004 (in Greek).

2 'Impacts of gold mining in Halkidiki', soshalkidiki.files.wordpress.com/2012/11/impacts-of-gold-mining.pdf.

3 See video: www.youtube.com/watch?v=AU1Xc3cv3as.

4 See video: www.youtube.com/watch?v=4RIbWbVt4Bg&list=UUoKjW4kyoLEVTMtEIIvutBQ&index=55.

5 soshalkidiki.files.wordpress.com/2013/04/women_en.pdf.

## References

Amnesty International (2012) 'Policing demonstrations in the European Union', www.amnesty.org/pt-br/library/asset/EUR01/022/2012/en/1e06df7d-6878-40e0-8e82-d07605e9a6e9/euro10222012en.pdf accessed, 23 March 2014.

Benos, A. (2012) *The impacts on health from large scale mining activities such as gold mining*, soshalkidiki.files.wordpress.com/2012/11/impacts-of-gold-mining.pdf, accessed 2 May 2014.

Grey, S. and D. Kyriakidou (2012) 'Greece's triangle of power', Reuters, www.reuters.com/article/2012/12/17/us-greece-media-idUSBRE8BG0CF20121217, accessed 23 April 2014.

HELLAS GOLD S.A. – ENVECO S.A. (2010) *Environmental Impact Assessment of the project 'Mining-Metallurgical plants of Cassandra's mines' by the Company 'HELLAS GOLD S.A.' in Halkidiki* (in Greek).

Panagiotopoulos, K. (2012) *Mining activity in the NE Halkidiki: adverse effects on soils, crops, livestock and agriculture* (in Greek).

Technical Chamber of Greece (2011) *Views of TEE/EKM for the project 'Mining – Metallurgical Cassandra Mines plants of the Company HELLAS GOLD S.A.'*, Department of Central Macedonia, Technical Chamber of Greece (in Greek).

Triantafyllidis, G. (2012) *Appearances of gold in Northern Greece and production by extraction of the rock: the fate of 'interchangeable metal' on water ecosystems* (in Greek).

The Right to Food (RTF) campaign in India has been mobilizing and advocating on hunger, malnutrition and food-related issues in the country for the last ten years. The RTF campaign's foundation statement asserts that it is 'an informal network of organisations and individuals committed to the realisation of the right to food in India' (RTFC n.d.). Over these years the RTF campaign has expanded into a wide network with members across the country representing different groups, including agricultural workers' unions, women's rights groups, Dalit rights groups, single women's networks, child rights organizations, those working with construction workers, migrant workers and homeless populations, and so on. These varied groups have come together in agreement with the campaign's belief that 'everyone has a fundamental right to be free from hunger and that the primary responsibility for guaranteeing basic entitlements rests with the state' (ibid.). The campaign has a small secretariat for coordination, a steering committee which takes decisions between conventions, while the agenda for the campaign is set in a National Convention that is open to all those who consider themselves members to attend.

### Judicial pressure and popular mobilization

The RTF campaign has its origins in a public interest litigation (PIL) filed in the Supreme Court in April 2001 by the People's Union for Civil Liberties, Rajasthan. The petition demanded that the country's gigantic food stocks should be used without delay to protect people from hunger and starvation (PUCL 2001; Drèze 2002; Guha-Khasnobis and Vivek 2006; Birchfield and Corsi 2010) (see also Chapter C3 on food sovereignty in India). Popularly known as the 'Right to Food case', this is now one of the longest-running mandamuses in the world. More than fifty orders have been passed, including some very significant ones such as universalization of school midday meals and the supplementary nutrition programme for children under six years, pregnant and lactating mothers and adolescent girls (RTFC 2008a). While some of these orders were path-breaking in their content, it was soon realized that for them to actually translate into action on the ground required pressure from the people. Different groups began to mobilize around the Supreme Court orders and came together to form the Right to Food campaign. Very soon, the scope expanded beyond the Supreme Court case towards building a larger public campaign for the right to food (Drèze 2002).

Through discussions and debates within its various constituencies the

**Image E8.1** March organized in 2012 by the Right to Food campaign in Sarguja, India (Right to Food campaign)

campaign began to understand the linkages between questions of access to resources and livelihoods and the right to food. The campaign argues that while demanding greater entitlements from the state, struggles have to be mounted to ensure that the compulsions of the present neoliberal economic order do not succeed in taking people away from what they have had access to over centuries – access to resources such as forests, land and water (RTFC 2008b, 2010, 2014). There needs to be constant pressure and mobilization for a more equitable model of development in which economic growth is not based on exploitation but rather creates equal opportunities for all.

At the same time, in the context of the general onslaught on public services and the role of the state in welfare provision, it is necessary to continuously fight for what is due to the people even if it provides only temporary reprieve. The campaign has therefore focused on bringing in and strengthening legislation and schemes such as the National Rural Employment Guarantee Act (NREGA), the Integrated Child Development Services (ICDS), the Midday Meals (MDM) scheme and the Public Distribution System (PDS) (Khera 2013), while at the same time working in solidarity with movements related to land rights, opposing coercive displacement, forest rights, fighting social exclusion and so on (RTFC 2009).

The activities of the Right to Food campaign involve developing resource material for grassroots organizations in the form of pamphlets, primers, booklets; generating 'evidence' from the field on the status of hunger, starvation and implementation of government schemes; mobilizing people from across the country and leading public action in the form of protest demonstrations, rallies, public hearings, sit-ins (*dharnas*); advocating with media, academics, politicians and parliamentarians on policies and legislation, and so on.[1]

### National legislation on food security

In the last four years (2009 onwards) the primary agenda on which the Right to Food campaign has focused is the National Food Security Act (NFSA). The Congress party in its election manifesto in 2009 promised to bring in a Food Security Act (Indian National Congress 2009). Once the government was formed under its leadership, it also declared this to be one of its priorities.[2] In the following four years there was intense debate on what such an Act should contain. The RTF campaign also actively worked to bring pressure on the government to introduce a Bill that was comprehensive in its approach. The Act that was finally passed was highly inadequate; however, it was still seen to be a step forward in the struggle for right to food (RTFC 2013; Aggarwal and Mander 2013). Some of the major challenges faced by social movements working with a rights-based approach in the context of globalization, privatization and liberalization can be highlighted from this experience.

While the government and all political parties took a narrow view of food security, reducing it merely to distribution of subsidized foodgrains to the poor (Sinha 2014), the campaign argued that one must take a more comprehensive approach, including issues of agricultural production, access to resources,

**Image E8.2** People's forum organized by the RTF campaign in New Delhi (Right to Food campaign)

livelihoods, minimum wages and so on (RTFC 2009). There was vibrant discussion within the campaign on whether it is possible to have a single piece of legislation which addressed these broad structural issues or whether the opportunity given by the promise of a Food Security Act should tactically be utilized to gain as much as possible within the framework of entitlements through public programmes.

The Right to Food campaign then drafted its own version of the Act. The draft was called the 'Food Entitlements Act' and not the 'Food Security Act' because it was believed that food security was a broader concept, as mentioned above. The campaign's draft demanded a decentralized procurement mechanism, a universal and expanded public distribution system including cereals, pulses, millets and oil, special provisions for vulnerable groups such as feeding programmes for children, social security pensions for the aged and disabled, portability of entitlements for migrants and so on. The draft also listed broad principles related to coercive land acquisition, protecting small and marginal farmers, a moratorium on GM crops, food production and availability and so on (RTFC 2009).

## A minimalist approach to food security

All along, the friction between this comprehensive approach and the minimalistic framework set by the government has remained. Even though the RTF campaign and allied civil society networks talked about linking production, procurement and distribution issues, the debate in policy circles and the media was largely restricted to whether the Public Distribution System (PDS) should be universal or not and what the extent of coverage should be. This was also an important debate needing serious engagement.

On the other hand there was an onslaught from the right-wing media against the idea of the Food Security Act, saying that it would destroy the economy by being a burden on the fiscal deficit and distorting the food market. Many influential voices, even from within the government, were opposed to the PDS itself and proposed that it be dismantled and replaced by direct cash transfer (Dutta 2012; Mehrotra 2011; Kotwal et al. 2011). In this context, the campaign was forced to defend the PDS and its role, the need for state intervention on hunger and malnutrition, even while there were no takers for the entire comprehensive approach that was laid out in the campaign draft.

Therefore, in some ways the boundaries of the debate were already set. Even though the campaign tried to expand these boundaries, in hindsight it could be said that it was not very successful in doing so. While there is no doubt that the NFSA has great potential to improve the PDS and therefore access to food for a large majority of people in some of the poorest states in the country, it remains to be seen how effective the implementation will actually be. On the other hand, there is the criticism that such legislation serves only to legitimize a fundamentally anti-poor state which gets away with yielding very little. Parallels of similar tensions can be drawn with other socio-economic rights as well. Movements working on 'health for all' are forced to engage with 'Universal Health Coverage', those working on 'education for all' have to accept some access to education before talking about a 'common school system', and so on. Campaigns and social movements need to continue reflecting on how most effectively to negotiate with the system for small changes in such a manner that they take us towards the long-term goal rather than dilute the vision itself. This also raises basic questions on the relation between civil society and the state and whether civil society must restrict itself to a confrontational approach or be willing to engage in dialogue, and the issues that arise once dialogue begins to become an option.

### Building solidarity across different movements

A related issue is one of the mobilization capacity of campaigns such as the Right to Food campaign. While many of the groups that are part of the campaign work directly with thousands of people, some also being membership based, demonstrating this strength in the form of bringing all the people together in one place is a challenge. Considering that most of the time the people who are part of these organizations are also those who belong to some of the most marginalized social and economic communities, logistics and funding for mobilization become a serious restriction.

The Right to Food campaign's secretariat is run on the basis of individual donations received only in rupees and all events are also financed either by

**Image E8.3** Street play in New Delhi in support of the RTF campaign (Right to Food campaign)

individual donations or some support from participating organizations for provision of food, lodging and so on (RTFC 2008b). Funds from donor agencies are not accepted. This funding policy has been important in ensuring that the campaign's positions are formed on the basis of the beliefs of the constituents and not under pressure from any external considerations. It has also helped in maintaining the credibility of the campaign.

Secondly, with a predominantly corporate-influenced media and an apathetic middle class, it has been demonstrated that a large number of people on the streets protesting against inflation or demanding land rights make headlines only for the traffic jams caused, with no immediate response from the state. Therefore while a protest demonstration with over five thousand participants led by the Right to Food campaign does not get any attention, neither does one with over 50,000 participants led by the main trade unions (Srinivasan 2011). This is not to argue that there is no meaning in popular mobilization of this sort, but that this is a challenge that movements have to grapple with. Strategies for communicating the need for structural change, albeit incremental, not just to politicians and policy-makers but also to the media and the general public at large need to be developed.

In the RTF campaign's experience one issue that managed to get the sympathy of the non-poor was that of defining the poverty line. The absurdity of a poverty line as low as 32 Rupees (half of a US$) per person per day in urban areas, at a time of high inflation which was affecting people across classes, was something that everyone took notice of. On this issue, the street action by the campaign found widespread support from the media and the general public at large, with the government being forced to make a statement that poverty lines will be revisited.[3] However, the demand for a universal PDS on the basis that one of the reasons targeted schemes fail is precisely because they are based on such ad hoc criteria, failed to resonate with the people as much.

In relation to the NFSA as well it can be argued that the campaign to some extent managed to influence the Act. Although the final Act is nowhere close to what the campaign had demanded, in comparison with the government's own initial drafts, which did nothing but legislate for the PDS in its current form, the NFSA includes an expanded PDS, delinks it from the poverty line, includes universal maternity entitlements, nutrition for children and a framework for grievance redressal (Government of India 2013). This expansion was possible because of multiple factors, with the RTF campaign also playing a role. The challenge now for the campaign is to move on and consolidate so that the gains made so far fructify on the ground, and also that the larger vision is not lost and the fight for that continues.

In sum, the RTF campaign's experience highlights the strengths of a loose network of organizations and individuals coming together on one issue and at the same time the difficulties in engaging with the state and the public at large on structural causes.

## Notes

1 See the website of the Right to Food campaign, www.righttofoodcampaign.in, for details on the various activities of the campaign.

2 See the president's speech to the parliament, pratihtmlbhapatil.nic.in/sp040609.

3 See www.righttofoodcampaign.in/below-poverty-line/articles for a collection of articles in the media on this issue.

## References

Aggarwal, A. and H. Mander (2013) 'Abandoning the right to food', *Economic and Political Weekly*, XLVIII(8).

Birchfield, L. and J. Corsi (2010) 'Between starvation and globalization: realizing the right to food in India', *Michigan Journal of International Law*, 31(691): 691–764.

Drèze, J. (2002) *The Right to Food: From Courts to the Streets*, www.righttofoodindia. org/links/articles_home.html, accessed 25 March 2014.

Dutta, A. (2012) 'Direct cash transfer will be a game changer, says Kaushik Basu', *The Hindu*, 20 December, www.thehindu.com/todays-paper/tp-national/tp-otherstates/direct-cash-transfer-will-be-a-game-changer-says-kaushik-basu/article4220188.ece, accessed 25 March 2014.

Government of India (2013) *National Food Security Act*, New Delhi: Government of India.

Guha-Khasnobis, B. and S. Vivek (2006) 'Rights-based approach to development: lessons from the Right to Food novement in India', WIDER Research Paper no. 2006/X, Helsinki.

Indian National Congress (2009) *Lok Sabha Elections 2009 – Manifesto of the Indian National Congress*, incmanifesto.a-i.in/manifesto09-eng.pdf, accessed 25 March 2014.

Khera, R. (2013) 'Democratic politics and legal rights: employment guarantee and food security in India', IEG Working Paper no. 327, New Delhi.

Kotwal, A., B. Ramaswami and M. Murugkar (2011) 'PDS forever?', *Economic and Political Weekly*, XLVI(21).

Mehrotra, S. (2011) 'Introducing Conditional Cash Transfers (CCTs) in India: a proposal for five CCTs', IAMR Occasional Paper

no. 2/201, New Delhi: Planning Commission, Government of India.

PUCL (2001) *PUCL v. Union of India & Ors – Initial Petition*, www.righttofoodindia.org/case/petition.html, accessed 25 March 2014.

RTFC (2008a) *Supreme Court Orders on the Right to Food: A Tool for Action*, New Delhi: Right to Food Campaign Secretariat.

— (2008b) *Right to Food Campaign: Collective Statement*, www.righttofoodindia.org/data/rtf_campaign_collective_statement09.pdf, accessed 25 March 2014.

— (2009) *Food Entitlements Act, 2009 – Draft of 12th September 2009*, www.righttofoodindia.org/data/rtf_act_draft_charter_sept09.pdf, accessed 25 March 2014.

— (2010) *Fourth National Convention on Right to Food and Work – Rourkela: Resolutions*, www.righttofoodindia.org/data/summary_resolutions_fourth_national_convention_right_to_food_act, accessed 25 March 2014.

— (2012) *Right to Food Campaign's Critique of the National Food Security Bill 2011*, www.righttofoodindia.org/data/right_to_food_act_data/events/March_2012_general_note_final_18_february_2012.pdf, accessed 25 March 2014.

— (2013) *Right to Food Campaign rejects the National Food Security Bill cleared by the Cabinet*, www.im4change.org/latest-news-updates/right-to-food-campaign-rejects-the-national-food-security-bill-cleared-by-the-cabinet-20034.html, accessed 25 March 2014.

— (2014) *Ahmedabad Declaration*, Declaration issued at the end of the National Right to Food and Work Convention, Sanand, Ahmedabad, 1–3 March 2014.

— (n.d.) *Foundation Statement*, www.righttofoodindia.org/foundation.html, accessed 25 March 2014.

Sinha, D. (2014) 'Demanding a comprehensive food security legislation', *eSocialSciences*, forthcoming, www.esocialsciences.org/commentaries/Commentaries.aspx.

Srinivasan, R. (2011) *Media's (Lack of) Coverage of Workers' Rally in Delhi*, www.pragoti.in/node/4300.

Aboriginal community-controlled health services (ACCHS) have been the torch-bearers for Comprehensive Primary Health Care (CPHC) in Australia and have been one of the key vehicles through which the Aboriginal community has been able to engage in the struggle for health. This struggle has, from its inception, combined collective action to gain greater access to primary medical care and social and preventive programmes with addressing the broader, underlying social determinants of health.

### Development of Aboriginal community-controlled health services (ACCHS)

Following a long colonial period characterized by conflict, dispossession, marginalization and large-scale decimation from massacres and communicable diseases that Aboriginal people had previously not been exposed to, in the 1960s a grassroots Aboriginal movement formed in collaboration with non-Aboriginal activists. This social movement led to the successful 1967 referendum and subsequently a new positive period in Aboriginal affairs was established – the era of self-determination (Anderson 1997: 123). The 1967 referendum gave Aboriginal people citizenship for the first time and also gave the Commonwealth government constitutional power to make laws in relation to Aboriginal people. As citizens, Aboriginal people were better able to advocate for their citizenship rights, including access to healthcare, education and government transfer payments that had previously been denied to them.

Aboriginal community-controlled health services developed within this context with the first ACCHS being established at Redfern in Sydney in 1971. This was inspirational to many Aboriginal communities around the country and many similar services were established in the following few years (Bartlett and Boffa 2005).

These new ACCHS were initially started with either no government funding or small seeding grants. The Central Australian Aboriginal Congress (Congress), for example, was established in 1973 as an advocacy body and initially focused on the lack of shelter for Aboriginal people living around the small, remote, mainly non-Aboriginal town of Alice Springs. People were living in humpies (temporary shelters made from tree bark and branches) and the provision of tents was the beginning of action to properly address poor living conditions that were so much part of the poor health at that time. Within eighteen months Congress had established a community health programme, including a medical service as a response to the high levels of ill health in the community and the fact that the mainstream hospital system was seen as part of the colonial state and had been implicated in the forced removal of Aboriginal children. At this time there was no primary care, and general practitioners became the main or only source of primary medical care for both Aboriginal and non-Aboriginal people (Bartlett and Boffa 2001).

Following the initial wave of establishment of Aboriginal health services, by the mid-1970s these services formed the National Aboriginal and Islander Health Organization (NAIHO) as their umbrella body. It was realized that in order to gain greater strength in political advocacy for change there was a need to network and join forces. In 1977, NAIHO developed a National Black Health Plan that advocated for a coordinated and collaborative approach to the project of improving Aboriginal health (Foley 1982). While this plan was never adopted by governments, it was a crucial document in terms of uniting health services around a vision of better health, strengthening their input into government policies and influencing those policies. It was one of the first expressions of the critical role that ACCHS were to play in the struggle to improve Aboriginal health through better-informed Aboriginal health policy development.

### Flag-bearer of Comprehensive Primary Health Care

Seven years after the emergence of ACCHS in Australia, international commitment to primary healthcare (PHC) as a policy model was formalized in 1978 with the Alma Ata declaration on PHC (WHO 1978). The significance of the Chinese model of barefoot doctors in inspiring the Declaration is well known; less well known is the participation of Aboriginal NAIHO representatives in the drafting of the Declaration. When PHC was further endorsed as a key strategy by the World Health Assembly in 1981, the Aboriginal community-controlled health service model in Australia was already a powerful expression of the Alma Ata vision for CPHC.

However, from the beginning, in Australia as in other First World nations, there was ongoing tension between the delivery of selective PHC programmes targeting particular areas, such as medical care, immunization and maternal and child health, on the one hand, and resourcing communities to deliver comprehensive PHC programmes according to their own priorities on the other (Baum 1995). Australia had not developed a national primary healthcare policy and had very much retreated from the commitment given at Alma Ata to CPHC (NCEPH 1992). Resourcing the capacity of Aboriginal communities to use their health service as vehicles for the broader political struggle on these types of issues was not something that government was comfortable with, and there were attempts to restrict the role of Aboriginal health services to primary medical care with some selected programmes.

It was in this context that NAIHO was defunded in the mid-1980s by the

Commonwealth minister for Aboriginal affairs, following extensive criticism of the government of the day for its failure to make progress on key Aboriginal health priorities. However, NAIHO continued the struggle for Aboriginal health improvement with funding from philanthropic institutions. In 1991 it ceased functioning to make way for the new National Aboriginal Community Controlled Health Organization (NACCHO), which was established as part of the implementation of the National Aboriginal Health Strategy. Since then ACCHS have gone on to develop umbrella organizations at the state and territory levels, such as the Aboriginal Medical Services Alliance of the Northern Territory (AMSANT) (Bartlett and Boffa 2005).

It is Aboriginal people and their communities who have most vigorously and consistently developed the PHC model in Australia through the ACCHS. These services were instrumental in lobbying for the National Aboriginal Health Strategy (NAHSWP 1989), built on the principles of the PHC policy model for Aboriginal health advancement.

### The struggle to be part of the 'mainstream' health system

However, by the early 1990s ACCHS around the country became frustrated about the lack of focus on health service development, the failure to implement the National Aboriginal Health Strategy, the lack of effective joint health planning, and an almost exclusive focus on environmental health to the detriment of resourcing primary healthcare services. There was a strong view at the time that health services of all types, including primary healthcare services, would make no difference to Aboriginal health advancement compared with environmental health issues. In the Northern Territory (NT), Aboriginal health services had a long history of an informal alliance, and in 1994 this alliance was formalized with the formation of the Aboriginal Medical Services Alliance, NT (AMSANT). A major focus for AMSANT was how to advocate for more appropriate administrative and funding support to Aboriginal community-controlled primary healthcare services. At that time the role of Aboriginal health services was seen as 'supplementary' to that of the mainstream health system, which did not provide CPHC to anyone, let alone Aboriginal people (O'Donoghue 1995).

However, ACCHS saw their role in delivery of PHC to Aboriginal communities as central and not merely supplementary. Indeed, the NAHS embraced a strategy intended to have ACCHS established in all communities, and was seen as an important aspect of addressing Aboriginal health disadvantage. Further, many ACCHS were the major (and sometimes only) providers of PHC services to their communities, but they were not getting specific funding support.

As a result of these concerns, Congress and the National Centre for Epidemiology and Population Health published a monograph that analysed the Aboriginal health system, identified barriers to progress, and suggested how these could be addressed (Bartlett and Legge 1994). This provided a basis for AMSANT and NACCHO to further develop their lobbying campaign to highlight the problems with existing practices, and to call for the transfer of administrative and funding responsibilities to the Commonwealth Department of Health (Bartlett and Boffa 2005).

### Welfare colonialism

One of the key problems with the administrative arrangements for Aboriginal health at that time was that they perpetuated a type of 'welfare colonialism' whereby funding for Aboriginal health came only from a special Aboriginal-specific programme and not from the much greater mainstream funding sources within the health department. In addition to this, the funding arrangements were such that Aboriginal organizations from different sectors were forced to compete with each other for the same funds, and this undermined the previous community-level collaboration that had existed in advocacy on the broader social determinants of Aboriginal health. Intersectoral collaboration was replaced by intersectoral conflict (Bartlett and Legge 1994). As the then director of Congress explained (Delaney 1994): '... when you are at a negotiating table you have to look after your own organisation or your interest. And sometimes that can create ill feeling ... It is all designed to take the heat off the minister ... and point it at the blacks. We're blaming our own mob. And I think that's a brilliant strategy, for the government to make us fight ourselves.'

Administrative responsibility for funding for Aboriginal health was transferred from the Aboriginal affairs portfolio to the health portfolio in 1995, and it was this transfer which then enabled the key health policy decisions that led to the Aboriginal health improvement that is now occurring quite rapidly in the Northern Territory. The key policy changes were:

1 The establishment of a special section of the Commonwealth Health Department that focused on Aboriginal health with special expertise, especially in primary healthcare.
2 The establishment of a specialist umbrella Advisory Council to advise the health minister of the day on Aboriginal health issues.
3 The adoption of a national plan to improve Aboriginal health through the National and Torres Strait Islander Strategic Framework and a national approach to reporting on progress in Aboriginal health through the Aboriginal Health Performance Framework.
4 The development of the Framework Agreements in Aboriginal Health which included the establishment of the state and territory joint planning fora involving all levels of government and the Aboriginal community-controlled health sector as partners. An era of partnership with Aboriginal health services in health planning rather than conflict began.
5 Much greater access to mainstream health funding systems for Aboriginal

people, including the Australian health insurance scheme known as Medicare and the Pharmaceutical Benefits Scheme for access to essential medicines. The total level of funds for Aboriginal health, including health services, has increased from around $54 million per year prior to the transfer in 1994 to more than $1 billion per year now.

6   Improvement in the inter-sectoral relationships between Aboriginal community-controlled health services and Aboriginal community-controlled organizations in other sectors, which have led to more effective action on the social determinants of health (Hogan et al. 2006).

7   The establishment of a range of special programmes that were fully integrated into comprehensive PHC, including eye and ear health, the Social and Emotional Well Being programme, the Stolen Generations Counselling programme, the Sexual Health and Blood-borne Viruses programme, quality improvement, chronic disease and many others.

8   The establishment of national reporting tools such as the national Key Performance Indicators (nKPIs).

A less tangible outcome of these changes was a greater recognition of the need to respect the special expertise that had developed within Aboriginal communities in different sectors. This helped lead to clearer articulation of Aboriginal perspectives in national dialogue, the opening up of Aboriginal participation in the mainstream government departments and also in mainstream culture and economy, and a stronger expression of solidarity of non-Aboriginal Australians with the Aboriginal struggle. While institutional racism remains widespread and economic interests continue to press for further dispossession (particularly in northern Australia), the improving health status of Aboriginal people speaks of slow but real (albeit uneven) progress in confronting the social determinants of health. This progress has been informed and in some degree driven by the ACCHS but it is largely now carried in a much more dispersed way by achievements by individuals and organizations in many sectors.

### Improvements in health outcomes

The Northern Territory especially was able to utilize all of these key changes to transform the health system, primarily because much of the thinking that led to these health system reforms came from within the Aboriginal community-controlled health sector in the NT, which was led by AMSANT. Figure E9.1, from the recent Council of Australian Governments (COAG Reform Council 2013) Indigenous Reform Council report, shows that there has been a more than 30 per cent decline in all-cause mortality for Aboriginal people since 1999 and the NT is now on track to close the Life Expectancy Gap by 2031.

In this period, in the Northern Territory, there has been improved access to primary healthcare, with average per capita funding increasing from $700 per person in 1999 to more than $3,000 per person in 2013 (ibid.).

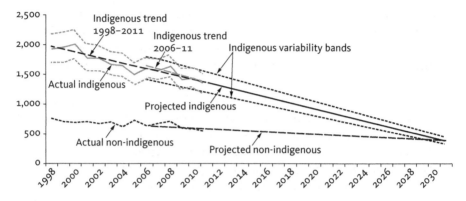

**E9.1** Death rates per 100,000 standard population, Northern Territory

Another part of the progressive realization of the CPHC vision has been the increasing iterations of what has become known as 'core primary healthcare services'. There have been three iterations of the core primary healthcare services model with the most recent and comprehensive version produced in 2011 in which there are five service domains (Northern Territory Aboriginal Health Forum 2011):

1 Clinical Services
2 Health Promotion
3 Corporate Services and Information
4 Advocacy, Knowledge, Research, Policy and Planning
5 Community Engagement, Control and Cultural Safety.

Defining core services is part of defining the progressive realization of the right to health as the obligation on governments to ensure access to evidence-based services and programmes according to need is made more explicit. Australia has the resources to ensure all of the services and programmes outlined in this core services model are accessible through Aboriginal community-controlled health services. This includes services and programmes in areas such as early childhood, family support, alcohol and other drug treatment, and aged and disability care, along with the more familiar clinical, maternal and child health, chronic disease and other services. Resourcing all of the core services will enable CPHC to make its maximum contribution to closing the gap.

This health improvement story for Aboriginal people demonstrates the important role that ACCHS have played in the broader struggle for Aboriginal health improvement and in the progressive realization of the CPHC care vision of health for all in Australia. They still remain the torch-bearers for CPHC in a nation where this service model has been undermined in all other areas. They continue to work to promote health across sectors and not just treat illness (Baum et al. 2013).

## New challenges

The struggle for Aboriginal health improvement now faces a new challenge as the Australian government, along with those of many other rich nations, responds to the global financial crisis with tough new austerity measures that may make it hard to maintain the current investment in primary healthcare services and will certainly make it hard to secure increased funding. It will be important over the coming years to advocate for a more evidence-based approach to the economic crisis using the evidence that 'austerity kills' in public health terms as well as the reality that countries that adopt more progressive taxation and redistributive polices have a stronger economy with greater employment, as well as better health and education systems (Marmot et al. 2014). Now more than ever the struggle for health equity within and between countries is embedded in the political economy of health on a global scale and this reinforces that part of the Alma Ata declaration that states: 'Gross inequalities in the health status of people, both between and within countries are politically, socially and economically unacceptable and require a new world economic order dedicated to achieving more equitable health outcomes' (WHO 1978).

## References

Anderson, I. (1997) 'The National Aboriginal Health Strategy', in H. Gardner (ed.), *Health Policy in Australia*, Melbourne: Oxford University Press, pp. 119–35.

Bartlett, B. and J. Boffa (2001) 'Aboriginal Community Controlled Comprehensive Primary Health Care: the Central Australian Aboriginal Congress', *Australian Journal of Primary Health*, 7(3): 74–82.

— (2005) 'The impact of Aboriginal community controlled health service advocacy on Aboriginal health policy', *Australian Journal of Primary Health*, 11(2): 1–9.

Bartlett, B. and D. Legge (1994) 'Beyond the maze: proposals for more effective administration of Aboriginal health programs', NCEPH Working Paper no. 34, Alice Springs/Canberra: Central Australian Aboriginal Congress/National Centre for Epidemiology and Population Health, Australian National University.

Baum, F. (1995) 'Goals and targets for health: their limitations as an approach to promoting health', *Aust. J. of Primary Health Interchange*, 1(1): 19–28.

— (2002) *The New Public Health*, Melbourne: Oxford University Press.

Baum, F., T. Freeman, G. Jolley, A. Lawless,

M. Bentley, K. Varrto, J. Boffa, R. Labonte and D. Sanders (2013), Health promotion in Australian Multidisciplinary Primary Health Care Services: case studies from South Australia and the Northern Territory', *Health Promotion International*, 8 May, doi: 10.1093/heapro/dat029.

CAAC (Central Australian Aboriginal Congress) (1998) *Core functions of Aboriginal primary health care*, Alice Springs: CAAC.

COAG Reform Council (2013) *Indigenous Reform 2011–2012. Comparing performance across Australia*, Report to the Council of Australian Governments.

Delaney, A. (1994) 'The tap that Richo built', Background briefing, ABC Radio National, 13 March.

Foley, G. (1982) 'Aboriginal Community Controlled Health Services – a short history', *Aboriginal Health Project Information Bulletin*, 2: 13–15.

Hogan, E., J. Boffa, C. Rosewarne, S. Bell and D. Ah Chee (2006) 'What price do we pay to prevent alcohol related harms in Aboriginal communities? The Alice Springs Trial of Liquor Licensing Restrictions', *Drug and Alcohol Review*, 25 May, pp. 1–6.

Marmot, M., E. Bloomer and P. Goldblatt

(2014) 'The role of social determinants in tackling health objectives in a context of economic crisis', *Public Health Reviews*, 35(1), www.publichealthreviews.eu/upload/pdf_files/13/00_Marmot.pdf, Accessed 15 March 2014.

NAHSWP (National Aboriginal Health Strategy Working Party) (1989) *A National Aboriginal Health Strategy*, March, Canberra: Australian Government Printing Service (AGPS).

NCEPH (National Centre for Epidemiology and Population Health) (1992) *Improving Australia's health: the role of primary health care*, Final report of the Review of the Role of Primary Health Care in Health Promotion in Australia, by D. G. Legge, D. N. McDonald and C. Benger, Canberra: NCEPH, Australian National University.

Northern Territory Aboriginal Health Forum (2011) *Core Functions of Primary Health Care: a Framework for the Northern Territory*.

O'Donoghue, L. (1995) 'Aboriginal health: an ATSIC perspective', Research Section Occasional Paper no. 1, Canberra: AIATSIS, pp. 4–5.

United Nations (1979) *General Assembly Resolution 34/58*, New York: UN.

WHA (World Health Assembly) (1979) *World Health Assembly Resolution WHA3230*, Geneva: WHA.

WHO (World Health Organization) (1978) *The Declaration of Alma Ata*, Geneva: World Health Organization.

— (1998) *Social Determinants of Health: The solid facts*, ed. R. Wilkinson and M. Marmot, Copenhagen: WHO Regional Office for Europe and WHO Healthy Cities website, www.who.dk/healthy-cities/.

# CONTRIBUTORS

**Abigail Speller**, postgraduate scholar, Faculty of Health Sciences, Simon Fraser University, Canada

**Alex Faulkner**, University of Sussex and Health Action International

**Alexandra Bambas Nolen**, Coordinating Centre for Global Health, University of Texas Medical Branch (UTMB), Galveston, Texas, USA

**Alexandro Sacco**, ForoSalud, Asociación Latinoamericana de Medicina Social (ALAMES) and People's Health Movement, Latin America.

**Alexis Benos**, Laboratory of Hygiene and Social Medicine, Aristotle University, Thessaloniki (Greece)

**Alison Katz**, independent researcher, Geneva, Switzerland

**Ambareen Abdullah**, postgraduate scholar, School of Social Work, Tata Institute of Social Sciences (TISS), Mumbai, India

**Amit Sengupta**, People's Health Movement, India

**Angelo Stefanini**, Centre for International Health, University of Bologna (Italy)

**Anna Marriott**, Health Policy Adviser, Oxfam GB

**Anne-Emanuelle Birn**, Dalla Lana School of Public Health, University of Toronto, Canada

**Anne-Marie Thow**, Menzies Centre for Health Policy, School of Public Health, University of Sydney, Australia.

**Anuj Kapilashrami**, Global Public Health Unit, School of Social and Political Sciences, Queen Margaret University, Edinburgh, Scotland, UK

**Armando de Negri Filho**, World Social Forum on Health, Brazil

**Arne Ruckert**, Research Associate, Globalization and Health Equity, Institute of Population Health, University of Ottawa

**Asa Cristina Laurell**, independent consultant and physician, Mexico

**Baijayanta Mukhopadhyay**, People's Health Movement, Canada

**Belgacim Sabri**, Tunisian Right to Health Association, Tunisia

**Bridget Lloyd**, People's Health Movement, South Africa

**Camila Guigliani**, People's Health Movement, Porto Alegre, Brazil

**Chiara Bodini**, Centre for International Health, University of Bologna (Italy)

**Claudio Schuftan**, People's Health Movement, Vietnam

**David Legge**, School of Public Health, La Trobe University, Victoria, Australia, and People's Health Movement

**David McCoy**, Queen Mary University, London, Medact and People's Health Movement, UK

**David Sanders**, School of Public Health, University of the Western Cape, South Africa, and People's Health Movement, South Africa

**David van Wyk**, Bench Marks Foundation, South Africa

**Deepa Venkatachalam**, Sama, Resource Group for Women and Health, and People's Health Movement, India

**Diane McIntyre**, Health Economics Unit, University of Cape Town, South Africa

**Dipa Sinha**, Centre for Economic Studies and Planning, Jawaharlal Nehru University (JNU), New Delhi, India, and Right to Food Campaign, India

**Dirk van Duppen**, Doctors for the People, Antwerp, Belgium

**Donna Ah Chee**, Central Australian Aboriginal Congress Aboriginal Corporation, Alice Springs, Australia

**Eduardo Espinoza**, Ministry of Health, Government of El Salvador

**Egmont Ruelens**, Doctors for the People, Antwerp, Belgium

**Elias Kondilis**, Laboratory of Hygiene and Social Medicine, Aristotle University, Thessaloniki (Greece)

**Eugene Cairncross**, Department of Chemical Engineering, Cape Peninsula University of Technology, Cape Town, South Africa

**Farah M. Shroff**, School of Population and Public Health, Faculty of Medicine, University of British Columbia, Canada

**Fran Baum**, Southgate Institute for Health, Society and Equity, Flinders University, Adelaide, and People's Health Movement, Australia

**Francine Mestrum**, Network of Global Social Justice, Belgium

**Garance Upham**, Safe Observer International, France, and People's Health Movement, France

**Germán Alejandro Crespo Infantes**, Ministry of Health and Sports, Government of Bolivia, and Asociación Latinoamericana de Medicina Social (ALAMES), Bolivia

**Guddi Singh**, paediatrician in the NHS, UK, Medact, London, and People's Health Movement, UK

**Halkidiki Collective**, Halkidiki, Greece

**Hani Serag**, People's Health Movement, Egypt

**Héctor Javier Sánchez Pérez**, Observatorio de Muerte Materna de Chiapas, Colegio de la Frontera Sur (Ecosur), Mexico

**Indranil Mukhopadhyay**, Public Health Foundation of India (PHFI), India

**Jagjit Plahe**, Department of Management, Monash University, Victoria, Australia

**Jessica Hamer**, Oxfam GB

**John Boffa**, Central Australian Aboriginal Congress Aboriginal Corporation, Alice Springs, Australia

**José León Uscátegui**, Mission Barrio Adentro, Government of Venezuela

**K. M. Gopa Kumar**, Third World Network (TWN), India

**Linda Mans**, Dutch Human Resources for Health (HRH) Alliance and Wemos Foundation, Amsterdam, Netherlands

**Louis Reynolds**, Education Development Unit, University of Cape Town, and People's Health Movement, South Africa

**Marcos Arana Cedeño**, Instituto Nacional de Ciencias Médicas y Nutrición Salvador Zubirán, Comité Promotor por el Derecho a una Maternidad Segura y Voluntaria de Chiapas, Mexico

**Mariette Liefferink**, Federation for a Sustainable Environment, South Africa

**Mary Galvin**, Department of Anthropology and Development Studies, University of Johannesburg, South Africa

**Mathieu Poirier**, health researcher, Léogâne, Haiti

**Matthew Anderson**, Department of Family and Social Medicine, MMC/AECOM, Bronx, New York, USA

**Mauricio Torres**, District Department of Health, Bureau of Social Participation and Citizen Services, Bogotá, and Asociación Latinoamericana de Medicina Social (ALAMES), Colombia

**Mohammad Ali Barzegar**, People's Health Movement, Iran

**Monica Riutort**, Peel Committee on Sexual Assault, Women's and Children's Health Systems, Ontario, Canada

**N. B. Sarojini**, Sama, Resource Group for Women and Health, and People's Health Movement, India

**Nila Heredia**, Minister of Health and Sports, Bolivia, and Asociación Latinoamericana de Medicina Social (ALAMES)

**Patrick Durisch**, Déclaration de Berne – Berne Declaration, Switzerland

**Pol de Vos**, Public Health Department, Institute of Tropical Medicine, Antwerp, Belgium

**Radha Holla Bhar**, Breastfeeding Promotion Network of India (BPNI) and International Baby Food Action Network (IBFAN) Asia

**Rafael Gonzalez Guzman**, Department of Public Health, School of Medicine, Universidad Nacional Autónoma de Mexico (UNAM), and Asociación Latinoamericana de Medicina Social (ALAMES)

**Remco van de Pas**, International Health Policy Unit, Institute of Tropical Medicine, Antwerp, Belgium

**Ronald Labonte**, Faculty of Medicine, Institute of Population Health, University of Ottawa, and Department of Community Health and Epidemiology, University of Saskatchewan, Canada

**Sara Javanparast**, Flinders University, Adelaide, Australia

**Sharon Friel**, National Centre for Epidemiology and Public Health, Australian National University

**Shilpa Modi Pandav**, independent researcher, India

**Shradha Pant**, postgraduate scholar, School of Social Work, Tata Institute of Social Sciences (TISS), Mumbai, India

**Sophia Kisting**, occupational medicine specialist, Cape Town, South Africa

**Sue Fawcus**, Department of Obstetrics and Gynaecology, University of Cape Town, South Africa

**Susana Barria**, People's Health Movement and New Trade Union Initiative, India

**T. Sunderaraman**, Public Health Resource Network and People's Health Movement, India

**Thomas Gebauer**, Medico International, Germany

**Thomas Schwarz**, Medicus Mundi International, Basle, Switzerland

**Tim Reed**, Health Action International, UK

**Vijay Prashad**, Trinity College in Hartford, USA

**V. R. Raman**, Health Governance Hub, Public Health Foundation of India (PHFI), India

# INDEX